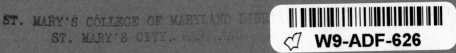

Egypt Under Nasir

GAMAL ABD AL-NASIR

Egypt Under Nasir

A Study in Political Dynamics

BY R. HRAIR DEKMEJIAN
State University of New York at Binghamton

State University of New York Press
Albany, 1971

Egypt Under Nasir

First Edition

Published by State University of New York Press
Thurlow Terrace, Albany, New York 12201

International Standard Book Number 0-87395-080-1 (clothbound)
International Standard Book Number 0-87395-180-8 (microfiche)
Library of Congress Catalog Card Number 70-152520

Printed in the United States of America

To my mother Vahidé
and my late father Hrant,
an Armenian Dashnak revolutionary

Contents

Illustrations

Tables

Acknowledgments

To an extent one's first book represents the repository of intellectual influences acquired during the last phases of academic training. This is particularly true if one has had the good fortune of being instructed by a number of highly competent and dedicated teachers. Among those toward whom I feel a deep and abiding sense of loyalty and gratitude are Professors G. Lowell Field, Louis L. Gerson, Harry J. Marks, and Max B. Thatcher of the University of Connecticut, and Murray Levin of Boston University. An even greater intellectual debt is due to Professors John S. Badeau, J. C. Hurewitz, Charles Issawi, Majid Khadduri, and Dankwart Rustow of Columbia University, who guided the early phases of my research since 1962 and at various times acted as valuable critics. I am particularly grateful to Professors Hurewitz and Rustow for their persistent encouragement and efforts to have the present study published in book form.

No less significant were the opportunities accorded by the State University of New York at Binghamton administration, the Department of Political Science, the Southwest Asia—North Africa Program, the Harpur Foundation, and the Center for Comparative Political Research. A research trip funded through the efforts of Dean Peter Vukasin and my colleagues, Walter Filley and Don Peretz, provided me with a first-hand opportunity to study the Egyptian political process at close range. Additional funds for research came from the Research Foundation of State University of New York, and the Center for Comparative Political Research under Arthur Banks. Throughout I was fortunate to have the help and council of many colleagues at the State University of New York at Binghamton, especially Professors Rebecca Grajower, Michael Cohen, Safia Mohsen, Harry Gyman, Louis Gawthrop, Paul Smith, David Peterson, Khalil Semaan, Nathan

Hakman, Robert Jordan, Arthur Banks and Eduard Ziegen-hagen. I also acknowledge my debt to Dean Arthur Goldberg of the University of Rochester, who taught me how to write English-language papers in political science during our undergraduate careers at the University of Connecticut. The bibliographic assistance of our librarian, Jalal Zuwiyya, was most valuable. Equally important was the help of my friends, Professors Matti Moosa of Gannon College and Vartan Artinian of Harvard University, especially regarding Arabic language sources.

My list would be incomplete without mentioning the role of my students, both graduate and undergraduate, who helped materially and intellectually at every stage of research and writing. Among them I would like to single out Mtshana Ncube, Taysir Nashif, Aram Nigogosian, Virginia Rober, Robert Tostevin, Bana Barazi, Samuel Dolgow, Sally Kellam, James Leighton, and Zvi Klopott. My faithful friends, Ohannes Bezazian, Ray Thompson and Vartkes Baboghlian, were always a steady source of assistance and reassurance. Most importantly, I owe an inestimable debt to my assistant, Margaret J. Wyszomirski, without whose devoted efforts this study would have been immeasurably poorer.

In view of the painful uncertainties of the publication process, conscientious and competent editors are an author's best friends. I was indeed fortunate to discover such persons in Norman Mangouni, Director of the State University of New York Press, and Mrs. Margaret Mirabelli, who served as copy editor. I am particularly thankful for Mr. Mangouni's efficient and prompt stewardship of the manuscript despite shortages of time and staff. In this connection it is fitting to remember the anonymous readers and evaluators of this work while in manuscript form; although their critical comments prompted countless revisions, the quality of the final product was bettered considerably.

As for my wife and boys, something more than mere gratitude is necessary for the many deprivations they endured during the writing of this volume. Throughout my trials and tribulations all four of them—Anoush, Gregory, Armen, Haig—were a source of inspiration and strength.

June 1971   *R. H. Dekmejian*

Egypt Under Nasir

"Nasserism's first property is motion."
        —MALCOLM KERR

*"Political action is not undertaken by
angels but by human beings. Political
leadership is not a ruthless and sharp sword
but rather a process of balance . . .
between various possibilities and, in many
cases, between obvious risks."*
        —GAMAL ABD AL-NASIR

Prologue

GAMAL ABD AL-NASIR of the United Arab Republic died of a coronary thrombosis on 28 September 1970. His sudden departure at a most critical juncture in Middle Eastern history drew the curtain on the first phase of the Egyptian Revolution of 23 July 1952; it also marked the end of what might be termed as the Nasirite era of Arab nationalist development—a period of intense political activity and social change that Nasir initiated and symbolized.

The present study traces the evolution of the Egyptian political system from the 1952 Revolution, through the June 1967 War, to Nasir's death and its aftermath. In view of Nasir's unique and pervasive role in Egyptian politics, the primary focus of inquiry is the leader himself as he interacted with the political environment of the fifties and sixties.

Circumstances of crisis, no less than peculiar personal attributes, propelled Nasir toward a revolutionary career based on charismatic leadership—a highly spiritual interaction between leader and followers rivalled only by two figures in Arab history—Salah al-Din and the Prophet Muhammad. In the short space of eighteen years Nasir carried out a successful coup d'état, won the power struggle with Nagib, propounded Pan-Arabism, defied the West and the East, led the Arab revolutionary movement, founded a new order in Egypt, intensified Arab resistance toward Israel, and fought two unsuccessful wars against the Jewish state without losing office. What follows is an inquiry into the dynamic factors that shaped Egyptian politics under Nasir.

1
The Framework of Analysis

ONE central characteristic of transitional systems undergoing accelerated and comprehensive social change is the persistent instability that pervades their political life. Of the multitude of variables that affect stability, the behavior of political elites is often of primary importance, particularly as this relates to the twin problems of legitimacy and control.

In view of the relative longevity of the present Egyptian leadership in difficult circumstances, any meaningful analysis of the political system would have to explore the processes by which they acquired and successfully exercised power. While approaching the system through the conceptual avenues of legitimacy and control gives an elitist bias [1] to this study, one may offer two compensating explanations. Considerably more data are available on elites in non-Western political systems than on groups, classes, or the popular base. Secondly, elite behavior is often politically more significant than mass behavior in developing states.

In order to define the term legitimacy and its relationship to authority one may refer to Professor Dahl's analysis which assumes that once in positions of power and influence leaders will strive for legitimacy. Thus, when the influence of a leader is accepted as legitimate, he is said to have authority. According to Dahl the fundamental reason why leaders try to convert rule by naked force to authority—which is legitimate—is because this form of rule is more reliable, durable, and generally efficient.[2]

Fundamentally, the quest for legitimacy is the process by which elites strive for mass acceptability on the basis of some ideological justification for their positions of leadership. To the extent that the people accept these ideological justifications, the leadership is considered legitimate. At the general level, the particular strategy that a leader follows to acquire legitimation is usually determined by his relationship to the prevailing ideological milieu. Max Weber identifies a trilogy of "pure" types of authority, each type requiring a different strategy for legitimation. In a traditional society where justification for authority is grounded in commonly held norms and practices that have been routinized over time, a new leader must seek legitimacy by intimately associating himself with the prevailing value system. In a society where authority is exercised by virtue of legality, in accordance with certain shared, rational rules and laws, a leader must adhere strictly to the ideological maxims that govern the system. These situations apply when the leaders in question do not oppose the existing "traditional" or "legal-rational" systems. If a leader is committed to the destruction of the status quo, his subsequent quest for legitimacy must proceed along lines substantially different from those prevalent in the previous system. One possible way such a leader may legitimize his rule is by what Weber calls charismatic authority.[3]

In the attempt to appraise the evolution of Egyptian politics since the Revolution of 1952, it becomes apparent that certain earlier notions need modification in the light of subsequent developments. Although a military dictatorship at the outset, the system after 1956 began to develop additional characteristics that helped promote stability and continuity. These new features included the emergence of the highly personalized leadership of Gamal Abd al-Nasir and the concomitant appearance of new ideologies, elites, and institutions. In view of the manifest complexity of these systemic changes and the centrality of Nasir's role, more conventional modes of analysis were found inadequate; hence the resort to a more comprehensive conceptual framework partially based on Weber's notion of charismatic authority.

Charisma has been given diverse meanings and interpretations by different scholars [4] because of its elusiveness and the psychological inability of democratic man to conceptualize such a foreign experience. At least in one respect Weber's writings can be cited as a source of ambiguity. In discussing the relative importance and interaction of the psychological and the social aspects of charismatic authority, he emphasized the former: [5] ". . . a certain quality of an individual personality by virtue of which he is set apart from ordinary men and treated as endowed with supernatural, superhuman, or at least, specifically, exceptional qualities." [6] In this sense, therefore, charisma is a "gift of grace" that exists independently from the social context. Yet Weber went on to recognize the need for the social acknowledgment of charisma without which the leader's possession of this gift becomes insignificant.[7] Although an individual may feel in himself the possession of gifts of grace, these become relevant only when recognized by others. Therefore, as in the works of Davies, Etzioni, Friedland, Willner and Willner, Rustow and others,[8] charisma is viewed here as a relationship between leader and followers rather than a personal attribute of the leader himself.

A Developmental Scheme

It appears that the incidence of charisma is tied to the interaction of a variety of complex factors. From an examination of the literature on charismatic leadership (theoretical as well as case studies), one may develop an historical-empirical type framework of general applicability. In order to render the concept more operational, one may identify these factors and arrange them in a developmental cycle. These interacting factors or preconditions include:

1. A situation of acute social crisis characterized by the pathological response of society to a breakdown of the existing mechanisms of conflict resolution.[9] In such times irrational, schizophrenia-like disorientations occur creating a deep sense of psychological dependence and heightened expectation.[10] At the political level, a crisis in legitimacy engulfs the system, its leaders, ideology, and institutions. The prevailing milieu of mass alienation, social atomization, and identity crisis renders the populace vulnerable to mass appeals.[11]

2. The appearance of an exemplary personage without whom the charismatic relationship will not begin. And vice versa, the process cannot be initiated without circumstances of turmoil, regardless of a leader's charismatic potential. The simultaneous oc-

currence of these initial prerequisites may trigger the charismatic process depending on a number of intervening variables related to the way in which the leader projects himself upon the society in crisis. The intervening variables which appear during the self-revelation of the potential charismatic are performance-message, personal qualities, and opportunity to propagate.

The leader reveals himself through heroic performance and a messianic message. These two components are mutually reinforcing; the leader's performance may represent the unfolding of his message, or the message may contain his program for heroic activity.

The initiation of the charismatic relationship depends on whether the leader's performance-message fits the crisis situation. If the leader's performance and message are not correctly attuned to the cultural ethos and the deeply felt needs [12] and expectations of the crisis-torn society, the process will not begin. The leader's performance should be of a type that is regarded as exemplary, extraordinary, or heroic by the leader's own society. The accompanying message typically contains a bold prescription to remedy the prevailing crisis situation, as well as a utopian promise for the future. While attuned to the needs and problems of the existing society, the message also includes values and modes of behavior significantly different from those in practice. Yet this revolutionary nature of the message does not preclude the selective incorporation of certain of the prevailing values and symbols. In this sense there is a latent blend and continuity between the old and the new; the leader may selectively invoke history, myth, and past heroes to reinforce the sanctity of his mission. To capture a mass audience, he propagates the highlights of the message in simple and explicit terms. On the basis of these promises—reinforced by heroic activity—the leader establishes an initial charismatic bond with the masses.

The personal qualities of the leader constitute another dynamic variable in promoting the leader-follower interaction. A leader's possession of exemplary qualities is always determined by his own society, according to its peculiar culturally-derived criteria. In terms of his own milieu, the potential charismatic is an outstanding personality, endowed with great dynamism, sensitivity, and resourcefulness. These personal gifts become instrumental in imparting to his followers the values and maxims of the message.

Judging by more universal criteria, he is also a revolutionary inclined to take major risks. Being a product of his own crisis-torn environment, he is an acutely alienated individual. Usually his alienation can be traced back to an unstable family life and failures or sufferings experienced in society, i.e., inability to gain social mobility, imprisonment, identity crisis—factors that propel him toward revolutionary action. In this sense he is a marginal who draws to himself other alienates or marginals who eventually become the core of his movement dedicated to enlarge his following (gemeinde) to include the alienated masses.

Finally, the leader-follower interaction may be aborted if the leader is denied the opportunity to propagate and perform. While a leader may possess a charismatic following before acquiring high office, in certain cases charisma is systematically developed after a position of power is achieved.[13] Often this is accomplished through the skillful use of the mass media—a new factor nonexistent until the present century.[14] One may realistically expect the ruling elite to attempt silencing the potential charismatic as soon as he begins to propagate his message. Under such conditions the aspiring charismatic almost inevitably needs a secure base. He may remove himself and his initial followers from the area of the ruling elite's control, or if circumstances permit, he may move against them and capture political control. However he obtains a secure base, it will provide the leader an opportunity to spread his word and demonstrate his heroic abilities.[15] As Weber points out, continuous success is imperative for charisma perpetuation since it validates the leader's charisma in the eyes of his followers. The effective interaction of the foregoing factors results in an initial charismatic bond.

3. The leader can now proceed to effect a value transformation on the basis of the legitimacy flowing from the nascent charismatic relationship. Increasingly he exercises a diffuse and intense influence over the normative orientations of the masses.[16] As Professor Etzioni points out, in contrast to other types of authority under which the public's criteria remain unchanged, the charismatic is able to effect a significant change in his subject's value system.[17] Thus, the leader fills the value-belief vacuum cre-

ated by the social crisis with his own belief system or ideology as promulgated in his message. As the new values, perspectives (*Weltanschauung*), and policies of the leader find acceptance among the masses, they can be said to become subject to *his* charisma and he becomes *their* charismatic leader. In view of this reciprocal relationship, the notion that the charismatic ". . . is always the creation of his followers," [18] becomes a half-truth. It is necessary to add: to the extent that the leader has succeeded in imparting his values to his followers, they are *his* creation.

One of the most distinctive characteristics of charismatic authority that sets it apart from traditional or legal-rational types is the highly spiritual link that develops between the leader and his followers. Based on a bridge of leader-inspired values, the charismatic relationship places the leader "in communion" with his adherents—in a state of intense spiritual union. In this context, the charismatic performs certain psychological functions; [19] he gives his faithful a feeling of comfort, consolation, and a sense of belonging. Indeed the charismatic relationship is a two-way process from which both leader and followers receive fulfillment and satisfaction.

4. The final stage in the evolution of charismatic authority is "routinization." The term denotes the leader's efforts to establish a new order based on the legitimacy derived from his charisma. [20] Thus, the new organizational forms and processes that he inaugurates will bear the halo of his blessing. The legitimacy popularly ascribed to these institutions flows not only from his heroic record and exemplary qualities, but, more basically, from the value transformation that he has caused to take place. In other words, whatever the leader proposes will find general acceptance and legitimacy since these constitute the implementation of his ideology which his people have come to share.

Logic suggests that to insure stability, routinization should occur at the height of the charismatic relationship, before inevitable reverses or the passage of time erode the leader's charisma. [21] However, not all charismatics are successful routinizers; by temperament and experience some are not inclined to undertake bureaucratic-administrative endeavors. [22] Indeed, effective routinization requires a painful psychological readjustment on the leader's part. If he is able to make this transition at the height of the charismatic relationship, he can then establish a new order which is likely to survive his death or the eventual weakening of the charismatic bond. Early routinization may also facilitate the succession process after the leader's departure.

Clearly, effective routinization is imperative to stabilize an inherently unstable charismatically-conditioned socio-political order. Because of his messianic behavior, the charismatic generates expectations bordering on the miraculous. As a socializing force the leader not only greatly increases the number of people involved, but also the intensity of their involvement. Given the strength of the bond, at the outset, immediate psychological payoffs—dignity, sense of belonging—may be sufficient to maintain the leader's hold on his followers. In the long run, however, they will expect him to deliver social, political, and economic payoffs as well, through routinization of various mechanisms for need satisfaction. At this stage, the leader's following is transformed into a movement or party to serve as a rule-stabilizing agency.

At the culmination of the process the leader will have presided over a transition from charismatic authority to a system increasingly reliant upon rational-legal means of legitimacy; with the passage of time, the system may also acquire traditional legitimacy as well. Also his power will become progressively depersonalized within the framework of a highly bureaucratic system.

A number of problems remain regarding the general concept of charismatic leadership and the identification of charismatics. The first concerns the frequent criticism that the charismatic typology compares "good" and "bad" men,[23] and therefore is morally objectionable. A related problem arises when one considers David Easton's attempts to differentiate between "genuine" and "spurious" charisma, the sole criterion being ". . . a genuine sense of calling" that the leader would experience.[24] The main weakness of this typology is the virtual impossibility of empirically distinguishing between the genuine and the spurious, since most leaders invariably claim to have received the calling. The ultimate judgment of whether the leader is good or bad or genuine or spurious lies solely with his followers. The opinions of outsiders or non-communicants who have not succumbed to the leader's charisma are irrelevant. Whatever the leader's personal qualities or morality, the fact remains that these *were* acceptable to his followers and proved instrumental in convincing them of the truth of his message. Therefore, the analysis of a particular charismatic relationship should center on the objective identification of the leader's qualities and maxims and the reasons for their popular acceptance. Finally, one should consider the wealth of recent literature on psycho-historical studies on individual leaders.[25] However, considering the paucity of reliable and detailed psychological data on Abd al-Nasir of Egypt, these psycho-analytic approaches have not been utilized in the present study.

The foregoing framework can be useful in clarifying some of the conceptual difficulties associated with the usage of the term charisma. It helps to differentiate popular leaders from charismatic types. Although popularity derived from heroic or exemplary performance can contribute to the fostering of the charismatic relationship, it is not synonymous with charisma. One may identify a number of popular leaders or potential charismatics (e.g., Generals Nagib and Eisenhower), who failed to proceed beyond the first stage of the scheme since they lacked a message.[26] The intense spiritual relationship engendered by the followers' absorption of the charismatic's message is lacking in the case of popular leaders.

The framework also helps to identify another category of leaders, common to the newly independent states of Afro-Asia. Such leaders have often progressed through the initial phases of the scheme by successfully propagating a message and achieving independence, yet they have failed to complete the process by not achieving routinization of new organizations and processes (e.g., Kwame Nkrumah, Ahmad Sukarno).[27] The resultant absence of genuine social change and the accompanying decrease in social payoffs are likely to weaken the charismatic bond and promote instability.[28]

Legitimacy and Force

It follows from Dahl's analysis that the higher the degree of legitimacy, the easier it is for an elite to maintain control without frequent resort to force. Conversely, as legitimacy decreases, the continued maintenance of control more and more comes to depend on coercive means. It follows that at a given moment the leadership sustains its position of control by a combination of acquired legitimacy and threat and/or use of force. Thus the basic relationship:

$$\text{Control (C)} = \text{Force (F)} + \text{Legitimacy (L)}$$

where C is held constant,[29] and F and L are interdependent variables inversely proportional to one another.

It should be noted that over a given time span, the relative proportions of legitimacy and force vary in a given political system depending on leadership performance, as well as a multitude of other internal and external factors. If, for instance, component $F > L$, and continues to increase, C becomes more and more dependent on F, creating a condition of increasing instability. On the other hand, if $L > F$ and continues to increase, C increasingly becomes dependent on L; the resultant trend would be toward stability.

The foregoing relationships may be useful as criteria in differentiating the so-called developed systems from emerging nations of the non-Western world. Thus, in systems where elites, ideologies, institutions, and processes are institutionalized over a relatively long period of political development, such as in the United States, Britain, and even the USSR, the fluctuations of legitimacy and force are not likely to be of great magnitude. Especially in constitutional systems such as the United States and Britain, the likelihood of a major and sharp drop of the legitimacy curve is almost negligible, except in rare moments of great crisis. If individual elites happen to lose legitimacy, similar elite types replace them without any significant harm to the legitimacy of institutions and the system as a whole. In contrast, the frequency, magnitude, and consequences of a drop of elite legitimacy in the newly developing states are relatively great as a direct result of the manifold weaknesses of the newly born ideologies, institutions, and processes, which themselves lack the strengthening aura of legitimacy. When institutional legitimacy is already weak, and the initial legitimacy that elites acquire during the struggle for independence begins to erode, instability sets in.[30] Force is in-

Figure 1. *Control Based on Increasing Force*

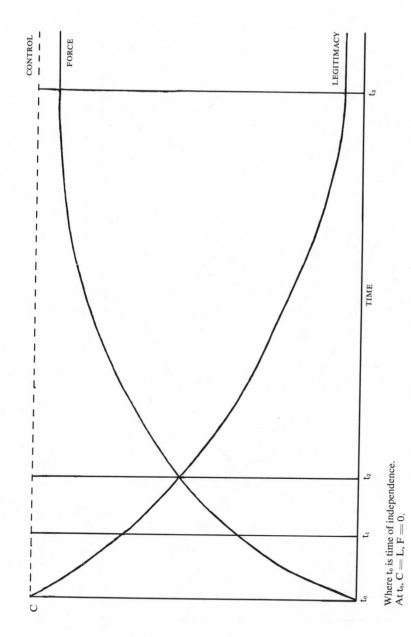

Where t_0 is time of independence.
At t_0, $C = L$, $F = 0$.

* Realistically "0" can never be reached.

11

Figure 2. *Control Based on Increasing Legitimacy*

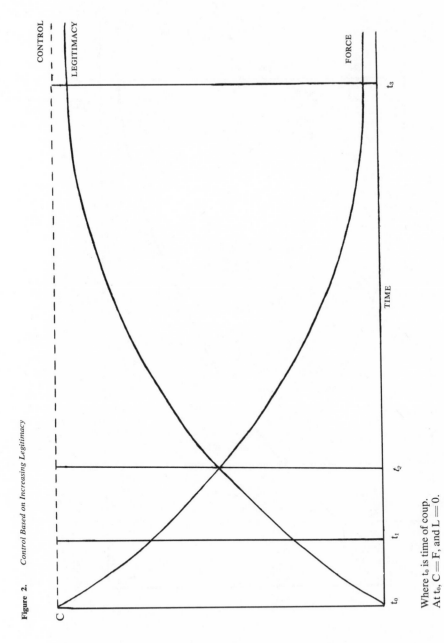

Where t_0 is time of coup.
At t_0, C = F, and L = 0.

* Realistically "0" can never be reached.

12

creasingly relied upon as a means of control, a process that usually culminates in the overthrow of the ruling elite (e.g., Egypt 1922–1952; Syria 1946–1949; Iraq 1921–1958; Ghana 1957–1966). This process is graphically represented in Figure 1.

In contrast, elites that acquire power through coup d'état—the application of maximum force—will begin ruling on the basis of a low level of legitimacy in most cases, except when charisma is present or the overthrow is the result of a popularly based revolution. Therefore, in coup d'état regimes, productive elite strategy requires a progressive reduction of the application of force and the concomitant rise in legitimacy. Graphically the process is represented in Figure 2.

Whatever combination of strategies elites utilize to acquire legitimacy, rarely can they completely dispense with the threat or actual use of force. Indeed, in the real world of politics, control through legitimacy is almost always augmented by varying degrees of coercive power, since invariably some groups or persons will fall outside the pale of that legitimacy. Even in situations of maximum legitimacy the force component is held in reserve to put down marginal opposition elements if the need arises. In that sense force maintained in reserve, or potential force, becomes a constant and may be differentiated from the actual application of force, which varies.[31]

Admittedly it is difficult to determine empirically the precise mix of legitimacy and force at particular instances during the development of a political system. The problem is especially acute when measuring the legitimacy component in the absence of suitable data, particularly surveys, which are difficult to acquire in many developing countries, such as the UAR. Under such circumstances, one must rely on indirect and less accurate indices to gauge legitimacy.

The problem is equally real in the appraisal of charismatic legitimation. In cases where charisma is an important factor, a common pitfall has been the tendency to overemphasize charismatic legitimacy at the expense of the coercive and organizational aspects of political control. Too often a leader's success in rulership is conveniently ascribed to charisma thereby hiding many of the other dynamic factors contributing to his rise. The task of the analyst then is to identify and weigh as carefully as possible the

Chart 1. *The Charismatic Process*

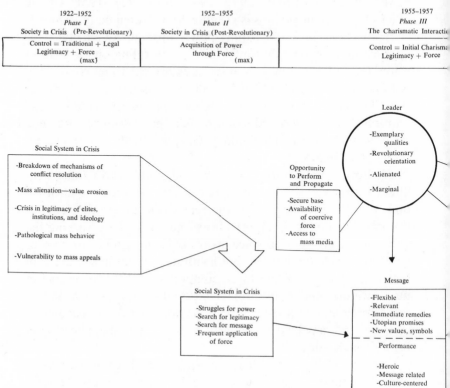

1922–1952	1952–1955	1955–1957
Phase I	*Phase II*	*Phase III*
Society in Crisis (Pre-Revolutionary)	Society in Crisis (Post-Revolutionary)	The Charismatic Interactic
Control = Traditional + Legal Legitimacy + Force (max)	Acquisition of Power through Force (max)	Control = Initial Charisma Legitimacy + Force

Social System in Crisis

-Breakdown of mechanisms of conflict resolution

-Mass alienation—value erosion

-Crisis in legitimacy of elites, institutions, and ideology

-Pathological mass behavior

-Vulnerability to mass appeals

Opportunity to Perform and Propagate

-Secure base
-Availability of coercive force
-Access to mass media

Leader

-Exemplary qualities
-Revolutionary orientation
-Alienated
-Marginal

Social System in Crisis

-Struggles for power
-Search for legitimacy
-Search for message
-Frequent application of force

Message

-Flexible
-Relevant
-Immediate remedies
-Utopian promises
-New values, symbols

Performance

-Heroic
-Message related
-Culture-centered

14

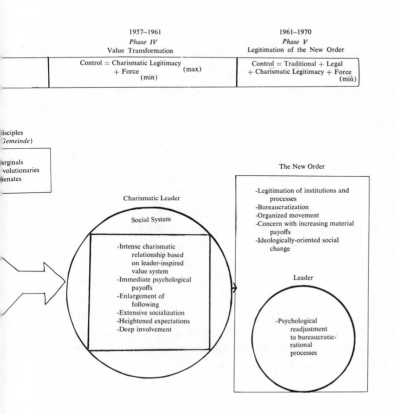

1957–1961
Phase IV
Value Transformation

1961–1970
Phase V
Legitimation of the New Order

Control = Charismatic Legitimacy
+ Force ———— (max)
(min)

Control = Traditional + Legal
+ Charismatic Legitimacy + Force
(min)

isciples
(Gemeinde)

arginals
volutionaries
ienates

The New Order

Charismatic Leader

Social System

-Intense charismatic
relationship based
on leader-inspired
value system
-Immediate psychological
payoffs
-Enlargement of
following
-Extensive socialization
-Heightened expectations
-Deep involvement

-Legitimation of institutions and
processes
-Bureaucratization
-Organized movement
-Concern with increasing material
payoffs
-Ideologically-oriented social
change

Leader

-Psychological
readjustment
to bureaucratic-
rational
processes

15

ever changing proportions of the twin interacting elements of control—legitimacy and force—and explain elite behavior in those terms.

The dynamics of the Egyptian political system since 1952 are to be analyzed within the foregoing conceptual framework which combines the proposed charisma scheme with the coercive and organizational facets of rulership as outlined in Chart 1 (pp. 14–15). The various aspects of crisis in pre-revolutionary Egyptian society are further explicated in Chapter 2, corresponding to Phase I of the chart. Chapter 3 focuses on the early policies of the military government, with special emphasis on the Nasir-Nagib power struggle and the role of the civilian political groups (Phase II). The emergence of Nasir as a consequence of particular international developments (i.e., Baghdad Pact, Bandung, arms deal, Suez War) and the accompanying appearance of new ideologies, myths, and symbols are treated in Chapters 4, 5, 6 (Phase III). The process of value transformation or ideological change is analyzed in Chapters 7, 8, 9 (Phase IV). The leadership's efforts to build the institutions of the new order (e.g., Arab Socialist Union, National Assembly) are set forth in Chapters 10 and 11. The final chapters analyze the strengths and weaknesses of the political system under conditions of severe external and internal stress since the mid-1960s.

2

A Background of Protracted Turmoil

A MULTITUDE of factors combined to create a condition of protracted and intense crisis in Egyptian society in the three decades prior to the military coup of July 1952. On the political scene, there existed a state of continuous crisis caused by the three-cornered power struggle between the monarchy, the Wafd Party, and the British imperial presence. The first contender in the struggle —the non-Egyptian Muhammad Ali dynasty—aimed at the perpetuation of its autocratic rule. Britain's interests centered on the preservation of what had been since 1882 her preponderant position in Egypt. The nationalist opposition to these status quo forces came from the Wafd Party under Sa'd Zaghlul which pursued the dual aims of securing independence from Britain and limiting the monarchy's autocracy in the system.

The nationalist forces represented by the Wafd consisted of the landowners, the rising capitalist class, religious leaders, and affluent lawyers. Operating from such a narrow base,[1] and armed with a nationalist ideology directed against Britain, the Wafd was successful in skillfully mobilizing mass support among certain important sectors of Egypt's population—peasants, bureaucrats, students, small businessmen, and the urban masses. The hard-won independence from Britain in February 1922 represented an accomplishment of great magnitude, since it was the very first victory of a truly native Egyptian elite against foreign domination. Thus, the aura of legitimacy derived from this success remained with the Wafd even after the death in 1927 of its first leader, Sa'd Zaghlul. Yet neither its popularity nor its impressive showing at the polls were sufficient to enable the Wafd to rule the country. What prevented the Wafd from effective and continuous rulership was the crown, and to a lesser extent the British government. Palace intervention manifested itself in repeated violations and suspensions of the constitution promulgated in 1923. The Wafd was kept out of power from 1930 to 1936 when it won a substantial electoral victory reflecting popular opposition to the palace. In the subsequent ten years (1936–1946) the power struggle continued unabated. A number of lesser political parties that had come into being since 1924—Sa'dists, Liberal Constitutionalists, the Union Party, People's Party—were largely ineffectual.[2] Under King Faruq, the arbitrary dissolution of parliaments, the dismissal and appointment of cabinets, and the formulation of policy independently from the government, became routine practices.

The preoccupation of the Wafd and the lesser political groups with the power struggle left large areas of political thought and action unattended. Indeed, parallel to the political chaos was the crisis among intellectuals caused by the impact of modernization on a traditional Islamic society.[3] The problem involved nothing less than the creation of a comprehensive national philosophy to guide the subsequent transformation of Egypt. The gates to *ijtihad* [4] that had been opened by Shaykh Muhammad Abduh in the late 1800s remained open with no national consensus in sight. Not only were the intellectuals unable to reach a consensus, but there was no political leadership capable of effectively presiding over this crucial process of ideology formation and forging a new synthesis of thought. In view of its inability to hold power and the self-centered orientation of its narrow-based leadership, the Wafd did not fulfill this key role in the Egyptian political system. As a result the emerging nationalist ideology was not supplemented with a comprehensive creed of societal change.

It was in this situation of political *immobilisme* that a new urban class seeking upward mobility entered the Egyptian political stage in the early 1930s. The frustration that soon beset this nebulous class [5] proceeded directly from the existing social, political, and economic conditions in society. In a milieu marked by the erosion of the traditional Islamic value system, there was no available ideology to adopt. The anti-British nationalism of the Wafd offered no solution to their social and economic problems. Indeed, the chaotic system could not adopt or absorb the new groups by creating congruent relationships between it and the ruling elites. What was needed was not only economic and social reform but political recognition of the emerging class. The Wafd recognized the new class only to the extent of soliciting its votes but did not grant it a voice in the high councils of the party. This denial of upward political and social mobility, coupled with the Wafd's failure to deal effectively with the crown and the British, alienated the new emerging social groups from the grand party of Sa'd Zaghlul and his successor, Mustafa al-Nahhas. Faced with an unresponsive power structure that also forbade independent political organization, the new classes were forced to look for means of action outside the existing system. The movement that most successfully responded to their needs and aspirations was the Ikhwan al-Muslimin—the Muslim Brotherhood.

The phenomenal success of the Ikhwan in transforming itself from a small reformist society (1928) to a revivalist mass movement can be ascribed to its ability to perform precisely those functions in which the political parties had dismally failed.[6] The Ikhwan's novel formula was the unity of thought and action: it provided its followers with a total ideology identifying the ills of society and prescribing measures to remedy them. The propagators of this indigenous creed based on fundamentalist Islam not only advocated total social, economic, and political reform, but proceeded to demonstrate these in their own subsidiary enterprises. The Brotherhood provided each follower with specific tasks and duties thereby creating in him the *esprit de corps* of the indoctrinated believer who was also a participant with vested interests.

The period from 1945 to 1952 can best be described as one of protracted violence where, due to the progressive decrease in traditional-legal legitimacy, there was increasing reliance on force as a means of control. The chain of political assassinations by the Ikhwan and the Green Shirts were an unmistakable sign of deepening crisis. The only institution that had not been directly involved in the conflict before 1948 was the military establishment. While the junior officer ranks had been widely infiltrated by the Ikhwan, the communists and others, the military had not been utilized to settle the domestic political power struggle. Indeed, the king regarded the army as his own exclusive preserve of power. He controlled it through personal selection of senior officers for the high command and the screening of candidates entering the Military Academy. Several developments, however, alienated the military from the crown.

The year 1936 marked the beginning of an important policy change for admission to the Military Academy—a change destined to have far-reaching consequences for the political system. This policy instituted by the new Wafd government made it possible for native Egyptians of non-aristocratic or non-Turkish origin to gain entrance into the academy. It was no mere coincidence that all eleven founding members of the Free Officers group (1949) entered the academy in the three years after 1936.

Dissatisfaction among these young officers against Britain and the government developed early during World War II and drove them to conspiratorial activity. However what really alienated them was the humiliation of Egyptian arms in the Palestine War of 1948. The defective arms scandal and the arbitrary fashion in which the army had been committed to battle focused the wrath of the defeated officers upon the king and the palace-appointed leadership.[7] Furthermore, their distrust of civilian authority was reinforced during the Suez Canal crisis of October 1951, when the newly elected Wafdist government encouraged army participation in anti-British guerrilla activities. While some officers seem to have been involved in the government's attempt to divert the attention of the army away from domestic politics, the Free Officers Executive Committee under its chairman, Lt. Col. Gamal Abd al-Nasir, refused to respond.[8]

Much has been written about the history of the Free Officers movement prior to the seizure of power in July 1952, manifesting a wide range of diverse accounts and interpretations.[9] From these, several valid generalizations emerge.

The Association of Free Officers, established in 1949, was one of several conspiratorial groups within the army. Among these were Anwar al-Sadat's group that later joined the Free Officers and Mustafa Kamal Sidqi's terroristic organization. Also there existed a large group of officers organized by the Ikhwan, under Muhammad Labib.[10]

The Free Officers shared no common ideology except anti-British nationalism and dissatisfaction with the existing state of affairs. Many had been deeply influenced by the fundamentalist Islamic doctrines of the Brotherhood,[11] while others were leftists. In any case, members of the group were not permitted to retain membership in other organizations.

Despite the constant assertion that the Free Officers were "the sons of the people" and therefore of "humble origin," [12] this was not wholly the case. Since a secondary education was required to enter the Military Academy, it is clear that they came from families that could afford the expense of such schooling. Apparently, the Free Officers came from reasonably affluent middle class families of peasants, clerks, and other officials. None came directly from the poorer masses of Egypt, although in contrast to most earlier ruling elites they were ethnically Egyptian and in that sense could be considered "sons of the people." Furthermore, although seven percent of the officers corps were Christian, all of the principal Free Officers were Muslim. Not even a single Copt could be found among them.[13]

The distinguishing qualities of the Free Officers group that gave it certain advantages vis-à-vis competing conspiratorial organizations and the existing power structure, included:

1. Unity among the inner core of eleven officers, reinforced by past ties of schooling and combat as well as by their shared revulsion toward the status quo.

2. Effective leadership by the chairman of the Executive Committee, Abd al-Nasir, and the utilization of the cell system. Thus, a good deal of power was concentrated in the hands of the few who controlled certain key units of the army.

3. The ability to gather intelligence through strategically placed contacts about the plans of other secret societies, the high command, the palace, and the key embassies. At the hub of this communications network [14] was Nasir himself.

4. The ability to move quickly and boldly to preempt the actions of competing groups and the palace. Indeed, especially after witnessing the Free Officers strength in the Officers' Club elections, the king was preparing to crush them. Their boldness in being the first group to act guaranteed them success. Considering the weak state of the power structure, any one of the several officers' groups could have conceivably effected the coup, if they had moved first. What the various historical accounts do not

mention is that the other two major officers' groups had been on the decline during 1950–1951, while the Free Officers were gaining momentum.[15] One of these—Capt. Mustafa Kamal Sidqi's band of twenty-three officers—because of their continuous terroristic involvement had come under constant surveillance and harassment by the authorities that resulted in the group's partial breakup. On the other hand, the Brotherhood had dissipated its energies in the guerrilla campaign against the British in the Canal Zone. Government action against the Brethren was especially harsh, since of all the conspiratorial groups this was the largest and most powerful outside and inside the army. In addition, the Brethren in the army were left leaderless after the death of Muhammad Labib in 1951.

3
The Advent of
Military Dictatorship

THE coup that was to become a revolution came on 23 July, after months of internal crisis that had culminated in the burning of Cairo on 25 January 1952. Three days after the coup, King Faruq was forced to abdicate in favor of his son and was sent into exile. The swift and bloodless takeover ended over two millenia of foreign rule and brought to power a truly Egyptian elite. The ease with which the traditional power structure was brought down manifested the organizing skill of Abd al-Nasir and the weakness of the regime.

From the outset, the officers' behavior as rulers testified to their total lack of a program for concrete political action. Indeed, the first broadcasts of the coup contained only vague notions of what was to be done. The initial message proposed one negative and one positive action: "to cleanse the nation of tyrants" and "to restore constitutional life," both in the name of the people. As in other military coups, the clear implication of these early pronouncements was that in the absence of any other agent, the army had acted to set things right and would then return to the barracks. At first there existed no reason to suppose otherwise. The Free Officers Executive Committee renamed itself the Revolutionary Command Council and asked former Prime Minister Ali Mahir to form an all-civilian government. Soon, however, because of the ill-defined nature of the relationship between the RCC and the civilian cabinet, serious conflict developed culminating in Mahir's resignation on 7 September 1952. The prime minister was not prepared to accept the role of blind executor of RCC policies, which seemed too radical to the conservative civilians on the cabinet. The three policies that manifested the RCC's desire to establish popular bases of legitimacy and support for the revolution were agricultural reform, the abolition of monarchial rule (19 June 1953), and reorganization of political groups. In September 1952 the Agrarian Reform Law [1] was put into effect by a new all-civilian cabinet of apolitical technocrats under the "Leader of the Revolution," General Muhammad Nagib. In view of the historical land ownership structure in the valley of the Nile, this limited redistribution of land to the fallahin was a revolutionary act of some consequence. It enabled the regime to establish a link with the peasant masses and reduce the economic power of the landed aristocracy. However, the greater political significance of the Agrarian Reform Law lay in its being a demonstration of RCC power in the face of vehement opposition from the once powerful landlords and former civilian elites.

A far more explosive problem was reform of the political parties. Indeed, the issue involved nothing less than a delimitation of the civilian role versus the military role in government—an issue that kept Egyptian politics in turmoil until mid-1954.

The coup of July 1952 had been an affair exclusively organized and directed by eleven [2] junior officers, relatively unknown outside the military establishment and lacking widespread popular support. Their last-minute desperate efforts to recruit General Nagib to lead the revolt as front man did not flow from Lt. Col. Abd al-Nasir's wish "to yield the place of honor to an older man," [3] as Colonel al-Sadat asserts, but was designed to surround the Free Officers group with a halo of legitimacy and recognition which they sorely lacked. Indeed, Generals Aziz al-Misri and Ahmad Fu'ad Sadiq had been contacted earlier for the leadership position and were found less receptive.[4] Besides the scarcity of recruitable leaders, the Free Officers choice of Nagib had been prompted by the general's distinguished performance in the Palestinian War [5] and his known sympathies with the aims of his junior colleagues. In view of this background and his assigned role as Leader of the Revolution, popular attention automatically centered on Nagib, who by September 1952 held the offices of premier, war minister, commander-in-chief, and RCC chairman. Such achievements as agrarian reform and the abolition of the monarchy were credited, not to the relatively colorless [6] military figures of the RCC, but to their leader. In addition to being one of the few Egyptian heroes of the 1948 War, Nagib's fatherly bearing and reputation as a humble pious Muslim contributed to his popularity among the people. In the eyes of the Egyptian masses, he was the hero-general appearing in a time of acute crisis with a message of salvation who would now change the miserable status quo. Indeed, in terms of milieu, personality, and performance, General Nagib possessed considerable charismatic potential. To establish the causes for his subsequent failure to become a truly charismatic leader, it is necessary to analyze his role in the power struggles of 1953–1954.

By mid-August 1952, it was quite apparent that the RCC's order of July 31 to political groups "to purge undesirable elements," had not been taken seriously by the Wafd and the lesser political parties.[7] As to the Brotherhood, in view of its great organizational power and numerous adherents among the military, the RCC chose not to consider it a political party. The short period of accommodation [8] that followed was terminated (August 1952) when the RCC rejected the Brotherhood's demand of veto power over new legislation. Soon it became clear that the officers would accept neither the Brotherhood's ideology, nor its organizational machine. Instead, the RCC went directly to the people to organize support by sending its members on extensive speaking assignments between September 1952 and June 1953. Meanwhile the regime began to unfold its new policy toward the civilian political groups. The initial action was in response to a challenge from the least powerful of all civilian political organization—the extreme left—in the form of the Kafr al-Dawwar labor revolt of 13 August 1952.[9] The vigorous suppression of the unrest and the subsequent hanging of its two ringleaders seemed to indicate the regime's desire to set a forceful example for other civilian groups contemplating counter-revolutionary activities. The next blow fell on the larger political groups. In January 1953 all parties were dissolved and their assets confiscated. The inauguration of the Liberation Rally on 23 January 1953, was an attempt to fill the vacuum between the regime and the masses and contain political unrest perpetrated by the civilian groups. The launching of this mass organization and the simultaneous announcement of a three-year "transitional period" under military dictatorship, revealed the RCC's intention to stay in power. The establishment of the Republic on 19 June 1953, formalized direct military rule as four leading RCC members took over key ministries in the government: Gamal Abd al-Nasir, deputy premier and interior minister; Abd al-Latif al-Baghdadi, war minister; Abd al-Hakim Amir, commander-in-chief; Salah Salim, minister of national guidance and Sudanese affairs. General Nagib was made president of the Republic and prime minister.

In retrospect, it seems that the assumption of direct rule by the military was related to the new alignments emerging within the RCC and the army itself. One central problem was the growing popularity of General Nagib whose moderate public pronouncements contrasted sharply with the militant words and actions of his younger colleagues. Indeed, the general must have felt that his source of power and legitimacy extended far beyond the narrow clique of young officers and embraced the dispossessed civilian groups and the Egyptian masses. In the circumstances, the takeover of important cabinet positions by Abd al-Nasir and his three colleagues can be viewed as an attempt to demonstrate explicitly and publicly their actual possession of power. Yet their main base of strength—the Army Officer Corps—was not secure, even after repeated purges of potential military counter-elites. One such action seems to have taken place on 25 September 1952, when 450 Wafdist officers were retired.[10] Action was also taken against the influential artillery colonel, Rashad Muhanna, the leader of an abortive 1947 revolt, who had refused to join the Free Officers at a critical stage of the July coup. Due to his deep involvement with the Ikhwan [11] and his attacks on the RCC's agrarian measures, Muhanna was removed from the Regency Council on 17 January and placed under house arrest. In the same month Muhanna was implicated in an anti-RCC plot along with the brothers, Lt. Col. Muhammad Husni al-Damanhuri and Capt. Hasan Rif'at al-Damanhuri, and sentenced to life imprisonment.[12] As the RCC's two-front conflict with General Nagib and the civilian political groups intensified during 1953, a coalition of such strange bedfellows as the Brethren, Leftists and Wafdists emerged, cutting deeply into the ranks of the army and the RCC itself. The leadership of this pro-Nagib alliance rested with the Supreme Council of the Brethren which had itself split into factions favoring and opposing cooperation with the military regime.[13] Essentially, therefore, the ensuing struggle between the military and the Brotherhood involved two internally split centers of power, each attempting to exacerbate the existing conflicts within the opposition group.

The opening shot finally came from the Brotherhood in January 1954 in the form of large-scale student and labor disorders protesting the February 1953 Anglo-Egyptian agreement on the Sudan and calling for *jihad*—holy war—against the British garrisons in the Canal Zone.[14] The RCC responded on 14 January by imprisoning 400 Brethren including the Supreme Guide. Apparently this action did not weaken the organization seriously, since the anti-RCC front continued to precipitate serious disturbances in February-March 1954.

General Nagib's sudden resignation on 25 February, prompted by policy disagreements within the government, brought a great outpouring of anti-RCC public sentiment and threats of mutiny among army officers and Sudanese frontier guards.[15] While the evidence about RCC's infighting is sketchy, the pro-Communist RCC member, Khalid Muhyi al-Din and other cavalry officers supported Nagib against the pro-Abd al-Nasir forces.[16] Considering the split in the army and the solid organizational support granted him by the Brethren-Leftist-Wafdist alliance, General Nagib loomed as the greatest threat to the faltering power of the RCC's pro-Nasir majority. Three days later Nagib was reinstated in office amid great popular jubilation. But instead of remaining at the helm of power in Cairo to consolidate and even maximize his new strength, the general soon journeyed to face the uncertainties of a political celebration in the Sudan. Meanwhile, as the new military governor of Egypt, Colonel Abd al-Nasir presided over the thorough liquidation of pro-Nagib elements in the army. However, the colonel's most remarkable feat had been his success in retaining the loyalties of most RCC members during the trying days of late February.

Interaction of Policy and Power

To discerne the precise factors responsible for Abd al-Nasir's acquisition and preservation of leadership within the RCC and
among the larger group of pro-RCC officers will continue to be a
difficult task as long as inside sources remain unavailable. Even
after the lapse of eighteen years there exists little hard evidence
on the proceedings within the RCC and on the period of Nagib's
ascendancy in general.[17] However, it is evident that between the
July 1952 coup and Nagib's triumphant return to power in late
February 1954, the attrition in RCC membership was limited to
officers marginal to the inner core. The original membership of
the RCC after the coup consisted of:

> Muhammad Nagib
> * Gamal Abd al-Nasir
> * Abd al-Hakim Amir
> * Salah Salim
> * Gamal Salim
> * Kamal al-Din Husayn
> * Hasan Ibrahim
> * Abd al-Latif al-Baghdadi
> * Anwar al-Sadat
> * Khalid Muhyi al-Din
> * Zakariyya Muhyi al-Din
> * Husayn al-Shafi'i
> * Ahmad Anwar
> * Kamal al-Din Rif'at
> Ahmad Shawqi
> Abd al-Mun'im Abd al-Ra'uf
> Lutfi Wahid
> Yusif Sadiq

The attrition process seems to have been a gradual affair.
Prior to the February 1954 disturbances, at least three of the

* Denotes thirteen core RCC members who had had close ties prior to
the July coup.

members—the Leftists, Shawqi and Sadiq,[18] and the Muslim Brother, Abd al-Ra'uf—had left the fold to engage in conspiratorial activities. While Shawqi and Sadiq, in their capacity as commanders of key units on the night of the coup, had perhaps contributed most to the takeover, they were latecomers to the inner circle.[19] On the other hand, Abd al-Ra'uf seems to have spiritually left the Free Officers group sometime between 1949 and 1952, before his final departure in 1953. Thus, the only inner core member who temporarily deserted the pro-Nasir majority was the Leftist, Khalid Muhyi al-Din, who threw his lot in with General Nagib. All the remaining twelve RCC members stood solidly behind Nasir.

The phenomenal solidarity of the inner group with Abd al-Nasir is often explained in terms of his natural gifts of leadership and the cohesiveness of the core forged in military training, battle, and revolt. On the other hand, Nagib is seen as an older man with a traditional outlook, whose association with the younger officers prior to the coup had not been intimate. While these explanations are correct, they only supplement the truism that, in the final analysis, leadership and power depend upon policy—the latter being the appeals of competing leaders designed to maximize their support for the purpose of achieving power. In the context of the Nagib-Nasir struggle for power, as in other situations,[20] policy choices helped determine the winner in the contest. It should be remembered that, essentially, the competing policies centered on the role of the military in Egyptian politics. While the popular general's advocacy of "a return to the barracks" might have eventually guaranteed him the presidency in a civilian context, it directly threatened the vested interests of the ruling military elite. In the crucial confrontation with Abd al-Nasir within the RCC and the army, Nagib was bound to lose since his choice of the policy of explicit opposition to military rule showed a total lack of sensitivity to the quest for power inherent in the ambitious young officers. Thus, they had no choice but to throw in their lot with Abd al-Nasir.

To be sure, in the struggle for leadership, the skilful choice of issues and the related elements of sensitivity to power and timing are as relevant to constitutional systems,[21] as they are to authoritarian conditions; the major difference being in the consequences of failure. Thus, Dwight Eisenhower's inability to understand and utilize these power-preserving devices resulted in indecisive rulership; such a failure for Abd al-Nasir would have surely meant a permanent loss of power.

The temporary defeat of the Nasirite faction in late February 1954 was brought about precisely because of the RCC's insensitivity toward the element of timing. While defection within the RCC and its military supporters had been cut to a minimum, by his resignation on 23 February, the general had forced upon his opponents an enlargement of the scope of conflict to include the suppressed groups and the masses. When one considers the subsequent outpouring of popular support for Nagib, the RCC's acceptance of the general's resignation demonstrated a clear-cut case of erroneous timing. Indeed, Abd al-Nasir and his followers had permitted Nagib to precipitate the struggle at a time of their relative weakness on two fronts. First, the purge of pro-Nagib elements within the army had not been completed, and second, the RCC and its emerging leader did not yet possess organized popular support among the urban masses.

The RCC's main effort to gain civilian support centered on unionized workers and students. Simultaneously, the RCC purged pro-Nagib and leftist elements within the army [22] and initiated a campaign to reduce Nagib's popular and organizational strength through pressures, imprisonments, and propaganda. These dual goals of building student-labor mass support and undermining pro-Nagib and especially Ikhwan power were partly pursued within the institutional structure of the Liberation Rally. This organization served as a "school" to indoctrinate the masses and counterbalance Ikhwan students and other anti-Nasir elements in street demonstrations. After these preparatory steps, in response to the mounting anti-RCC campaign [23] in the newly freed press, suppressive measures were relaxed and by 9 March, Nagib once again became prime minister. Encouraged by the existing political climate, Nagib pressed the RCC for a gradual demilitarization of the government and the election of a constituent assembly. In a surprise move on 22 March, the RCC rejected these measures and adopted a resolution promising an end to military rule by 24 July, restoration of political parties, and free elections for a constituent assembly to elect a president.[24]

Shocked by the resolution, the general could clearly discern its meaning. Nagib could not vote against the resolution, since it was he who was the great champion of parliamentary rule. Indeed, such opposition on his part would permanently eliminate the support he had from diverse civilian political groups. Yet voting for Nasir's resolution would cast him in the role of destroyer of the revolution in the eyes of the army and its civilian supporters. Fully aware of the detrimental effects of both alternatives to his position, the general reluctantly chose to vote for the resolution.

As expected, the sudden announcement to end the revolution shocked its supporters and crystallized the anti-Nagib sentiment both in and outside the army. By picturing the general as the foe of the revolution, the RCC effectively alienated him from his remaining supporters in the army.

While preparing its next move, the RCC released scores of political prisoners, including the Supreme Guide of the Ikhwan, Hasan al-Hudaybi. Meanwhile, the old political parties were seriously engaged in reactivating themselves in preparation for parliamentary rule. The time had come for the RCC to display its following in the streets—a type of support that it had lacked in the previous contest of power. Well-organized mass demonstrations by students and workers belonging to the Liberation Rally were held in several strategic areas of Cairo, in support of continued RCC rule. This was followed by a paralyzing strike of pro-RCC transport workers, which on 29 March spread to other parts of Egypt. Next, the army, the navy, and the police expressed their strong support of the RCC. It all seemed a carefully staged show of popular pro-Nasir support. Indeed it was. The street mob—that formidable and ever-present force in Middle Eastern politics—which had been one of Nagib's major weapons against the RCC, was turned against him. On 28 March, "bowing to popular demand," the RCC reversed its decision of 25 March and announced that it would continue to rule until the end of the transitional period (January 1956), the political parties would again be outlawed, and the elections would be postponed; instead, a vague "national consultative council" would be created.

The old political parties reacted vehemently but ineffectively to the sudden reestablishment of military dictatorship. The student demonstrations organized by the Brethren, the Wafdists and the communists, were quickly dispersed and the universities were closed down. On 18 April, Nasir once again became prime minister and chairman of RCC, while Nagib retained the presidency. During the subsequent trials of Brotherhood leaders, Nagib was implicated and placed under house arrest on 14 November 1954. The contest for power between Muhammad Nagib and Gamal Abd al-Nasir had ended with the latter's victory.

The ascendancy of pro-Nasir forces in the spring of 1954 marked the beginning of institutionalized military rule in Egypt. Yet this initial success did not fully secure Nasirite power, which was still endangered by the remaining opposition groups, especially the Ikhwan. In the attempt to destroy its opponents, the first step in the regime's strategy was to reduce the weaker organizations. Consequently, the Wafd, Liberal Constitutionalists, and the Sa'dists received the first blow; their leaders were deprived of political rights for ten years and excluded from executive positions in various organizations. Significantly, the Ikhwan leadership was not included in this category. Always true to the time-tested formula of divide and rule, once again Abd al-Nasir postponed the final reckoning with the Brethren. Meanwhile, successive blows were administered to Ahmad Husayn's Misr al-Fatat, Mustafa Kamal Sidqi's National Democrats, and Wafdist students. More important perhaps, the military dictatorship made a good start toward the depoliticization of students—a significant achievement in Middle Eastern politics. Under the newly appointed minister of education, Kamal al-Din Husayn, many student agitators and forty university professors were purged.[25]

Though preoccupied with internal problems of power perpetuation, Prime Minister Nasir moved decisively to settle the question of British military presence in the Canal Zone. The ensuing mildly pro-Western policy precipitated immediate opposition from the communists and the Brotherhood. In line with his previous practice, Nasir first retaliated against the much weaker communists by arresting 252 party members on 31 May 1954.[26] The conflict between the Brethren and the government did not intensify until the initialling of a Heads of Agreement with Britain on 27 July 1954, which provided for the complete evacuation of the Canal Zone within twenty months, while giving Britain the right to return if Turkey or Arab League nations were attacked.[27] Soon it became evident that this agreement, which had been negotiated by Abd al-Nasir personally, was being used by the Ikhwan to rally opposition against the regime both in Egypt and the rest of the Arab world. In his "open letter" of 2 August, addressed to Abd al-Nasir, al-Hudaybi called the agreement "treasonable"; later he toured the Arab countries denouncing the prime minister as a "traitor to the national cause." [28] This attempt of the Supreme Guide to bring external and internal pressure on the regime was not very successful in terms of undermining Abd al-Nasir's power in Egypt. Yet throughout the summer, the regime took no decisive steps against the Ikhwan, but limited itself to neutralizing the Brotherhood's commando groups in the Canal Zone and publicly answering the charges of treasonable conduct. Meanwhile Brethren propaganda continued to praise General Nagib as the "Savior of the country," whose opposition to the Canal agreement was no secret.[29]

Throughout the summer and early fall the uneasy coexistence of the regime and the Ikhwan persisted. On the night of 26 October Muslim Brother Mahmud Abd al-Latif fired eight shots at Premier Abd al-Nasir during a speech in Alexandria. This unsuccessful and badly organized assassination attempt provided the regime with the opportunity to crush the Ikhwan. Before dawn the leaders of the movement were arrested, and eventually 4,000 members were taken into custody.[30] The key members of the organization were brought before a special "people's tribunal" consisting of Gamal Salim, Husayn al-Shafi'i, and Anwar al-Sadat. The proceedings somewhat resembled the Stalinist show trials of the 1930s and the Czechoslovak trials of the early 1950s. Apparently under torture, the once proud Brethren were reduced to broken wrecks, and when subjected to intensive questioning most of them pleaded guilty to charges of subversive activity,[31] and implicated many "undesirables" including President Nagib who was subsequently put under house arrest.[32] What emerged from these show trials, which were given wide publicity through the government-controlled mass media, was another category of "enemies of the people," to be added to such earlier enemies as the Wafdists, the royalists, and the communists. Despite a Brethren offer to terminate all counter-revolutionary activity in return for the release of its arrested members,[33] the regime pressed on with the trials. Six of the defendants were executed and Supreme Guide al-Hudaybi was imprisoned for life. As far as it is known the alleged organizer of the attempted plot, Lt. Col. Abd al-Ra'uf, was never caught.

The suppression of the Brethren removed the last and most powerful of Egypt's political organizations, at least temporarily.[34] The systematic pulverization of these groups secured the new regime and demonstrated its ability and willingness to use its power decisively to crush opponents. The stage was set for the regime's self-avowed intent to begin the process of social transformation, if indeed this was its immediate aim.

A Quantitative Survey of Crises (1947–1955)

The progressive deterioration of Egypt's political-social fabric between 1947 and 1952, and the subsequent power struggles until 1955, can be illustrated by a quantitative study of reported events or acts of coercion and violence. These conflict indicators include instances of large-scale imprisonments, violent strikes and demonstrations, suppressions, killings and assassinations, plots and purges—all involving a large measure of violence.[35] For the sake of convenience the reported occurrences are weighed equally; the "Chronology" of the *Middle East Journal* is used as the main source.

An analysis of Figure 3 shows the sharp jump of frequency of acts involving the manifestation of coercive power between 1947–48. These were due to the defeat in Palestine, the Sudan question, and the deep cleavages in Egyptian society. The relative calm of 1949 and 1950 may be indicative of the last concerted effort of the ruling traditional-legal elites to maintain control in a situation of minimal legitimacy. Even during this brief lull before the storm some aspects of the next phase of turmoil—the Suez crisis, the arms scandal, etc.—were coming into sharp focus. Thus the sharp rise in the number of reported cases of violence during 1951 and the first half of 1952 shows the progressive inability of the system to contain its internal dis-

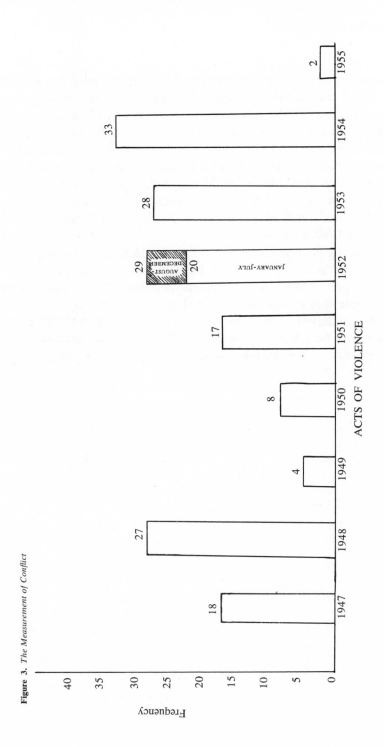

Figure 3. *The Measurement of Conflict*

ruptive forces in an atmosphere of Ikhwan-led guerrilla warfare against the British. It should be noted that during the seven months prior to the July coup, twenty acts of violence were committed in contrast to the previous high count of twenty-seven for the entire year of 1948. This pointed to an unprecedented intensification of the crisis leading to the military takeover. It was ironic that in the midst of this turmoil, King Faruq made what was to be his last attempt at self-legitimation when he proudly announced on 6 May 1952, the tracing of his ancestry to the Prophet Muhammad.

During the remaining five months of 1952, the violence count dropped to nine, but during 1953 it rose to a high of twenty-eight, and in 1954 to an unprecedented thirty-three, reflecting the struggles for power, the suppression of the political parties, and the liquidation of the Ikhwan. In sharp contrast, the 1955 count stood at two, testifying to the totality of military control under Nasir, as well as to the nascent legitimacy of his rule.[36]

4

The Emergence of
Charismatic Authority

WITH the elimination of all organized opposition, the "political" phase of the revolution was complete. According to Abd al-Nasir's timetable, the "social" revolution would be the next order of business in Egypt.[1] However, for a variety of reasons the latter phase was postponed until 1961. While it is difficult to ascertain all of the reasons behind the regime's failure to undertake thoroughgoing social transformation in the mid-1950s, several factors are apparent. The first of these was the existing ideological and organizational vacuum. The Western democratic ideology, with its constitutional forms, had been discredited;[2] in its stead, no substitute ideology, myth, or institution was introduced by the military. Indeed, in their preoccupation with internal power struggles until mid-1954, the officers had not had an opportunity to develop a comprehensive blueprint for social action. Although they had crushed the various opposition groups, the resultant void was not filled with new cadres for social control and organization, except those borrowed from the army. As models, the totalitarian systems of the right and the left were equally unattractive. The bloody excesses of the Nazis and their subsequent defeat in World War II dispelled the early fascination of certain Egyptian civilian and military leaders with the German experience. Similarly, the Stalinist terror, coupled with the anti-nationalism and atheism of communist ideology, found few firm adherents among the military elite.[3] In fact, considering the lack of ideology and experienced cadres, the totalitarian alternative was not a viable one in the mid-1950s. Finally, the elite faced the classical problem of all successful revolutionaries—the critical transition from destroyers to builders—that required a total psychological metamorphosis; and for military officers, specialists in the arts of destruction, this task was doubly difficult. Yet it was clear that both after the July coup and in the wake of Nasir's victory over Nagib, the officers almost intuitively felt the need for new bases of legitimacy. Significantly, until early 1955, the military pursued its quest for self-legitimation almost exclusively through a continuation of traditional and legal-rational means, as their predecessors had done before them. The cooptation of General Nagib to invest the July coup with the legitimacy of his heroism and senior officer status constituted one example. After the takeover, both in its pronouncements and actions, the junta maintained a degree of adherence to legal-rational means which involved a semblance of constitutional freedoms and periodic relaxations of control. Thus, at the outset, the RCC released hundreds of political prisoners, abolished the king's secret police, lifted press censorship, punished corruption, installed civilian cabinets, initiated land reform, passed labor and social legislation, and repeatedly promised an early return to full constitutional rule. Yet as the Nagib-Nasir rivalry intensified, the hard-won legitimacy derived from the preceding acts went to the general. As the crisis of legitimacy engulfed the Nasirites, they were compelled to legitimize their sole instrument of mass support—the Liberation Rally—by emphasizing its "teaching of religious observance and orthodoxy" to the youth.[4] This use of Islamic orthodoxy—a traditional legitimizing device—was especially revealing since it was designed to neutralize the Ikhwan's anti-RCC campaign being waged throughout Egypt and the neighboring Arab states. It was in this context that early in 1954 RCC spokesman, Major Salah Salim, began to make vague references to ". . . some sort of Arab unity" and ". . . a simultaneous federation of Arab states . . . ,"[5] a theme which in later years became a major ideological tool in the Nasirite quest for Pan-Arab legitimacy.

If anything, the crisis in legitimacy loomed greater than ever after Nagib's overthrow and the Brotherhood's suppression. While relying heavily on force as its main instrument of control, the regime continued to use the old combination of traditional and legal-rational devices of self-legitimation. In concrete terms these included Prime Minister Nasir's pilgrimage to Mecca (7 August 1954) where he met the leaders of Sa'udi Arabia and Pakistan and issued the call of Islamic unity against the West.[6] In September, RCC member Anwar al-Sadat called an Islamic congress in Cairo to stress the regime's orthodoxy, and two months later (17 November) the Council of the Ulama' at Al-Azhar went on record denouncing Ikhwan terrorism and supporting the regime. At the same time, as a grand gesture, the presidency was offered to the highly respected octogenarian, Lutfi al-Sayyid, who declined the post. Throughout, the regime increasingly aligned itself with popular opinion by making anti-British pronouncements, bringing to trial certain spies for Israel, and reiterating its promise to restore constitutional life by January 1956. Thus, by early 1955, having entrenched itself through military power, the regime was still groping for traditional and legal legitimacy on the bases of the old value systems of Egyptian nationalism, and Islamic orthodoxy. If there was in Nasir's mind a scheme to build a radically new foundation for rule legitimacy through a massive ideologically-conditioned social-economic transformation, it was not made explicit at this stage.

Foreign Policies as Sources of Legitimacy

For the Nasirites the year 1954 was one of victory over internal challenges—a victory accomplished primarily through the military's superior coercive power. In contrast, the eventful year 1955 may be regarded as a turning point during which almost inadvertently the military elite began to discover a new base for legitimacy—the leader's popular appeal. This appeal was generated by Nasir's phenomenal success in the international arena during 1955 and 1956.

Nasir's diplomatic prowess affected a change in the leadership's primary focus of interest from the domestic to the foreign plane; subsequently the revolutionary dynamic registered a perceptible shift from Egypt to the Pan-Arab level. Yet, even without the new order of priorities, simultaneous action on both the home and foreign fronts would have been difficult because of the elite's small size and the limited capabilities of the emerging system. Indeed, considering the initial reluctance of the ruling military to incorporate large numbers of civilians at the top, the large-scale decision-making required by a two-front revolution would have been practically impossible,[7] even if an ideology of internal transformation existed.

There is little evidence that, initially, the military elite planned extensive foreign involvement; to a large extent this was dictated by external factors. Ironically, it might even be said that Nasir's very enemies—the Brethren, Israel, the West—inadvertently projected him into the international plane. The gains registered in foreign policy had three major interrelated effects. First, Nasir's successful performance in international affairs brought him great popularity among Egyptians and the masses in other Arab lands as well. Second, the leader's newly gained Pan-Arab popularity and the increasing primacy given to Egypt in the Arab world initiated an elite-inspired ideological revolution: Egyptian nationalism evolved into Arab unity nationalism.[8] Third, Abd al-Nasir's adoption and propagation of the new ideology of Arab-unity nationalism (Cairo-centered) as his own personal message brought about a substantial normative change in the belief system of Egyptians.[9] Increasingly, Egyptians began to look at themselves as Arabs, thus sharing and adopting their leader's belief system. Therefore, charismatic authority can be said to have emerged at the moment when Nasir's popularity derived from successful diplomacy enabled him to modify significantly the beliefs of his people. And to the extent that the leadership had internal support derived from charismatic legitimacy, it did not feel initially the need for additional legitimational props achieved through large-scale internal transformation. As Figure 3 indicates, during 1955 the number of acts involving force or violence decreased greatly, illustrating not only the government's ability to liquidate the opposition by force, but also the new legitimacy that the regime had acquired. After the mid-1950s, control came to depend increasingly on a rising legitimacy component.

The End of Egypt's Splendid Isolation

Egypt's political isolation from the Arab East, since the time of Muhammad Ali and for centuries prior, began to break down after the 1930s. A variety of factors—political, economic, cultural—were responsible for bringing independent Egypt closer to the Arab lands beyond the Sinai.[10] Ideologically, by the late 1930s, the Westernist-Pharaonic phase had given way to an intellectual movement seeking reidentification with the Islamic ethos [11]—a development that rekindled the Islamic-Arab past and caused Egyptians to relate more actively to other Muslim-Arab states. At a more pragmatic level, this trend had been strengthened by the establishment of the British-conceived Arab League and by King Faruq's pro-Arab and Pan-Islamic policies. Moreover, in view of historical precedent and geopolitical factors, Egypt could be expected to show a strategic interest in lands beyond the Suez.

The Arab-Israeli War of 1948 marked the culmination of this process, whereby for historical, strategic, and emotional reasons the Palestine issue became permanently wedded to Egyptian foreign policy. The joint defeat of Arabs and Egyptians strengthened their existing ties of mutual identification and widely publicized in Egypt the threat of Israel.

Finally, it can be argued that after 1952 the actions of the Ikhwan forcefully directed the regime's attention to other Arab countries. By waging a vigorous campaign in Arab lands against the Canal Zone Agreement and the alleged anti-Islamic orientation of Nasir's regime, the Ikhwan enlarged the scope of conflict to include Muslim Arabs outside Egypt. While the prospect of British departure was generally well received, the subsequent ruthless suppression of Brethren leaders in Egypt seems to have shaken Egyptians and other Arabs alike. In view of the furor created in Syria, Jordan, and Iraq, and especially considering the detrimental effect of this on Muslim Egyptians, it seems logical to assume that some of Nasir's subsequent policies were designed to appease the Muslim majorities at home and abroad.[12]

While the foregoing developments eroded Egypt's isolation from the Levant, it was not until 1955 that she was drawn into active involvement in inter-Arab politics. This turbulent period of Egyptian history may be viewed as one of continuous and heightened interaction between foreign policy, external events, and the leadership performance of Nasir. The external factors that projected the Egyptian revolutionary dynamic and its leader to the Pan-Arab level included the Baghdad Pact, the Bandung Conference, the arms deal with the Soviet bloc, and the Suez crisis of 1956.

Soon after the Anglo-Egyptian agreement (Februrary 1953) on the Suez Canal, there seems to have been a general expectation in the West that eventually Egypt could be brought into a Middle East defense network directed against the Soviet Union.[13] Still preoccupied with internal problems of power consolidation, Abd al-Nasir apparently hedged until 24 February 1955, when Turkey and Iraq suddenly announced the conclusion of an alliance with the West. Prime Minister Nuri al-Sa'id of Iraq had taken the lead in reaching an accommodation with the West without waiting for Abd al-Nasir, who viewed the action as an attempt to disrupt Arab solidarity,[14] reintroduce British influence in the Middle East, and weaken Egypt's position in the Arab League. The virulent Egyptian propaganda attack that ensued against Nuri Pasha found enthusiastic support among other Arabs and had the effect of nearly isolating Iraq in the Arab East. Through a series of bilateral defense agreements, Sa'udi Arabia, Syria, and Yemen linked themselves to the Egyptian defense system.[15] Egypt's negative stand toward the proposed Baghdad Pact increased her influence and popularized Abd al-Nasir in the Arab world. By his refusal to be pushed into a treaty arrangement with two ex-imperial powers—Britain and Turkey—Abd al-Nasir had placed himself within the prevailing stream of Arab sentiment, which focussed on the desirability of concluding defense agreements against Israel and not the more distant Soviet Union.

In terms of sustaining and extending his influence and popularity, the Egyptian leader's first act of defiance of the West was a move in the right direction. Indeed, consciously or unconsciously he had chosen an issue—refusal to join a Western-sponsored pact. And through the utilization of the centrally-controlled mass media, he had made the issue the passionate concern of Egyptians and other Arabs. Clearly, in the Arab-Egyptian milieu of the mid-1950s, there existed a crisis situation to be exploited by a sensitive leader, through the skillful choice of issues that would arouse strong feelings among the masses. In view of the near complete alienation of many Arabs from the West,[16] the most relevant issue a sensitive leader could espouse would be a general policy of anti-Westernism. And the choice of this issue at a time of growing frustration among Arabs, as was the case in the early 1950s, illustrated the emerging leader's remarkable sense of timing.[17]

The popularity Nasir gained from his confrontation with the West was instrumental in laying the preliminary groundwork on which future charismatic legitimacy would rest. Yet defiance of the West, however heroic in Arab eyes, essentially constitutes a negative act. When the leader manages to supplement such defiance with the positive act of acquiring recognition and respect at the international level, his popularity would certainly increase among his people. At the first summit meeting of Afro-Asian ex-colonial states held in Bandung, Indonesia, in April 1955, Abd al-Nasir was treated as the leading representative of the Arab world and emerged as one of the key figures of the conference. Success at Bandung marked the beginning of Nasir's subsequent addiction to "summitry"—a practice utilized especially by leaders of developing nations to distract the people's attention from their not-too-happy domestic condition to external successes. But more significant perhaps, was Nasir's reeducation at Bandung and other conferences under the influence of such men as Jawaharlal Nehru and Josip Broz Tito. As a result, in terms of adopting a policy toward the bi-polar world and developing an external ideology, the Egyptian leader became a leading proponent of the doctrine of positive neutralism and non-alignment.[18] In view of prevailing sentiment, the anti-Westernism and anti-colonialism implicit in positive neutralism would find widespread support in the Arab world. Nasir's prominent role at Bandung and his adoption of anti-Westernist positive neutralism seems to have had a great impact on the Arabs. Indeed, Bandung ushered in that phase of the charismatic process when a leader begins to create an image of himself embodying qualities highly esteemed by his society.[19] This is reflected in the following lines:

> The name of Nasir has become a part of our country's
> name . . . it has become our symbol of the enormous evo-
> lution that occurred in the Arab East and Africa. It has
> also become a symbol of the cooperation of three
> continents—Africa, Asia, and Latin America.[20]

The development of charismatic leadership is directly dependent on the leader's continued success in achieving victories. The
one failure amongst Nasir's string of victories was the challenge
of Israel. Until February 1955, Egyptian policy toward Israel
had been relatively less aggressive than that of other Arab states.
Fully cognizant of his army's weaknesses and preoccupied with
domestic problems, Abd al-Nasir had limited himself to a policy
of keeping the Suez Canal and the Gulf of Aqaba closed to shipping bound for Israel. When Israel attacked Gaza on 28 February
1955, declaredly to suppress commando raids, and subsequently
remilitarized the Al-Awja area in September–November, the
Egyptians were in no position to retaliate.[21] These actions constituted a serious problem for the emerging leader, since they demonstrated the weakness of his forces. If the Egyptian regime was
to maintain its position in the Arab world and, indeed, to stay in
power at home, it needed to acquire modern armaments to build
a strong fighting force. Defense of the Suez Canal after the British
departure, Israel's growing might, and pressure from his own military were additional factors that led Nasir to seek modern arms.
When it became apparent that the West was reluctant to supply
these under terms financially and militarily acceptable to Egypt,
Nasir turned to the Soviet bloc and concluded a satisfactory armaments agreement in September 1955. While this setback of the
West gave a major advantage to the Soviet Union, it also contributed heavily to Abd al-Nasir's popularity among Arab masses.[22]
Through the arms deal, the military defeat at Gaza was turned
into a political victory, further enhancing the leader's position.
The West's denial of large-scale modern arms had been a major
grievance for Egyptians and other Arabs alike since their defeat
by Israel in 1948. Arms acquisition had been a passionately felt
need which Nasir satisfied by responding positively to the Soviet
offer. In Arab eyes he once again succeeded in defying the West
and winning another victory. In deepening the emotional bond

between the leader and the led, Nasir's third successful performance had reinforced popular faith in the eventual success of the leader's movement.

As the three year "transition period" ended in June 1956, a new constitution was promulgated and Nasir was elected president. With the termination of martial law, the RCC dissolved itself and its members resigned their military commissions. Meanwhile, Nasir's policies in the Arab world were clashing headlong with the interests of the Western powers. With France there was the thorny problem of Egyptian support to Algerian revolutionaries; with Britain, the violent Egyptian campaign against Middle East monarchies increasingly angered the Eden government. Moreover, Nasir's repeated threats about the possibility of withholding Arab oil from Europe were not conducive to normal relations; neither were a series of Egyptian diplomatic moves which progressively alienated the American leadership. These included the rejection of the Baghdad Pact, the Soviet arms deal, adherence to positive neutralism, and the recognition of the People's Republic of China. Apparently, Nasir did not expect a forceful American reaction to his moves. He may have thought that regardless of his actions the Americans would fulfill their promise to finance the construction of the Aswan High Dam if only to block a Soviet effort in that direction. This appraisal did not take into account the thinking of the chief pilot of United States foreign policy, the avidly anti-neutralist John Foster Dulles. The secretary of state's abrupt withdrawal of the offer, followed by a similar British move, greatly angered Abd al-Nasir, who retaliated by nationalizing the Universal Maritime Suez Canal Company on 26 July 1956.[23]

The official reason given for the nationalization was the need to use Canal profits in place of the withdrawn Anglo-American aid to build the High Dam. However, the resort to such a potentially dangerous form of retaliation seems to have been dictated by political and perhaps psychological reasons.[24]

The psychological compulsion to get even cannot be lightly dismissed in the behavior of such revolutionaries as Fidel Castro and Abd al-Nasir. Indeed, all reverses and rebuffs from stronger powers are regarded as affronts to their personal dignity requiring some sort of immediate retaliation. But more important than the personal were the ideological and political reasons to retaliate. The ideological compulsion to retaliate is inherent in revolutionary systems. While all modern governments claim to govern in the name of progress, revolutionary dictatorships and movements tend to deify and monopolize it. In such cases, the idea of progress is given an aggressive content which may manifest itself in expansion of territory, propagation of ideology, and maximization of power, both domestically and internationally. Since these revolutionary regimes base themselves on the idea of continuous expansion at the expense of some internal or external adversary, any slowdown or reverse in progress is regarded as a threat to their own existence. Even if the revolutionary dynamic is stalled, the leadership usually endeavors through symbolic acts and propaganda to show its followers evidence of continual progress.[25] Whenever possible, reverses and defeats are countered by acts of retaliation, or otherwise minimized, or hidden from the eyes of the public. However, because of the very nature of the Dulles rebuff, which was blunt, sudden, and explicit, it was impossible to minimize or obscure it through the use of propaganda techniques. Arabs and Egyptians saw the challenge as one transcending Abd al-Nasir's person and directed against the whole emerging ideology and practice of Egyptian-led Pan-Arab nationalism. Thus, any response on the part of Abd al-Nasir would have to be conditioned by the ideological and aspirational requirements of his movement. Finally, in terms of domestic political needs, a form of dramatic response was necessary. Since the system had come to rely on diplomatic victories as internal props, the Dulles challenge would certainly damage the elite's domestic power position.

While the ensuing attack by Israel, Britain, and France rallied wide support for Abd al-Nasir, the defeat of his forces by Israel [26] seriously hurt his international prestige. Yet for a variety of reasons his prestige at home and among Arabs remained undamaged and indeed his charismatic appeal registered an upswing. Probably what saved him was the ill-conceived Anglo-French attack, just after Israel's lightning campaign. Under the circumstances, Abd al-Nasir was cast in the role of the hero-martyr, desperately fighting two major European powers in addition to Israel. With the subsequent withdrawal of the invading forces, followed by the Egyptianization of British and French holdings, a total military defeat was turned into a resounding political and moral victory. For a people so recently under colonial rule, the humiliating withdrawal forced upon the invaders by the U.N. and the two super-powers amounted to a victory of the first magnitude. The net gain for Israel, considered by Egyptians as a "tool" of Western imperialism, was the opening of the Tiran Straits and the termination of commando activity through the establishment of UNEF units on Egyptian soil.[27] However, these concessions were not visible to most Egyptians due to the physical remoteness of the Sinai; also, the Israeli gains were considered minimal when compared with the aggressors' complete withdrawal, continuing Egyptian control of the canal, and their success in denying Israel passage through the waterway.

Yet the army's inglorious performance in the Sinai had to be explained. As it turned out the regime did not acknowledge the defeat of its forces by Israel, but termed it a "tactical withdrawal" ordered by Nasir after the Anglo-French attack.[28] Almost certainly, the withdrawal had been ordered after substantial Israeli gains. However, the Egyptian explanation for the pullback pointed to the fear of entrapment of the army between the Israelis and the Anglo-French forces.[29] The resistance shown by the Egyptians against the latter at Port Said is celebrated every year as a symbol of the nation's will to fight.[30]

5

The Ideological Imperative

ONE major reason for the West's deep-seated myopia toward the non-Western world is the failure to understand and appreciate the avid ideological orientation of the developing countries. Having achieved a high degree of integration, the need to emphasize ideology has diminished among Western nations. If the West has entered the era of "end of ideology," [1] the non-Western world of developing countries is in what may be called the "beginning of ideology."

Various analysts have suggested that material and social advances are not sufficient to insure successful nation formation; national integration is seen as the crucial element. The two factors impeding the integration process are the absence of a strong sense of personal and national identity and the lack of a congruous relationship between subjects and rulers.[2] The function of the socialization process is to counteract these impediments by inculcating the citizenry with a set of dominant values and myths —an ideology that in turn will provide a foundation for the development of consistent attitudes toward the elite and the state. But this crucial process cannot even begin without the benefit of an ideology, that minimum group of values and beliefs usually lacking in many emerging nations. Indeed, even to begin the task of nation-building a minimum of ideology seems imperative.

Once the leadership adopts a working ideology, the socialization process begins to operate by building consistent attitudes, which in turn serve to strengthen the citizen's sense of personal adequacy and solidarity with the group.[3] In the initial stage of nation-building, ideology reinforces the individual with a set of defenses against his external world. It provides him with an interpretation of reality which is congruous with that held by the ruling elite and transforms him from a traditional subject into a participant citizen.

Beyond its solidarity and identity-producing roles, ideology unites thought (beliefs) and action. It legitimizes action by basing it on superior morality and rationality.[4] In this sense, ideology becomes an instrument of rule in the hands of an elite, since it justifies the elites' exercise of power. In time, after an ideology is widely propagated and internalized, it acquires its own dynamism, whereby it restricts thought and limits action.

The political creed that has provided the minimum ideological requirements of the developing states is nationalism—the earliest and the most basic of all modern ideologies. By mobilizing mass support, nationalism has prepared the ground for contemporary revolutionary ideologies which depend on the mass consciousness of the citizenry.[5] While nationalism still provides the essential "take-off" ideology for the newly formed nation-states, it alone cannot produce a detailed action program needed for large-scale internal transformation. What has changed in the modern context is the nature of the people's aspirations and expectations. Present-day nationalists expect not only a strong nation-state, but one that is able to improve their economic and social position in a short time. Clearly, traditional nationalism is found wanting; it has to be supplemented by more modern comprehensive ideologies, which provide a total program of external and internal change.[6]

The military revolutionaries of 1952 were the direct heirs of the Egyptian nationalism fashioned by Mustafa Kamil, Sa'd Zaghlul, and Mustafa al-Nahhas. However, this nationalist ideology, which had been the motive force behind the Egyptian nation-building process, was becoming outmoded in terms of the political and social conditions of mid-twentieth century Egypt. Indeed, if it were not for the continued British presence and the rise of Israel, Egyptian nationalism might have outgrown its usefulness earlier in the century. But preoccupation with Britain and a narrow class base bound the pre-1952 Egyptian elites to Egyptian nationalism and blinded them to the need to supplement it to meet the requirements of modern times. These were traditional elites operating within the confines of a traditional nationalism and employing worn-out tools of rulership. The power struggle between the various competing elites, which was compounded by the palace and the British, and the absence of new ideology impeded the socialization process and therefore nation-building. Even if the socialization of the citizenry had been effectively pursued, there was no explicit and positive ideology which could mobilize the people behind the leadership. The ideals of liberalism and parliamentary democracy could not fill the ideology gap because these were not commonly held values. Lacking a firm commitment to these ideals, the traditional Egyptian elites had done little to utilize them as ideological tools. More significant, perhaps, was the manifestly ambivalent character of nationalism among Egyptians. The field research undertaken by Patricia Kendall [7] during 1951 reveals a pervasive vagueness and indecisiveness among professionals that included doctors, teachers, engineers, lawyers, and journalists—a key subelite group in the social structure. Their conception of Egyptian nationalism not only lacked specific content beyond the achievement of complete independence from Britain, but also a concrete program to achieve this aim. Given the high degree of ambivalence at that level of society, one could infer that the attitude at lower levels was more ambivalent, perhaps bordering on indifference. Alienated from the West they admired, these professionals manifested deep feelings of self-doubt and social inferiority—all indicative of a serious crisis in identity.

The 1948 Egyptian defeat in Palestine dramatically illustrated the failure of the leadership to guide the country from "nationalist-statehood" to "nation-statehood." [8] The high degree of ideological commitment that produces loyal supporters and effective fighters for the nation-state had not sufficiently permeated even the army ranks.

The military organizers of the July 1952 coup were fired essentially by the same ambiguous nationalism that had motivated the traditional elite groups they had overthrown. Without any doubt their primary purpose in taking power had been to realize the main ideals of Egyptian nationalism—the building of a strong, independent nation-state. Five years after the coup, the balance sheet indicated a very uneven development in the political system. The haphazard measures of the military at the outset were token reforms and not the implementation of a comprehensive creed of action. The military incorporated its inherited Egyptian nationalism into the nebulous "Six Principles" of the revolution published in January 1953 and reiterated by Abd al-Nasir at Bandung.[9] Two of these principles—the liquidation of imperialism and the building of a strong army—were pursued almost immediately as a part of the officers' nationalistic creed. The remaining four—the ending of feudalism and capitalism, and the establishment of social justice and democratic life— represented the bare outlines of an internal ideological program, the implementation of which was indefinitely postponed. The subsequent shift in revolutionary action from the domestic to the international stage was accompanied by a parallel redirection of ideological development whereby Egyptian nationalism evolved into Pan-Arabism. While the prerequisite conditions to effect this evolution already existed in the Egypt of late 1954, the final and official adoption of Pan-Arabism was due to Abd al-Nasir's subsequent diplomatic success. In the absence of a ready-made doctrine of external conduct, the pragmatically developed and successfully applied foreign policies of the leader hardened into the official ideology of the Egyptian elite. This was in obvious contrast to the Soviet case, where in theory, and often in practice, policies are derived from Marxism. As Nasir's victories evoked overwhelming Arab approval, his policies were propagated in the name of Pan-Arabism. This initiated a change of beliefs and identity among Egyptians who started adopting their popular leader's new ideology and regarding themselves as Arabs living in Egypt. To the extent that this transformation occurred among the populace, Abd al-Nasir had become charismatic.

It is difficult to assess the degree and extent of the ideological transformation from Egyptianism to Arabism among Egyptians. While the period from 1954 to 1957 may have been too brief to effect thoroughgoing change, one should also consider the combined impact of the leader's victories and Pan-Arab popularity on an emotionally charged Egyptian people. Whatever the extent of belief transformation at that stage, it is important to note that the resulting socialization of Egyptians was being effected in terms of the charismatic leader's newly adopted ideology of Pan-Arabism. In other words, Egyptian nationalism had been supplemented by another nationalist ideology—Pan-Arabism—which also lacked a creed of internal change. As a result, the socialization that was being carried on in the name of Arab unity nationalism (Pan-Arabism) did not touch the more immediate day-to-day social and economic needs of Egyptians. While identification with the charismatic leader gave the masses a sense of pride and dignity, it did not appreciably affect their social and economic position. As a result, the process of socialization and therefore nation-building was bound to be incomplete and to a degree superficial.

The 1956 defeat in the Sinai demonstrated that, as in 1948, the Egyptian soldier still lacked the spiritual preparation necessary for effective combat. The forces of a developing nationalist state once again had met those of a fully developed nation-state and were found wanting. That sense of deep loyalty to country, the hallmark of the nation-state, had not developed sufficiently in the Egyptian fighter. It seems that the crucial socialization process by which a set of dominant values are inculcated in the citizenry had not started functioning properly, since ideology-formation and propagation in late 1956 was barely in the take-off stage. The ideological deficiency had been temporarily and imperfectly compensated by the nascent Pan-Arab charisma of the leader, which served as a poor substitute for the missing full-scale ideological transformation. What emerge are two interrelated weaknesses of charismatic leadership. A charismatic leader cannot operate indefinitely with a semi-developed ideology; that is, charisma by itself is not an effective and dependable instrument of rule and national integration. To make himself the major agent of the nation-building process, the leader must supplement his charisma with a comprehensive national ideology. This is the stage when the leader's nebulous message is converted into more or less concrete ideological maxims to be inculcated in the citizenry thereby creating a sense of national identity and a congruous ruler-subject relationship.

A related shortcoming was Nasir's heavy reliance upon dramatic exploits in foreign affairs as sources of legitimacy without a corresponding effort to develop ideological-organizational support through internal social change. Any single major external reverse could easily have damaged his position of leadership permanently. If it had not been for the faltering Anglo-French attack and the subsequent United Nations' pressure on Anglo-French-Israeli forces to withdraw, Abd al-Nasir could have found himself in such a perilous position, especially in view of his defeat by Israel.

For Britain, France, and Israel, the Suez crisis should have been equally instructive. Apparently, they thought that a limited military campaign would be sufficient to topple the Egyptian leader before anyone else could intervene.[10] The inadequacy of this plan was the failure of Western strategists to take into account the changed nature of the Egyptian political system. The Egyptian system in 1956—as the Cuban during the Bay of Pigs invasion—was not a traditional dictatorship that could be overthrown internally by the limited application of external force. Despite the urgings of British broadcasts from Cyprus and leaflets dropped by bombers, no one attempted to overthrow the government. Once the opposition political groups had been eliminated and the masses mobilized in support of a popular leader, there remained no internal political force to challenge Nasir's rule. Thus, while the lag in the socialization process had seriously harmed the Egyptian war effort in the Sinai, the slowly advancing Anglo-French campaign on the heels of Israel's attack strengthened the people's identification with the charismatic leader. Significantly, during the crucial period between the war's end and the Anglo-French-Israeli evacuation, no overt internal challenge developed against Nasir. While force had been available to maintain control, the leader did not have occasion to resort to it. Apparently his popular legitimacy derived from charisma was great enough to sustain him until the achievement of political victory in the form of his enemies' withdrawal from Egyptian territory.

Attempts at Party Organization

The military debacle of 1956 should have amply demonstrated to the ruling elite the inherent weaknesses of the existing political system. As it turned out, it was only partially instructive. The behavior of the ruling elite during the first decade of the revolution demonstrated that they would react decisively only when confronted with a clear and present threat to their position. Lacking ideological guidelines and experience in the arts of rulership, they could not behave otherwise. Policy was improvised pragmatically, as the need for action became forcefully apparent.

Until 1957, the charismatic presence of the leader apparently blurred the elite's view of the manifold internal weaknesses of the system. The leader's charisma, coupled with the elite's monopoly of force, had seemed more than sufficient to sustain power domestically and even manifest power externally. Apparently, the need for organized institutional arrangements as internal props was not acutely felt. Thus, beyond repeated distractions by foreign affairs and the lack of cadres and experience, the delay in launching a mass organization can be explained only in terms of the leadership's failure to perceive the immediate necessity for such a structure.

By the time of the Suez War in the fall of 1956, the regime's first attempt at mass organization—the Liberation Rally—had proved unsuccessful. Certain Egyptian historians of the 1960s are reasonably candid in their critical analysis of this organization. They point out that it lacked bold leadership, experienced cadres, efficient organization, and comprehensive ideology.[11] More significantly, the early revolutionaries are criticized for failing to give the Liberation Rally sufficient attention, importance, or even the semblance of political power, especially since it had been created "to keep the people busy, and give them something to think about and prevent a vacuum."[12] The Liberation Rally did succeed in neutralizing Wafdist, Brotherhood, and Communist influences among the masses and in creating massive mob support for the RCC during the power struggles of 1954. Once these utilitarian goals had been accomplished, one may safely assume that, in the pragmatic view of the elite, the organization had served its main purpose and could be disbanded.

The second abortive attempt to form a party organization—the National Union—did not come about until May 1957, about six months after the Egyptian defeat in the Sinai. The ills that rendered it ineffective and precipitated its demise in the fall of 1961 were essentially the same as those affecting the Liberation Rally. The new organization was repeatedly characterized as a "school," one that was to become "a liaison between the government and the people." [13] However, in 1957, as in 1953, there was no explicit hint as to how this liaison function was to be performed. If the National Union was to serve as a school for the masses and as an agency of societal reconstruction, it lacked a detailed curriculum and a comprehensive program of change. In short, the deficiencies in ideology persisted. Since the days of the Liberation Rally, ideological development had been uneven. While Egyptian nationalism had evolved into Pan-Arabism, the development of an ideology of social change was minimal beyond the new formulation of constructing "a socialist, democratic, cooperative society." [14] In the absence of a clear definition of this formula and a precise method for its achievement, Abd al-Nasir's new scheme could not be properly considered an ideology of internal transformation. If the failure in the Sinai had in reality alerted the elite to the necessity of initiating genuine internal transformation through the use of a strong mass movement, the National Union was not the answer. Clearly, it lacked a "total" ideology that would give it internal cohesion and clarity of purpose. The fact is that the elite's quest for ideology was still in progress with no consensus in sight. Furthermore, it appears that the leadership failed to perceive large-scale social change as being necessary to maintain its position of power. Thus, the National Union was bound to be another holding operation to keep internal problems dormant and maintain control.

The ideological, structural, and organizational shortcomings of the National Union, have been objectively acknowledged in recent Egyptian historical scholarship [15] and to a degree by Nasir himself. These, coupled with the "part-time" attention [16] given to the organization by the leadership, rendered it totally unprepared for the difficult tasks that lay ahead within the larger context of the short-lived Syrian-Egyptian union.

Myths, Charisma, and Ideology

In a sense, both ideological development and the evolution of charismatic leadership are processes of myth-making. According to the French syndicalist, Georges Sorel, a myth is "a body of images capable of evoking sentiment instinctively." [17] The myth does not easily lend itself to rational analysis, for it is based on intuition, instinct, and belief. It is specifically designed to create cohesion, inspiration, and dynamism in a revolutionary movement.[18] To Sorel, all great social movements were based on the pursuance of myths. Christianity's myth was the vision of the Kingdom of God; the myth of liberalism envisioned a society embodying liberty, fraternity, and equality. In the hands of Sorel's most famous disciple, Benito Mussolini, the myth was equated with the nation.

From the point of view of the socialization process, effective myth-making is a necessary prerequisite for successful national integration. Since myths serve as the popularizers of ideology, the two should be regarded as inseparable. Myth-making simplifies the doctrinal intricacies of the ideology bringing the doctrine to the level of the masses.

Nasir's success in mobilizing Arabs behind his movement should be attributed, in large degree, to his remarkable myth-making ability. The first important myth that he advanced in creating a revolutionary movement was the greatness of the Egyptian, and later, Arab nation. When in 1955 Egypt's security necessitated a closer identification with other Arab countries, Abd al-Nasir adopted the Ba'athist myth of Arab unity. In more recent years Egyptian ideologues have supplied Pan-Arabism with a theoretical rationalization and historical foundation and made it an integral part of Nasirite ideology. But in essence Pan-Arabism (Arab unity) remains a myth in the Sorelian sense despite its ideological embellishments, because many Arab writers agree that it is primarily based on "feeling." [19] Such a myth cannot be easily refuted by conventional logic, and therefore constitutes a potent instrument in the hands of the Egyptian elite to mobilize the Arab masses and drive them to revolutionary action.

In contrast to the wide scholarly attention given the role of myths in the study of ideology, the relationship of myths to charisma remains largely unexplored. Both in terms of origin and political utility, myths and charisma are inextricably intertwined. In the first place, myths and charisma share a common nonrational base of intuition, instinct, belief, and emotion. As such, these two concepts do not readily lend themselves to rational analysis. On a pragmatic level, the development and perpetuation of charisma seems to be intimately dependent on the leader's myth-making ability. An aspiring charismatic generates two types of myths: those relating to his message and those pertaining to his own role in propagating the message.

The first are essentially ideological myths which simplify, define, and concretize the nebulous message. The myths of Arab unity and the Pan-Arab state belong in this category. Simultaneously, however, a leader of charismatic propensity carves out for himself a central role in the movement that is dedicated to the implementation of the ideological myths. The Arab-Egyptian case clearly illustrates that the original Ba'athi developers of the myth of Arab unity could not effectively fulfill the leadership role, which subsequently devolved onto Gamal Abd al-Nasir. Indeed, the myth of Arab unity had been around long before the emergence of the Egyptian leader. By Nasir's own admission, what the Arabs needed was a leader who could fill the "role in search of a hero." [20] As a result Abd al-Nasir acquired a personal myth—the imperative of an Arab hero leader—who could actively pursue the ideological myth of Arab unity. While it has been the usual Egyptian practice to base this leadership imperative on historical precedent (e.g., Salah al-Din) and the rationally determined needs of today's Arab world, in times of crisis the myth of divine appointment was invoked in order to shore up the leader's position:

> Fellow countrymen, I have given my life to this Arab Revolution and my life will last for this Arab Revolution. I shall stay here as long as God wants me to; to fight with all my efforts for the sake of the demands of the people. I shall give my whole life for the people's right to life. This nation has given me support of which I never dreamt, and I have nothing to give it except every drop of my blood.
>
> Fellow countrymen, the hour of the revolutionary work has struck. We shall work by the will of God, and by the will of God, we shall be victorious.[21]

In a practical sense Nasir's role in relation to Arab nationalism has been singular. His major and undeniable contribution was the transformation of the remote abstraction of Arab unity into an immediate psychological reality. By popularizing and focussing the Arab quest for transcendence into political activism, the historical myth of a Pan-Arab state assumed psychological presence in the Arab mind for the first time. This transformation was accelerated and reinforced constantly by the leader's pronouncements and more importantly by his political performance. When in February 1958 the first step of the "inevitable" process was brought about with the union of Syria and Egypt, Gamal Abd al-Nasir emerged as supreme hero of Arab history, "sent by destiny" as "messenger" and "implementor" of a revolutionary philosophy.[22] Despite Syria's secession, Nasir persisted in identifying himself with the historical myth of Arab unity. What resulted was the blending of myths and the charisma of the leader; the legitimacy, sanctity, and timelessness associated with a myth is transferred to the leader. The constant identification of leader with myth usually culminates in the charismatic leader himself becoming a "symbol and myth"—a customary reference to Abd al-Nasir in Egyptian publications.[23]

In early 1958 all indications were that Abd al-Nasir was at the zenith of his popularity among Arab masses. The Eisenhower Doctrine, aimed at isolating him, had failed, as pro-Egyptian elements challenged pro-Western Arab regimes in Lebanon and Jordan and subsequently succeeded in achieving the formation of the UAR and promoting the Iraqi revolution of June 1958. He had made himself the leader of a Cairo-based revolutionary movement, which had the nebulous aim of uniting all Arabs from Morocco to the Persian Gulf. However, at that stage the Egyptian president was an incipient revolutionary, ideologically and organizationally ill-equipped to lead a genuine revolutionary movement throughout the Arab world. While Pan-Arabism had been adopted as an external ideology, no corresponding revolutionary doctrine of internal transformation had been formulated, much less implemented. Indeed, Egypt, the "base" of the revolution, had experienced only partial change; by 1958 only the official Pan-Arab ideology of the elite had been widely politicized among Egyptians. While this accelerated Arabization of Egyptian society constituted a massive ideological transformation in itself, it hardly touched the crucial socio-economic substructure of society. Thus, in 1958, Abd al-Nasir was attempting to extend to other Arab lands "the Arab Revolution in Egypt," which had not really occurred in his own country. As it turned out, after the Syrian-Egyptian union the major issue was precisely the shape to be given united Arab society. Confronted with a multitude of difficulties in ruling Syria, the increasing need for homogenizing the two societies became clear. It was thought that the creation of two politically, socially, and economically similar societies would insure the preservation of unity under Abd al-Nasir. During 1960 several "socialist" controls were placed on Syria's comparatively free economy and in September 1961 the nationalization of the private sector and land redistribution was accelerated. Meanwhile, the regime's organizational structure, the National Union, had become bogged down in both regions of the UAR and infiltrated by a host of new and old opponents—Ba'athists, large landowners, capitalists—who were instrumental in Syria's secession in September 1961.[24] Clearly, an inexperienced elite had tried to extend its frontiers of power by relying on the leader's charisma and a semi-formulated ideological and organizational base. While Nasir's charisma, coupled with the Arab unity component of his ideology, had been sufficient [25] to effect the union, these same factors could not sustain it indefinitely. As soon as internal change was introduced into Syria, which had become a restive police state, the system broke apart. A haphazardly conceived and untried program of change had been put into practice by an external regime that could not muster in Syria [26] (as it could in Egypt) a coercive force great enough to effect the desired transformation and keep the union from dissolving. In the final analysis, as the Syrians discovered, Abd al-Nasir's myth of Pan-Arabism was incongruous with its Egyptian practice. Abd al-Nasir, the great myth and charismatic mythmaker, was no more than an imperfect ruler in the Syrian context.

The Political System After the Secession

It would be no exaggeration to state that the social revolution in Egypt occurred not in 1952, but in 1961. Since that date there have been serious attempts to routinize charismatic authority through the implementation of a socialist ideology.

While it is operationally difficult to develop quantitative indices for measuring variations in the charismatic bond, it can be safely stated that the Syrian secession had a damaging but not irreparable effect on the position of Abd al-Nasir. In view of this great reverse, the widespread belief in the leader's abilities and the validity of his message could have waned or even disappeared if remedial action was not taken immediately. It is a credit to Nasir's acute sense of power preservation that he instituted remedial measures almost at the heels of the breakup. Simultaneous action was needed on many fronts. He had to minimize the damage to his Pan-Arab image, especially in view of the repressive Egyptian performance in Syria. This was done by refraining from military action in Syria, restoring Egyptian-held Syrian funds, and not blocking Syrian reentrance into the U.N. and the Arab League. These actions were accompanied by the Egyptian leader's display of fatherly benevolence and tolerance toward "the Arab people in Syria," who allegedly were being threatened with the intrigues of reactionaries and imperialists operating from Israel. Abd al-Nasir's words clearly reflected his "concern" toward Syria even after the secession.

> I ask all popular forces who still abide by the United Arab Republic and by Arab unity to understand now that national unity within the Syrian homeland is the prime consideration. Syria's strength is strength for the Arab Nation and Syria's dignity is dignity for the Arab future. Syria's national unity is a pillar of Arab Unity . . . May God help beloved Syria, guide its footsteps and bless its people. This United Arab Republic will remain . . . to support every Arab struggle, every Arab right and every Arab aspiration.[27]

To minimize the damage to his position Nasir further asserted that the union was only an "experiment"; he went on to reaffirm his faith in the "inevitability of history" and in the "unity between the peoples of the Arab Nation."[28] He also clearly restated his continuing role "as a soldier in the service of the Arab Nation."[29] Thus, in addition to the charismatic compulsion to react in a Pan-Arab manner, what emerged was the related ideological compulsion to continue in the path of Arabism. A disillusioned Nasir could not disown the ideology of Arab-unity nationalism which he had adopted and nurtured, since his commitment to it had been too complete. Any attempt to disavow Arabism and fall back on Egyptian nationalism would have obliterated his charisma abroad and seriously undermined his power at home. Thus, despite the fact that a major defeat had been brought about by pursuing the goals of Arab unity in Syria, Nasir was forced to uphold Pan-Arabism and operate within its bounds, if only to safeguard his remaining power in Egypt. Military power and charisma, on which the regime had relied since 1955, were in the process of blending. But in addition to force and charisma the regime had begun to rely on ideology to sustain its power. In this respect the political system may be regarded as having entered Phase IV of the Charismatic Process (pp. 15–16).

Following attempts to repair the leader's charismatic image, attention focussed on the state of the base—Egyptian society. Nasir's most immediate concern was to secure the regime's position in Egypt, after the serious shock of the Syrian secession. While hard evidence is lacking of a simultaneous internal conspiracy in Egypt, the need "to protect the Revolution" from internal enemies was repeatedly stated in the Egyptian press.[30] Beyond this immediate consideration, there was the long-range problem of enlarging the popular base to gain wider legitimacy for the ruling elite. The externally stalled revolutionary dynamic had to be switched to internal revolutionary action to justify and consolidate the leadership's power.

After the autumn of 1961, the Egyptian political system followed the general pattern of development outlined in Chapter 1. As stated in the analytical framework, the inherent instability of charismatic authority flows from the atrophy of charisma which occurs when the leader's image of infallibility cannot be maintained in the face of inevitable reverses. Therefore, the stabilization of the system requires the early infusion of the leader's personal legitimacy into new political, social, and economic structures. In Egypt this effort was not undertaken in earnest until after the dissolution of the Syrian-Egyptian union. Thus, the evolution of the political system since 1961 reflected a belated effort by Nasir to seek wider popular and organizational support in the face of waning charisma brought about by repeated external reverses. These included his inability to deal with the Syrian Ba'athists, the unpopular war in the Yemen, the overthrow of Ben Bella, and the costly confrontations with West Germany and the United States. The Syrian secession was only the beginning of the process of charismatic atrophy.

In a limited sense, the attempts to routinize charisma after 1961 resembled those of 1957, which culminated in the abortive National Union. However, there were three important differences in the two situations. In the Pan-Arab sphere, the Syrian secession was a more serious and damaging crisis than the 1956 defeat in the Sinai. In contrast to 1957 Nasir had developed a comprehensive program of internal change—Arab socialism. Finally in October 1961, there was a much fuller realization of the need for serious internal organization and change.[31] Some of these notions are reflected in the president's speech delivered on 16 October 1961:

> . . . we committed a gross mistake. . . . We formed the National Union to act as a frame encircling the conflict between classes. . . . Reactionary elements which infiltrated into the National Union managed to paralyze its revolutionary effectiveness . . . consequently, the most important thing today is the popular reorganization of the National Union to change it into a revolutionary organ in the hands of the national people. . . . The National Union should be opened for the laborers; the farmers; the intellectuals; the professionals; the owners whose property is not based on exploitation; to the officers and soldiers who represented the vanguard on July 23.[32]

These six legitimate categories of people were to constitute a "single hard-working class," in a society "where the rule of social justice is to be established on the law on God." [33] The dispatch with which the new socialism was put into effect after mid-October 1961 reflected the regime's seriousness in building a new and wider base of domestic power. The net effect has been the weakening of the Egyptian bourgeosie, the destruction of the large landowners, and the establishment of etatism over an officially sanctioned unity of workers, peasants, intellectuals, professionals, and soldiers. After the initial restructuring of Egyptian society excluding capitalist and landowning interests, the rest of the legitimate classes were to cooperate within the new political framework of the Arab Socialist Union, which came into being in December 1962. Subsequent events were to show that the Egyptian approach to party formation was only partially successful.

The Paucity of Dissent

The authoritarian nature of the system, coupled with the dependence of most intellectuals on government jobs, made the voicing of dissent a rare practice. One major source of criticism was emigré intellectuals such as Ahmad Abu al-Fath and Anwar Abd al-Malik who lost no opportunity to brand the ruling regime from the comfort of a foreign land.[34] However, for those living in Egypt, criticism was possible either by the method of implication or through the proposal of "constructive" suggestions designed to better the existing state of affairs. A major exponent of this rare breed of dissenters is Shaykh Khalid Muhammad Khalid, whose literary fame and advanced age permit him a degree of freedom uncommon to lesser intellectuals. In one of his more recent works, Khalid concerned himself with the pervasive "crisis of freedom" that he found in all existing political systems regardless of ideology. While expressed in general terms, his constant emphasis on individual freedoms and "peace of mind" constituted a critique of the Egyptian political system by implication.[35]

In his specific treatment of Egypt, Khalid is concerned with making socialist Egypt more democratic. His general prescription is a more vigorous implementation of the Charter with respect to personal freedoms.[36] Specifically, he proposes: a loyal opposition in a more dynamic legislature, complete separation of powers, an independent press to act as a check on government, popular elections of governors, freeing of prisoners, complete freedom of discussion.[37] These were the same themes that Shaykh Khalid had so eloquently stressed during the debates of the National Congress of Popular Forces in November 1961; [38] significantly, certain of these proposals became the central issues during the reformation period succeeding the June 1967 War.

6

The Revolutionary Present and the Recasting of the Past

The Search for Ideology

ONCE the elite perceives the central role of ideology in nation-building, it is faced with the extremely complex problem of developing a suitable ideology. The experience of most developing countries indicates that finding an ideology is no simple task. In its quest for ideological guidelines each political elite operates within certain parameters, which are peculiar to each new political entity. In the Egyptian case there were certain preconditions that shaped ideological development in the formative years of the revolution.

1. The relative absence of a firm ideological commitment beyond Egyptian nationalism on the part of the military elite at the time of the 1952 power seizure. Most of the leaders to a large extent were fairly open-minded and willing to study and experiment with alternative ideological maxims. Being confirmed pragmatists by virtue of military training, the officers consistently reiterated their desire to be pragmatically eclectic: to borrow only those ideological maxims which in their opinion would ideally fit the Egyptian milieu. This notion is clearly reflected in the following statement by President Abd al-Nasir:

> It is no easy task for we have to design the structure of our new society as we build it. Our circumstances differ from those of other nations and this is why we cannot imitate the pattern of any other society; as each community follows the mode of evolution and the pattern best suited to its circumstances. Our blind imitation of any system would

ignore the nature of our society and the different factors influencing it and would thus be incompatible with the needs
of this people.

We are required to study the experience of other nations
and to benefit by it but under no circumstances can we
copy it. This is why we say that we not only build our
society but we also design its pattern as we go. This pattern
is modified by the nature and circumstances of our changing societies and its requirements. This is why it is a continuous process. The broad lines of this pattern are socialism,
cooperation and democracy, and our task is to adapt these
principles to our circumstances and to proceed with the
work of building a growing integrated society.[1]

2. The character of the cold war and Egypt's colonial experience, coupled with the pragmatic approach of the military leaders, had the cumulative effect of making complete ideological
alignment with the West or the Soviet Union increasingly unattractive. By late 1955 the leadership seems to have realized the dis-
advantages and dangers implicit in choosing one or the other of
the competing ideologies and/or power blocs, and indeed the
immense profits to be gained from abstaining in such a choice.
This produced a neutralist ideological orientation externally and
subsequently an eclectic socialist doctrine for internal transformation.

3. The leadership and power vacuum in the Arab world.
During the years 1953–1955 the Egyptian elite perceived the appalling lack of effective and well-entrenched leaders in the Arab
East. Clearly, there was a role waiting to be filled at the Pan-
Arab level. As soon as the Nasirites were entrenched in a relatively stable country, they began to show clear intentions of fill-
ing this role. The central cultural and political position that this
most advanced and populous of Arabic-speaking countries enjoyed made it possible for a relatively popular leadership to act
as leader of the Arabs. The many benefits to be derived from this
leadership role in terms of increased domestic popularity and foreign respect could not go unnoticed by Abd al-Nasir. Hence developed the Arab unity aspect of Nasirite ideology.

4. The last significant factor affecting the type and manner of

ideological development is the Egyptian-Arab past—a subject that brings into consideration the function of history in the process of establishing a nation-state.

The crucial relationship between ideology and modern nation-building cannot be fully explained without considering the role of history. It is often said that modern history begins where historians become concerned with the future as well as with the past.[2] Indeed, in order to see what lies ahead, modern man can only look into history, which he ultimately interprets in terms of his present and future perceived needs and aspirations. However, this constant process of interaction between past, present, and the projected future becomes relevant only when people begin to develop a collective consciousness, aspiration, and concern about the future. As soon as an ethnic entity begins to ask itself about the kind of future life it desires to lead, it begins to reexamine and rediscover and/or invent the past, all depending on its present and future perceived needs.

By definition revolutionary movements are based on a radical rejection of pre-revolutionary forms of social and political organization and thought. This rejection is imperative not only to justify the revolution but also to sharpen the ideological tenets of the movement on which the new society is to be built. It is in this sense that history and ideology-formation are inextricably related; the past influences ideology formation and implementation and in turn is recast by the ideological and pragmatic realities of the present.

The degree to which a particular country's past is rejected or reinterpreted usually depends on the nature of the leadership's ideology, the extent of the latter's entrenchment, and the character of its people's historical experience. Thus, if a revolutionary elite already possesses a ready-made ideology of a Marxist type (e.g., USSR), the rejection of past societal structures and practices is bound to be almost total. In the case of the Egyptian military regime, this type of development was not possible because of the existing ideological vacuum, as well as the junta's insecure power position until its entrenchment in 1954–1955. Even if the officers had initially possessed an ideological compulsion to criticize the past, this would have been suicidal especially if such criticism had involved the Islamic heritage.[3] A total critique of the past

would have been imprudent and indeed unnecessary. The Nasirites soon discovered that the retention of a slightly reinterpreted
form of Sunni Islam coupled with a peculiar form of Arab unity
nationalism would prove beneficial to their cause. As the officers
were exposed to socialist influences on the one hand, and began
to manifest Pan-Arab tendencies on the other, the crucial ingredients for the new ideology came into sharp focus: selected portions of a revived and reinterpreted Egyptian-Arab past had to
be merged with certain elements of Islamic thought which in turn
had to be fitted into the modern Nasirite conception of socialism.
This conscious attempt to relate and base a modern ideology on
the past makes the Egyptian experiment in ideology-building a
pioneering effort that may serve as an example for other developing countries. Moreover, the notion of basing the present on certain more or less solid foundations of the past endows the ideology and the system with a certain continuity and legitimacy and
therefore a built-in stability and strength.

The degree to which a revolutionary movement rewrites history is directly related to its present internal and external needs
and to its future ideological commitment to rebuild society. The
deeply felt need of totalitarian revolutionary elites to rewrite history is clearly illustrated by the Soviet and Chinese examples.
While in a general sense Chinese and Soviet history-writing has
been shaped by the officially held maxims of Marxist ideology,
political and psychological needs felt by the elites have, at times,
exercised considerable influence. It will suffice to recall the
Stalinist revision of Russian history, glorifying certain portions of Russia's imperial past (e.g., Peter the Great), in order to
meet the urgent need for reviving Russian nationalism to counter
the German onslaught during World War II. In the case of China,
the present nationalist policy of the Maoist leadership makes
it necessary to reemphasize the territorial and military grandeur
of the ancient empire, including the "civilizing" role of such
non-Chinese dynasties as the Yuan (Jenghis Khan) and the
Ching (Manchu).[4] The Hitlerite revival of the Teutonic past
and Mussolini's glorification and mimicry of imperial Rome
reflected the ideological, psychological, and policy needs of these
leaders.

Attempts to reinterpret the past are not limited to modern totalitarian systems, but have been the constant preoccupation of historians throughout world history. Diverse interpretations result because each historian invariably views the past through the shaded glasses of his own ideological and social milieu and tends to stress those aspects of history which best fit the value system of his own society. As E. H. Carr observes, Gibbon's hero was the philosopher-king, Marcus Aurelius, while nineteenth century Social Darwinist historians preferred Julius Caesar. In the modern epoch of large-scale planning and organization, the greatness of Augustus Caesar has been rediscovered.[5]

The third world of developing countries soon discovered the utility and necessity of rewriting history to lay the foundations of national integration and nation-building. A pioneer among this group of countries was Kemalist Turkey.[6]

There is no doubt that in the 1920s Kemalist Turkish historians were faced with an impossible task of history writing. Indeed, much of the Turkish past was nothing but a burden; no meaningful tie could be established with the immediate Ottoman-Caliphal past, since it had been newly overthrown. It was still less possible to use the pre-Ottoman Turkic past in view of the Moscow-Ankara rapprochment of 1920 and the necessity to suppress the remaining Pan-Turkist leaders of the previous Ittihad regime. Moreover, under external threats to annex parts of Anatolia, a historical tie had to be established with the land. The new republic was faced with the problem of being unhistorical. Clearly, if no valid connection could be made between the past and the present, a historical anchor had to be created. As a result the Kemalist historians Turkified the ancient Hittites.

In terms of the immediate political-military needs of the Kemalist Revolution in the 1920s, the question of historic authenticity became almost irrelevant. While modern Turkish history-writing has witnessed notable attempts to reintroduce authenticity, it seems clear that in terms of early Kemalist needs the "Turkification" of the Hittites was a necessary step. Even more difficult is the position of certain newly formed African states, since in the virtual absence of a recorded past, outright history-manufacturing can be anticipated.

It is no exaggeration to state that despite the rich past of the land of the Nile, revolutionary Egypt found itself to a large extent unhistorical. A large portion of the Egyptian past was irrelevant to the ruling elite except in a negative sense. At the most general level, reinterpretation of history was prompted by the necessity to strengthen the legitimacy of the Nasirites in Egypt and subsequently the Arab world. As the Revolution's new ideological action program came into sharper focus in the late fifties, historical precedent was utilized to broaden its popular acceptability and legitimacy. Specifically, historical reinterpretation aimed at justifying and legitimizing the July 1952 coup, the subsequent Revolution, and the Pan-Arabist, socialist orientation of the regime. This process was further influenced by the Egyptians' world-view which had been shaped by their old and new historical experiences. These included the Ottoman and Western imperial heritage, the centrality of Sunni Egypt in the Islamic realm, and the contemporary relationship of Egypt vis-à-vis Israel, Africa, and the Arab states.

While the foregoing interrelated factors placed certain limits on historical reinterpretation, on the whole, the Egyptian case lacks the extreme rigidity prevalent in Russian, Chinese, and Kemalist historiography. To cite a fitting example, there exists a wide divergence of views about the beginnings of Arab nationalism—a subject that has given rise to lively debate among Egyptian historians in the last few years. Thus, Arab nationalism is variously described as having originated with Islam, Salah al-Din al-Ayyubi, or even the Napoleonic conquests, to mention a few.[7] Yet there seems to be no official (governmental) attempt to uphold a single orthodox view on the subject to the exclusion of all the others. When this general Egyptian laxness is contrasted with the furor generated over V. M. Molotov's "erroneous formulation" in 1955 concerning the building of socialism in the Soviet Union, the rigidity and dogmatism of the Soviet approach becomes glaringly apparent.[8]

The Egyptian laxness may be traced to the relatively permissive attitude of the regime resulting from ideological unsophistication and preoccupation with more pragmatic problems. It should be stressed that Egyptian ideological development is still in its formative stages, possessing broad formulations but lacking in detail. In the circumstances, it is not surprising that ideology and its historical roots have not hardened up to the present time.

It seems that the regime will not object to diverse historical interpretations of nationalism so long as all Egyptian historians are
agreed on the more general ideological maxims, e.g., the pur-
suit of a Cairo-centered Pan-Arab State. In other words, while
an ideologically determined historiography has begun to develop, there is no evidence of placing historical research in a
strait-jacket.

History as a Tool of Rule Legitimation

While for the Kemalist Revolution the Turkish-Ottoman past
seemed a burden, a reinterpreted Egyptian-Arab past became a
blessing for Nasir. One of the main difficulties in finding an historical anchor for the Revolution was the persistence of foreign
rule in Egypt since early times. Indeed, Abd al-Nasir was the first
ethnic Egyptian to rule in Egypt since the demise of the phar-
aohs. The mere fact of Nasir's Egyptianness conferred substantial
legitimacy upon him and his revolution. However, the foreign origin of most pre-1952 Egyptian rulers created considerable difficulties in the attempts of modern Egyptian historians to link the
revolutionary present with the non-Egyptian past of Egypt.

In order to justify the July 1952 coup and subsequent military
rule, the immediate past had to be rejected. Indeed, nothing
could be an easier task. The ruling Muhammad Ali dynasty was
of Ottoman-Turkish origin, and in view of its performance in rulership, it remained very vulnerable to attack. Muhammad Ali is
criticized not only as a foreign intruder but also as a self-seeking
despot who based his rule on essentially foreign elements. His
modernization and expansion are viewed as destructive, since
these needlessly consumed the country's strength.[9] Finally, Muhammad Ali is accused of confiscating fallahin property, thus
reinforcing the old feudal relationships; a condition that was not
reversed until the Nasirite revolution.[10] The corruption and inef-
ficiency of his successors is said to have left Egypt open to colonial domination, formalized by the British occupation of 1882.
In this context, the Urabi revolt is officially [11] regarded as a
twofold protest against Britain and the alien Khedivate, which

was being supported by imperialist monopolies. Yet despite the assertions of the Charter and various historians [12] that a continuous revolutionary connection between Urabi and Abd al-Nasir exists, the former has often been criticized as an "unenlightened revolutionary, lacking organizational and planning skills befitting a soldier." [13] It should be emphasized that this mildly controversial assessment of Urabi Pasha does not extend to such popular figures as Mustafa Kamil (praised as a true nationalist) and Shaykh Muhammad Abduh (glorified for his religious reformism).[14] For the Nasirite revolution, however, the more recent past (World War I and after) was of greater consequence.

A thorough revaluation of the 1919 revolt seems basic and necessary for the Nasirite historian since it gives him a convenient *raison d'être* for the military power seizure of July 1952. To be sure, the nationalism manifested in 1919 is recognized as "genuine," yet the revolt itself is judged a "failure" necessitating a second revolution in 1952.[15] The failure is attributed to the Egyptian leadership of the period, which "overlooked the needs for social change" and failed to rearrange the economic substructure of society by the redistribution of wealth.[16] At the political level, the 1919 leadership is criticized for "compromising with the imperialists and the palace," instead of "decimating imperialism as done after 1952." [17] Thus, the Anglo-Egyptian treaties of 1922 and 1936 are considered shameful compromises showing the leaders' ignorance of the subtle methods of imperialism.

Two additional charges are leveled at the leaders of post-World War I Egypt. The first is the unpardonable sin of blindly forcing on Egypt an inherently "alien" form of government—the European multi-party parliamentary system.[18] The second charge is more significant in view of the ideological necessities of the present. It is the failure of the old elites to understand the true nature of Arab-Egyptian history—"they were incapable of deducing from history the fact that there is no conflict whatsoever between Egyptian patriotism and Arab nationalism." [19] While there is no direct critical reference to Sa'd Zaghlul in the Charter, it is obvious that the charge is squarely directed against him and his colleagues. The isolationist attitude that Zaghlul manifested as the leader of the Egyptian *wafd* (delegation) to the Paris Peace Conference had irked other Arab leaders. This fact, coupled with the relative Egyptian disinterest in the rest of the Arab world until the formation of the Arab League, constitutes a potent weapon in Ba'athist hands to question the Arabness of Nasirite Egypt.[20] The only reason Zaghlul was spared official criticism was the regime's reluctance to discredit an immensely popular Egyptian hero.

The fragmentation of the Arab East after the First World War under the mandate system is partially explained in terms of the old elite's lack of "vision beyond the Sinai." In other words because of Egyptian unwillingness to lead the Arabs, "the danger of the Balfour Declaration which set up Israel . . . tearing Arab territory apart . . ." was not clearly perceived.[21]

Considering the Pan-Arabist ideological compulsion to relate Egypt intimately with the rest of Araby, Egypt's Arabness is constantly reiterated in Nasirite historiography. The Charter goes on to view the "Arab Nation" as one whole, as if there existed an organically intimate relationship between Egypt and other Arab lands, in the post-World War I period.[22] Thus, the main element that enables Egyptian historiography to give a semblance of unity to this period is the similar experiences of Egyptians and Arabs under Western imperialist rule. This unifying factor is projected in two directions: into the past, to unify Arab history and into the future, to reinforce the regime's present ideological position to lead the Arabs in quest of the Pan-Arab state.

The official critique of the parliamentary period (1922–1952) serves as justification for the 1952 takeover and the subsequent Nasirite rule. The post-1919 leadership is charged with being inept, lacking revolutionary zeal, compromising with imperialism, and permitting its party ranks to be infiltrated by the palace, "big landlords," "parasites" and "opportunists." [23] This "deviation" of the remaining revolutionaries produced corrupt political parties with "superficial differences," which accepted "from the intruder . . . a mere scrap of paper bearing but a trace of pseudo rights" and made democracy a "shameful farce." [24] Because of the civilian politicians' infighting and lack of unity and identity with the people, the Nasirite historians justify the subsequent liquidation of political parties and the substitution of the National Union and Arab Socialist Union schemes.[25] The actions of Abd al-Nasir are not seen as spontaneous or arbitrary but as the unfolding of historical forces—"the tendency for progress"—which inevitably brought the demise of old elites.[26]

The various political groups active on the pre-1952 Egyptian political scene, including Sa'd Zaghlul's Wafdists, are represented as elites who became increasingly alienated from the people by letting themselves be corrupted by the palace, the imperialists, and the monopolists. Such instances as King Faruq's vehement defiance of His Majesty's High Commissioner in 1942 until the arrival of tanks at the palace and his reluctance to go to war on the side of the Allies are not brought out; neither is the Wafd's record of strong opposition to Britain.

The official Egyptian attitude regarding World War II is one of negative abstention. Indeed, the whole conflict is seen as irrelevant to Egypt and the Arab world, where "the people expressed themselves through obstinate refusal to take part in the war." [27] To be sure, Colonel Anwar al-Sadat's [28] account of the prevailing pro-German sentiment (manifesting itself in General Aziz al-Misri's abortive attempt to reach the German lines) is not included in the Charter. Instead, the Germans are labelled "racialists" who were at war with Anglo-French imperialism. The conspicuous absence of any reference to Egyptian-Arab sympathies toward the Axis can be easily explained in terms of the image that the leadership wants to create, in addition to foreign policy imperatives. In the light of the mass extermination of Jews in Germany, the Egyptian dedication to remove Israel is sometimes labelled a "racialist" policy—something Egyptian spokesmen have consistently rejected.[29] Moreover, any identification with Nazi Germany would seriously harm Egypt's world image; even the "friendly" Soviets might find it difficult to support such a regime.

In the final analysis, it seems evident that the Egyptian reinterpretation of World War II history, as presented in the Charter, is a modified application of Lenin's theory of imperialism. By regarding the war as "a strife over the colonies and markets between racialism and Anglo-French imperialism," [30] the authors of the Charter (consciously or unconsciously) have converted a portion of Lenin's doctrine to fit their view of World War II—something that even the Soviets have not attempted since they were party to the conflict. As to the Soviet Union's role in the war, the Charter remains conspicuously silent.

The unity imposed by Nasirite historians on the common experiences of the Arabs in the first half of the twentieth century culminates with the Egyptian involvement in the 1948 War against Israel. The simultaneous Egyptian and Arab attack on Israel and their joint humiliation suffered in defeat pervades all Egyptian literature dealing with the subject. Indeed, this joint involvement is all-important to the Egyptian Pan-Arab historian, because it is the sole historical anchor in modern times intimately connecting Egypt with the Arab East. To discover a similar political connection one has to trace back at least to the tenth century.[31] The emphasis placed on the joint humiliation by Israel implies a future uniting of the Arabs for the purpose of erasing the injustices of the past. Thus, one of the main functions of the Egyptian ideologue-historian clearly emerges: to unify the Arab past to build a united Arab future.

The years between 1948 and 1952 are seen as the "preparatory stage" during which the necessary preconditions for the revolution were developing. This period is characterized as one in which the increasing anger and humiliation of the masses was being transformed into "revolutionary consciousness" waiting to be unleashed. The rise of anti-British terrorism, the multiplication of secret organizations, the "peasants' rebellions . . . against serfdom," and the burning of Cairo are all related to the rising popular anger.[32] Against this background, the role of the Free Officers on 23 July 1952 is described as that of "a popular tool" which "by taking the side of the popular struggle" occupied "its natural place in the country." [33]

The use of the term, "its natural place," to describe the army's role in the take-over of July 1952 is closely related to the legitimation of military rule. Egyptian history since Muhammad Ali has been recast to show the historically inevitable necessity [34] and therefore the legitimacy of the military takeover and entrenchment. Once firmly focused on July 1952, the Egyptian historian proceeds to relate all past failures and injustices—Ottoman rule, imperialism, Urabi's defeat, the Wafd corruption, the Palestine debacle—to the new regime's promises to rectify the legacies of the past and thereby legitimize itself. Thus, history as such becomes a progression toward and background to the revolution. As the external and internal injustices multiply, the revolutionary consciousness of the people is said to increase to the point where the immediate precoup period is characterized as one of mass revolutionary fervor that permeated throughout the width and depth of society.[35] The fact that little revolutionary consciousness existed among Egypt's masses at the time was irrelevant since this historical reality would not contribute to the legitimation of the new regime. Though the episode of July 1952 was a mere coup engineered by a small clique of officers, it had to be given the aura of a legitimately conceived and broadly based act "that was not accidental but rationally planned," [36] "not a coup but a genuine revolution." [37]

While a coup denotes an accidental, inherently illegitimate, and therefore temporary state of affairs, a mass-supported revolution implies legitimacy and therefore permanence both domestically and in the Arab world. Once the coup was transformed into a revolution, the next big step involved the conversion of a purely Egyptian experience into a Pan-Arab revolution by recasting the Arab and Egyptian past into a united whole. With the past historically united, the unity of the future would become desirable, logical, and perhaps even possible.

Historical reinterpretation was not confined to the prerevolutionary period but also included the first three years of military rule. The official account of the years 1952–55 depicts the struggle for power between the ruling military officers on the one hand, and the political parties and the Ikhwan, on the other. The charges levelled against the latter are, of course, "fanaticism" and "terrorism." The Wafd and the smaller parties are pictured as corrupt and unwilling to purge themselves.[38] Because of this corruption, constant infighting, and lack of unity, the parties were dissolved. Egyptian writers claim that the Wafd—the majority party before the revolution—in reality "did not represent the people." [39] A more significant aspect of the historiography of this period is the phenomenon of the "unperson"—the omission from historical accounts of the names of now-fallen central personages. The major "unperson" in modern Egyptian history, of course, is General Muhammad Nagib.

Reshaping the Distant Past

In order to legitimize the new Pan-Arabist orientation of the
Egyptian regime, historical reinterpretation had to reach deep
into Arab history. If modern Egypt was to serve as the great unifier of the Arabic-speaking world, the Egyptian and the Arab past
had to be unified to some degree; certain common historical experiences had to be emphasized and others reinterpreted or deemphasized. In view of the objective realities of the past, the
Nasirite historian's task of selectively relating Egyptian history to
that of other Arabic-speaking peoples' was a most ungrateful
one. These difficulties resulted not only from the diversity of the
past but also from the narrow ideological limits of the present
within which the historian had to labor. Indeed, the ideological
requirements of the Nasirite version of Arab unity nationalism
were formidable. These included: 1) the widely held Arab ideological goal of achieving Arab unity; 2) the Egyptian goal of realizing a Pan-Arab state centered on Cairo; 3) the officially pro-
claimed Arabness of modern Egypt, which necessitated the
assumption that Egyptians had been Arabs and acted as Arabs
within the ancient realm of Islam; [40] and 4) the continuing alienation and animosity of Egyptians and Arabs toward Christian
West Europe.

In the light of modern experience, the incompatibility of the
second goal with the first in the minds of some non-Egyptian
Arabs has been amply demonstrated. Yet despite the secession of
Syria from the United Arab Republic and the almost continuous
tension between Abd al-Nasir and the Ba'athists, Sa'udis, and
Hashemites, the Egyptian president managed to sustain an un-
equalled position of leadership. The Nasirite conception of Egypt
as "the base" [41] for the Arab revolutionary struggle remains valid
and relevant both as an ideological tenet and a practical fact.

In general terms, the Nasirite historian endeavors to recast the
Arab-Egyptian past within two interconnected molds. First, he
views the historic conquests and civilization of Islam as a purely
Arab affair, thereby converting the historical unity of Islam into

Arab unity. Then he proceeds to emphasize those periods in which Arab power radiated from Egypt. In terms of the present ideological and strategic needs of the UAR, the two foregoing positions are most logical, though historically somewhat inaccurate. If future Arab unity is to be achieved, much of Islamic history has to be "Arabized"; [42] if Egypt is to be the base for future Arab unity, it must claim to have fulfilled such a function in the past.

The Arabization of the military and intellectual glory of the Islamic civilization was no difficult or even novel task for Egyptian historians, since it has been general practice in modern Arab literature. The tendency among Arab historians to treat important Muslim intellectual and military personalities—Berbers, Turks, Kurds, Syrians, Persians—as Arabs, antedates Nasirite historians. The real difficulty lay in finding historical anchors for a Cairo-centered movement of Arab unity—a difficult task considering the realities of Islamic history. A cursory survey will readily reveal that the Cairo-centered Nasirite historian did not possess a real choice; the imperatives of his present narrowed his choice to the adoption and glorification of only one period, one dynasty, and one ruler—Salah al-Din al-Ayyubi.[43]

In terms of geographical location and ethnic makeup, the first three successive periods of Islamic history not only fail to qualify for Nasirite adoption, but even constitute a threat to the claim of Egyptian leadership in modern Araby. Egypt's relationship to the Rashidun based on Medina, the Umayyads at Damascus, and the Abbasids at Baghdad was that of a non-Arab, conquered territory. As such these would provide historical justification for rival Arab-unity movements centered on Arabia and the Fertile Crescent.[44] The period of political independence achieved under the short-lived Tulunid and Ikhshidid Dynasties is equally useless as an historical foundation for modern Egypt. Although this marked the emergence of Egypt as a sovereign state for the first time since Ptolemaic days, the dynasties in question were founded by Turks.[45] To the modern Arabized ideologue of Egypt, the Tulunid-Ikhshidid era constitutes nothing less than one of foreign imperialism. Moreover, these dynasties could not serve as models for Arab unity, since their power did not extend to the whole of today's Arab world.[46]

The advent of Fatimid power in Egypt is also irrelevant to modern Egyptian historiography. The controversial genealogy and legitimacy of Fatimid Caliphs,[47] compounded by their Shi'ism and non-Egyptian origin, disqualifies these rulers as meaningful historical anchors for today's Sunni Egypt. In addition to these factors, the modern ideological utility of the Fatimids would be limited since at no time did the dynasty rule all of the eastern Arab world.

In contrast, the reign of Salah al-Din al-Ayyubi fits most of the ideological requirements of modern Egyptian historian-ideologues. To begin with, Salah al-Din terminated the "illegitimate" caliphal rule of the Shi'i Fatimids in Egypt and replaced it, at least nominally, with that of the Sunni Abbasids. Thus, as the supreme champion of Sunni Islam, his subsequent acts of establishing hegemony over the Arab East could be regarded as legitimate endeavors carried out under caliphal authority. What is particularly significant to the Egyptians is the fact that Salah al-Din established his first power base in Egypt, then proceeded to unify the shattered realm of Islam, with the exception of "un-Arabized" Persia.[48] Thus, for the first time in history, Egypt became the base of united Islam which, in the absence of Persia and Turkic territories of the north, could be regarded as a union of Arab and Arabized Muslims and not one of diverse, heterogeneous Islamized peoples. Although his rule over Syria, Iraq, and Arabia had been extended from his Egyptian base, Salah al-Din has not been regarded in these lands as an Egyptian conqueror. His "unflinching" and victorious struggle against the Crusaders —"the first wave of European colonialism"—automatically makes Salah al-Din the modern symbol of unity for Arabs and Egyptians alike,[49] particularly in their opposition to the Christian West. Thus, the acts of this Arabized Kurd are of immeasurable utility to the Nasirite historian, because for the first time in history a newly Arabized Egypt became united with the Arab East under Egyptian supremacy.

The choice of Salah al-Din as a primary historical focus is also determined by the Egyptian's view of their present situation. The Western imperial presence still constitutes a continuing affront to national dignity. The protection extended to Israel, "a bastion of imperialism," and the limits placed on Egyptian ambitions by

American power are equated with the Crusaders' invasion of the Middle East. As a result, what essentially was regarded as a religious conflict between Islam and Christianity is now revived; only Islam is replaced by Arab nationalist ideology and the Christian Crusaders by Western imperialism. In the Arab perception, Israel becomes an extension of the West as were the Frankish kingdoms of Syria-Palestine during the Crusades. In this context, it is emphasized that "Salah al-Din kindled the Arab revolution . . . which is still continuing." [50] Yet the Egyptian *raison d'être* for reviving the past and "continuing" Salah al-Din's "revolution" is not the subjection of Arabs to Western pressures only, but also the West's unwillingness to forget the past. Reference is often made to General Allenby's pronouncement upon entering Jerusalem in 1918 that "the Crusades have come to an end." Another instance frequently cited is General Gouraud's words at Salah-al-Din's tomb at Damascus—"We are back Salah al-Din." [51] Indeed, preoccupation with this interpretation of the Crusades is even reflected in the Charter.[52] The implied similarity between the success of the united struggle against Europe under Salah al-Din and the necessity for creating such a united movement under Abd al-Nasir is clearly reflected in most of the literature on the subject. The special relationship between Egypt and the rest of the Arab East achieved by Salah al-Din works against the allegation that Egypt's historical experience was isolated from that of Arabs in Syria, Palestine, Iraq, and Arabia. Moreover, the legitimacy and acceptance enjoyed by an Egyptian-based leader, as was Salah al-Din, serves as an important precedent to clothe the Nasirite movement of Arab unity with the cloak of historical legitimacy.

The memory of Salah al-Din and his role as Arab unifier and victor against the Crusaders were recalled by President Nasir on many occasions, especially during the Syrian-Egyptian union.[53] His visit to Salah al-Din's tomb in Damascus on 28 February 1958, and adoption of Salah al-Din's eagle as the UAR national emblem symbolized Abd al-Nasir's identification with the sultan.

The unification of the Egyptian-Arab historical experience by Egyptian historians also affects their interpretation of the subsequent Mamluk-Ottoman era. Muslim unity in opposing and defeating the Crusaders becomes a unity of suffering under the

Turkic groups; the Christian enemy is replaced by a Muslim one
—"Ottoman colonialism disguised in the form of the Caliphate." [54] The Egyptian evaluation of the Turks and Turkish
rule reflects the historial Arab-Egyptian enmity toward Turkic
rulers and the pro-Western, pro-Israeli, and pro-Iranian position
of Turkey during the cold war years. The Turk is pictured as an
"unpolitical animal" who rules by the sword; [55] essentially he is a
foreigner in the Near East, having arrived there not peacefully
but by "invasion." The Ottoman period is characterized as one of
darkness for Arabs and Islam because the Turks "had no interest
in civilization"; [56] they usurped the Caliphate and imposed a co-
lonialist and reactionary rule that led to the isolation of Arabs
and the disintegration of their civilization.[57]

Other Aspects of Historiography

The historiography of present-day revolutionary Egypt also reflects a distinct trend toward "Egyptocentrism" and "Arabocen-
trism." Moreover, even the histories of lands and peoples unrelated
to the Arab-Egyptian past are interpreted through the ideological
coloration imposed by the present revolutionary milieu. A few
examples are sufficient to illustrate these points.

First, the emphasis placed on the debt of the West to Islamic
civilization is somewhat exaggerated. In contrast, the corresponding Arab debt to Greco-Roman civilization is given only brief
mention. All the Arab civilizing traits, including nationalism,
were "copied" by the West and in that process lost their moral
content through aggressive and unjust use.[58] The renaissance in
Italy is seen as the result of the acquisition of Arab knowledge
through Sicily. And not to be outdone by the Chinese and Scan-
dinavians, the strong possibility of Arab navigators discovering
America before Columbus is suggested.[59]

There seems to be a tendency to judge the historical behavior
of certain European states in terms of present UAR relationships
with these states. For instance, Portugal receives unfavorable
treatment because of its present rightist ideological orientation
and continued possession of African colonies. Their discovery of

a sea route to India is said to have caused the decline of Arab lands. Vasco da Gama's "fanatical ruthlessness" in India (now a friendly state) also receives special emphasis.[60] It should be remembered that the issue here is not the validity of these interpretations, but the fact that they reflect the Egyptian mode of looking at the past in terms of the present. And if one accepts Leibnitz's dictum that "the present is saturated with the past and pregnant with the future," Egyptian attitudes on history are important for their potential role in shaping the future.

In the absence of survey research, it is hard to determine the degree to which the new historical analysis has become a part of the Egyptians' belief system and world outlook. At the level of the political and intellectual elites, the new historiography appears to be more than a manipulative political device—indeed, some of its major portions seem to flow from conviction and therefore form an integral part of the elite's world view (*Weltanschauung*). Given the fact that the new history is an integral part of all school curricula, one would expect it to shape the socialization and world view of the new generation.

In the final analysis, the role of history in the modern Egyptian context is that of a weapon to defend the regime and justify its present policies. In this respect the similarities between Sino-Soviet and Egyptian historiography are more than striking. While in Marxist historical scholarship the historian must wage war against "bourgeois falsifications," [61] the Egyptian historian has to guard against the "wrong analyses" [62] of Western and other historians. Moreover, like their Soviet counterparts, the Egyptians are confirmed simplifiers and unifiers of history, without toleration for complicated, diverse, or pluralistic interpretations of the subject. While they declare themselves ardent believers in the cyclical determinist theory of history—i.e., the past glory of united Araby will inevitably happen again in the future—in actual fact the direction of their historical process is reversed. The ideological compulsion and commitment to the Pan-Arab state of the future shapes present actions and recasts the past. For the Egyptians, Leibnitz's dictum is reversed: the present is saturated with the future and pregnant with the past.

7

Pan-Arabism and the Arabization of Modern Egypt

The Non-Muslim Minorities

IDENTIFICATION with the Arab past for realizing future Arab unity could not be accomplished without Arabizing the Egyptian present. As late as 1955, when the Egyptian leadership began to assume a definite Arabist orientation, the historical process of Arabization (*isti'rab*) of Egypt had not been completed. Indeed, the people of the Nile Valley had never been fully acculturated into the Islamic-Arab civilization that had come to Egypt with the Muslim-Arab conquest (*futuh*) of the seventh century. While the simultaneous processes of Islamization and Arabization did replace much of the old Hamitic-Christian-Byzantine [1] culture, islands of resistance remained until modern times. The successive waves of foreign rulers—the Shi'a Fatimids, Turkic dynasties (Ikhshidids, Tulunids, Mamluks, Ottomans) and Europeans—had slowed down the force of Islamization and Arabization. Meanwhile certain new ethnic groups began to arrive, often with the explicit encouragement of various rulers. These included diverse Turkic groups, Armenians, Syrian Christians, Greeks, Italians, Jews, and others. [2]

With the advent of Egyptian nationalism, the Turkic groups either left or became assimilated with relative ease since they were already Muslims. However, certain of the non-Muslim minorities had historically resisted assimilation. The purely Egyptian nationalism of Ahmad Urabi, Mustafa Kamil, and Sa'd Zaghlul might have been able to accommodate such diverse non-Arab, non-Muslim groups as the Greeks, Armenians, Italians, and

Jews. As citizens of Egypt, their minority status could have been tolerated under a nebulous ideology of Egyptian nationalism. But with the adoption of Pan-Arabist integrative policies by the Nasirite elite after 1955, the possibilities of mutual accommodation began to recede. While consenting to an "Egyptian" label, these minorities had little desire to become Arabized. Moreover, the special status and privileges granted these groups under the Fatimids, Ottomans, Britons, and the Muhammad Ali dynasty contributed further to the ambiguity of their position. The increasingly militant and serious tenor of the regime's Pan-Arab ideology could not help but threaten many of these historically insecure communities. This element of insecurity became more pronounced when the theoretically secular regime not only accommodated traditional Islam, but also incorporated some of its teachings in the official ideology.[3] The revival of the anti-Christian Islamic past in the press and certain books [4] gave the new regime a nonsecular coloration in the eyes of non-Muslims.[5]

There has been little evidence of an official program of minority assimilation. Any seemingly anti-minority action flowed naturally from the new leadership's self-image as reflected in its ideology. Now that the foreign monarchy and imperialist subjugation were ended, the new leadership viewed itself as the embodiment of the age-old Egyptian dream—to be ruled by Egyptians. If its claim of being genuinely Egyptian was to be taken seriously by the overwhelming majority of the people, then the elite had to rebalance the traditional structures of access, status, and privilege which heavily favored the minorities. As a result, the relatively strong Coptic representation in the governmental bureaucracy and the top political leadership of the pre-1952 period was reduced in favor of Muslims. As to the other non-Christian groups, many of their special privileges derived from the old Ottoman *millet* system were taken away, as was their prominent economic position.[6] Furthermore, the revolutionary leadership did not offer the kind of special access to the top that the Greeks, Italians, and Syrian Christians possessed during the monarchy.[7] The army officers did not make a practice of relying on the advice and help of leading non-Muslim subjects as did the rulers of the Muhammad Ali dynasty. This alienated the ethnic groups since the absence of these men deprived them of a sense of identification with the system. However, in all fairness, the regime did strive to accord other types of formal and informal recognition to certain minorities. These included presidential appointment of various Christians to allotted seats in the National Assembly as well as official meetings between governmental figures and minority functionaries.

The Egyptianization-Arabization process has been most deeply felt in minority schools as well as those supported and operated by Christian missionaries. A law promulgated in 1958 brought these school systems under the close supervision of the Ministry of Education which must approve all courses, prescribe textbooks, and conduct seminars for teachers of history, civics, and related subjects.[8] These courses are now taught in the Arabic language. Nevertheless, minority newspapers, particularly Greek and Armenian, have continued to flourish.

In general, the effect of the new order on the non-Muslim minorities has been a steady wave of emigration from Egypt. Interviews clearly show that the only factor delaying a mass exodus is the strict official ban on taking capital out of the country. There is even evidence to indicate that for the first time in history [9] Copts are leaving Egypt in growing numbers.[10] Assuming that present trends continue, the various non-Muslim groups are bound to disappear by emigration and in the case of Copts also through assimilation.[11] As the process continues, the Egyptian body politic will become still more homogeneous both linguistically and religiously.[12]

Isti'rab and Muslim Egypt

Historical experience has demonstrated that the existence of a homogeneous society with common bonds of religion, history, and language tends to facilitate the nation-building tasks of nationalist elites. In comparison with most African, Asian, and Latin American developing societies, the Egyptian is highly homogeneous. Over 90 percent of Egyptians are Sunni Muslims and unlike other Arab countries Egypt is not burdened by sectional, sectarian, or racial strife. Although internally homogeneous, one of Egypt's main problems in the 1950s and 1960s was the quest for credibility as an Arab nation. The question bluntly posed by the Syrian Ba'athists begged for an answer: were the Egyptians really Arabs?

It should be emphasized that in traditional Islamic society the question of a Muslim's ethnic background was not as significant as in the modern nationalist environment. During the course of Arab history, the question of ethnic identity was raised only when the Arabization process could not keep up with the more rapid pace of expanding Islam. In other words, the conflict between Muslim Arabs and other Muslims—Persians, Berbers, Turks—came into being when Arabizing influences, in contrast to Islamization, encountered stiff resistance. In the case of Egypt, after the Ayyubids, the country was ruled by unassimilated but Muslim Kipçak and Oghuz Turkic groups. While concrete historical evidence is seriously lacking, it seems that the process of Arabization was arrested during the 500 years of Ottoman-Turkish rule, until its revival in the twentieth century. Yet before the advent of the Ottomans, Arabizing forces seem to have been vigorous enough to cause the replacement of Coptic by Arabic as the spoken language of the Copts around the sixteenth century.[13]

When Egypt awakened from the slumber of the Turkic period, characterized as the "dark ages" [14] in modern Egyptian historiography, it found itself in an alien milieu of nation-states. The reawakened Muslim Egyptian intellectual of the late nineteenth and early twentieth centuries was a man without historical bearings —he was in a sense unhistorical. He needed time to rediscover Egypt's past and then choose and identify himself with certain of its portions. Indeed, the only fact he knew about himself was that he was a Muslim, and as such he concentrated on making the al-Azhar, the center of Islamic learning. The questions as to whether he would regard himself as a pharaonic Egyptian, an Ottoman, or an Arab remained to be resolved. A brief look at the literature of the period reflects the continuing indecision and crisis among intellectuals. The great diversity of opinions expressed necessitates a closer examination.

Lacking a sense of national identity, the initial reaction of Egyptian intellectuals to European imperialism (political and economic) manifested itself in the Pan-Islamic movement presided over by the non-Egyptian, non-Arab, Jamal al-Din al-Afghani. While a movement to revive Arabic literary masterpieces had begun in Khedive Isma'il's days, the ideological framework of opposition to foreign influence continued to be Pan-Islamic even during Colonel Urabi's revolt against the Turkish-Circassian military leadership. As European intellectual influences on Egypt intensified, a number of diverse movements came into being to replace the worn-out tenets of Pan-Islamism. By the beginning of the twentieth century the obsolescence of this doctrine was demonstrated by the successive attacks of Ottoman nationalists [15] and Pan-Turkists,[16] leaving its continued advocacy to the universally despised Sultan Abdulhamid. In the political arena, the nationalist movement of Mustafa Kamil had begun to manifest a strongly secular current, independent of Pan-Islamism.

In a general sense, the problem of the intellectual was to relate in an effective way the realities of the Egyptian present to the Islamic past. The Egyptian present consisted of a growing nationalist fervor brought about by the British presence and the increasing intensity of European intellectual influences. The response of the Egyptian intellectual was similar to his Turkish counterpart; he advocated adoption of the thought and institutions of the West European countries in the hope of simulating the intellectual, economic, and military progress of his imperial masters. In this sense, the prevalent trend was toward Europeanization, and in the intellectual realm the influences at work mostly came from France and Britain and to a lesser extent from Germany, Italy, and Russia. Thus, under the strong influence of French revolutionary literature and British social thought, the intellectuals assumed a Western cultural orientation, an uncompromising rationalist approach, and a seemingly firm dedication to liberal-nationalist thought and institutions. However, the transition had to be made within the context of Islamic society. The rationalist epistemology and the secular nature of the model European nation-state soon brought these Westernist writers in conflict with the traditional precepts of Islam and the accepted interpretation of Egyptian-Arab history. Thus, if an Egyptian nationality was to be created, the historic concept of the larger Muslim *ummah* (community) had to be reinterpreted in a drastic manner; Islam, the religion, had to be declared separate from the state. The group that attempted this transformation included such thinkers as Ali Abd al-Raziq, Ahmad Amin, Abbas Mahmud al-Aqqad, Taha Husayn, and Tawfiq al-Hakim.[17] Once Islam as religion was effectively separated from the historic concept of the Muslim state, the Egyptian intellectuals could argue that the unity imposed on the newly Islamized lands was nothing but the utilization of Islam as an ideology of conquest by the Umayyads and the Abbasids. This meant nothing less than a radical rejection of the Arab past and complete dissociation from "the Arab subjugators" of Egypt.[18] Thus, linguistic and religious similarity was not taken to mean cultural identity, much less political unity. In the circumstances, the conquests of equally "extra-Egyptian" rulers such as the Shi'ite Fatimids, the Turkic Tulunids, and Mamluks were portrayed as valiant Egyptian attempts to assert their independence against the eastern Arab centers of power in Damascus and Baghdad.

But the attempt to dissociate from Islamic-Arab unity was indeed a negative act. As Professor Nadav Safran observes, "it was still necessary to provide a positive ideological rationale for a specifically Egyptian nationalism. . . ."[19] In the attempt to endow the new state with a distinctive Egyptian "cultural personality," the pharaonic past was revived and refurbished. Among the intellectuals who advocated an "Egypt First" policy based on pharaonism were some of the country's foremost journalists, especially Fikri Abaza, Ihsan Abd al-Quddus, Mustafa Amin—who continued to press their case well into the early period of the revolution.[20]

This Westernizing-Egyptianizing phase of intellectual and political history has, at best, only a historical significance to the contemporary observer of the Egyptian scene. In terms of popular following and official sanction, most of the painfully constructed tenets of the Westernizing phase seem outdated for modern Egyptian society; their primary importance lies in the reaction they created. It was this reaction against the Westernizing movements that was destined to shape the intellectual, social, and political structure of Nasirite Egypt.

As in the evolution from Pan-Islamism to Westernism, the reversion to the Muslim ethos came as a result of newly developing forces and conditions that unfolded in the early thirties. These included a general alienation of Egyptian intellectuals from their former ideal—the West. The more familiar they became with the content of Western civilization, the more glaring seemed the weaknesses of Europe, and the wider the gap between the theory and practice of liberal democracy. Increasingly, the wholesale adoption of a Western life style seemed less and less attractive. Meanwhile the performance of the constitutional regime (1922–1952) had been disastrously poor; the political and economic expectations of a rapidly expanding population were unfulfilled.

In these frustrating circumstances a group of intellectuals led by Muhammad Husayn Haykal effected a reversion to the spiritual tenets of traditional Islam, in the absence of other attractive alternatives. In contrast to the subsequent revolutionary period, the remaining alternatives of totalitarian communism and fascism must have seemed unattractive mainly because of their atheism and ruthlessness,[21] in addition to being essentially Western and therefore foreign. This conscious backtracking by Haykal harkened to such thinkers as Rashid Rida, Muhammad Abduh, and Jamal al-Din al-Afghani. In essence, it amounted to a total rejection of everything Western except science and technology [22]—a conclusion that the Ottomans and Muhammad Ali had reached in the early 1800s without the guidance of intellectuals.

The anti-Western trend that began with Haykal—a former Westernist—included an attack on the very concept of nation-statehood. The modern state system was characterized as one of "mutually competing units" bent on destruction.[23] During the 1930s and after, Haykal's Pan-Islamic alternative of "divine unity" bringing all Muslims within the fold seemed meaningless, since no such desire could be detected among non-Arab Muslims. Indeed, as it subsequently developed, Haykal's revival of Islamism in opposition to Western liberalism could relate itself only to other Arab countries. Because of its limitation to Arabic-speaking countries, the new Pan-Islamic movement reinforced the Islamic ties between Egyptians and Arabs, and as such constituted a force working against Egyptian isolation; in this way it influenced the emerging ideology of Arab unity nationalism. In the context of the modern nation-state system, the step from Pan-Islamism to Pan-Arabism did not prove to be a difficult one. Since the achievement of a religiously based unity became impossible, a secular uniting of Arabic-speaking nation-states seemed the logical alternative. And in this union of states, a reinterpreted and limited form of Pan-Islamism would still be applicable—the Islamic heritage could serve as a common cultural bond between various Arabic-speaking Muslim lands.[24]

In terms of epistemology, the revolt against the West brought down the earlier dedication to reason and replaced it with rampant emotionalism, spiritualism, and romantic traditionalism. The correlation between similar developments in Europe and Egypt in the mid-1930s was not, perhaps, accidental. Indeed, in the rise of Italy and Germany, the Egyptians could not fail but observe the mounting of what seemed a successful challenge to liberal democratic regimes that included Great Britain—the arch-enemy of Egypt. In terms of cultural orientation, the elaborately constructed edifice of the Western-inspired Egyptian "cultural identity," that included pharaonic, Greek, Roman, and Islamic elements, was dismantled and replaced by an Islamic core, subsequently to be crowned by an Arab superstructure.

Finally, by the late 1930s, the economic aspects of Egyptian liberal democracy came under heavy criticism. The attack centered mainly on the big landowning class, which was increasingly identified with the existing political parties.[25] While some astute critics of the social system like Khalid Muhammad Khalid observed that the blame for the misery of the masses should be placed chiefly on "oriental capitalism," the West continued to be denounced as "materialistic." [26] Clearly, a replacement for the existing Oriental-Western capitalist and feudalist system had to be found. But the anti-Western milieu that prevailed in the period of reaction did not prove conducive to the adoption of welfare-statist or other non-Marxist socialistic solutions. Similarly, the atheistic aspect of communism prevented it from becoming a viable choice. Therefore, the only solution that could be advanced was an attempt to reexamine and reapply the economic tenets of early Islam. The resulting concept of Islamic socialism as formulated by Shaykh Muhammad al-Ghazzali [27] became the major ideological position of the Ikhwan regarding the social and economic reorganization of Egyptian society.

On the eve of the officers' coup, the evolution of ideology had made a full circle. Yet in the process, the broad swings of the ideological pendulum had encompassed a variety of concepts and doctrines, some of which were incorporated into the official ideology of the Nasirite regime. In this sense therefore, there is a continuity between pre-1952 intellectual currents and those of the Nasirite period, despite the claims of the revolutionary regime to the contrary. In terms of political structure and ideology, the new Egypt has many deep roots in the old Egypt—more than the official ideologues would grant. In many ways the pre-1952 intellectuals were preparing the ideological groundwork for revolutionary Egypt. The concepts and doctrines that survived the revolutionary takeover included:

1. An authoritarian ideological-religious legacy in the context of dictatorial rule, in reaction to the liberal democratic ideology and its constitutional practice.

2. The retention of the basic tenets of al-Ghazzali's Islamic socialism; but within a more secular and broader context.

3. The mass aspect and emotionalism of fundamentalist movements like the Brethren.

4. The adoption and incorporation of anti-Westernism into the new revolutionary ideology. (This included the concept of borrowing from the West only scientific knowledge.)

5. The utilization of the Islamic theory of Dar al-Harb in the modern context of the regime's opposition to imperialism.

6. The reapplication of a secularized and limited Pan-Islamism within the framework of the Arab-speaking world. This includes the reinterpretation of the historical Islamic *ummah* into an Arab *ummah,* and the projection of this "fact" of the past into the future utopia of Arabs—the Pan-Arab state. In other words the Islamic unity of the past is transformed into Arab unity, through historical reinterpretation, and is applied to the Arab-Egyptian present and future. Indeed, this development was revolutionary in terms of offering leadership to the Arab world. With respect to Egypt, it meant nothing less than a commitment to the total Arabization of Egyptian society and culture. Thus, the Arabization process that started with the Islamization of the valley of the Nile after the Arab conquest is reaching its culmination under official guidance and encouragement.

Without doubt, the concepts and formulations of intellectuals would remain unimplemented theories unless they are adopted and applied by a relatively legitimate elite working in a receptive environment. To be sure, that was the relationship of Rousseau to the French Revolution, and that of Locke and Montesquieu to the American Revolution. The nature and direction of the intellectual metamorphosis of most well-known Egyptian writers—al-Aqqad, al-Hakim, Haykal, Amin [28]—had evolved to such a point where an intelligently eclectic and legitimate political leadership could transform these ideas into practice. Even the last lonely hold-out—the Westernist Taha Husayn—would eventually capitulate and seek employment from the new rulers, as did the rest of his colleagues. The new leaders, born in this period of diverse and free *ijtihad,* were a part of the new evolution in thought. Through their seizure of power and perpetuation of rule, they made themselves the great culminators of the process. Out of the various schools of thought expressed in the last seventy years, a consensus—an *ijma'*—finally emerged in the late 1950s. Yet significantly, the final process of reaching the *ijma'* of Arab unity and socialism was presided over by neither the *ulama'* nor the intellectuals, but by young army officers. For the present, the gates of *ijtihad* thrown open by Shaykh Muhammad Abduh in the 1880s have been slammed shut firmly and resolutely by the elites of the new order in Egypt.

The Evolution of Nationalist Thought

The foregoing analysis suggests that monocausal explanations are insufficient to account for the evolution of Egyptian nationalism into Arabism. Instead, one may discern a convergence of factors affecting the process of ideological change. To recapitulate, Egyptian nationalism had been found inadequate, both in theory and practice, not only by many intellectuals but later by the political elites themselves. Its content and underpinnings imparted a sense of artificiality and irrelevance with respect to the existing Egyptian ethos. Regardless of its ancient glory, anchoring modern nationalism on the pharaonic period had a ring of unreality, especially to Muslim Egyptians. The weakness and ambiguity of its pharaonic foundations might have been overcome had it not been for the "foreignness" of its content; the adoption of a secular path was too abrupt a departure from the Islamic reality of Egyptian society. The wholesale borrowing and duplication of European ideas and forms not only reduced their general legitimacy but also caused strong intellectual reaction. Finally, Egyptian nationalism in practice was a great disappointment for leaders and masses alike. The ruling elite, with the exception of Sa'd Zaghlul, did not adhere to it seriously; there were no systematic and protracted attempts at ideological propagation and socialization. Soon, two of Egypt's leading politicians, Azzam Pasha and al-Nahhas Pasha, began to oppose it. The constitutional forms of Egyptian nationalism produced continued chaos within the three-cornered power struggle between the king, the Wafd, and the British. Moreover, there was little thought of providing Egyptian nationalism with an ideological component for social change to increase its internal relevance. Finally, its ultimate goal—full independence—remained unfulfilled. Hence, the search for alternatives.

Yet, Arab nationalism as an alternative did not readily emerge. First, Haykal attempted a return to Islamism marked by the rejection of the Western elements of Egyptian nationalism. This reidentification with the Islamic ethos, coupled with the cultural centrality of Egypt in the Arab orbit, pointed the way to a less secular, more militant, and non-Western ideological path— Arab nationalism. But while the groundwork for the transition to Arab nationalism had been laid decades ago, its actual adoption was largely determined by political considerations in the larger Arab sphere.

Arab nationalist intellectual trends made their appearance in Egypt in the 1930s. In the next decade Arabism began to compete against Egyptian nationalism with the support of King Faruq and political leaders, such as al-Nahhas Pasha and Azzam Pasha.[29] While Egyptian willingness to join the Arab League in 1945 may be regarded as a manifestation of Arabizing trends, it hardly represented widespread grassroots pressure. By all indications, public and intellectual opinion was mixed. Ultimately, the leadership's decision to join was based primarily, but not exclusively, on diplomatic and security calculations. Similarly,

Egypt's involvement in the Palestine War of 1948 was prompted by security calculations coupled with the king's desire to distract attention from the prevailing domestic turmoil toward the foreign front. However, the subsequent defeat of Egyptian arms brought vociferous denunciation of Pan-Arabism and demands to withdraw from the Arab League. This produced a reidentification with Egyptianism and a relapse into isolationism which persisted until 1953 (see Figure 4). Yet despite these tendencies Egypt signed a collective security pact with the Arab states in 1950. In the early post-revolutionary period, Arab nationalism once again emerged as a competitor of Egyptian nationalism. However, it was not until the threat which the Baghdad Pact posed to Egypt's leading position in the Arab world that a more definitive and genuine commitment to Arabism was made by Nasir. Therefore, the final decision in favor of Arabism was taken in response to an external threat and against a divided domestic public opinion base where Arabism was gaining gradual ascendency. Subsequently, Nasir's personal identification with Arabism pushed the remaining supporters of Egyptianism into the background until the aftermath of the June War.

A quantitative analysis of nationalist ideology graphically reveals the decline of Egyptian nationalism and the concomitant rise of Arab nationalism. The specific technique employed to measure the changing intensity of these phenomena over time was content analysis [30] of Egyptian radio broadcasts between 1 January 1952 and 31 December 1959. The broadcasts included local newspaper articles, speeches of government leaders, official statements, as well as news analysis and editorial comment by radio announcers—a total of 15,515 news items.

In the broadcasts, the general theme of Egyptian nationalism was characterized by specific references to "unity of the Nile Valley," "sons of the Nile Valley," "Egyptian people," "Egyptian territory," "Egypt will destroy," "glory and dignity of Egypt." In each case the emphasis focussed exclusively on the Nile Valley in the Sudan and Egypt. In contrast, the themes denoting Arab nationalism were used in the context of a Pan-Arabist identification with the peoples of other Arab states. These themes included "the Arab nation from the Atlantic Ocean to the Arab Gulf," "Arab Egypt," "Arab solidarity," "Arab people of Egypt." Regardless

Figure 4. *Ideological Change (Yearly Index)*

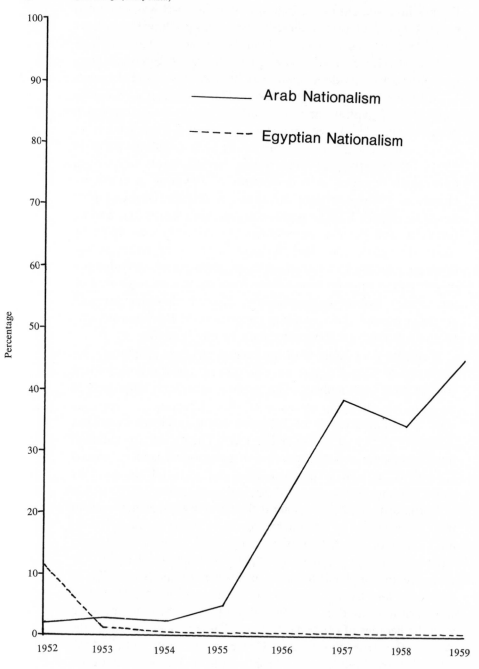

Figure 5. *Ideological Change (Monthly Index)*

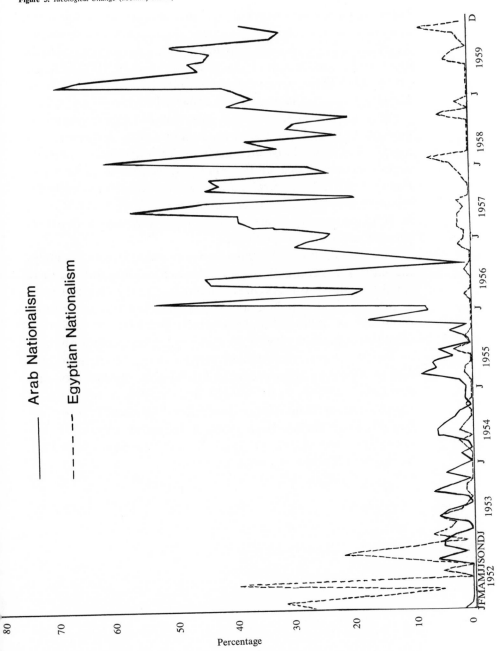

of the frequency with which a particular theme occurred within a news item, it was counted only once. The frequency of themes in a given month or year were divided by the total number of news items in the same month or year and multiplied by 100 yielding a percentage. These percentages were plotted against time from January 1952 to the end of December 1959.

As Figure 4 indicates, the predominant theme expressed through April of 1953 was Egyptian nationalism. However, during 1953 the cumulative frequency of Arab nationalism already slightly exceeded that of Egyptian nationalism, as recorded in Figure 5. After 1953, Arab nationalism maintained its yearly cumulative preponderance over Egyptian nationalism and starting in 1955 registered a sharp increase while Egyptian nationalism became relatively insignificant.

This evolution of nationalist thought, which closely resembles the shift of Turkish nationalism (Ahmet Riza) into Pan-Turkism (Ziya Gökalp, Yusuf Akçura), should not be regarded solely as an artificial shift of policies by Abd al-Nasir but also as a normal evolution of political thought which preceded it. Indeed it would be a mistake to view serious ideological evolution purely as tactical change in Egyptian foreign policy. It is more correct to regard external events as crystallizers, accelerators, and developers of Pan-Arab thought and action. A reversion to Egyptian nationalism was not discernible until after the June War. Yet this trend has not been overly pronounced; certainly it was not of the same magnitude as the Kemalist reversion from Pan-Turkism to Turkish nationalism.

8

The Nasirite Theory and Practice of Arab-Unity Nationalism

THE ideology (*aqida*), propounded by Gamal Abd al-Nasir [1] and pro-Nasirite ideologues, has two interrelated aspects. The first, Arab-unity nationalism or Pan-Arabism, concerns those doctrines of the ideology that are related to the external world. The second main aspect, Arab socialism, involves those doctrines which are primarily related to the transformation of Egyptian-Arab society.

Nasir as Pragmatic Ideologist

The precise role of Nasir in Egyptian and Arab ideological development is not easy to assess empirically; still more difficult to uncover is his real motivational base, the internalized set of beliefs that determined his attitudes and behavior.

The nature and scope of Nasir's personal contribution to the development of Pan-Arabism and Arab socialism is discernible only to a degree. In the early period, beginning in 1955, his contribution was pragmatic; ideology flowed from his successful performance as leader. This particularly applied to Pan-Arabism and positive neutralism, both of which became official ideology after Nasir had demonstrated their utility as policies.

Similarly, the regime's drift toward socialism during the late 1950s had been pragmatically determined, but only to a point. Nasir's early experimentation with semi-etatist measures that stopped short of a full-scale socialist commitment had been generally without success. His attempt to create a partnership between the state and a reluctant Egyptian entrepreneurial class as a means of instituting accelerated economic development ended in failure; nor did this scheme receive the necessary economic-political support from the West. As is often the case, American concern primarily centered on Egypt's external orientation rather than on its internal evolution. Therefore, the growing unattractiveness of the Western model, coupled with the elite's propensity to extend the scope of its power, pushed the system toward a socialistic orientation. The final adoption of Arab socialism (1961), however, marked the end of the pragmatic phase; indeed, many of the new policies had not undergone a successful testing period, in contrast to Arabism and neutralism. The leadership had adopted an official ideology which was to be propagated, tested, and implemented at the same time. To the extent that Arab socialism was not derived from Egyptian national experience, Nasir's contribution to ideology-formation was less pragmatic and more theoretic. In other words, in promulgating Arab socialism, Nasir was operating as an ideologist with an untested methodology.[2]

While it is safe to assume that Nasir personally took a major role in the new ideological formulations, it is next to impossible to determine the extent of his own contributions as a man of ideas. It would seem that the development of various doctrinal intricacies and justifications were the work of intellectuals in and outside the government (see Chapter 9).

What were Nasir's personal values and attitudes that constituted his motivational base? In endeavoring to seek an answer by analyzing his ideological pronouncements, it should be remembered that one of the foremost functions of ideology is that of a tool to promote elite legitimation and control. However, a leader's espousal of a particular ideology does not automatically mean that he believes in all of its values. Nonetheless, for a person as intimately identified with ideology-building as Nasir, one may assume a relatively high correlation between personal beliefs and personal ideology.

One method of inferring a leader's beliefs is to contrast ideology with practice. Here, the pitfall is that political practice may be shaped by determinants other than formal ideology or the leader's own values. Nevertheless, one can tentatively identify several of the more basic beliefs Nasir internalized. These included: 1) belief in Egyptian nationalism and its concomitant values of national power, dignity, and prestige; 2) belief in social justice for his people, whom he regarded as the victims of centuries of political and economic exploitation; 3) commitment to rapid modernization; and 4) belief in a sense of personal mission to accomplish the above goals.

The beliefs, values, and attitudes that Nasir came to possess were the end products of the socializing influences that he experienced through life. The sum total of direct and indirect learning experiences within his family, school, occupation, no less than the influence of major political events helped shape Nasir's basic beliefs and view of the political world.[3]

Reliable and detailed information concerning Nasir's early years is unavailable, beyond the fact that his family life was generally unstable. This was characterized by the strained relations between young Nasir and his father especially after the death of his mother.[4] After his father's remarriage, it appears that Nasir's homelife became particularly unhappy as he was sent away to live with relatives.[5] Thus from the beginning one can discern the crisis conditions that fostered alienation in Nasir's person. As he stepped from his family crisis situation into the larger, Egyptian crisis milieu of the 1920s and 1930s his alienation deepened and intensified. Born to a father of Sa'idi peasant stock [6] from Upper Egypt, one might safely consider Nasir a marginal in terms of Egypt's urban, middle class—the status to which the family aspired.

The rejection of authority that had characterized Nasir's home life also manifested itself in school. His formal education was marked by numerous transfers and generally undistinguished performance. The country's political ferment had disrupted the educational process and Nasir soon found himself more preoccupied with student demonstrations than booklearning. In terms of political socialization, the beatings, injuries, and jailings that he experienced as a student demonstrator were more influential than his schooling. Clearly, the primary theme of this learning process was Egyptian nationalism directed against Britain. The examples set by the main personalities of the anti-British struggle—e.g., Mustafa Kamil, Sa'd Zaghlul—were instrumental in inspiring young nationalists like Nasir. More direct was the influence of the virulently nationalistic General Aziz al-Misri, one of Nasir's teachers at the military academy.

Major political events also left their mark on the political psyche of the budding revolutionary. Among these were the Anglo-Egyptian Treaty of 1936 and the denigration by Sir Miles Lampson (Lord Killearn) of Egyptian sovereignty in February 1942 by the use of tanks to force the dismissal of the pro-Axis prime minister. These events constituted direct affronts to Nasir's sense of national and personal dignity. The last of these socializing events—the Palestine War of 1948—set him on an irreversible course to overthrow the system.

The rootlessness and mobility that characterized Nasir's family and school life also appeared in his career as political agitator. At one time or another he joined most of Egypt's political movements—Misr al-Fatat, the Wafd, the Brethren—without being able to find a permanent political niche because of disagreement with their policies and leadership. The only organization that could possibly offer some satisfaction to his nationalistic aspirations was the army. After an initial rejection, Nasir was admitted to the Military Academy. His subsequent career as an officer only sharpened his revolutionary zeal.

With the passage of time and the acquisition of experience as ruler, Nasir developed a secondary category of more specific beliefs and values, all derived from his original belief system. The most important of these, Arab-unity nationalism, evolved out of Nasir's earlier ideal of Egyptian nationalism. Indeed, when he was fighting in the Arab-Israeli War of 1948, the colonel seems to have been primarily preoccupied with Egyptian nationalism. Nevertheless, the active Egyptian involvement on the Arab side could not help but crystallize in the mind of the "hero of Faluja" the general notion of Arab solidarity. In Part III of the *Philosophy of the Revolution,* the first traces of the evolution of Egyptian nationalism into Arab-unity nationalism begin to appear. This work of Abd al-Nasir, first published in pamphlet form in 1953, illustrates that the evolutionary process from Egyptian to Arab nationalism may have been taking form in Nasir's mind, before external events (e.g., Baghdad Pact) motivated him to espouse openly the cause of Arab nationalism. Though it is difficult to assess the depth to which Nasir internalized Arabism, the intensity of his identification with the doctrine, as well as the high priority he eventually gave to its achievement, even to the point of hurting his own Egypt, make it difficult to doubt his sincerity. Other derivative value systems that Nasir embraced included positive neutralism and Arab socialism. His neutralism flowed directly from his commitment to nationalism, the preservation of national dignity, and realization of national power. Similarly, one can suppose that Arab socialism was grounded in Nasir's sense of social justice; there is no evidence to indicate that he had strong socialist leanings, either before or after the revolution. After its adoption in 1961, Nasir increasingly used socialist terminology; however, it is not clear to what extent the new ideology shaped his world outlook and perception. Other ingrained values included both admiration for and deep resentment and suspicion of the West; admiration for the West's modern achievements in terms of power, technology, and a high standard of living; resentment, over Britain's imperial role in Egypt and the West's continuing support for Israel. Had it not been for Israel, one might have expected his attitude toward the West, especially the United States, to change over time. Nasir's deeply held anti-Israeli attitudes reflected the hurt personal dignity of a proud nationalist, as well as the wounded collective dignity of the Arabs he symbolized. This notion, coupled with Nasir's revolutionary personality and his ingrained view of Zionists as perpetrators of injustice in the Arab world, made him psychologically unable to reach a long-range settlement with an ascendant Israel, even if his people would have permitted him to do so. His attitude may have changed in the event of Arab gains in battle—a situation that would sufficiently restore national dignity to have allowed Nasir to conclude peace.

Pan-Arabism: Sources and Development

Chapters 6 and 7 dealt with the establishment of historical anchors for the Nasirite Pan-Arabist ideology. This section explicates the main ideological tenets of Arab-unity nationalism (Cairo-centered) as promulgated in the Charter and in the writings of some of its foremost proponents, both Egyptian and non-Egyptian.

Epistemologically speaking, Arab-unity nationalism is traceable to four interrelated sources—intuition, rationalism, experience, and tradition. Abd al-Nasir and other proponents of the ideology repeatedly stated that the tenets of Arab unity reside in Arab hearts.[7] In their efforts to ascertain the existence of the "feeling" of nationalism, most Arab theorists resort to the epistemological tool of intuition; [8] they would have to follow the dictates of the heart. While the process of discovering the fundamental truths of the ideology is a private endeavor for each Arab, the collective will of the Arab people was to be articulated by the leader of the nationalist movement, Gamal Abd al-Nasir, who himself relied on intuition (in addition to other means of gauging the popular will) as an epistemological tool to "read" the hearts of the people and interpret their aspirations. The heavy reliance of Nasir and Nasirite ideologues upon the intuitive approach should not be surprising considering that nationalism is the child of emotion and feeling. In pursuing the broad aims of the ideology, the Nasirites are, at times, less concerned with the practical and the rational and more with the desirable.

Despite the intensive use of the intuitive approach, there is also an attempt to base the ideology on reason. The major exponent of the rational approach is the ex-Ba'athist, Abdallah al-Rimawi, who attacks the Ba'athist ideologue, Michel Aflaq, as an unscientific romanticist.[9] Essentially, al-Rimawi agrees with Aflaq's thesis that Arab nationalism is "a matter of feeling," [10] yet he hastens to add that "Arab nationalism has passed the romantic stage and is now realistic." [11] Moreover, al-Rimawi regards contemporary Arab nationalism as a rational (*aqlaniyyah*) and pragmatic movement "which is derived from life." [12] However, this rationalism is not based on what the Nasirite ideologues call "conventional logic," but on "revolutionary logic" because only the latter is considered truly responsive to Arab needs. The "revolutionary will" of the people, as represented by the "revolutionary vanguard" (i.e., the Free Officers), defies the use of conventional logic since this "could have tempted it through bargaining, compromise and reform ideas inspired by charity and donation." [13] Instead, the people's revolutionary will choose total revolution.[14] What emerges is a rejection of moderation (which is prompted by conventional logic) and a firm commitment to radical change, which gives the ideology its revolutionary dynamic.

Although the term "revolutionary logic" is not clearly defined, it is believed to help the revolutionaries objectively assess the position of Arab nationalism at a given stage of development in relation to other forces at work in the world arena. The revolutionary logic seldom seems to rely on *a priori* reasoning. Instead, the rational determination of evolving policy—and therefore ideological development—is based on the lessons learned from the Arab revolutionary experience. This pragmatic approach of Abd al-Nasir and the Nasirite ideologues to the short-term development of Arab nationalist ideology should be considered a distinctive feature of Egyptian intellectual and social thought. All endeavor is described as being "experimental," including the Arab revolution itself.[15] This reliance on empiricism may be considered a natural development, considering the absence of a ready-made ideology. The alternative of borrowing non-Arab ideologies is vehemently opposed since these "have not arisen out of the nature of national experience." [16]

The fourth basic source from which ideology is derived is the history of the Arab people. Abd al-Nasir conceived of Egypt as circumscribed by three circles: Arab, African, and Muslim. Of the three, the Arab circle was unquestionably the most significant for him because "this circle is as much a part of us as we are a part of it, that our history has mixed with it and that its interests are linked with ours. . . . We have suffered the same hardships, lived the same crises. . . ." [17] The stress therefore is placed on the common historical experience of the Arabs. In view of these common traditions and present realities, Abd al-Nasir concluded that Arab unity could be achieved because ". . . the region is one, and its conditions, its problems, and its future and even the enemy are the same. . . ." [18] The UAR Charter reiterates the soundness of Arab unity in more explicit terms:

Unity . . . is identified with the Arab existence itself. Suffice it that the Arab Nation has a unity of language, forming the unity of mind and thought. Suffice it that the Arab

Nation is characterized by unity of history creating unity of conscience and sentiments. Suffice it that the Arab Nation enjoys unity of hope, the basis of the unity of future and fate.[19]

Other writers proceed a step further to maintain that Arab unity is a necessity in the present world environment. They point out that in this age of large power blocs, Arab unity is imperative because of economic, political, geographic, and especially military reasons.[20]

As Egyptians became increasingly committed to Arab-unity nationalism, the Nasirite ideologues introduced the element of inevitability.[21] They held that the historical process would inevitably culminate in a perfect final stage of Arab development (which is the final stage of the ideology)—the Arab nation.[22] Thus, in the tradition of Marx and Hegel, history is viewed as an inevitable process, in this case moving toward Arab unity.[23]

It is readily recognized that the path to ultimate union is long and is composed of several stages, which are not clearly defined. The lack of a preconceived timetable and precise definition of future stages can be traced to Nasirite unwillingness to be tied down by theoretical chains, but to create each phase of development pragmatically, in a gradual manner. So far as it can be ascertained from the UAR Charter, two successive stages of development must be concluded before the utopia phase of total Arab unity. The first step consists of the formation of nationalist governments "representing the will and struggle of the people within a framework of national independence." [24] It is assumed that an Arab government truly responsive to the popular will would be well disposed toward unity. The second phase is that of the unification of two or more Arab states.

In advocating the second stage, the drafters of the Charter advise extreme caution. Recalling the bitter experience of Syria's secession from the UAR, they warn against "speeding up the various stages of development towards unity" which would create "economic and social loopholes that could be exploited by elements opposed to unity. . . ." [25] Instead, they urge "practical efforts to fill the economic and social gaps stemming from the difference in the stages of development of the various peoples of the

Arab Nation." [26] The cautious attitude of the UAR in 1962 was a far cry from its pre-1961 policy of precipitous Arab unity. As such it represented a shift in tactics, based on an objective analysis of empirical data—the experience of the Syrian secession.

Of the two stages leading to ultimate union, the first is considered by far the more important at the present time. Indeed, UAR policy in the sixties actively encouraged the formation of revolutionary Arab governments "based on popular will." The type of regime proposed by Nasirite ideologues for other Arab countries as a first step toward Arab unity is outlined in the Charter:

". . . any nationalist government representing the will and struggle of the people within a framework of national independence . . . , in the sense that it eliminates every contradiction between that government and the ultimate goals of unity." [27]

In reality the Egyptian ideologues are proposing the establishment of Arab regimes closely resembling the Egyptian system which they regard as the only Arab state where the foregoing requirements are found.[28] This is nothing less than an invitation to imitate the Egyptian experience in social and political development. Once such regimes are firmly in power it is believed that they will strive to follow the dictates of their people, which, as in the UAR, invariably point in the direction of Arab unity.

The Nucleus State

While Arab unity is considered an "inevitable process of nature" [29] that will eventually end the present "artificial" separation of Arabs, it still needs leadership. In his *Philosophy of the Revolution,* Abd al-Nasir had both intuitively and rationally discovered a double role to be filled—that of an Arab hero-leader and that of an Arab country to take the lead in unifying the Arabs. His actions demonstrated that Nasir assigned this dual leadership role to himself and to Egypt.[30]

The Egyptian assumption of "the historic responsibility" [31] to achieve Arab unity is based on several factors. The Nasirites argue that a revolution needs a secure and strong base if it is to succeed. Because of "natural and historical factors" only Egypt can act as a base to effect Arab unity.[32] These factors include Egypt's possession of economic wealth, size, population, stability, experience, and religious-intellectual leadership in the Arab world. Hence, these writers see the Egyptian assumption of Arab leadership as a natural development. In this context, the policies of Egypt—"the nucleus state"—and the interests of the Arab nation are regarded as identical, and the UAR is declared capable of realizing the goals of Arab-unity nationalism.

Nasirite ideologues are extremely sensitive to charges of Egyptian imperialism and interpret these as attempts to discredit Nasir's Arab nationalist movement. The Charter solemnly declares that "unity can not . . . be imposed" and "that coercion of any kind is contrary to unity." [33] This, however, did not restrain Egypt from encouraging pro-Nasir unionist elements in various Arab countries. While the Charter declares that the UAR will not be drawn into local disputes and leaves it to local elements to prosecute the "actual struggle" in their respective countries, it also considers it a "duty to support every popular nationalist movement that tends to unity." [34]

During the years of the Syrian-Egyptian union, the nucleus or "vanguard" state came to include Syria—an inclusion which gave Nasir's mission as unifier of Arabs not only territorial reality but also historical legitimacy. On numerous occasions he paid tribute to Syria's traditional primacy in the Arab sphere: "Syria has always been the heart and center of Arabism from where the call for Arab Nationalism and Arab Unity began." [35] Nevertheless, in a real sense, the base remained where Nasir was—in Cairo.

It is important to note that the Nasirite call to Arab unity was not primarily directed at the respective Arab governments but to their citizens. The Charter reiterates this policy in most explicit terms:

> The UAR, firmly convinced that she is an integral part of the Arab Nation, must propagate her call for unity so that it would be at the disposal of every Arab citizen, without hesitating for one minute before the outworn argument that

this would be considered an interference in the affairs of others.[36]

Thus, while on the one hand the UAR calls for a policy of noninterference between Arab states, on the other it directly appeals to "every Arab citizen" to rally behind the so-called "popular, progressive elements" which are invited to dismantle the existing Arab governments. The UAR still intends to cooperate with other Arab regimes within the context of the Arab League. But since the league is an association of governments, it cannot serve the "noble and ultimate objective" of Arab unity and as such is considered an institution of limited utility.[37] Therefore, peaceful association with other Arab governments within the league is at best a short-range policy which is subordinate to the simultaneously pursued long-range policy of uniting "the nationalist popular progressive movements" of the various Arab countries.

This dual policy of ephemeral cooperation with Arab governments at one level, and the simultaneous advocacy of their popular overthrow at another,[38] would seem inconsistent in terms of what Nasirites call conventional logic. Yet to these followers of revolutionary logic, the dual policy seems totally consistent with the "real" aspirations of the Arab people, which is seen as seeking unity within the UAR fold.

Nevertheless, the Egyptian assumption of leadership in achieving Arab unity cannot be regarded simply as a manifestation of Nasirite imperialism. It should be remembered that even prior to Nasir's rise, there existed considerable Arab support for Egypt to take the leadership role. With the rise of Nasir, the former pro-Egyptian sentiments spread and intensified throughout the Arab world, in response to the appeal of the charismatic leader. Especially in Syria, Iraq, and Jordan, grassroots pro-Nasir sentiment pushed the local elites toward reaching accommodations with Egypt that ranged from outright union to alliances. The unionist elements in the various Arab countries viewed any hesitation by their rulers to join Arab unity schemes as covert identification with Western imperialism and Zionism. Clearly, the duty of the Arab nationalist was to overthrow these "reactionary" regimes —an effort for which he sought UAR support. Since such support was not always forthcoming, the UAR has often been criticized by non-Egyptian Arab revolutionaries.

The precise governmental system of the future united Arab state remains a debatable point. The Egyptian-Syrian union of 1958 indicated Nasir's preference for a unitary state. The ideological justification for such a system is based on Arab history. It is pointed out that a loose federal system is alien to Arab historical experience and that a unitary state with administrative decentralization is the only suitable form of government "because in the past the Arab State was one, governed by one universal government." [39]

The first experiment in constituting a unitary state failed when the Syrian Region seceded from the UAR. The abortive attempt of April 1963 to form a federal union between Egypt, Syria, and Iraq [40] illustrated Abd al-Nasir's willingness to experiment with a federal system. But the subsequent Syrian and Iraqi reluctance to implement the Union Accord of 17 April 1963 put an end to federation schemes until the late 1960s.

Positive Neutralism

The doctrine of positive neutralism [41] had become the foreign policy of the Egyptian state even before its adoption as part of Nasirite ideology. When the success of this policy was demonstrated after mid-1955, positive neutralism was automatically regarded as an integral part of the official guiding ideology of Abd al-Nasir's revolutionary movement.

Since the development of Egypt's positive neutralism coincided with Nasir's attempt to claim the leadership of Pan-Arabism, this doctrine of non-alignment in international politics was made a part of the ideology of Arab-unity nationalism. The extension of the foreign policy of the nucleus state to the whole Arab nationalist movement was no arbitrary superimposition by the Nasirites. Having experienced an imperial past similar to Egypt's and facing a common "western-sponsored" enemy, Israel, the sentiment for neutralism already existed in other Arab countries,[42] prior to the rise of Abd al-Nasir. Therefore, other Arab nationalists welcomed and applauded the Egyptian adoption of positive neutralism as a doctrine to define the external outlook of the Arab unity movement.

The emergence of positive neutralism as a basic tenet of Egyptian foreign policy was the result of a variety of factors, some of which predated the coup of July 1952. Indeed, if positive neutralism is viewed as a specifically anti-Western movement, its real roots are to be found in the historic Muslim resentment against the emerging power of Christian Europe. This resentment was most strongly manifested first, not by the Arabs, but by Turkish nationalist thinkers around the turn of the century.[43] However, in contrast to the Arab nationalists of mid-twentieth century, the Turkish nationalists' resentment of Christian Europe did not evolve into a deep feeling of anti-Westernism. Instead, under the decisive guidance of Mustafa Kemal, the Turks became avid Westernists. After World War II the American readiness to accord her protection against the Soviet Union made Turkey a somewhat grateful member of the Western alliance system until the early 1960s.

The Arab experience with the West was of a totally different nature. Most Arabs regarded the continued presence of Britain and France in the Middle East as the negation of the solemn promises of independence given to them during World War I. The accumulated anti-Western feeling manifested itself in Rashid Ali al-Kaylani's revolt in Iraq (1941), the Arab Revolt in Palestine (1936–39), and in secret Egyptian attempts to seek ties with the advancing German forces.[44] The British action forcing King Faruq to remove Ali Mahir from the premiership for his refusal to declare war on the Axis powers also increased anti-British feeling among Egyptians,[45] as Nasir himself testified. However, what contributed most to the Egyptian-Arab alienation from the West was the latter's role in helping establish the Israeli state; after the Arab defeat in the 1948 war, blaming the West became a psychological necessity. Egypt's reluctance to support the UN intervention in Korea and its opposition to Western-sponsored joint Middle Eastern defense organizations [46] were indicative of the developing anti-Western mood before the Revolution.

As the inheritors of such a legacy, the military rulers of Egypt did not have a free hand to make radical policy changes. Any attempt to introduce a pro-Western foreign policy would have seriously harmed the domestic position of the junta. In addition to the domestic risks involved, the deep-seated anti-British feeling of the Free Officers and their lack of loyalty to Western democratic traditions made closer association of Egypt with the West more difficult. It was naive for the West to expect these young revolutionaries to forget the imperial past and ally themselves with Britain, a bitter enemy, against the relatively distant Soviet Union. In the circumstances, therefore, the pursuance of neutralism was natural for Egypt. Yet in the first two years of their rule, the Free Officers refrained from following this seemingly natural course of development because of their preoccupation with domestic power preservation and Egypt's existing treaty relations with Britain. Several new factors were needed for the development of Egyptian neutralism. First, the domestic power struggle between the supporters of Muhammad Nagib and those of Gamal Abd al-Nasir had to be settled. Second, relations with the West had to deteriorate sufficiently to permit Egypt to turn to the USSR. Third, the evolving neutralism of Egypt had to find support and indeed respectability among certain newly emerging non-aligned nations. Fourth, the Soviet leadership had to show a readiness to assist neutralist countries [47] in general and Arabs in particular, in the context of their growing anti-Israeli orientation.

At the outset Egyptian neutralism was of a peaceful and moderate nature. Whatever foreign policy the junta generated in its first two years of existence was the work of Abd al-Nasir more than anyone else in the ruling elite. Because of his preoccupation with domestic contests of power, Nasir seems to have kept his foreign involvement to a minimum. The neutralism of this period was specifically directed at gaining concessions from the West and placating the anti-British sentiments of various Egyptian leftist groups and the Muslim Brethren. The concessions which Egypt wanted were arms and loans from the United States and a treaty with Britain effecting the quick withdrawal of her forces from the Suez Canal base.

Thus, despite the contention of contemporary Egyptian writers who insist that neutralism was the policy of the military revolutionaries from the very outset (July 1952),[48] it was not until later that the first signs of this policy emerged. This is clearly indicated in the content analysis of Radio Cairo broadcasts as presented in Figures 7 and 8. Not until December 1952 did neutralist themes appear. They continued intermittently at a low frequency until February 1954. The cumulative count of neutralist themes was still lower during 1954 reflecting the preoccupation with the Nasir-Nagib power struggle, the Brotherhood's purge, and Egyptian expectations of economic and military aid from the West. Nevertheless, during this period, Nasir repeatedly stressed "that today's Egypt is not the Egypt of yesterday" and that "Egypt . . . refuses to give its friendship except to those who realize that it is a nation of freemen, who prefer to perish than have their sovereignty and freedom infringed upon." [49]

The year 1955 constituted a main turning point in the evolution of Nasirite neutralism, from a quiescent to a positive or active phase. Significantly, it coincided with Nasir's rise as charismatic leader (see Figure 6, p. 112) and the decisive ideological shift from Egyptian nationalism to Arabism (see, Figure 4 p. 94). The shift to a more dynamic neutralism seems to have grown out of the Egyptian frustration at the West's reluctance to grant it sufficient importance. In short, Egypt wanted to receive all the economic and military aid given to the West's allies (e.g., Turkey) without undertaking the responsibilities of the Western alliance system. The conclusion of the Baghdad Pact in February 1955, between Iraq and Turkey, further accelerated Egypt's march toward neutralism. Indeed, more than any other factor, the Western efforts to lure the Arab states into the new security system contributed to the development of a more aggressive neutralism. Viewing the Baghdad Pact as a Western attempt to destroy the Egyptian-led security system of the Arab League,[50] Abd al-Nasir was provoked into a more aggressive policy than he had chosen to follow previously. This new phase of neutralism displayed two additional characteristics of the doctrine. The first was the final and explicit rejection of involvement in foreign military pacts. The second and less apparent characteristic was the Egyptian attempt to claim the Arab world as its own sphere of influence to the exclusion of both the West and the East.

Another factor that contributed to the development of the ac-

Figure 6. *Centrality of Nasir as Reflected in the Media*

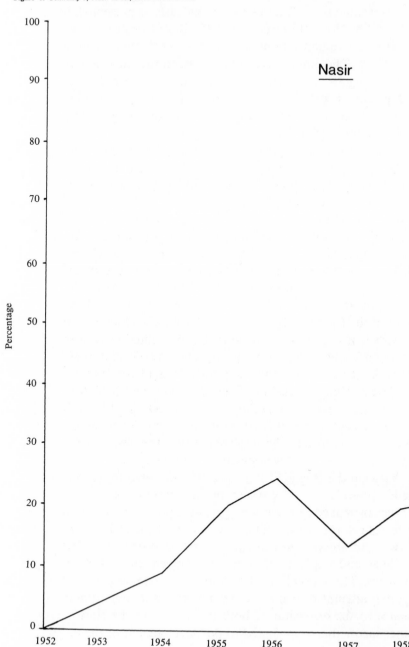

tive phase of Egyptian neutralism was the encouragement and inspiration derived from the emerging Afro-Asian bloc. After progressively alienating itself from the Western camp, Egypt was anxious to augment its international standing by associating itself with the neutralist states which met at Bandung, Indonesia, in April 1955.

It appears that the importance of the Bandung Conference was underestimated by the West. This meeting which brought together the representatives of ex-colonial countries had the effect of strengthening their self-confidence. The impact of Bandung on Arabs generally and on Abd al-Nasir particularly was of still greater proportions. The Egyptian leader was accorded great honors as the head of the Arab delegations and the conference accepted the Arab point of view on the Palestine question.

In the developing Nasirite policy of neutralism, Bandung is regarded as an all-important cornerstone. Its great impact on Egyptians is revealed in the writings of historians and ideologues alike who claim that the "positive" element of the country's neutralist policy stemmed from Bandung,[51] and revealed itself in "the nationalization of the Suez Canal, reemphasizing the real meaning of the Conference." [52] Although in October 1960 Nasir credited the Syrians as the initiators of the doctrine,[53] the Egyptians have since come to regard themselves as the pioneers of positive neutralism and nonalignment; [54] as such they find it natural to claim for Egypt a leading role in the neutralist bloc.

After mid-1955, Nasir's neutralist policy acquired a more pro-Soviet (anti-Western) orientation as the USSR began to extend generous amounts of military (September 1955), diplomatic (1956 Suez War), and economic (Aswan) assistance. In terms of frequency, neutralist radio pronouncements further increased during 1956 (Figures 7 and 8), especially just before (May–August) the Suez crisis.

The success of Nasir's policy of active neutralism had two direct effects on subsequent ideological development. First, in view of the repeated victories that neutralism had brought Egypt, this policy was made an integral part of Nasirite ideology: a successful policy was transformed into a doctrine. Second, as Egypt's neutralism began to gain wide support among other Arabs, Abd al-Nasir proceeded to link his policy in early 1957 with the ideol-

Figure 7. *Positive Neutralism (Yearly Index)*

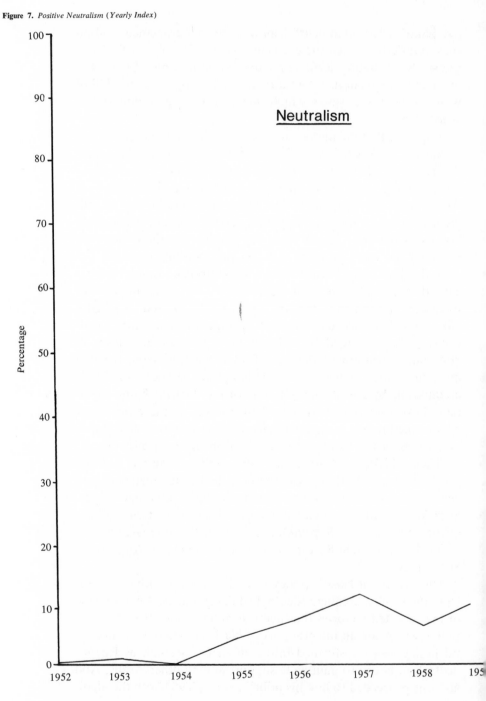

114

Figure 8. *Positive Neutralism* (*Monthly Index*)

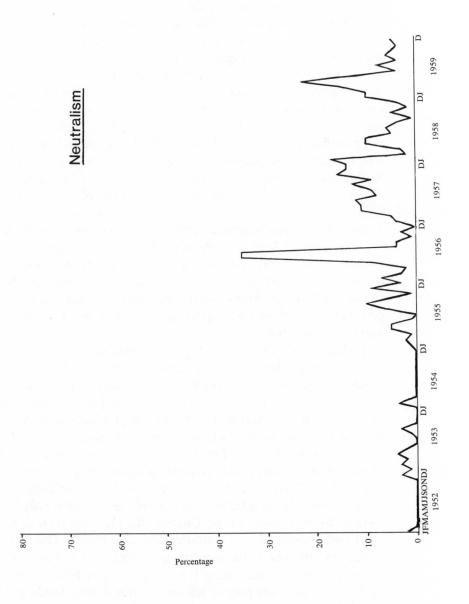

115

ogy of Arab-unity nationalism,[55] which he had gradually adopted. In this manner, the Egyptian policy of positive neutralism was extended to the Nasir-led Arab unity movement and made into a doctrine defining the future relationship of Arabs toward the non-Arab world. The simultaneous growth of neutralism and Arab nationalism can be shown by comparing the graphs represented in Figures 4 and 7.

The Egyptian and indeed the Arab conception of positive neutralism primarily involves the free pursuance of self-determination and the maximization of political independence. Despite solemn pronouncements that positive neutralism contributes to safeguarding peace,[56] this doctrine should be viewed as an attempt to thwart the extension of non-Arab influences in the Arab world, until such time when a strengthened Egypt can unite the Arabs on its own terms and assume a leading role in world affairs.

Both the Charter and most Arab writers proclaim peace as the supreme goal of Arab positive neutralism. Yet it is naive to assume that the moral goal of peace transcends Arab considerations of self-interest. Clearly, peace at any price is unacceptable to the UAR and to Arabs in general. Therefore, one might suggest that the Arab desire for peace is applicable only to a limited number of situations.

To begin with, the desire for peace is obviously motivated by the fear that the Arab countries, along with the rest of the world, would be destroyed in a thermonuclear exchange.[57] They also desire peace to avoid big-power intervention in the Arab world. If future foreign intervention is to be countered effectively, peace is necessary to give the Arabs time to develop military strength. Finally, peace is necessary for Arab economic development and prosperity. However, world economic progress and prosperity are regarded as "indivisible" since peace cannot "be stabilized in a world, where the standards of the people vary enormously." [58] Indeed, to the authors of the Charter, the clash between developed and underdeveloped countries seems inevitable. Therefore, to preserve the peace, the developed countries have to assist the underdeveloped in narrowing the prosperity gap between them by breaking the monopoly of science, by transferring funds spent on nuclear weapons to peaceful development, and by refraining from forming economic blocs.[59] Clearly, what the UAR ideologues advocate is nothing but "inter-national" socialism in which developed nations would transfer large portions of their wealth to underdeveloped lands. It is believed that the levelling of national wealths in the world would guarantee peace.

The UAR Charter advances two reasons why the advanced nations should aid the underdeveloped nations. First, the Charter regards such assistance as a moral duty of the wealthier countries. However, this moral obligation is not based on considerations of charity but on the "historical" fact that "underdevelopment was imposed" on the poorer countries by the imperialists. Therefore, the extension of economic aid by the advanced imperialist countries "constitutes the human atonement for the age of imperialism." [60] Without giving any reason, the Charter further states that the "non-imperialist" countries also should share in the process of atonement.[61]

The second reason explicit in the Charter for assisting the poorer countries is preservation of peace, which is another moral argument. However, this argument carries an implied threat that peace is untenable without economic aid. The failure of the advanced countries to share their wealth and knowledge with the developing states may polarize the world community into antagonistic blocs of haves and have-nots. A second possible interpretation involves the widely held Western assumption that lack of foreign aid brings domestic instability in developing countries, making them vulnerable to great-power manipulation. In other words, the Egyptians seem to be telling each .of the superpowers that their reluctance to extend aid will lead to domestic instability, making Egypt susceptible to Soviet or American domination, depending on the identity of the power that happens to be engaged in that particular situation. Finally, the Arab advocacy of peace stops at the door of Israel which is regarded as "an imperialist cancer." The struggle against this state is considered the logical continuation of the general war against imperialism,[62] and therefore is viewed as a just war *par excellence.*

In the final analysis the doctrine of positive neutralism emerges as a shield in the hands of the revolutionary leadership of Egypt to exclude great power intrusion from what it considers to be its own special sphere of influence. The deterioration of Soviet-

Egyptian relations in 1959 indicated Abd al-Nasir's determination to oppose the increase of communist influence in Syria and Iraq. What had started as a policy of positive neutralism directed primarily against the West, assumed, during 1958, an anti-Soviet orientation as well, thereby justifying to a certain degree its appellation of neutralism.

As a shield to fend off non-Egyptian intrusions into Arab affairs, the role of positive neutralism has been essentially defensive. While it has shown great aggressiveness in reaction to external provocation, in the absence of the latter, positive neutralism has manifested itself in such projects as sponsoring neutralist bloc conferences and conducting a UAR policy on the international scene designed to guarantee the continued flow of economic assistance from the West, and military and economic assistance from the East. At any given time, the relative position of Nasir's neutralism depended on his perceptions of the attitudes of the big powers. Thus, during the years of the Syrian-Egyptian union (especially in 1959) the UAR displayed a higher order of neutralism as Nasir and Khrushchev traded charges concerning the imprisonment of Egyptian and Syrian communists. In contrast, ever since the June '67 War, the neutralist component of Egyptian foreign policy has declined as the UAR has come to rely upon the Soviets for military survival.[63]

9

The Nasirite Theory and Practice of Arab Socialism

HISTORICALLY, the relationship between political power on the one hand and economics and geography on the other has been extremely close in the Nile Valley. Indeed, a study of Egyptian history substantiates, to a large extent, the theories of geographic and economic determinists, who attempt to explain the accumulation of political power in terms of geographic and economic factors.

The outstanding geographic factor in Egypt is the Nile, flowing through its narrow valley situated at the eastern extension of the Sahara Desert. The historic dependence of the population on the flooding of the river for its livelihood constitutes the single most important economic factor. The economic need to control this process of natural irrigation necessitated the development of centralized political authority at a very early date.[1] From antiquity, Egypt had a deeply entrenched tradition of centralized state control over factors affecting its economy.

With the advent of the Muhammad Ali dynasty, the historic trend toward large-scale state control accelerated. The extensive irrigation projects constructed by the Egyptian government and the British further intensified state control. However, the government's role in industrial development was reduced to a minimum after the collapse of Muhammad Ali's large-scale schemes, chiefly because of British opposition to Egyptian industrialization. In addition to irrigation, it was only in the field of transportation and communication that the state was able to achieve a controlling position from the very outset. This included the building and operation of ports, telegraphs, and an excellent system of railways. On the whole the government's large-scale involvement in irrigation, transportation, and communication was successful; and as such it set a precedent for the mass nationalization drive of the 1960s when state control became universally regarded as a magic solution for all economic problems.

Government's Role in the Economy (1920–1952)

In the post-World War I period state involvement in the economy remained at a minimum. Preoccupied with securing political independence and burdened by the capitulations, the government's role was limited to encouraging the development of private enterprise.

It was not until the 1930s that the government became more active in the economic field. Independence was already achieved, and the depression had concretely demonstrated the need for state regulation of the *laissez-faire* system. Egypt's ever-growing population and the need to protect its infant industries constituted additional factors that necessitated government involvement in the economy. The road to a greater economic role was opened in 1930 when Egypt regained its fiscal autonomy. The tariff reform of that year gave the country's industry much needed protection from competing European manufactures. After 1930, duties on foreign imports (textiles, shoes, glass, sugar) were repeatedly raised, insuring the survival of Egypt's industries.[2]

Other fields of limited state involvement in the industrial sector included research, prospecting, and the extension of subsidies, loans, and credit to various firms through the Misr Bank and later through the Industrial Bank. While the government sponsored the reorganization of certain enterprises and the formation of some cartels, it usually stopped short of interfering in the production policies of the various firms.

An important area of involvement was agriculture where the government attempted to increase production and diversify crops. After 1931 agricultural credit was extended through the

Banque du Crédit Agricole and the Crédit Hypothecaire Agricole.

Another area of limited state control was insurance. In 1939, the predominantly foreign insurance firms were compelled to keep in Egypt at least 60 percent of their reserves; this percentage was substantially raised in 1950.[3] The tendency toward Egyptianization was further manifested in 1951 when a new law completely Egyptianized the National Bank's board of directors and extended partial government control over policymaking.

With the advent of World War II, government activity in the economic field began to increase. In 1939 exchange control was imposed on foreign transactions and imports were subjected to licensing, except those from the sterling area. Growing shortages and inflationary pressures prompted the government to resort to a variety of deflationary devices including floatation of loans, budget surpluses, an increased tax rate, sales of gold, and price controls. After the war the government retained the exchange control system. Also, import licensing was made more flexible, to be utilized by the state as a means of regulating its foreign-exchange reserves. This was followed by the promulgation of Law No. 119 in 1948 which replaced the sterling-exchange standard with a managed currency.[4] Indeed, many of the measures enacted during the war years were retained and even intensified. Government action was directed toward more progressive taxation, social legislation, and Egyptianization. The government repeatedly intervened in the futures market to buy cotton at fixed minimum prices and found itself burdened with large quantities of cotton after the Korean War boom in 1951.

In summary, the prerevolutionary period was marked by increasing government involvement in the economy which took four different forms:

1. Complete state ownership and control:
   Transport
   Communications
   Irrigation
   Suez Oil Refinery

2. Partial state control or ownership:
   Bank du Crédit Agricole
   Crédit Hypothecaire Agricole
   National Bank
   Egyptianization of various firms
3. Regulatory state activity:
   Progressive taxes
   Price controls
   Acreage restrictions
   Buying cotton
   Exchange control
   Import licensing
   Loan floatation
   Budget surpluses
   Rationing
   Requisitioning
   Sales of gold
4. General state assistance:
   Tariffs
   Research
   Pilot projects
   Prospecting
   Subsidies
   Credit
   Cartels
   Banking

The Revolutionary Period: The Capitalist Phase (1952–1956)

The evolution of Egyptian socialism before 1961 was a slow process marked by groping, indecisiveness, and experimentation. The UAR Charter readily admits that "the revolutionary march" started without a complete theory, leaving the elite to depend solely on the famous "six principles." [5] It would have been more correct to state that the revolution had no theory at all, since even the much-venerated six principles did not go beyond general statements opposing feudalism, monopoly capitalism, and recognizing the need for social justice.

In the absence of a theory of internal change, the economic and social policies developed by the leadership reflected the regime's need to preserve its dominant power position. At least in the first years of their rule the Free Officers seemed primarily interested in the political results of their economic and social policies. Increasing production, humanitarian considerations, and the need to divert investments from agriculture to industry were, at best, secondary factors. These priorities were illustrated in the Agrarian Reform Act of 9 September 1952.

The main features of the act consisted of limiting individual land holdings to a maximum of 200 *faddans* (slightly more than 200 acres) and expropriating the rest for redistribution among the fallahin. The government was to pay for the expropriated land in bonds bearing three percent interest, redeemable within thirty years, and the fallahin were to repay the state in annual installments during the same period. The law further provided for the formation of agricultural cooperatives, workers' unions, and regulated tenant-landowner relations.[6]

When the reform decree was implemented, the government acquired 500,000 *faddans* of excess land holdings, of which 430,000 *faddans* were distributed to 120,000 landless farmers.[7] In political terms, the junta had delivered a formidable blow to the large landowners whose economic power made them potentially dangerous to the ruling group. Conceivably these landowners could have financed anti-Nasirite factions within the army.

The second political effect of the agrarian decree involved the peasantry. In attempting to raise the social and economic status of the fallahin through land distribution, the junta initiated a long-term campaign to bring this class into the body politic as a source of potential support.

Ideologically, the agrarian reform of 1952 represented a concrete step against "feudalism" and toward the redistribution of wealth. But in other fields of national life, radical reform remained at a minimum. Aside from such modestly welfare-statist measures as rent control, progressive taxation, and anti-corruption laws, no basic reshaping of the domestic economic order was attempted in the early years of military rule.

In addition to promulgating the Agrarian Law, the immediate concern of the government after July 1952 was to achieve economic stability. The problems inherited from the chaotic pre-revolutionary period included such important items as the budget, cotton, and the balance of payments.[8] In order to deal with the huge budget deficit of 1951–1952, the regime reduced expenditures and raised income taxes and certain duties. Also, the large deficit in the 1952 balance of payments was reduced by raising customs duties and clamping on stricter import controls.

However, the most surprising change was the government's policy of encouraging foreign investments. Under various laws passed in 1953 and 1954, the 1947 provisions covering the transfer of profits and capital were relaxed, new concessions were granted, and foreign interests were permitted to gain majority control of companies.[9] In effect these laws constituted nothing less than a reversal of the government's former policy of Egyptianization and indeed a relaxation of state controls over certain foreign companies.

The regime also moved to encourage capitalist development by facilitating domestic capital investment, especially in industry. Duties were raised on competing manufactured goods and reduced on machinery and raw materials. Companies which showed promise of growth were exempted from taxes on profits. Simultaneously the government began to participate more directly in certain sectors of economic life by providing some capital for the establishment of various enterprises which included an iron and steel company and a commercial bank.

The Revolutionary Period: The Socialist Phase (1956–1967)

A variety of external and internal factors contributed to the transformation of the Egyptian economy from a mixed-capitalist to a socialist system. Politically and economically, Egypt was increasingly alienated from the West in a series of diplomatic encounters during 1955 and 1956; i.e., the Baghdad Pact, the tripartite arms embargo, the High Dam controversy, the nationalization of the Suez Canal, and the Anglo-French-Israeli attack. The internal factors contributing to the transformation consisted of the elites' disappointment with the existing capitalistic system, their subjection to external left wing ideological influences, their need to gain popular acceptance, and the compulsion to destroy the remaining islands of independent economic power.

While in his early speeches Nasir advanced various utopian and welfare-statist ideas bordering on socialism, he stopped short of advocating a purely socialist formula for internal change. These included the desire to close the gap separating the classes by making the rich help the poor and instituting a government composed of all classes to rule over one big, happy family—Egypt.[10]

By 1955 the internal power struggle had been resolved in favor of Nasir without any reference to leftist doctrines of internal change. According to Professor Binder, it was only after his visit to Bandung that the colonel began to use the term socialism as a means of achieving social justice.[11] It is possible that the socialism practiced by some of the nations present at Bandung had favorably influenced Abd al-Nasir. After Bandung, capitalism came under increasing attack and the new anti-capitalist orientation of the government was made an integral part of the six principles of the revolution.[12]

Decrees issued during 1955 and 1956 did not reflect the government's emerging socialist ideology to any great extent. However, the granting of social security to workers, the extension of state control over the fertilizer trade, and the export of certain agricultural products were indicative of the future direction of change. In the same period the government participated in the mining and petroleum industries and nationalized the Suez Canal Company.

The Constitution of 1956 reiterated the regime's determination to achieve social justice by raising the standard of living, providing old-age benefits, public health, and social insurance. However, it contained no provision indicative of comprehensive socialist development. Under Articles 8 and 11, the rights to private economic activity and private property were declared inviolate. But it was also made clear that these rights would be strictly limited by considerations of the general good.[13] Overall, the 1956 Constitution institutionalized moderate etatism in a mixed socialist-capitalist economy.

The year 1957 marked the beginning of a government drive to increase its control over the country's finances. Law No. 153 prohibited the founding of any insurance company without government authorization. In line with the regime's announced intention of eliminating foreign influences, two Egyptianization laws were issued, providing for the reorganization of the largely foreign-owned commercial banks and insurance companies into Egyptian joint-stock companies. Moreover, the ownership of capital shares and the direction and management of these organizations were to be transferred to Egyptian subjects.[14]

In the same year a number of organizational laws were issued, manifesting the regime's desire to introduce comprehensive economic planning, a prerequisite for socialist development. The agencies created under these laws included the Economic Development Organization, the Supreme Council for National Planning, and the General Organization for Execution of the Five-Year Plan. The most important of these state agencies, the Economic Development Oganization, was charged with the distribution of public funds in various fields of economic activity to insure uniformity of purpose. Also, this organization was given wide authority to set up new companies and supervise other public organizations put under its control.[15]

Finally, under Law No. 152/1957, 74,000 *faddans of waqf* (religious endowments) lands were requisitioned for distribution to peasants.[16] In 1958, by Law No. 168, the Agrarian Reform Law of 1952 was amended, reducing interest on both the landowner compensation bonds and the price of distributed lands, from 3 percent to 1½ percent. At the same time, the period for redeeming state bonds and paying for distributed lands was extended from twenty to forty years.[17] This action lightened the burden of payments both on the state and the fallahin, at the expense of the former landowning class.

In industry, additional laws promulgated in 1958 extended and intensified the state's control. Law No. 28/1958 gave the Ministry of Industry increased authority over new industrial establishments by subjecting them to license. The ministry was charged with issuing obligatory specifications for production and permits for industrial expansion.[18] Clearly, this law contained sufficient authorization to serve as the legal framework for effecting total state control of industry at a future date. Moreover, under Law No. 114/1958, restrictions were clamped on the boards of directors of commercial companies, whereby no one person could hold more than one directorship and no director could receive more than £E 2,500 per annum.[19]

However, despite increasing state controls in the private sector, in 1958, Abd al-Nasir still spoke of a partnership between capital and government.[20] It is obvious from the president's speeches that even as late as November 1958, he had not committed himself to a clear ideological position on domestic change. The Egyptian leadership still seemed to be examining the various alternatives of development and eclectically and empirically adopting only such policies considered suitable for the Egyptian milieu. While the broad guidelines of the new society were announced to be "socialism, cooperation, and democracy," [21] the precise meaning attached to these terms remained undefined.

The years 1959 and 1960 were marked by increasing etatism. By Presidential Decree No. 258/1959, thirteen public utility companies were put under the control of the State Audit Department. Under Law No. 232/1960, the national economy was to be regulated and coordinated by a comprehensive plan of development for the declared purpose of raising the standard of living.[22] The most significant development of 1960 was the nationalization of three leading banking institutions—the National Bank of Egypt, the Bank Misr, and the Banque Belge.[23] Once this step was taken, the eventual nationalization of the remaining financial institutions became a certainty.

Another sector that became subject to nationalization during 1960 was the publishing industry. Under the authority of Law No. 156/1960, the state took over the four leading publishing houses of Cairo—Al-Ahram, Al-Akhbar, Ruz al-Yusif, Al-Hilal.[24] The regime justified its action by contending that "the people's ownership of the political and social guidance media is inevitable in . . . a socialist, cooperative, democratic society" because "capital should have no domination over these important media, since such domination may result in deviations contrary to the aims of society. . . ." [25] Therefore, the government was basing its takeover on the fear that the privately owned publishing media could be utilized to undermine the revolution and indeed the regime itself. However, an examination of major Egyptian newspapers would indicate that, since the entrenchment of the new regime in 1954–55, the press generally had become an obedient instrument of the government. There was no political need, despite Nasir's assertion to the contrary, for resorting to state ownership, when the regime already effectively controlled the publishing field. Clearly, the reason lay in the growing etatist attitude of the governing elite, which had moved away from advocating a mixed socialist-capitalist system and was increasingly adopting socialist etatism. In the absence of an easy method for accelerated development, it seems that the Egyptian leadership viewed increased state ownership of the means of production as a necessary precondition for economic success.

The most revolutionary period of internal social change in Egypt was the year 1961. After years of indecision, Nasir was now ready to implement the long-promised social revolution. The swiftness and decisiveness with which the social revolution of 1961 was launched clearly indicated that the leadership's ideological development had reached a relatively stable and solid stage, whereby a precise formulation of immediate and future goals would be possible. Yet the new ideological goals of the elite were not divulged to the public until actually enacted in the form of laws. A brief analysis of these laws is therefore necessary for ascertaining the new content of the ideology and the extent of state control of the economy.[26]

In March and April of 1961, the regime set up four organizations which were to serve as the foundations for the subsequent nationalization of the economy. The most important of these was the Misr Organization, established to pursue economic development through investments in commerce, finance, agriculture, and industry. It acted as a holding company for virtually all nationalized or partially nationalized organizations, except those established by the General Organization for the Execution of the Five-Year Industrial Plan. The others were brought under the Nasr Organization, which functioned as a separate industrial holding company. The field of finance was placed under a supreme council. The task of general policy-making for all state economic enterprises was given to the Supreme Council for Public Economic Organizations. Subsequent developments showed that these intricate organizational structures were intended to extend state control as well as state management and ownership over a large sector of Egypt's economy. Indeed, they were designed to make the state the supreme capitalist in the land.

The revolutionary laws and decrees issued in 1961 are too numerous to discuss in full in the present context; therefore, only the more important ones are presented. The first group consisted of general regulatory laws.

Controls placed (June–July 1961) on cotton sales, exports, and imports,[27] were followed by closure of the two stock exchanges and the futures market, whereby no shares could be sold. Another regulatory law (No. 114) limited the boards of directors of various firms to a maximum of seven members, two of which were to represent the employees.[28] Law No. 134 authorized the minister of industry to assign production quotas to industrial firms. In December, the whole public business sector was grouped into thirty-eight public organizations and brought under a Supreme Council for Public Organizations headed by President Abd al-Nasir. The council was empowered to define production targets, insure coordination, approve budgets, and supervise general progress.[29]

A second group of laws concerned state ownership of business. One of the most sweeping measures was Law No. 117 of 20 July, which nationalized the remaining banks and insurance companies, as well as forty-two industrial, commercial, and other firms.[30] On the same date, Law No. 118 provided for the partial (50 percent) nationalization of eighty-three establishments. Another sweeping measure was Law No. 119 which limited individual ownership to a maximum of £E 10,000 in 145 listed companies. All excess holdings were to be transferred to the state in return for fifteen-year, 4 percent government bonds. The businesses affected were very diverse—textiles, cigarettes, soap, paper, plastics, minerals, glass, pharmaceuticals, and real estate. Additional laws issued in July nationalized the Khedivial Mail Line, the Cairo Trainway Company, the Lebon Company, and four cotton-pressing firms.[31] Under Republican Decree No. 1203, firms with 25 percent or more of state ownership were forbidden to assign contracts exceeding £E 30,000 to companies which did not have at least 50 percent state ownership. Also, private contractors were forced to apply for a minimum of 50 percent ownership, since they were not permitted to be given contracts by companies which were 25 percent or more state-owned. Finally, between October 1961 and January 1962, the property of 850 "reactionaries" was sequestered.

Another group of laws involved the redistribution of personal income. Law No. 111 of July decreed the distribution of net profits of commercial organizations and Law No. 113 limited salaries to £E 5,000 per year. Law No. 115 placed a tax rate of 90 percent on incomes above £E 10,000.[32] Additional laws were passed placing a graduated tax on residential rent income and limiting each worker to one job of forty-two hours per week.

The fourth cluster of socialist laws centered on agriculture and land ownership. Under Law No. 127 of July 1961, individual land ownership was reduced from 200 to 100 *faddans* and the excess distributed among landless peasants. Law No. 128 provided a 50 percent reduction of price and interest on land distributed under the old agrarian reform laws. Law No. 1250 stipulated that future loans to farmers would be free of interest charges.

Briefly, the extent of state ownership and control of economic life was as follows as a result of the laws and decrees of 1961. There was preponderant state ownership and control of manufacturing and mining, except petroleum, and some small industries. Moreover, government ownership of public transport and control of financial activity and foreign trade was almost complete. Irrigation, communications, and most educational institutions had been in government hands from the outset. To be sure, the means of production were nationalized to the extent that the public sector of the economy became preponderant. Nevertheless, certain large islands of privately owned enterprise were permitted to remain. While large department stores were nationalized, a significant portion of the internal retail trade was left in private hands. Indeed, this is one area where government control has been difficult to achieve.

A more important sector of private ownership is agriculture. While the bulk of the land belongs to individual owners, large areas are supervised by the government and other lands are farmed by producer's cooperatives. The government, nevertheless, exercises a considerable amount of indirect control over agriculture through its monopoly of credit, fertilizers, irrigation, machines, and cotton purchases.

Small hotels, cafes, and places of entertainment remain in private hands, as are most residential buildings, the rents of which are strictly controlled. Finally, the professions have not been nationalized, although many of their members work for the state.

During 1963 the trend toward increasing government ownership and control over the economy continued without let up. In July 1963, four hundred apartment buildings, eight contracting, transport and navigational companies, and fourteen pharmaceutical firms were nationalized. On 12 August 1963, the Minister of Industry, Dr. Aziz Sidqi, listed 240 firms to be taken over. These included tanneries, flour mills, transport, food processing industries, dairies, and manufacturers of rubber, textiles, candy, and soft drinks.[33] On 17 November 1963 six landholding companies that had been partly nationalized in 1961 were completely taken over. Simultaneously, the Ministry of Supply attempted to crack down on the middlemen.[34] The regime's nationalization policy was pursued through 1964 and 1965. During March 1964, eleven trading companies (Law No. 51) were taken over and 155 other establishments (Laws No. 52, 120, 123) were nationalized.[35] As to agrarian reform, by the fall of 1965, a total of 647,000 *faddans* had been distributed to 273,000 families, although a large number of landless peasants remained.[36] Between 1965 and the June War the main thrust of governmental decrees was toward amalgamation and consolidation of insurance companies, banks, steel works, and other firms in an attempt to establish greater control.[37] The emergencies imposed by war and defeat further contributed to the enlargement of the state's authority in economic matters. These included austerity measures which led, beginning in 1969, to a general improvement in the economy.

In a general sense the laws of 1961–67 crippled the economic power of the industrial, financial, and commercial classes—the bourgeoisie of Egypt—and completely destroyed the remaining power of the once powerful landowner. The beneficiaries of the revolution have been some of the peasants and, to a certain extent, the workers. The other main beneficiary has been the regime, which now possesses overwhelming economic control in addition to military and political dominance. Although economic control has maximized the regime's power, it has also bestowed upon it the sole responsibility for future economic breakdowns.

Sources of Arab Socialism: Islamic Tradition

Having traced the implementation of the economic aspects of Arab socialism in Egypt, the analysis will now focus on its ideological bases and the type of society it strives to create.

In terms of epistemology, one primary source of ideology is tradition. In their attempts to create the historical bases for Nasirite socialism, Egyptian ideologues repeatedly invoke the theory of the Islamic state as outlined in the Qur'an and the *hadith* and the social practices that flowed from these. It is held that the divine injunction calling on "Muslims to help each other wherever possible" had been widely practiced under Muhammad and the "rightly guided" caliphs. Indeed, the regime's present position on monopoly, social justice, property, and taxes is justified on the basis of Islam. Thus, socialism is said to have existed in the Islamic state from the very beginning.[38]

The inherently socialistic nature of early Islam is found in the primitive communism that existed in the *ummah* (community). The concepts and practices that Egyptian ideologues refer to include the following: 1) equality—Islam dictates equality among believers; 2) social justice—this is based on the religious duty to help the poor by paying the alms tax (*zakat*); the Prophet's and Umar's practice of sharing bounties equally and taxing the rich to help the poor are cited; 3) prevention of monopoly—this is based on the unlawful status of usury in Islam and the opinions given by jurists (*fuqaha'*), who condemn the concentration of money and food in the hands of the few. Thus, all the vital necessities of life, the existing "public utilities" and "means of production" are to be publicly owned; 4) the limited right to property—the right to property is limited by the interests of the *ummah* as outlined in the Qur'an. Particular reference is made to instances of public ownership of land in early Islam.[39]

The Synthesis of Nationalism and Socialism

The difficulties implicit in mating a nationalist ideology with socialism may have been one major reason for the Egyptian hesitation in embracing the latter as a creed of internal transformation. Indeed, this task required the relating of a purely nationalist and therefore exclusive ideology—Arab nationalism—with one possessing a worldwide appeal—socialism.[40]

While not denying the ideological tie existing among various socialist movements, because of their prior commitment to Arab nationalism, the Egyptian ideologues were faced with creating "organic" bonds between the two ideologies they adopted. Beyond labelling the socialism of Egypt as "Arab," they needed to demonstrate that Arab socialism flowed naturally from the general tenets of Arab nationalism.

In order to accomplish this fusion, Egyptian ideologues searched history for what they considered to be the seeds of socialism in the Islamic-Arab context. Thus, Nasirite identification with the "socialism" of early Islam grants Egyptian socialism historical legitimacy and religious sanction. Moreover, such an identification neutralizes criticism arising from the popular notion equating socialism with atheism and communism. Criticism from traditional Arab sources [41] is likewise rendered ineffective. Finally, the conscious relating of Egyptian socialism to early Islam has an Arabizing effect on the whole eclectic structure of the ideology; its Arabness and its "spiritual bases" in Islam combine to reinforce its distinctiveness from and superiority over various forms of European socialism.[42] It follows that the common historical roots of Arab nationalism and Arab socialism unite them in the modern context as a distinctly Arab ideology.

It is maintained that the historical roots of Arab socialist ideology accord it a moral and humanistic character. The constant stress of Nasirite ideologues on "spiritual values" indicates the seriousness and pride with which they regard these maxims. It is held that the diffusion of "values derived from the religions of the Arab Homeland" into Arab nationalist-socialist ideology has given these creeds an inner strength that will guarantee eventual victory.[43]

The Attack on Communism and Capitalism

In the social and economic fields, the foregoing spiritual values are thought to promote cohesion in Arab society and achieve co-operation among classes in order to realize the common good. More significantly, it is believed that the moral-spiritual substructure immunizes Arab nationalist-socialist ideology from the "malignancies" of "irreligious Communism and revisionist Western nationalisms." [44]

One should hasten to point out that the Egyptian attack on communism and Western capitalist-liberalism does not connote a rejection of the materialism found in these doctrines. It merely states that the theory and practice of these ideologies are based on a materialism devoid of spiritual content—and as such their maxims are not acceptable in their entirety to the Arabs. Instead the ideology of Arab nationalism-socialism concerns itself both with material prosperity and spiritual values and creates harmony between these seemingly antithetical forces.[45]

The crucial harmonization between materialism and spiritualism that Egyptian ideologues claim to have effected is made possible by the heritage of Islam—one that capitalism and Marxism do not possess.[46] Indeed, Marxism is seen as lacking a spiritual content; and in contrast to the Christian background of capitalism, the theory and practice of Islam constantly stresses the desirability of both material things *and* spiritual values. With the help of this dual legacy, it is held that the reconciliation of materialism and spiritualism can be easily accomplished in the context of modern Arab society.

Experience and Rationalism

As in the formulation of Arab nationalist ideology,[47] a major epistemological source of socialist doctrine is empiricism. While the initial reason for relying on experience was the military elite's lack of ideology, its subsequent importance came to lie in the distinctiveness that it gave Egyptian socialism. The starting point is again the peculiar historical-religious experience of the Arabs. Therefore, any ideology unrelated to the Arab-Egyptian past is vehemently rejected, since "the . . . solutions to the problems of one people cannot be imported from the experiences of another." [48] In the modern context, Arab "national experience" will reveal the needs of Arab society; in the process of pragmatically meeting these national needs ideology will develop. Apparently, the implication is that the task of rationally determining these needs ultimately will devolve on the leadership which is bound to take national experience into consideration. The epistemological sources of Arab socialism seem to fall into the following historical sequence: 1) revelation—the divine promulgation of Islam through the Prophet, as the primary source of knowledge; 2) tradition—the body of early Arab-Muslim thought and experience; 3) empiricism—the pragmatically derived knowledge of leaders, concerning the actual needs of Arab society; 4) rationalism—the rational assessment of these needs and the rationally determined doctrines and methods to fulfill them. It should be pointed out that in the epistemological derivation of Arab nationalism, the same categories are utilized with one major addition—intuition.[49]

While the Egyptian rejection of wholesale importation of foreign doctrines is specifically directed against communism and capitalism, the Charter explicitly states that an *a priori* assumption that all "previous theories . . . and . . . solutions" are false "would be fanaticism." [50] Thus, to the extent that various non-Arab theories and methods can be made to suit the Egyptian context, Arab socialism is eclectic. It will borrow individual theories and methods, but not a whole ideology. Yet anything that is borrowed automatically receives an experimental status, and not that of "rigid theories," [51] which impose a predetermined path.[52] Two explicit rejections of communism arise. First, a ready-made ideology prescribes a predetermined path, one that does not take into account differing national experiences. Second, Marxist ideology is seen as one forcefully "imposed" from above and not one "accepted" by the masses. While both arguments constitute a reaffirmation of nationalism versus Marxist internationalism, they may also reflect the Egyptian attachment to empiricism in contrast to communist "blind determinism." [53] In view of the trial and error road followed by Egypt since 1955, especially with respect to socialist development, the constant stress on empiricism as a guide to action seems fairly consistent. Nevertheless, when Nasirite ideology is considered in its entirety, its elements of empiricism and inevitability seem irreconcilable. Egyptian ideologues begin by rejecting predetermined ideologies in favor of building Arab socialism empirically and then proceed to proclaim "the inevitability of a socialist solution" [54] without any explicit awareness of logical inconsistency. A similar inconsistency becomes apparent in relation to the inevitability of Arab unity.

Nature of Arab Socialist Society

In order to determine the nature of man and society in Egyptian socialist ideology, it is necessary to discover how Nasirite ideologues view other political systems. Modern capitalist society is seen as one that organizes itself on private ownership and the preponderance of individual interest. The "superficial" reforms introduced from above are regarded as attempts "to alleviate the class struggle," and the retention of religion is viewed as "consolatory promise of eternal life." Moreover, all political organizations are said to "exploit the people." [55] On the other hand, Marxist society is regarded as the radical antithesis of capitalist society; its reforms are seen as being too drastic—religion is suppressed, classes are decimated, property is made public. Moreover, it is felt that all political power belongs to the vanguard of one class and the individual's relationship to the system is that of a nonentity.[56]

In contrast to these two extremes, Arab socialism is seen as striking "a virtuous balance," thereby creating a "third type of society." [57] The religious legacy of Islam is said to give Arab socialist society an inherent goodness and tolerance which assures the individual's "high place" in the system. What secured the "true" political and social freedom of the Egyptian man was the "revolutionary act" of July 1952. Both in the Charter and in other ideological treatises, it is repeatedly stated that the quest for political freedom without economic freedom—the opportunity to earn a living—is misleading and false.

The heaviest intellectual debt of Nasirite ideologues to orthodox Marxist theory can be detected in the unity with which they view the realms of politics and economics. What makes them thoroughgoing economic determinists is their "indisputable" belief that "the political system in any state is . . . a direct reflection of the prevailing economic state of affairs." [58] As such the interests that control the economic substructure will ultimately decide the nature of the political superstructure.

In order to substantiate this theory of economic determinism, the pre-1952 Egyptian social-political experience is subjected to intense analysis. Pre-revolutionary Egypt is pictured as a time when economic power was centralized "in the hands of an alliance between feudalism and exploiting capital." [59] Thus, the political system founded on a feudalist-capitalist substructure was nothing but a dictatorship of these exploiting classes over the Egyptian people. To these "enemies of the people" there has been added, since October 1961, the new category of "the exploiting bourgeosie" with "imperialist inspiration" remaining a pervasive theme. The new formulation which emerged is best expressed in the equation:

National Reactionism (al-Raj'iyyah al-Wataniyyah) =
Capitalists + Feudalists + Exploiting Bourgeosie +
Imperialist Inspiration.[60]

Therefore to change the political structure of the Egyptian state, the mere overthrow of the monarchy was not sufficient; the economic foundation had to be transformed by crushing the Dicta-

torship of Reactionism. Thus, the Nasirites agree with the communists on the necessity of transforming the economic
substructure. However, they diverge from the communists in
their view of the nature of the economic-social transformation.
The Nasirites begin by rejecting the Marxist concept of a classless society dominated by the proletariat [61] and instead promulgate a theory of "limited" class struggle. They mention that
"within a framework of national unity" [62] Arab socialist society
will include previously exploited and therefore "legitimate"
classes of people—farmers, workers, small businessmen, intellectuals, professionals, non-exploiting proprietors, and soldiers.[63]
Any notion of a class struggle among these "productive" classes
is vehemently attacked; it is emphasized that these are to cooperate fully within the national framework. The only struggle that
will develop inevitably and naturally is the one between these exploited classes and their former exploiters—National Reactionism (capitalists, feudalists, exploiting bourgeosie, imperialists).

What distinguishes the Nasirite concept of class struggle and
society from the Leninist-Maoist version of Marxist society [64] is
the inclusion of small businessmen, "non-exploiting" proprietors
and landowning peasants. Still another distinguishing factor is
the peaceful nature of the class struggle. To understand the
meaning of class struggle in Nasirite socialist ideology, one
should trace the evolution of this concept. Clearly, the term
"class struggle" gained increasing usage in Egyptian terminology
only after the Syrian secession and the implementation of the socialist laws of 1961. Indeed, as late as July 1961 when the socialist laws were promulgated, the UAR president was still talk-
ing in the name of fraternity, love, and national unity.[65] The
Syrian secession, that came in part as a reaction to socialization,
led to "an objective analysis" of class relationships in which the
inevitability of the class struggle became explicit.[66] As a result, it
was concluded that to prevent civil strife, "National Reactionism" had to be crushed; that is, it had to be "deprived of all its
weapons," by force, if necessary. In turn this accomplishment is
expected to pave the way to the peaceful solution of the class
struggle.[67] Despite the necessity of force at the initial stage to
"disarm" the reactionaries, the Egyptian emphasis on the peace-

ful nature of subsequent class struggles permeates most of the literature on the subject.

The Nasirite concept of class struggle does not imply a condition of "permanent purge" in the Stalinist sense.[68] The Charter states that the regime has no intention "of sacrificing whole living generations." [69]

Revolutionary Consciousness and the Individual

In a society where the class struggle is limited in scope (only to reactionaries) and method (peaceful, if possible), the permanency of the revolutionary dynamic can be maintained only by the elite's stress on revolutionary consciousness.[70] The main vehicles engendering such consciousness are the mass media and the educational institutions. The media constantly attacks "deviators from the Charter" and foreign and domestic "enemies of the people" [71] and attempts to make the individual aware of his duties and responsibilities to Arab socialist society.

The responsibilities of society, i.e., the state, are rather clearly formulated in the Charter. Thus, in a context of "social justice and equality of opportunity," society grants the individual freedom of speech and thought, freedom of religious belief, freedom from class exploitation, right to a job according to his abilities and interests, medical care and old-age insurance, and the right to free education which suits his abilities.[72]

In return for these rights, the Egyptian has certain obligations and duties toward the state and society. He is urged by the media to display an attitude of "cooperation"—a word repeated with great frequency in Egyptian literature. He is expected to pursue actively the ideological goals of the political system by acting as a "son of one national front." [73] Indeed, the heavy stress on "social solidarity and a single value system" demonstrates the regime's distrust of pluralistic tendencies.[74]

Egyptian socialist literature—from the Charter to textbooks for thirteen-year olds—is permeated with the Kantian concept of the "categorical imperative" or the Hegelian "man's station and duties," expressed in the terminology of modern authoritarian systems. The Charter states that "every citizen should be aware of his defined responsibility in the whole plan, and should be fully conscious of the definite rights he will enjoy in the event of success. . . ." [75] The suggestion that the "rights" to be enjoyed depend on the fulfillment of responsibilities is quite explicit. If a citizen chooses to alienate himself from "the whole movement of society," he forfeits his right to direct "the great historical task of building . . . a cooperative, socialist, democratic society." [76]

Needless to say, in a system that requires "each individual to be a servant of society" the concept of Lockean individualism is severely attacked. Thus, "people who are indifferent and think negatively" should be reeducated until their "habits, customs and thinking" are transformed.[77]

Productive Knowledge and the Sanctity of Labor

An individual's native intelligence and acquired knowledge are looked upon as social commodities. The acquisition of "knowledge for its own sake" is rejected; it must serve a social-economic function. The intellectual should not indulge "exclusively in contemplation" and theorizing but should transform his knowledge into productive work.[78] The parallel notion of art for art's sake, especially in the realm of literature, is vehemently rejected.[79] This constitutes a reiteration of the doctrine of socialist realism in which the artist expresses the sentiments of his people, especially those of laborers and peasants.[80]

The preoccupation of Nasirite socialist ideology and the educational system with production makes it imperative to stress the primary role of human labor in society. Creative work is seen as the only means to achieve the material-moral utopia projected by the ideology. The Charter points out that "labor is an honor. It is also a right, a duty and a sign of life." [81] However, it also emphasizes that for labor to be socially productive, it must be channeled into the context of organized and planned national action. As in other aspects of life, the responsibilities and duties of each producer "must be clear to him so that he may . . . know his exact position" in the machinery of production.[82] Therefore, a primary task of socialist education should be to destroy the prejudice against working with hands and replace it with the "sanctity of productive work." [83]

Yet the ideal socialist laborer is required to do more than perceive his precise station in society and fulfill his productive functions. Indeed, he must develop "mental clarity" to be able to relate "thought and experience." In other words the worker's relationship to his job must not be passive; he should constantly reassess his position vis a vis the national action by exercising "constructive criticism and brave self-criticism." [84] The similarities to Soviet terminology hardly need stressing.

Limited Right of Property

After 1961 a new system identifying three types of property ownership emerged. These included: 1) public property—outright government ownership which makes the state the supreme capitalist of the land; a common term describing this is *al-Ra'smaliyyah al-Wataniyyah*—national capitalism; 2) cooperative property —including lands and property held jointly by members of cooperatives; 3) individual or private property—which is protected from expropriation if "non-exploiting." Ownership of land is limited to 100 *faddans* per family. Ownership of buildings is subjected to progressive taxation and rent controls which place it beyond exploitation. However, private property can be nationalized if the public interest requires it. At all levels, "the people"—that is the state—will exercise general supervision and control over all types of property.[85]

A major area within the private sector is agriculture. Egyptian socialism vehemently rejects the communist theory and practice of full-scale collectivization. The "revolutionary solution" advanced is that of "increasing the number of land owners." [86] Particular reference is made to the agrarian reform laws of 1952 and 1961 under which nationalized lands were distributed to farmers. This application of socialism is said to be based on a study of the "real" circumstances of the agricultural problem in Egypt.

Though the farmer is liberated from landowners, usurers, and middlemen, he is not the absolute master of his new domain. The farmer is expected to function within the system's control, since "this revolutionary attempt at solving the agricultural problem . . . cannot be consolidated except by agricultural coopera- tion." [87]

Revolution, Science, and Free Will

The literature of Nasirite socialism since 1961 is replete with ref- erences to "science." One may safely state that Egyptian social- ism now possesses a scientific syndrome, whereby "scientificness" is regarded as the main tool to solve all problems. At one level science is considered an imperative prerequisite to progress and material well-being; the ideological promises of the coming uto- pia of plenty are to be realized through the application of science to all fields of production.[88] Moreover, science is regarded as a weapon against imperialism though it is admitted that "our oppo- nents still possess more scientific knowledge than we do." [89] It is emphasized that socialism is not based on charity and feelings of pity, but on a scientific attitude. In view of other attempts to base socialism on Islamic charity, this is an obvious contradic- tion.

At another level Arab socialism is called "scientific," since "it is the suitable style for finding the right method leading to progress." [90] Here "science" is used in a methodological sense, whereby it permits one "to analyze the relation between eco- nomic and social forces. . . ," [91] and "to understand the objec- tive conditions in Arab countries." [92] However, when the "sci- entific view" is applied to Arab history and is said to yield the modern need for unity,[93] the whole scientific approach may be regarded as bordering on scientism.

What particularly complicates the meaning of "science" is Abd al-Nasir's use of it to denote general knowledge: "Religions have all been the science of divinity, delivered to the Prophets through sacred inspiration." [94] The peculiar nature of this usage would have been insignificant if the president had not included "religious science by inspiration" in a speech dealing with "scientific socialism." While it is clear that the scientific nature of socialist thought and action does not exclude the possibility of gaining knowledge through divine inspiration, the problem points to the need to reconcile scientific methodology with traditional Islam. In this respect, however, one major historical conflict in Islam seems to have been resolved at least at the ideological level. The constant assertion of the primacy of human will over the environment is indicative of the modernized attitude of the elite. An ideology that recognizes the Arab man's right to determine the destiny of his nation and the Arab peoples' ability "to impose their will on life" [95] cannot tolerate the traditional belief in fatalism and predestination. Obviously, an age-old conflict has been settled within the context of Arab socialism in favor of free will.

10

Routinization of Charisma: The First Phase

The Arab Socialist Union (1962–1968)

IN MANY ways Egypt's third attempt at party organization, the Arab Socialist Union, was a more serious and concentrated undertaking than the National Union or the Liberation Rally. From the outset, the regime seemed to proceed with considerable efficiency under constant prompting from Nasir himself, who more than once spoke of a desire to transfer his office to the ASU headquarters or to resign the presidency to devote his energies to full-time party work. This was an auspicious beginning since it appeared that the president clearly perceived the need for a political organization and genuinely wished to see it instituted; however, this was not the case with many of his subordinates.

Aside from presidential support, the new political organism was aided by the final emergence of a comprehensive ideology. Thus the ASU could become a more ideologically oriented movement than its predecessors, possessing greater cohesion and a more focussed action program. However, these two advantages were counterbalanced by two interrelated obstacles which had had an abortive influence on the previous party structures. The first was the continuing lack of competent cadre sufficiently dedicated to the cause and possessing the necessary organizational skills to build the ASU. The second obstacle was the military's pervasive presence in the system which had stifled the effective development of the National Union.

In terms of administrative expertise, the available sources of recruitment for ASU cadres in 1962 consisted of the military, leftist intellectuals, and bureaucrats. Of these only the leftists had the necessary ideological preparation but the regime did not favorably regard their presence in large number in the ASU.

As plans for the new organization unfolded, certain structural similarities to single-party totalitarian models became at once apparent, despite the leadership's vehement denials.[1] Structurally, it was pyramidal, composed of four levels. At the very bottom were the basic units (7,000 in number) in each village, factory, school, and city quarter. The second level—the *markaz*—constituted a grouping of several basic units. All the *markaz* units within each governorate were brought under the Governorate ASU Congresses and its committees. At the highest level of authority was the General National Congress (1,500 members). Since this congress was to meet only once every two years, it elected a General Central Committee [2] of the ASU (250–300 members) that would convene at least twice a year. As this body was also unwieldy it would elect a twenty-five member Supreme Executive Committee —the real center of power at the top of the pyramid.[3] Beyond its select composition, which included some of the regime's leading personalities, the power of the Supreme Executive Committee derived from its formal functions. These included the day-to-day implementation of decisions, the exercise of overall political guidance in the ASU, and responsibility for dealing with matters pertaining to rank-and-file members.[4] Although never explicitly stated, the organization was designed to function according to the Leninist principle of democratic centralism, whereby the system would ensure the downward channeling of orders from the top and the upward flow of information from lower levels. Thus, it would perform the functions of aggregation, adjudication, integration, and communication.

However, the fundamental question confronting the regime was not structure but leadership. For a number of important reasons the leadership vacillated between creating an elitist or a popular organization and finally attempted to accomplish both with limited success.[5]

In the beginning all citizens except feudalist and capitalist elements were considered eligible for ASU membership. This resulted in a massive onrush of applicants causing the regime to terminate all recruitment in February 1963.[6] The organization that emerged after the screening process had six million members, 50 percent of whom were said to be workers and peasants; of the total, 250,000 were women.[7] However, sources published during 1968 indicated that the six million figure was either a gross overestimation or that about a million members had been purged during 1964 through stricter screening processes. These figures place the total ASU membership, in 1964,[8] at about 4,800,000 which had risen to over five million by June 1968.[9] In view of the fact that Egypt's total voting population is slightly over seven million, of whom five million are ASU members, the non-elitist character of the party becomes explicit. This conclusion is further reinforced when one compares the proportion of party members in the total population of Egypt to that of the Soviet Union which possesses an elitist party. While one out of six Egyptians is an ASU member, only one out of eighteen Soviet citizens is in the CPSU. The regime's unwillingness to build a purely elitist party was frankly attributed to the danger that those unable to gain entrance would turn to communist or neo-Islamic organizations.[10] What had emerged was a huge organization, designed to pre-empt potential centers of opposition by rechanneling and containing conflict while at the same time giving its members a sense of belonging and a semblance of participation. Yet despite all official pronouncements against elitism, the ASU was said to have "a qualitative and not a quantitative character." [11] In fact two "vanguards" existed within the larger organization. The first was a category of "active" members numbering one-half million that was to represent "the most dynamic and unselfish elements" of society and the "catalyst" of the ASU.[12] The rest were labeled "adherent" or "inactive" members, who had the right to elect but could not be elected. To gain "active status," these "active aspirants" would have to give "proof of their lack of self interest," manifest dynamism, and a willingness to cooperate for the general good.[13]

Beyond the active militants of one-half million, about 20,000 "socialistically cultured individuals" were to be carefully chosen and trained to become what the president called "a self-reliant inter-communicating cadre." These were to constitute the ASU's "political vanguard" or "vanguard organization" (Al-Tanzim Al-Tali'i), the full-time party professionals (apparatchiki), whose identity would be secret. To provide intensive political training, in May 1965, the ASU Supreme Executive Committee opened the Institute of Socialist Studies headed by Dr. Ibrahim Sa'd al-Din.[14] Among the aims of the institute were the teaching of social and political theory and the application of Arab socialism to concrete problems in factories and villages.[15] Several thousand vanguard members have been trained at the institute, but it is doubtful whether the total number of graduates has reached the officially projected goal of 20,000 individuals.[16]

At all levels of the party structure the principles of collective leadership, majority rule, criticism, and self-criticism were to operate. Overbearance and individualistic or dictatorial tendencies were to be avoided. Within the general framework of building a socialist society, the objectives of the ASU would be to maintain the revolutionary drive by educating and organizing the masses. The educational and problem-solving functions of ASU cadres were seen as necessary to gain the people's confidence, thereby substituting obedience (and therefore control) based on fear with one grounded on conviction.[17] ASU members were instructed to set an example for the people through personal sacrifice and upright behavior.

The ASU was also to fight passivity and deviation and prevent the "infiltration" of capitalist, feudalist, reactionary, opportunistic, and foreign elements.[18] Abd al-Nasir used the term "deviationist" in reference to Egyptian communists.[19] Asserting that their activity was a subject of his personal interest, the president declared the ASU an instrument "to foil communist activity" in Egypt.[20] His expressed desire was to see communists "grow into good citizens" and become believers in the National Charter. During 1965 a novel official policy emerged regarding the relationship of communists to the ASU and the political system as a whole. Two types of communists were identified: those who could be absolved and those who were beyond salvation. Abd al-Nasir stressed the importance of differentiating between Egyptians "who were once communists" and those who refused to change. Apparently, the former had expressed a willingness to join the ASU and would be permitted to do so. During his 1965 visit to the Soviet Union, Abd al-Nasir was reportedly successful in persuading the Soviet leadership to order the dissolution of the Communist Party in Egypt and the incorporation of its membership into the ASU. Some pro-Maoist party members who disobeyed the Soviet order reportedly were rearrested during August 1965.[21]

The Party Leadership

Since its inception in 1962, the top organs of the ASU have been the focus of almost constant change. At the highest level was the Supreme Executive Committee of the ASU, the membership of which until March 1964, is indicated in Table 1.

Table 1
ASU Supreme Executive (1962–1964)

BACKGROUND	MEMBERS
Officer	Gamal Abd al-Nasir, Chairman
Officer	Abd al-Latif al-Baghdadi
Officer	Abd al-Hakim Amir (Mushir)
Officer	Zakariyya Muhyi al-Din
Officer	Anwar al-Sadat
Officer	Husayn al-Shafi'i
Officer	Kamal al-Din Husayn
Officer	Ali Sabri
Officer	Hasan Ibrahim
Civilian	Nur al-Din Tarraf (Dr.)
Civilian	Ahmad Abduh al-Sharabasi
Officer	Kamal al-Din Rif'at
Civilian	Mahmud Fawzi (Dr.)
Civilian	Abd al-Mun'im al-Qaysuni (Dr.)
Civilian	Aziz Sidqi (Dr.)
Civilian	Mustafa Khalil (Dr.)
Officer	Abbas Rudwan
Officer	Abd al-Qadir Hatim (Dr.)

The composition of this committee reveals a number of important clues to the nature of the evolving political system in general and the relationship of the nascent party structure to the government in particular. Most obvious is the fact that this group (twelve ex-officers and six civilians) included many of the old core Free Officers and the half-dozen civilians who became associated with them soon after the coup. A related factor of major significance was the simultaneous presence of these individuals in the governmental structure; the twelve members of the former Presidential Council and six of the former Executive Council constituted the total membership of the ASU Supreme Executive. An interlocking relationship thus existed at the top between the governmental and party structures, which is quite similar to the Soviet and other left-totalitarian systems. In other words, the governmental and party hierarchies converged at the very top.

This interlocking relationship continued after the governmental reorganization of March 1964 and the formation of the ASU Provisional Secretariat in December 1964. The latter body of twenty-two members consisted of the following:

Table 2
ASU Provisional Secretariat (December 1964)

BACKGROUND	NAME	GOVERNMENT POST	ASU POST
Officer	Zakariyya Muhyi al-Din	Vice President	Member
Officer	Husayn al-Shafi'i	Vice President	ASU Secretary General in Cairo Governorate
Officer	Hasan Ibrahim	Vice President	ASU Secretary General in Alexandria Governorate
Officer	Anwar al-Sadat	Speaker of the National Assembly	Member
Officer	Kamal al-Din Rif'at	Deputy Prime Minister for Scientific Affairs	ASU Secretary General in Giza Governorate and for Propagation of Socialist Ideology
Civilian	Ahmad Abduh al-Sharabasi	Deputy Prime Minister for Waqfs and Al-Azhar Affairs	Secretary of the Subsecretariat for Farmers Sector

Table 2 (Continued)

BACKGROUND	NAME	GOVERNMENT POST	ASU POST
Civilian	Nur al-Din Tarraf (Dr.)	Deputy Prime Minister for the Sector of Labor, Justice, and Youth	Secretary of the Subsecretariat for Trade Union Affairs
Officer	Abbas Rudwan	Deputy Prime Minister for Local Government and Services	Secretary of the Subsecretariat for Upper Egypt
Civilian	Anwar Salamah	Minister of Labor	Secretary of the Subsecretariat for Labor Affairs
Officer	Khalid Muhyi al-Din	—	Secretary of the Subsecretariat for Press Affairs
Civilian	Sayyid Mar'i	Vice President of National Assembly and Chairman of Misr Bank	Secretary of the Subsecretariat for National Capitalism
Officer	Sha'rawi Guma'a	—	Secretary of the Subsecretariat for Organization
Officer	Fathi al-Dib	—	Secretary of the Subsecretariat for Arab Affairs
Officer	Tal'at Khayri	Minister of Youth and Sports	Secretary of the Subsecretariat for Youth Affairs
Officer	Husayn Zu al-Fiqar Sabri	Counsellor at the Presidency	Secretary of the Subsecretariat for Foreign Relations

Table 2 (Continued)

BACKGROUND	NAME	GOVERNMENT POST	ASU POST
Civilian	Ali Sayyid Ali	—	Secretary of the Subsecretariat for Labor Affairs
Civilian	Husayn Khallaf (Dr.)	Minister of Foreign Cultural Relations	Secretary of the Subsecretariat for Socialist Propaganda and Culture
Officer	Abd al-Salam Badawi (Dr.)	Secretary General for Administration at the Presidency	Secretary of the Subsecretariat for Research
Officer	Abd al-Majid Shadid	—	Secretary of the Subsecretariat for Financial and Administrative Affairs
Civilian	Ibrahim Sa'd al-Din (Dr.)	—	Secretary of the Subsecretariat for Supervision of Higher Socialist Institute
Officer	Abd al-Fattah Abu al-Fadl	—	Secretary of the Subsecretariat for Publications and Membership Affairs
Officer	Ahmad Abdallah Tu'aymah	—	Secretary of the Subsecretariat for Bureaucracy
Officer	Kamal al-Hinnawi	—	Secretary of the Subsecretariat for Lower Egypt

Table 2 (Continued)

BACKGROUND	NAME	GOVERNMENT POST	ASU POST
Civilian	Ahmad Khalifah (Dr.)	—	Secretary of the Subsecretariat for Professional Affairs
Civilian	Abd al-Hamid Ghazi	—	Secretary of the Subsecretariat for Farmers Affairs

The officer-civilian breakdown—sixteen officers against nine civilians—indicated the regime's intention to retain a firm organizational hold on the developing party structure. However, it seems that in contrast to the leadership of the National Union there was greater reliance on civilian help. More significantly, Table 2 shows the full extent of the interlocking relationship and hierarchical convergence between government and party at the top. With the exception of the armed forces, almost every governmental organization and endeavor from the presidency to ideological propagation was represented in the ASU Secretariat. Those functionaries holding positions in the government were considered "part-time" members who nonetheless were expected to pursue their tasks within the secretariat as "complementary" to their basic work.[22] It was admitted that certain ministries were more closely involved with ASU organizational matters than others. In such cases (e.g., local administration, labor, youth), party and government work became exceedingly intimate.

A second category of members that can be identified from the listing consisted of those who did not hold governmental posts. These eleven individuals may be regarded as top party professionals who have devoted themselves to full-time ASU work.

During the fall of 1966 there were purges in the ASU's rank and file, and on 28 November the Supreme Executive was reduced from fourteen to seven. The remaining members were Nasir, Amir, Muhyi al-Din, Shafi'i, Sadat, Sabri, and Sulayman. As the new prime minister, Sulayman was the only new member of the party's top command. All seven members were ex-officers.

How successful was the ASU in the first five years of its existence? A fully satisfactory judgment cannot be made because of the difficulty of acquiring hard evidence through field research. On the other hand it is possible to reach some tentative conclusions based on the searching criticism made since June 1967 by Egyptian writers of differing ideological persuasions.

To begin with, the formal construction of the ASU was never completed; the crucial Central Committee never came into being.[23] This, coupled with the Supreme Executive Committee's inability to prepare the required number of competent cadres,[24] prevented the organization from sufficiently penetrating the major sectors and levels of Egyptian society. The result was the emergence of what the prominent Egyptian journalists, Ahmad Baha' al-Din and Muhammad Hasanayn Haykal, have called "centers of power," [25] large pockets of illegitimate authority in the political system.

Two other interrelated weaknesses of the ASU that drew press criticism after June 1967 were the leadership's practice of appointing ASU officials and the prevalence of "political careerism" in the organization.[26] According to Haykal, the lack of elected leaders opened a gap between the ASU and the masses, thereby harming its legitimacy.

During the first five years of its existence it became increasingly evident that the ASU was vigorously moving into an area of activity well beyond its formal responsibilities. Instead of fulfilling its political functions of policymaking and supervision, the organization was rapidly encroaching upon the government's administrative functions.[27] Also, there was overemphasis on making detailed reports to the higher levels in keeping with Egyptian bureaucratic tradition; and due to serious distortion these reports did not reflect an objective picture of public opinion.[28] Finally, the lack of interest and commitment among large portions of the membership constituted perhaps the ASU's single greatest problem. A convenient index is membership dues. In May 1968, only 40 percent of ASU members had paid their dues; significantly, most of these were workers and peasants, whose dues were fully paid only because of automatic payroll deductions.[29] Among agricultural workers and employees of small stores, only 2 to 3 percent had contributed, since they were not under a system of payroll deductions; yet delinquents were not expelled from the organization, and reportedly some even voted in the 1968 party elections.[30]

In the final analysis, any appraisal of the ASU's first phase of activity would depend on one's criteria and expectations. If extent of legitimacy is taken as a criterion, the answer is that due to the negative factors discussed above, the new organization had not been sufficiently legitimized to be a reliable vehicle of revolutionary continuity. Clearly, its mere sponsorship by the leader was not enough to fully legitimize it in the absence of effective organizational performance. On the other hand, if one uses a more modest criterion—its utility to the leader—then one may point to at least two instances of ASU effectiveness. The first was the role of the "political vanguard" in uncovering the Ikhwan conspiracy of mid-1965, as revealed by Nasir himself.[31] The second instance of effective performance came on the night of 9 June 1967, and during the subsequent months when the ASU helped rally the pro-Nasir masses [32] against various conspiracies emanating from the military and to a lesser extent from the secret police. Indeed, these were precisely the "centers of power" from which the ASU had been consistently barred—an action that was to have far-reaching consequences for the political system, as will be seen in Chapter 13.

The National Assembly (1964–1968)

One of the most significant developments in the political system since the mid-fifties occurred in the less visible area of legislative life.[33] The National Assembly's record since March 1964 is worthy of close scrutiny if one is to determine the nature and direction of political change in the UAR.

The National Assembly elected on 12 March 1964 was the third legislative body since 1957. Of its 360 members, ten were appointed by the president and the rest elected from an officially approved list of 1,648 candidates.[34] Thus, each of the 175 electoral districts was represented by two deputies. While it is difficult to ascertain the fact through biographical studies, Egyptian sources held that about 60 percent of its membership was composed of farmers and workers.[35] These figures are in sharp contrast to the composition of the National Assembly of July 1957–March 1958 and the subsequent UAR National Assembly of July 1960–September 1961, which were heavily weighted in favor of prosperous lawyers, businessmen, high ranking bureaucrats, officers, and landowners. In the case of the former, the workers had won a mere 3 percent of the 350 seats while peasants were virtually unrepresented.[36] The magnitude of the turnover in composition becomes somewhat clearer when it is noted that only 76 out of 360 deputies elected in 1964 had been members of the previous assemblies.[37] Thus, in the ideological context of Arab socialism, the Assembly is considered as representing "the working forces of the people" and not the exploiting classes of earlier days. However, as Professor Binder points out, the extent and importance of the changeover in membership was considerably more limited than official figures would indicate.[38]

Within the framework of a strongly presidential system of government, the Provisional Constitution of March 1964 accorded the legislature substantial powers that included balancing and supervisory functions vis-à-vis the executive branch. While the Assembly may be dissolved by the president of the republic, the former has the constitutional right to withdraw its confidence from the government or any one of its ministers—an act which will force resignation.[39] In addition to the right of its members to question the prime minister and his ministers, the Assembly is granted substantial powers over the budgetary process. Moreover, the power to nominate the president belongs to the Assembly; the nomination is then referred to the people for a plebiscite.[40]

While it may be too early to assess definitively the precise role of the new legislature in the developing system, the evidence since March 1964 is in sharp contrast with the previous legislative bodies under the revolution which were little more than rubber stamps.

The formal procedure for debate follows the British parliamentary practice whereby the members of the government are subjected to questioning by the deputies. One general category of questions raised during the Assembly's 1964–65 session was related to the deputies' desire to receive information and clarification on various matters such as health, insurance, tourism, TV transmission to remote areas, agricultural and industrial research,[41] and so on. Another group of questions involved complaints arising from specific cases of governmental mismanagement usually in a representative's home district. Some of the more important complaints were faulty construction of buildings, failure to relieve areas of flood disaster, and delays in making Port Said a tax-free zone.[42] Other complaints included the high price of locally manufactured clothing material and the shortages of schools, hospitals, and paved roads in villages. Finally there was the revealing outburst about army "participation" in the Transport Authority, and the "intervention of the military police in the incidents of the consumer cooperatives." [43]

Four Test Cases

Beyond these routine matters, four major areas of legislative action could be identified as indicators of the Assembly's growing effectiveness. These were the problems of supply and prices, higher education, the Yemeni War, and the budget.

The debate on supply and prices came at a time of heightened popular frustration resulting from acute shortages in food and consumer goods in general. During three successive days of discussions starting 30 November 1964, the government submitted an account of the measures taken to alleviate the situation and the deputies responded with a series of recommendations. The government's report, given by Deputy Prime Minister Dr. Ramzi Stinu, was built around the dual themes of refuting "foreign press allegations" that there existed a general crisis in the supply of commodities and stressing the regime's ability to cope with the basic shortages. The only crisis Dr. Stinu admitted was in the supply of meat, which would be available only three times a week.[44]

The Assembly's general reaction to the food crisis could best be described as restrained and even sympathetic. It limited itself to making a number of recommendations that related more to the betterment of the mechanisms of distribution than to the general problem of shortages in commodities. In view of the UAR's confrontation with the United States regarding American food shipments, the issue had become a matter of national pride and as such did not generate vigorous criticism. Also, there seems to have been a common realization among the deputies that under the circumstances there was little they could do to remedy the situation. Throughout the debate the government seemed to be in full control. Relying on its infinitely greater expertise in economic matters, it was a simple matter for the government to respond effectively to the inquiries and turn down some of the deputies' suggestions as economically unfeasible.

It was in an area requiring considerably less technical expertise—higher education—that the Assembly distinguished itself. The debate that began late in December 1964 brought into the open one of the most fundamental problems of the political system that seems to remain undefined: the relationship between governmental decrees and Assembly legislation dealing with the same subject. It appeared that the cabinet had issued a presidential decree and the minister of higher education had proceeded to implement parts of it by changing the length of certain university courses, prior to debate in the Assembly. By vehemently challenging the constitutionality of the act, the deputies reaffirmed the very basic right of parliament to consider and pass upon the proposals of the executive branch.

The deadlock was broken by the President (Speaker) of the National Assembly Anwar al-Sadat, who spoke of his behind the scenes manoeuvres "to put-off issuing the decree until the discussion was over," despite Premier Ali Sabri's objections.[45] What followed was the Specialized Legislative Committee's report which stated that the cabinet had been "in the process" of issuing the presidential decree. Thereafter the Assembly asked for the indefinite postponement of the issue but despite some floor opposition permitted the minister of higher education to deliver his statement on the partial reforms he had instituted. Operating under direct pressure from the universities, the deputies responded with a general attack on the government's program which was described as "reform by installments" and one favoring certain privileged classes in its policy of admissions. In the end, in an unexpected move, the premier promised to postpone the reforms of higher education for one year during which a plan for thorough overhaul would be produced in consultation with the Assembly. It was the Speaker's turn to rise and soften the blow of the government's setback by thanking everyone and suggesting that the Assembly may have been a bit "unfair." He subsequently submitted a resolution embodying the main points of the debate, which won unanimous approval from the deputies.[46]

In the final analysis what was described in the Egyptian press as a "storm" over higher education, in reality served to establish two basic precedents in the evolution of the political system. By insisting on its constitutional prerogative, the Assembly put the government on notice that it would not be short-circuited by a presidential decree. By forcing a temporary postponement of the decree, the Assembly was able to challenge successfully the government's limited program of educational reform in debate and force a year's delay for a more extensive reappraisal of Egyptian higher education.

To place things in proper perspective, it should be pointed out that the Assembly's victory was a limited one since higher education is not a strictly political area. The Assembly's exposure to what may be described as a politically sensitive subject occurred in February–March 1965 when First Vice-President, Field Marshal Abd al-Hakim Amir gave a detailed report on Yemen in closed session. While it is impossible to know what went on behind closed doors, two points are illustrative of the growing importance of the legislature. The first is that, despite some opposition, the deputies succeeded in persuading the Speaker to declassify and release a good portion of Amir's remarks including figures on expenditures and casualties since the start of the Yemeni War. Secondly, the very fact that the deputies were given a three-hour detailed report on the war showed the leadership's willingness to share with the deputies information that would give the latter a sense of importance.[47]

Another major area of Assembly activity was the budgetary process. An examination of the debates held during June 1965 concerning the government's new budget reflected an increasing sense of independence among the deputies. This is not to suggest that there were strong objections to the size of the budget or to all of its parts. On the contrary, the approval of such budget items as defense, the Joint Arab Command, and the Palestine Liberation Organization, was described as "routine." Thus, when the Assembly's Committee on Budget and Development demanded a reconsideration of the government's draft budget, this did not encompass all of the budget, but certain politically less sensitive, although important items. The committee asked for a reallocation of funds whereby additional sums would be channelled toward nutritive industries, mining, raw materials and equipment, harbour development, the General Organization for Co-operative Productions, and judges' salaries. These funds would come from reduced allowances for "higher officials," and the consolidation of various insurance, transport, and communications organizations, that the committee had singled out as needing reorganization. As a result of the lengthy deliberations that followed, the government was forced to submit a new draft budget.[48]

In purely statistical terms the legislature's performance was not unimpressive. During its session ending in late July 1965, apart from special occasions, fifty-one working meetings were held, during which 650 speeches were delivered. Of the 560 questions put to members of the government, 259 were answered on the spot, 16 received written responses, and the rest were postponed until the next session.[49] In addition, the specialized legislative committees and subcommittees seem to have been active. A total of 290 meetings was held and a series of trips were organized taking committee members to the field on "inspection" missions. For example, the National Defence and Security Committee visited the Yemen; the Foreign and Arab Affairs Committee went to Gaza; other specialized committees—Industry, Power, Agriculture—made trips to the sites of enterprises that came within their respective areas of specialization. These investigative functions of Assembly committees seemed to enjoy the explicit support of President Abd al-Nasir, who had proposed the hiring of "specialist accountants" to help the legislators supervise the work of all enterprises in the public sector.[50]

In assessing the record of the 1964–65 session, two points must be noted. While it is difficult to appraise with precision the extent of the Assembly's influence on government policy, it has been obvious that in certain areas this has been considerable and in others virtually non-existent. But the true measure of the 1964–65 session was its precedent-making ability—its successful attempt to carve out an area of action in the Egyptian political process.

The session of the National Assembly that opened on 25 November 1965 proceeded along the very precedents established in the previous year. Even before the formal opening there were hints that the new government of Prime Minister Zakariyya Muhyi al-Din would be brought under close scrutiny. During the summer months the Assembly Secretariat had compiled a report of all the recommendations issued by the legislature during the past session and all the promises of the ministers for action. This report was forwarded to the cabinet so that the prime minister "may prepare his statement in view of it." [51] By this act the deputies put the prime minister on notice that promises given by the previous Ali Sabri government were equally binding on the new cabinet.

In terms of parliamentary procedure, the new session was marked with a greater reliance on the committee system. There was a fuller realization of the potentialities of specialized committees to serve as agencies of intensive investigation, supervision, and time-saving. In view of the legislature's mounting workload and the increasing complexity of issues, the committees were seen as indispensable for sifting the multitude of problems and establishing priorities on matters to be discussed by the Assembly as a whole. Under this system the numerous citizen complaints would only be brought to the Assembly if they had some bearing on a general problem; as a result the committees would act upon a host of matters not considered important enough to warrant Assembly consideration. [52] A related development was the utilization of public hearings by the committees—a procedure originally suggested by President Abd al-Nasir, who cited the example of American congressional hearings. [53] These procedures tended to place increasing power in the hands of committee members and committee chairmen.

An illustration of this trend came early in December 1965 with the emergence of the powerful Committee of Reply (*Lajnat al-Radd*), composed of four subcommittees, under the general chairmanship of Sayyid Mar'i, the deputy speaker.[54] The function of this committee was to study the prime minister's report and formulate the Assembly's reply to it. When the report was finally read, it was obvious that the Assembly was bent on duplicating its critical performance of the previous year, only with greater vigour and forcefulness. After expressing its general approval of the government's program, the report went on to criticize in detail many of its portions. One major area of Assembly concern was the sweeping price increases which the report criticized as hurting the poor man more than the rich.[55] By basing itself on "an unmistakable, common feeling" prevailing in the population, the committee called upon the government to hold the price line and resist the attempts of certain merchants to justify higher prices especially on meats and vegetables.[56] In a similar vein, the committee report singled out for attack those in higher income brackets who were called upon to shoulder more "socialist responsibilities" through increased taxation thereby "bridging the income gaps." [57] Other major points of criticism included extravagance in governmental expenditures such as "unnecessary appearances," featherbedding in public organizations, malpractices among workers, profiteering, shortages of consumer goods, and sugarcoating reports in the government-controlled press. While the report contained endorsement for the government's foreign policy, its emphasis on the need to develop light industries in rural areas may have been intended as indirect criticism of Nasir's strong commitment to heavy industry.[58]

During the debate that ensued, the prime minister seemed to display a genuine effort to satisfy the deputies on many important problems. These included a proposal to form a joint cabinet-Assembly committee to supervise governmental expenditures and a promise to guard against merchants indiscriminantly raising the prices of goods. It was agreed by both parties that the price rises would affect only luxury items.[59] After making these and other concessions, the Muhyi al-Din government was given a unanimous vote of confidence.

In the final analysis there may have been more to the Assembly's vigorous reaction than would meet the eye. It may be argued with justification that by permitting the deputies to let off steam the regime used the Assembly as a safety valve in the face of widespread popular criticism arising from price increases, scarce goods, and bureaucratic bungling. It is also possible that Assembly attitudes critical of the government reflected similar attitudes among the top elite. In connection with the last point, no less a person than Minister of State for Parliamentary Affairs Abd al-Fattah Hasan stated that the government's report lacked frankness.[60] Moreover, there seemed to be continuing disagreement about the legislature's role with respect to governmental decisions and their implementation—an issue of major consequence for the developing system that had remained hanging since the last session. During the December 1965 debates it became apparent that some prices had been raised prior to Assembly debate and consent.[61] The discussions that ensued proceeded precisely along the lines of the stormy debates of December 1964 over the previous cabinet's attempt at educational reform prior to Assembly consideration. Once again, the deputies questioned the legality of governmental execution of decisions that had not been referred to the Assembly; and once again Speaker al-Sadat asserted that the government "had been in contact" with the Assembly before the issuance of the decrees as the law demands.[62] In the end, this basic issue went unresolved and the Speaker followed his previous practice of referring "the problem of before and after" to the proper legislative committee.[63]

During 1966, the Assembly registered a number of successes in shaping governmental policy. One such area was housing, the lack of which had reached critical proportions in the city of Cairo. In the heated debates of late March 1966, the deputies prevailed upon the government to take immediate steps to provide more housing by evacuating buildings occupied by the Housing Ministry and General Organizations, and converting them into residential apartments. Furthermore, the legislature was given ample assurances that new housing policies and laws would be designed to protect the poorer tenants.[64] The statutes that were subsequently passed (July 1966), reflected considerable progress toward meeting the deputies' demands, although some criticism still persisted in the press.[65]

In May 1966 the Assembly became preoccupied with a topic that came up unexpectedly—the Kamshish incident. This affair involving the murder by "feudalists" of a village-level Arab Socialist Union official assumed large dimensions once brought up in the Assembly. A study of the debates reveals that the incident provided a welcome opportunity to air a variety of suppressed feelings and viewpoints, all of which gave the outside observer a rare view behind the official curtain. Some of the deputies' criticism centered on the inadequacy of existing laws limiting land ownership which were seen as ineffective in curbing the accumulation of land holdings by "feudalist" families. As a result, there were strong sentiments expressed for a "revolutionary" solution to the problem by "liquidating feudalism" through further sequestration of land. While some deputies were guarded in their remarks, others seemed to be mounting a full-scale attack against the leading elements of the various sectors of Egyptian society by calling for a total purge. A sample of these statements is illustrative:

"Reshuffling trade unions, which are as yet the resort of many of the reactionaries who find in them a tool for domination."
"Making a political assessment of the work of members of the board of directors."
"Purging the press of treacherous elements."
"Reconsidering those who occupy key positions in the country."
"Chase out these traitors from companies, general organizations and the Government, and from the National Assembly itself."
"Feudalists should be isolated from villages and sent to working camps."
"There are some people who took part in the July 23 Revolution now driving first class cars and living in palaces, possessing large property." [66]

In view of the fact that the last category included many of the top leaders of the UAR one may conclude that certain Assembly members felt independent enough to criticize the very people who made their election possible.

The government's response to the Kamshish affair and to the deputies' biting criticism may be described as restrained and not too responsive in terms of meeting the specific demands made during the debates. While the Feudalism Liquidation Committee under Field Marshal Amir was in the process of investigating "crimes of feudalism against the people," there was no evidence of any extensive purges at any level of society. As to the vociferous demands for further limitations on land ownership, Marshal Amir explicitly rejected such ideas.[67] Interestingly, he came from a landowning family.

The final major concern of the Assembly in the 1965–1966 session was the new budget. While it was difficult to ascertain the extent of Assembly influence in the make-up of the budget, it seems that the role of the Planning and Budget Committee was considerable. A number of its recommendations were put into effect, such as checking the growing expenditure for tourism, reduction of funds allocated to certain ministries that had to be consolidated, and the stabilization of rising prices.[68]

Several tentative conclusions can be drawn from the foregoing analysis. The existing evidence strongly suggests that the National Assembly prior to 1967 was primarily intended to channel popular desires upward to the leadership on the one hand and to explain the elite's official views to the masses on the other. In this sense it served as a safety valve, an upward channel of communication, and a vehicle for popular education, all combined.

However, in terms of purely legislative functions, much remained to be achieved despite strong pressure from certain deputies. Indeed, as long as the elites' traditional rule by decree was not replaced by that of law, the Assembly could not be considered an effective checking and balancing agency. Furthermore, the invariable finale of "unanimity" after debate and the obvious limits on legislative involvement in foreign and military affairs pointed to areas of Assembly weakness with respect to the executive branch. Nevertheless, while in foreign and military affairs the UAR legislature could not even qualify as a debating society, it had asserted itself beyond the realm of debate and increasingly influenced policy formation on the domestic scene. Even when the National Assembly seemed to serve as a rubber stamp, unlike the Supreme Soviet [69] it did so *after* lengthy discussion.

When dealing with the UAR one should not forget the experimental approach of its leadership to matters political, economic, and social. The formation and functioning of the legislature was a closely controlled experiment in a transitional political system, the results of which have not yet emerged. What it represented was a cautious, gradual, if somewhat belated expansion of the originally small decision-making elite to permit wider participation in government [70]—a step that also indicated a further move toward civilianization of the former military regime. It was in this sense that Abd al-Nasir called the Assembly "enlightened group leadership," while al-Sadat referred to it as "the Revolution's new Council."

The emerging relationship between the Assembly and the government may be characterized as generally cordial, despite the temporary deadlocks discussed above. In this connection the single most important role was that of Speaker al-Sadat who at critical moments used his prestige to bridge the gap by acting as a benevolent intermediary between the opposing sides. No less a person than this early and senior member of the revolutionary officers' group could have presided successfully over the Assembly experiment. Regarding the relations between the Assembly and the presidency, there is little on record that is revealing save the president's own actions and remarks. Of particular importance were Nasir's periodic speeches to closed sessions of the Assembly, during which he reportedly chose "to reveal" a number of "secrets" on major external and internal problems.[71] This, coupled with the fact that he submitted himself to lengthy questioning on the Assembly floor, indicated Nasir's apparent commitment to the strengthening of the legislature.[72] If this was indeed the case, it reflected a belated realization that he would have to routinize his charisma by attaching it to various institutions—such as the National Assembly—thereby legitimizing them in the eyes of his followers. Nevertheless, the crucial problem—that of permitting a loyal opposition—remained to be resolved. All indications were that Abd al-Nasir, and the leadership generally, were painfully aware of the classical problem that defied a clear-cut solution: at what point does a loyal critic become a deviationist? The president indicated that "some go too far" [73] in criticizing the regime and al-Sadat emphasized that "the responsibility of the Assembly is not to fish for the mistakes of the Government." [74] But in channeling of such protest through the official structures of the ASU and the National Assembly, both found a reassuring and healthy sign. More significantly, during a speech in May 1965, Abd al-Nasir tentatively broached the possibility of organizing an opposition in the National Assembly and the ASU,[75] only to reverse himself in the less liberal atmosphere of mid-1966.[76] Also, it was reported that the ASU's leadership was considering the feasibility of introducing two competing lists of candidates running for election in each constituency, instead of the usual single slate, whereby the defeated group would form the opposition.[77] As it turned out, Egypt's economic difficulties at home and political confrontations abroad during 1966 dampened further experimentation toward liberalization. In the restrictive atmosphere of the postwar period, the Assembly's decline was not arrested. Finally, the increasing rivalry during 1968 between the newly organized ASU and the National Assembly culminated in the latter's dissolution in November 1968. The political consequences of this rivalry are dealt with in Chapter 8.

11
The Power Elite (1952–1969)

No INQUIRY into the nature of the political system can be complete without a study in depth of the composition of strategic elites. If charisma and its legitimacy constitutes one aspect of control, the political elite and the power it wields constitutes another.

The term political elite has been given a wide variety of meanings and interpretations since Pareto and Mosca. Even in Lasswell's pioneering work the definition of political elites remains ambiguous.[1] As Peter Bachrach points out, what is required "is the broadening of the concept of political elite to include authority as well as power." [2] This notion is implicit in the elite control formulation advanced in the analytical framework of this study (Chapter 1). The proposition that political control depends on a mix of force and acquired legitimacy ($C = F + L$) accommodates both the power and authority components of Bachrach's definition of elites. The force component corresponds to power—the coercive aspect of elite rule; the legitimacy component corresponds to authority—the popularly acceptable aspect of elite rule. It follows that political elites are those who exercise both authority and power which constitute the two inseparable elements of control.

The study of the Egyptian post-revolutionary political leadership in the context of the foregoing conceptual scheme brings into clear focus the various phases of the self-legitimation process. As emphasized earlier, the partial transition from the military dictatorship phase ($Force_{max}$) to one characterized by charismatic authority ($Legitimacy_{max}$) was followed by a stage of routinization. It might be posited that one of the most basic indicators of routinization in a charismatically conditioned military dictatorship is the degree of civilianization. Effective civilianization might imply a high level of legitimacy barring instances of incompetent performance on the part of civilian elites. An accurate assessment of the civilianization process necessitates a social background study of Egyptian political leaders since the revolution. Such a study would also reveal a number of related aspects of systemic evolution, especially those concerning the socialization of elites. For example, an analysis of changes in educational specializations may indicate a transformation in the elite culture. In the Egyptian case one can hypothesize that a primarily lawyer-oriented elite culture has been transformed into one where technological and revolutionary norms predominate.

Scope and Method

The political leaders studied include all cabinet-rank individuals —prime ministers, deputy prime ministers, ministers, deputy ministers—as well as presidents and vice presidents. The time period covers approximately sixteen years, beginning with General Nagib's first cabinet of 7 September 1952 and ending with Nasir's cabinet reshuffle of 28 October 1968. Aside from this primary focus, the study also deals with certain aspects of the bureaucracy; the ASU leadership is examined in Chapters 10 and 12. The concern with the top leadership—the commanding heights—is not prompted solely by its importance, but also because of the relative availability of data, in contrast to the difficulties involved in gathering survey-type data.

The first category—cabinet and higher level leaders—includes 131 individuals who held power for varying periods between September 1952 and through the cabinet changes of October 1968. The basic approach is empirical [3] and centered on several key questions: where do political leaders come from in Egyptian society; how do they become and how long do they remain leaders; what techniques do they use; how much cooperation and conflict is there among them; and what happens to them after they leave their rulership positions. In short, the inquiry centers on the sources, recruitment patterns, cohesion, strategies, tenure, and disposition of 131 leaders—factors that determine what is often called the "circulation of elites." [4] Specifically, the following categories of variables were used to accumulate detailed biographical and behavioral data for each of the 131 leaders.

A. Age: (1) at first political office; (2) at first cabinet office; and (3) at leaving cabinet office.
B. Occupation: (1) positions held before first political office; (2) before first cabinet office; and (3) after leaving cabinet office.
C. Education: by (1) level of achievement; (2) area(s) of specialization; and (3) name of educational institution(s).
D. Family identity and class by birth or by marriage.
E. Religion.
F. Geographical affiliation by birth, residence, or occupation.
G. Political career: (1) first office held and tenure; (2) sequence of offices including tenure in each, from first to last office in government.
H. Political identification with (1) party; (2) group; (3) class; (4) military; and (5) ideology.

Sources of Data

The systematic collection of accurate biographical data on a large number of political leaders constitutes a real challenge for the student of the Middle East and the non-Western world in general. Various *Who's Whos* provide only a small portion of the data needed on a limited number of leaders. Not only are published biographical references scarce, but what is available is often full of errors in dates, places, and career histories. Still more serious are the divergencies that are frequently found between the biographical accounts of various locally published newspapers and periodicals. Under these circumstances, it was necessary to gather as much data as possible on each leader from a number of English and French sources,[5] and then collate them with similar information found in the Egyptian and Lebanese presses.[6] Finally, the results were checked by several knowledgeable individuals situated in Egypt and the United States. Supplementary material was collected through native contacts, as well as by the author in the course of a personal visit to the UAR. Despite certain gaps, the data on 131 leaders is as complete as possible, given the obvious limitations of time and resources, and especially under the prevailing touchy political situation in Egypt.

In reconstructing a composite picture of the leadership since September 1952, certain categories of information presented special problems of acquisition and/or analysis. For example, the determination of what happens to leaders after cabinet office, i.e., disposition of elites, presented serious difficulties, illustrating Muhammad Hasanayn Haykal's (editor of *Al-Ahram*) fitting observation on "the secrecy of revolutionaries." Conflicting data made the identification of social background and ideology particularly difficult and ambiguous thus rendering certain conclusions tentative. At all stages, laborious and extensive detective work was necessary to find the missing parts of the puzzle.

Who's Who: Military vs. Civilians

In the way of background, it should be noted that after three experiments with all-civilian cabinets under Ali Mahir (July 1952) and General Nagib (September and December 1952), leading RCC members came forth to assume key cabinet posts in June 1953. What followed was a massive infusion of officers into key bureaucratic positions for purposes of control and supervision. Indeed, at least some of the politically unreliable bureaucrats of the old regime had to be replaced by persons who combined political loyalty and administrative expertise—qualities that were readily found mostly in military officers. While detailed information on the military's initial presence in the government is unavailable, overwhelming predominance is evident at the highest and intermediary levels.

In purely quantitative terms the precise degree of the military's presence at the very top of the power structure is reflected in Table 3. Out of an aggregate of 131 leaders, 44 or 33.6 percent had been military officers of various types, in contrast to 87 or

Table 3
Aggregate Breakdown: Military vs. Civilian

	Officer	MILITARY Officer-technocrat	Total	CIVILIAN	Total
N	27	17	44	87	131
%	20.3	13	33.6	66.4	100

66.4 percent who had a civilian background. However, one should not be misled by the two to one numerical superiority of civilians over officers; while it clearly illustrates the extent of the regime's reliance on civilian elites, especially in technical areas, it is not to be regarded as a valid index of their relative power. Most of these civilians were the tools of the military (the members of the RCC and subsequently the president himself). Since each lacked an independent power base, none of the 87 emerged as a political leader in his own right, not even during the turmoil of the postwar (1967) period. This, coupled with Nasir's persistence in placing ex-officers in key ministries, made the military the virtual master of the system.

To be sure, one of the peculiarities of recent Egyptian political life has been the appalling lack of political backbone among the civilian leadership. These were mostly men of great intelligence, efficiency, and expertise; they were also a singularly depoliticized lot, devoid of political and ideological consciousness and therefore unable or unwilling to present a counterweight to the military. In the various power contests at the top, the civilians, or at least some of them, tended to side with different factions headed by ex-officers; yet as far as one can discern, no civilian actually *led* a factional power struggle. The few who dared to stand up to the military were purged; the vast majority, more interested in high office than principles, complied with the military's wishes. The final cost to the system of the civilians' compliance and the military's aggressiveness was great in many respects, especially in the building of the ASU. The president's belated efforts to repoliticize the civilian center of the political spectrum (to which most of the civilian leadership belonged) after a decade of strenuous depoliticization, were not immediately successful. The conversion of docile technicians into politically conscious party men could not be accomplished overnight.

Obviously, the best index of the officers' position within the leadership is their control of strategic posts. Both of Egypt's presidents *—Nagib and Nasir—had been officers, as were all of the vice presidents. The five men who successively occupied the premiership—Nagib, Nasir, Sabri, Muhyi al-Din, and Sulayman—were also ex-officers. In addition, several key ministries —Defense, Local Administration, Military Production, and the Ministry of State (for Intelligence)—have been headed by officers from the very outset. Certain other ministries alternated between ex-officers and civilians, i.e., Foreign Affairs, Tourism, Industry, Power, High Dam, Information, Scientific Research, Communications, Agrarian Reform, Supply, Youth, Labor, Education, Social Affairs, Planning, Waqfs, Culture, and National Guidance. The highly sensitive Interior Ministry became the preserve of ex-officers such as Muhyi al-Din and Guma'a with the single exception of Abd al-Azim Fahmi, a police officer. Even the Ministry of Public Health has experienced a form of quasimilitary intrusion; Muhammad Nassar and Abd al-Wahhab Shukri have both been long identified with the armed forces as military physicians. The Ministry of National Guidance, the state's supreme propaganda agency, has been headed by ex-officers since 1958.

Ministries with uninterrupted civilian leadership included Justice, Public Works, Housing and Utilities, Irrigation, Commerce, Agriculture, Treasury, and Higher Education. These are highly technical areas, generally unsuitable for individuals of military backgrounds; to appoint an officer as Minister of Higher Education would have been ludicrous at the very least. Yet, in the final analysis, various means were devised to assure military control over these "civilian" ministries as well.

In retrospect, three basic control strategies have been discernible since the military's direct involvement in government beginning in 1953. The first and crudest strategy was outright takeover of key ministries by leading RCC members, who employed civil-

* Egypt's third president, Anwar al-Sadat, is also an ex-officer.

ians as sources of expert advice in second-level slots. In later years, as vice presidents and deputy premiers in charge of clusters of ministries, or "sectors," the leading officers continued to exercise direct supervisory functions over the subordinate ministries, which were often headed by civilians. Baghdadi, Shafi'i, Muhyi al-Din, Husayn, Rif'at, Abbas Rudwan, Abu al-Nur, and Hatim, all headed such superministries. The second strategy employed was to maintain a military presence in the civilian-led ministries by placing officers in number two positions. Depending on the organizational make-up of the particular ministry, the military appointment could come at the deputy minister (a cabinet post), or undersecretary (below cabinet) level. Such were the roles of Husayn Zu al-Fiqar Sabri (until 1964) and Mahmud Riyad (1964–1967), both of whom successively served as deputies to Foreign Minister Mahmud Fawzi, a civilian. Qurra's position as undersecretary to Supply Minister Ramzi Stinu was an example of military presence at the undersecretary level.

The military's most ingenious method to maintain control centered on the appointment of a new breed of officers identified here as officer-technocrats. Most of these men began to appear in leading positions in the late 1950s and soon achieved cabinet or higher status, often displacing civilians and other military men.

Who were these officer-technocrats who constituted 13 percent of Egypt's 131 top elite since 1952? According to the classification employed here, almost all had been officers who went on to receive non-military degrees in diverse fields—engineering, physics, political science, law, history, and journalism. Two of the officer-technocrats were military physicians. The best known was General Muhammad Nagib, an officer with a law degree. Other well-known officer-technocrats included ex-Premier Sidqi Sulayman, War Production Minister Abd al-Wahhab Bishri, Foreign Minister Mahmud Riyad, Cultural Minister Sarwat Ukasha, and ex-Ministers Salah Hidayat, Abd al-Qadir Hatim, and Mahmud Yunis.[7]

In essence, the rise of the officer-technocrats was the military's answer to its civilian critics. For now the military had trained its *own* experts to cope with the new and diverse complexities of an industrializing society. Through these men the military could extend its scope of effective control further than ever, simultaneously reducing its reliance on the civilian experts. Given the views and needs of the leadership, the officer-technocrats were bound to succeed; they combined and enjoyed the best of two worlds.

One of the best ways to study the evolution of the political system is to analyze the changing proportions of officers and civilians in the leadership since 1952. In the study of military-led revolutions such as Egypt's, there is no real substitute for the employment of rigorous, empirically based analysis. Data concerning certain elite background characteristics are presented in Table 4. Of particular significance is the cabinet-by-cabinet breakdown of the number and proportion of officers, officer-technocrats, and civilians. The general pattern that emerges quantitatively illustrates the increasing militarization of the leadership during the early fifties as well as the recent trend toward civilianization.

On 7 September 1952, General Nagib became prime minister at the head of an all-civilian cabinet, replacing the previous RCC-installed civilian government of Ali Mahir. In both the September 1952 cabinet and the reshuffled December 1952 cabinet Nagib was the sole officer—classified as officer-technocrat in Table 4 for possessing a law degree in addition to his military status. The picture began to change with the entrance of four additional officers into the June 1953 cabinet—Nasir, Baghdadi, Amir, and Salah Salim. Their deep distrust of civilian elites, combined with the growing popularity of Nagib, had brought forth four of the main architects of the July 1952 coup. The June 1953 cabinet marked the beginning of an upward trend in the military's presence at the top for the next two and a half years. During the Nagib-Nasir power struggles, in 1953 and 1954, the military component continued to increase from 26.3 percent in June to 40.9 percent in the reshuffled October 1953 government. A further increase to 45.8 percent in the April 1954 cabinet reflected the Nasirite consolidation of power against Nagib and his civilian supporters. Between June 1953 and April 1954 Nasir succeeded in packing the cabinet with his fellow officers by retiring pro-Nagib civilians. The September 1954 reshuffle marked a peak of 52.1 percent when for the first time the number of officers exceeded that of civilians.

Early 1956 saw the first attempts at civilianization, subsequently interrupted by the Suez War. This was reflected in the June 1956 cabinet, when the military suffered a loss of four posts dropping its total to a low of 36.3 percent. With the formation of the United Arab Republic the military component once again began to increase.[8] Taking the aggregate of the multi-level leadership (presidents, vice presidents, central and regional ministers), the military registered a less than 2 percent increase in the March 1958 government; in the October 1958 cabinet, however, the total of officers went up by over 10 percentage points to 48.5 percent. In both cabinets the president and all vice presidents were ex-officers. At the Central Cabinet level, the military predominated with 60 percent (in March 1958) and 58.8 percent (in October 1958) respectively. Only in the regional cabinet did the officer representation reach a low of 19.8 percent in March, only to climb to 37.5 percent in October 1958. With the abolition of the regional cabinet system in August 1961, the military component climbed further from 48.5 to 51.5 percent, a level that remained constant in the first post secession cabinet (October 1961). The maintenance of an officers' majority seems to have reflected the regime's reliance on the coercive force of the military to help keep the UAR united in August 1961 and to prevent a Syrian-style coup in Egypt in October 1961. A noteworthy development since October 1958 was the increase of officer-technocrats in cabinet posts. By September 1966 the officer-technocrats claimed 21 percent of the posts, which in June 1967 increased to an all-time high of 27.5 percent.

Having recovered from the shock of Syria's breakaway, a new phase of partial civilianization was started in 1962, culminating in the founding of the ASU. The regime's new commitment to etatism and rapid industrialization could not be achieved without a greater reliance on civilian expertise; hence the progressive decline of the military component to 47.1 percent in September 1962 and 36.3 percent in March 1964. Not since June 1956 had the military's presence dropped to 36.3 percent; also, at no time since 1964 has this low level been reached despite the strong civilianizing trends of 1968.

The disproportionately greater power the military elite wielded despite its decreasing numerical strength (1962 and 1964) bears repeating. For example, in the September 1962 two-level cabinet,

Table 4

Age and Background Characteristics of Each Cabinet

CABINET	AVERAGE AGE	BACKGROUND								RELIGION				TOTAL
		Officer		Officer-Technocrat		Total Military		Civilian		Muslim		Copt		
		N	%	N	%	N	%	N	%	N	%	N	%	
7 September 1952	50.4	–	–	1	6.3	1	6.3	15	93.8	15	93.8	1	6.3	16
8 December 1952	49	–	–	1	5.9	1	5.9	16	94.1	16	94.1	1	5.9	17
18 June 1953	44.7	4	21	1	5.3	5	26.3	14	73.6	18	94.7	1	5.3	19
4 October 1953	42.6	7	31.8	2	9.1	9	40.9	13	59	21	95.5	1	4.5	22
17 April 1954	40.9	9	37.4	2	8.3	11	45.8	13	54.1	23	95.8	1	4.2	24
1 September 1954	43.5	10	43.4	2	8.7	12	52.1	11	47.7	22	95.7	1	4.3	23
30 June 1956	43.1	7	31.8	1	4.5	8	36.3	14	63.6	21	95.5	1	4.5	22
5 March 1958	44.3	7	33.3	1	4.8	8	38.1	13	61.9	20	95.2	1	4.8	21
President and Vice Presidents		3	100	–	–	3	100	–	–					3
Central Cabinet		5	50	1	10	6	60	4	40					10
Regional Cabinets		2	19.8	–	–	2	19.8	9	89.1					11
7 October 1958	44.9	11	33.3	5	15.2	16	48.5	17	51.5	32	97	1	3	33
President and Vice Presidents		3	100	–	–	3	100	–	–					3
Central Cabinet		9	52.9	1	5.9	10	58.8	7	41.2					17
Regional Cabinets		2	12.5	4	25	6	37.5	10	62.5					16
17 August 1961	47.8	11	35.4	5	16.1	16	51.5	15	48.3	30	96.8	1	3.2	31
President and Vice Presidents		6	100	–	–	6	100	–	–					6
19 October 1961	45.9	10	34.4	5	17.2	15	51.6	14	48.2	28	96.6	1	3.4	29
President and Vice Presidents		5	100	–	–	5	100	–	–					5
29 September 1962	47.7	12	33.2	5	13.9	17	47.1	19	52.6	35	97.2	1	2.8	36
President and Vice Presidents		6	100	–	–	6	100	–	–					6

		No.	%	No.	%	No.	%	No.	%	No.	%	No.	%	Total
Presidential Council		10	83	—	—	10	83	2	16.3					12
Executive Council		2	8.3	5	20.8	7	29.1	17	70.7					24
24 March 1964	49.9	10	22.7	6	13.6	16	36.3	28	63.6	41	93.2	3	6.8	44
President and Vice Presidents		5	100	—	—	5	100	—	—					5
Prime Minister and Deputy Prime Ministers		3	24.9	2	16.6	5	41.5	7	58.1					12
Ministers		2	7.4	4	14.8	6	22.2	21	77.7					27
2 October 1965	51.1	13	31.6	6	14.6	19	46.2	22	53.5	38	92.7	3	7.3	41
President and Vice Presidents		5	100	—	—	5	100	—	—					5
Prime Minister and Deputy Prime Ministers		2	22.2	2	22.2	4	44.4	5	55.5					9
Ministers and Deputy Ministers		6	22.2	4	14.8	10	37	17	62.9					27
10 September 1966	50.5	13	34.2	8	21	21	55.2	17	44.7	35	92.1	3	7.9	38
President and Vice Presidents		4	100	—	—	4	100	—	—					4
Deputy Prime Minister's		1	20	3	60	4	80	1	20					5
Ministers and Deputy Ministers		8	27.5	5	17.2	13	44.7	16	55					29
19 June 1967	50.1	11	37.8	8	27.5	19	65.4	10	34.4	28	96.6	1	3.4	29
President, Vice Presidents, and Deputy Prime Ministers		4	80	1	20	5	100	—	—					5
Ministers		7	29.1	7	29.1	14	58.2	10	41.6					24
20 March 1968	50.2	8	24.2	5	15.2	13	39.4	20	60.6	31	93.9	2	6.1	33
28 October 1968	50.3	7	22.6	6	19.4	13	41.9	18	58.1	29	93.6	2	6.4	31

the Presidential Council (supreme policymaking agency) was 83 percent military in contrast to only 29.1 percent military representation on the Executive Council. Also, in the multi-level cabinet of March 1964, Egypt's largest cabinet (forty-four), the military scored 41.5 percent at the deputy prime minister level, but only 22.2 percent at the ministerial level.

The convergence of a multitude of economic and political problems in the mid-1960s—i.e., the Yemeni War, the economy, internal unrest—produced a protracted crisis situation leading to the 1967 war. The immediate effect of this turmoil once again produced a ten point upswing in the military component in the Muhyi al-Din government. This upward trend continued to an unprecedented high of 55.2 percent in Sidqi Sulayman's cabinet of September 1966. Finally, in the aftermath of the June War, the new cabinet under Nasir's premiership (19 June 1967) marked an all-time high of 65.4 percent in the military's presence. This peak was reached at a time of great internal instability accentuated by the attempted coup led by Marshal Amir. One might hypothesize that a military-dominated leadership could effectively control internal unrest and at the same time more easily neutralize further insurrectionist activity coming from a demoralized military establishment.

The popular reaction against the military after the 1967 defeat, coupled with the student-worker riots of February 1968, prompted Nasir to begin a far-reaching reorganization of political life, the first manifestation of which was the March 1968 cabinet. The number of civilians doubled with a concomitant decrease of 6 officers in a cabinet of 33 members. The sharp drop in the military component from 65.4 percent (June 1967) to 39.4 percent signalled the start of a new stage of demilitarization of the Nasirite regime. The trend toward increasing civilianization is expected to continue if all other factors remain constant. However, if developments since 1952 are a guide, internal and/or external crises are likely to increase the military presence at the top.

Age and Tenure

While political involvement may have come early in adult life, the attainment of first political office came somewhat later, at an average age of 40 (see Table 5). This would have been higher were it not for the intrusion of the young officers whose first political

Table 5

Age: Aggregate Count

	YEARS
Average age of cabinet members at time of first political office	40.1
Average age of cabinet members at first cabinet office	46.9
Average age of cabinet members at leaving cabinet office	51.5

office was a cabinet post. Moreover, the relative youth of the officers and certain of their civilian recruits kept the average age at first cabinet office just under 47. The average would have been still lower had it not been for Nagib and older civilians such as Yusif, Tarraf, Fawzi, and Sharabasi. On the other hand, despite the political longevity of the foregoing civilians, the average age at leaving cabinet office was a relatively low 51.5 years, reflecting the briefness of tenure at the top for many officials. As seen in Table 6 the overall average tenure in office was 3 years 8 months. Yet significantly the average tenure of officers and officer-technocrats was almost two years longer than that of the civilian leaders—4 years 11.5 months and 3 years 1 month, respectively. This fact reflects not only the military's durability and entrenchment but also its leading position with respect to the civilians.

Table 6

Tenure

	YEARS	MONTHS
Average tenure of cabinet members	3	8
Average tenure of officers and officer-technocrats	4	11½
Average tenure of civilians	3	1

An analysis of average age data of each cabinet bears few surprises (See Table 4). There is a sharp decline in age between Nagib's all-civilian cabinets of 1952 and the June 1953 cabinet because of the entrance of young RCC officers, including Nasir. With the influx of additional officers during October 1953 and April 1954 the average age level dropped to an all-time low of 40.9 from the previous high of 50.4. Since that time there has been an almost uninterrupted rise in average age as many of the permanent figures aged in office and new recruits were brought in mostly from older age brackets. The trend toward generally older cabinets continued until October 1965 when the average age reached an all-time high of 51.1 years surpassing the previous high of the first Nagib cabinet. Since that time average age has remained virtually constant at almost 50 years.

Educational Specialization

Inquiry into the educational backgrounds of elites can reveal important clues about the leadership's sense of priorities, the direction of socio-political change and the political system itself. Because the modernizing countries are attempting to achieve rapid development, the type and level of the elite's education assumes greater importance than is the case with modernized societies. One might even hypothesize that educational background is a more significant variable in the study of developing countries than it would be for developed systems. In the Egyptian case education has traditionally been a politically significant dimension; it has been more so after the revolution.

Table 7 presents an aggregate breakdown of educational specialization by fields. As in Table 3, the total military is divided into two main categories according to their educational specialization. The officer category contains 27 individuals whose primary field of formal study was military science in which they held at least one degree. While several of these pure military types also pursued nonmilitary studies, none of them actually completed the requirements for academic degrees. In contrast, the officer-technocrats went beyond a military education to obtain academic degrees in nonmilitary fields. There were a total of 17 officer-technocrats, 7 of whom specialized in engineering in preparation for a highly successful career in the cabinet. Of the remaining 10, 3 became political scientists, 2 graduated as medical doctors, and 2 others held law degrees. Journalism and history claimed one each; and finally, one became an atomic physicist.

Among the 87 civilian leaders, there were 19 engineers—the

Table 7

Educational Specialization by Fields: Aggregate Count

	N	%	N	%	N	%
Military					44	33.6
Officers			27	20.6		
Officer-Technocrats			17	13		
Military-Political Science	3	2.3				
Military-History	1	0.8				
Military-Engineering	7	5.3				
Military-Physics	1	0.8				
Military-Law	2	1.5				
Military-Journalism	1	0.8				
Military-Medicine	2	1.5				
Civilians					87	66.4
Law	16	12.2				
Law-Political Economy	3	2.3				
Criminology	3	2.3				
Engineering	19	14.5				
Sociology	1	0.8				
Educational Psychology	6	4.6				
Chemistry	4	3.1				
Agriculture	9	6.9				
Economics-Business	12	9.2				
Islamic-Arabic Studies	3	2.3				
Medicine	3	2.3				
Fine Arts	1	0.8				
Geography	5	3.8				
No College Education	1	0.8				
No Data	1	0.8				

Total 131

largest single specialization category. When 19 civilian engineers are added to the 7 engineer officer-technocrats, the total engineering specialization category numbers 26—almost equalling the pure military category. In percentage terms, the engineers represent over 20 percent of the total leadership since September 1952 and as such reflect the regime's singular commitment to rapid industrialization.

The stress on general economic development is further reflected by the relatively high number of agronomists (9), chemists (4), and economists (12 + 3). The 9 agronomists are indicative of

Table 8

Educational Specialization

PROFESSIONAL SCHOOLS

CABINET *	TOTAL MEMBERSHIP	Mili-tary N	%	Law N	%	Medi-cine N	%	Mili-tary/ College N	%
1. 7 September 1952	16	–	–	4	25	1	6.3	–	–
2. 8 December 1952	17	–	–	6	35.3	1	5.9	–	–
3. 18 June 1953	19	4	21.1	7	36.8	1	5.3	–	–
4. 4 October 1953	22	7	31.8	5	22.8	1	4.6	1	4.6
5. 17 April 1954	24	9	37.5	4	16.7	1	4.2	1	4.2
6. 1 September 1954	23	10	43.5	4	17.4	1	4.4	1	4.4
7. 30 June 1956	22	7	31.8	4	18.2	1	4.6	1	4.6
8. 5 March 1958	21	7	33.3	3	14.3	1	4.8	1	4.8
9. 7 October 1958	33	11	33.3	2	6.1	2	6.1	3	9.1
10. 17 August 1961	31	11	35.5	2	6.5	1	3.2	4	12.9
11. 19 October 1961	29	10	34.5	2	6.9	1	3.5	4	13.8
12. 29 September 1962	36	12	33.3	2	5.6	2	5.6	4	11.1
13. 24 March 1964	44	10	22.7	2	4.6	2	4.6	5	11.4
14. 2 October 1965	41	13	31.7	2	4.9	1	2.4	6	14.6
15. 10 September 1966	38	13	34.2	2	5.3	1	2.6	8	21.1
16. 19 June 1967	29	11	37.9	2	6.7	1	3.5	8	27.6
17. 20 March 1968	33	8	24.2	2	6.1	1	3	5	15.2
18. 28 October 1968	31	7	21.9	1	3.1	2	6.3	5	15.6

* Educational information on two cabinet officers is unavailable, as seen in cabinets number 1, 2, and 3. One cabinet officer had no college education; see, cabinets number 12, 13, 14, 15.

** The various college specializations are grouped into five fields. Technology includes engineering and agriculture. Humanities includes literature, Islamic stud-

Egypt's serious food problem. Among the social sciences, the more traditional field of geography (5) is overrepresented in contrast to sociology (1). The field of law claims a high proportion of the elites, especially when the 2 military lawyers are added to 19 civilian lawyers. But the fact that the number of lawyers falls short of the military or engineer categories clearly indicates their secondary role in Egypt, in contrast to many other countries, especially the United States. Finally, the presence of educational psychologists shows special concern with the educational process, while the 3 criminologists may indicate excessive systemic pre-occupation with police work.

A number of additional insights are gained by examining changes of educational specialization over time (see Table 8). As

COMBINATIONS: PROFESSIONAL & COLLEGE		COLLEGE **				
Military/ Law	Law/ College	Tech- nology	Human- ities	Social Science	Eco- nomics	Pure Science
N %	N %	N %	N %	N %	N %	N %
1 6.3	– –	1 6.3	3 18.8	1 6.3	3 18.8	– –
1 5.9	– –	2 11.8	2 11.8	2 11.8	2 11.8	– –
1 5.3	– –	3 15.8	1 5.3	1 5.3	1 5.3	– –
1 4.6	– –	3 13.6	1 4.6	1 4.6	2 9.1	– –
1 4.2	1 4.2	3 12.5	1 4.2	1 4.2	2 8.3	– –
1 4.4	1 4.4	3 13	1 4.4	– –	1 4.4	– –
– –	1 4.6	5 22.7	1 4.6	1 4.6	1 4.6	– –
– –	1 4.8	5 23.8	1 4.8	1 4.8	1 4.8	– –
– –	1 3.1	8 24.2	1 3.1	2 6.1	2 6.1	– –
1 3.2	– –	8 25.8	– –	3 9.7	1 3.2	– –
1 3.5	1 3.5	6 20.7	– –	3 10.3	1 3.5	– –
1 2.8	1 2.8	6 16.7	1 2.8	4 11.1	2 5.6	– –
1 2.3	3 6.8	10 22.7	– –	5 11.4	3 6.8	2 4.5
– –	3 7.3	9 22	– –	2 4.9	2 4.9	2 4.9
– –	2 5.3	7 18.4	– –	2 5.3	1 2.6	1 2.6
– –	2 6.7	3 10.3	– –	– –	2 6.7	– –
– –	4 12.1	7 21.2	– –	3 9.1	2 6.1	1 3
– –	3 9.4	7 21.9	– –	3 9.4	2 6.3	1 3.1

ies, fine arts, linguistics, philosophy, and journalism. Social Sciences includes political science, geography, history, sociology, educational psychology, education, and criminology. Economics includes business, commerce, finance, and political economy. Pure Sciences includes botany, chemistry, and physics.

stated previously, those with a purely military education became a permanent fixture after June 1953 despite fluctuations. Simultaneously there is an increase of officer-technocrats reaching a peak in the June 1967 cabinet. Technological specializations—agriculture and engineering—progressively climb until August 1961, and after 1964 several scientists (chemistry, physics, botany) make their debut for the first time. The percentages in the smaller categories—medicine, social science—fluctuate without clear trends.

The two fields of specialization that registered decline since September 1952 were humanities and law. After a high of 18.8 percent in September 1952, the humanities (literature, Islamic studies, fine arts, linguistics) declined and finally disappeared beginning in March 1964. After their preponderance in the December 1952 and June 1953 cabinets, the lawyers registered a precipitous decline in 1958; by October 1968, there remained only 1 in the cabinet. The numerical decline of lawyers and humanists since 1952 and the concurrent increase of officers, officer-technocrats, engineers, and scientists reflect basic changes in the Egyptian political culture. A heavily lawyer-oriented culture before the revolution, Egypt continued to rely on the services of lawyer-politicians in the early years of the revolution. With the advent of planned, accelerated socio-economic development that required technical specialists, the lawyer's utility gradually declined. As generalists the lawyers and humanists lacked the specialized training to cope with the new technological environment. Politically, the military-revolutionary milieu proved incompatible to the lawyer. Not only was he too closely identified with the pre-revolutionary political culture, but also his traditional "brokerage" functions were not needed in the new society. Legalistic, competitive politics, and economics had been replaced by ideological, revolutionary politics, and the lawyer became the odd man out; his status is not likely to change in the foreseeable future.

Educational Level

A striking aspect of the cross-national study of leaders is the relatively high level of education possessed by elites in certain developing countries. On the basis of preliminary investigations, it seems that the general educational level of cabinet-level leaders in a number of developing countries actually exceeds that of corresponding Western elites.[9] While the identification of the causal factors behind this phenomenon falls outside the scope of this study, it seems that countries committed to rapid modernization feel a greater actual and psychological need for highly trained experts at the top. To a large extent this has been the case in modern Egypt. As shown on Table 9, out of 131 leaders only 1 lacked a college education. A more impressive fact is the unusually high number of those holding doctorates—over 47 percent.

In other words there were almost as many doctorates as the B.A.s and M.A.s combined.

Table 9
Educational Level: Aggregate Count

LEVEL	NUMBER	PERCENTAGE
Cabinet members holding only B.A. degrees	38	29
Cabinet members holding M.A. degrees	29	22.1
Cabinet members holding M.D. and Ph.D. degrees	62	47.3
No information	1	0.8
No college education	1	0.8
Total	131	

Data reflecting the fluctuations of educational level since 1952 are found in Table 10. After a high of 25 percent in September 1952, the B.A.s decline sharply due to displacement by doctorates in December 1952 and the entrance of officers with M.A.s during 1953. The December 1952 cabinet is noteworthy since it marked an all-time high for the doctorates, exceeding 70 percent. The general trend set during 1953 was one of progressive decline for the doctorates resulting from the increasing number of officers (B.A.s and M.A.s) entering the cabinet. The low point for doctorates was reached in the September 1954 cabinet with only 30.4 percent of the total; the trend was sharply reversed with the limited demilitarization of June 1956, reaching over 42 percent in the joint UAR cabinets of 1958. After several fluctuations in the early 1960s, the doctorates reached a high of 47.7 percent in the layered 1964 cabinet where they displaced officers with M.A. degrees. The trend was sharply reversed under the consolidated Muhyi al-Din cabinet (1965), where doctorates dropped to 36.5 percent and the increased number of officers pushed up the M.A.s almost 10 percentage points, and the B.A.s 2 points. In the two cabinets preceding and following the 1967 war, the doctorates reached a low of 31 percent because of the large influx of officers and civilians holding B.A.s and M.A.s. Not until the March 1968 cabinet was the downward trend reversed. In response to antimilitary sentiments among the population as reflected in the February riots, Nasir brought into the cabinet 8 civilians holding doctorates. As a result, the B.A.s declined by 3 points and the M.A.s by 7 points; the number of doctorates rose by 20 points to 51.5 percent. The upward trend in doctorates continued in the October 1968 reshuffle, reaching 53 percent, but still far short of the December 1952 cabinet.

The headlong quest for doctorates in the last decade as a means for achieving social respect and political mobility has been characterized by Haykal as "a mockery." He describes the situation as one in which "those with doctorates wanted political office, and those in political office wanted doctorates." [10] There are already signs pointing to an excess of Ph.D.s in certain specializations. If this trend continues Egypt's Ph.D.s might find themselves within the ranks of the unemployed, as the lawyers had done earlier.

Table 10

Educational Level: By Each Cabinet [1]

CABINET	TOTAL NUMBER	BACHELOR N	%	MASTER N	%	DOCTORATE N	%
7 September 1952	16[2]	5	31.3	2	12.5	8	50
8 December 1952	17	4	23.5	1	5.9	12	70.6
18 June 1953	19	3	15.8	5	26.3	11	57.9
4 October 1953	22	3	13.6	8	36.4	11	50
17 April 1954	24	5	20.8	10	41.6	9	37.5
1 September 1954	23	6	26.1	10	43.4	7	30.4
30 June 1956	22	5	22.7	8	36.4	9	40.9
5 March 1958	21	5	23.8	7	33.3	9	42.9
7 October 1958	33	8	24.2	11	33.3	14	42.4
17 August 1961	31	8	25.8	10	32.2	13	41.9
19 October 1961	29	6	20.6	10	34.4	13	44.7
29 September 1962	36*	7	19.4	13	36	15	41.6
24 March 1964	44*	10	22.7	12	27.2	21	47.7
2 October 1965	41*	10	24.3	15	36.5	15	36.5
10 September 1966	38*	11	28.9	14	36.8	12	31.6
19 June 1967	29	7	24.1	13	44.7	9	31
20 March 1968	33	7	21.2	9	27.3	17	51.5
28 October 1968	31	7	21.8	8	25	16	53

1. The Bachelor's level includes all B.A. and B.S. degrees, military academy diplomates, and licentiates in law. The Master's level includes all M.A. and M.S. degrees, staff college, and graduate diplomas from insitutes. The Doctorate level includes all Ph.D. and M.D. degrees.
2. No information is available on one cabinet member.
* One cabinet member who served in each of these cabinets did not have a college education.

Place of Study

Despite France's great cultural influence on Egypt, a larger number of leaders went to Britain and the United States for purposes of study. Ideologically, however, French influence was perhaps greater than that of the U.S. and Britain—especially the influence of the French left. A partial explanation might be found in the primarily technical specializations studied in the U.S. and U.K. while almost all who went to France studied law and/or political economy.[11]

Table 11

Breakdown by Educational Institution and Country—Number of Degrees *

FRANCE		EGYPT		BRITAIN		UNITED STATES		MISC.	
10		148		22		16		6	
Montpelier	1	Ain Shams	1	Birmingham	3	Chicago	1	Germany	4
Paris	9	Al-Azhar	2	Cambridge	3	Columbia	2	Rome	1
		Cairo	78	Durham	1	Harvard	2	Vienna	1
		Military		Edinburgh	2	Illinois	1		
		Acad.	38	Leeds	1	M.I.T.	1		
		Staff		Liverpool	3	Ohio	1		
		College	29	London	5	Oregon	1		
				London		Syracuse	1		
				School of		California	4		
				Economics	1	Pennsylvania	1		
				Manchester	3	Wisconsin	1		

* This breakdown of the number of degrees (Bachelors, Masters, and Doctorates) in Table 11 represents only those which were positively identified. In certain cases, it was impossible to identify the institution granting the degree.

Possibly because of the language problem, only 4 Egyptian leaders studied in Germany, while Italy and Austria claimed one each. As far as it is known not a single one of the 131 received a degree from a Soviet institution or even stayed there for prolonged specialized training except official visits. Almost surely this will change in the next decade.

The largest share of higher education was borne by Egyptian universities, especially at the bachelor's and master's level and increasingly at the doctorate. In view of the high cost of foreign education, the increasingly diverse offerings at Egypt's five universities, and the well known reluctance of the foreign-educated to return to Egypt, one can anticipate a sharp decrease in the number of those studying abroad. Despite its obvious benefits, any significant decrease in foreign educational experience will tend to push the country's higher education into intellectual isolation and stagnation. The foreign education of 46 [12] out of the 131 leaders can be taken as an index of their foreign exposure; this will inevitably be reduced as educationally home-grown leaders replace them in future years. The result will be a narrowing of the elite's world view—a development that has already occurred among the officers and officer-technocrats, most of whom are locally educated.

Relationship of Specialization to Cabinet Post

A useful method to determine the importance of educational specialization in the acquisition and fulfillment of leadership roles is to measure the incidence of positive relationships between field of study and type of ministerial post held. In other words, is the minister doing what he was trained for in school. Operationally, certain difficulties arise when certain ministers are placed in charge of several, often unrelated ministries, simultaneously. In such cases unless a positive relationship exists between the leader's educational background and *at least one* of the ministries under his charge, he is not counted in the related category. Admittedly, it is difficult to deal with certain key educational categories, especially law and military science. With the exceptions of Justice and Foreign Affairs, a law degree is considered insufficient training for other posts. As for those with purely military educational backgrounds, a negative relationship is assumed except with respect to the Ministries of War, Interior, and State (security). For example, Kamal al-Din Husayn's military education is considered singularly unfitting for his position as minister of education. [13]

Table 12 indicates a relatively high percentage (68 percent) of ministers holding posts related to their respective educational

Table 12

Educational Specialization—Cabinet Post Relationship: Aggregate Count

	N	%
Ministers holding posts related to specialization	89	67.9
Ministers holding posts not related to specialization	28	21.4
Ministers holding both related and not related posts	14	10.7
Total	131	

specializations. If the same rigorous criteria are used on most U.S. cabinets, it is possible that the American percentage would be somewhat lower than the Egyptian. The unrelated category was swollen to 21.4 percent because of the military; also over 10 percent at different times had held posts both related and unrelated to their educational field.

There have been significant fluctuations over time in the percentages of the related versus unrelated categories, as seen in Table 13. Nagib's first cabinet consisted of highly educated, civilian specialists, who were placed at the head of ministries that correlated highly with their educational expertise; this was more

Table 13

Relationship of Educational Specialization to Ministerial Post

CABINET	RELATED		NOT RELATED		TOTAL
	N	%	N	%	
7 September 1952	11	68.8	5	31.3	16
8 December 1952	13	76.5	4	23.5	17
18 June 1953	14	73.4	5	26.3	19
4 October 1953	13	59.1	9	40.9	22
17 April 1954	12	50	12	50	24 (incl. Amir)
1 September 1954	9	39.1	14	60.9	23
30 June 1956	12	54.5	10	45.5	22
5 March 1958	14	66.7	7	33.3	21
7 October 1958	22	66.7	11	33.3	33
17 August 1961	22	71	9	29	31
19 October 1961	21	72.4	8	27.6	29
29 September 1962	24	66.7	12	33.3	36
24 March 1964	31	70.5	13	29.5	44
2 October 1965	28	68.3	13	31.7	41
10 September 1966	28	73.7	10	26.3	38
19 June 1967	17	58.6	12	41.4	29
20 March 1968	25	75.8	8	24.2	33
28 October 1968	24	77.4	7	22.6	31

so in the December 1952 government where the related group exceeded 76 percent. A slight decline occurred in June 1953, followed by further declines reaching a low of 39 percent in the September 1954 cabinet which reflected the increasing number of military men. This trend was reversed in the 1956 cabinet and a relatively high level of correlation between specialization and type of post was maintained after March 1958. The June 1967 cabinet registered a drop to 58.6 percent from a high of 73.7 percent for the previous cabinet, to a large extent the result of a high military presence. Finally, the reduction in the number of officers and the corresponding increase of civilian specialists in March 1968 brought up the related percentage to 75.8 percent; after the October 1968 reshuffle an unprecedented 77.4 percent was reached indicating a very high correspondence between educational field and ministerial post.

In summary, there existed an inverse relationship between the number of officers in cabinet posts and the degree of correspondence between educational field and type of ministerial office. However, in certain cabinets a low percentage resulted not only from the large number of ex-officers in charge of nonmilitary ministries, but also because the educational backgrounds of certain civilian ministers had little to do with the work of their respective ministries. The latter were appointed because of their political reliability.

Cursus Honorum or Pathways to Power

The determination of the different avenues or paths potential leaders take to reach the top requires systematic data on the career patterns of each individual leader. The crucial starting point for the elites' march to the top is original occupational background. A total of 8 occupational sources are identified on Table 14 and illustrated in the diagrammatical representations, Figures 9, 10, 11, 12, 13, 14, 15, and 16. The largest group is, of course, the military with 44 persons, or 33.6 percent of the entire leadership. Virtually all of these men, including the officer-technocrats, had been associated with the coup of July 1952. Their paths to the cabinet and higher-level posts differed considerably depending on their original positions in the Free Officers movement and their personal relationship with Nasir, to mention two of the more important determinants. With Nagib and Nasir leading the way in 1952 and 1953, eventually 16 of the officers entered the cabinet directly from the armed forces. Most of these were leading members of the Free Officers and the RCC. A second contingent of lesser known officers went from the military into various bureaucracies—ministerial, presidential, provincial, managerial —for the express purpose of establishing the regime's control over them. Of the 17 officers directly entering the bureaucracy, 8 subsequently entered the cabinet without holding intervening posts.

The diplomatic corps possessed a special attraction for the officers; 5 went directly from the military into ambassadorial posts, another reached there after holding a bureaucratic job. While at least 5 officers were deputies at various times before assuming cabinet office, two officers went directly into the National Assembly. Finally, there were those military men whose pathway to power went through the intelligence services. The lack of data on this aspect of political life makes it difficult to differentiate between intelligence activity in the military context and that pursued in the presidential bureaucracy. One suspects that organizationally the two often coincided. Whatever the case, a total of 4 officers were involved in intelligence work as their first jobs, and another 4 served in intelligence at some time prior to entering cabinet positions—a total of 8. There is evidence to indicate that at least 3 of the 8 intelligence men were directly associated with the presidential bureaucracy.

Less visible than the cabinet, the leaders of the party, or the army, the presidential bureaucracy was always a primary center of power in the political system by virtue of its closeness to Nasir himself. Significantly, as a path to cabinet office, the presidential bureaucracy has been used exclusively by those with military backgrounds. As far as can be discerned, not a single civilian's career pattern included the presidential bureaucracy prior to cabinet office. Only 1 civilian—Aziz Sidqi—retired to the presidential bureaucracy in between cabinet offices. Every single one of the 11 who passed through the presidency prior to cabinet office was an ex-officer. Representing 25 percent of the 44 ex-of-

Figure 9. *Career Patterns: Military as Original Occupation*

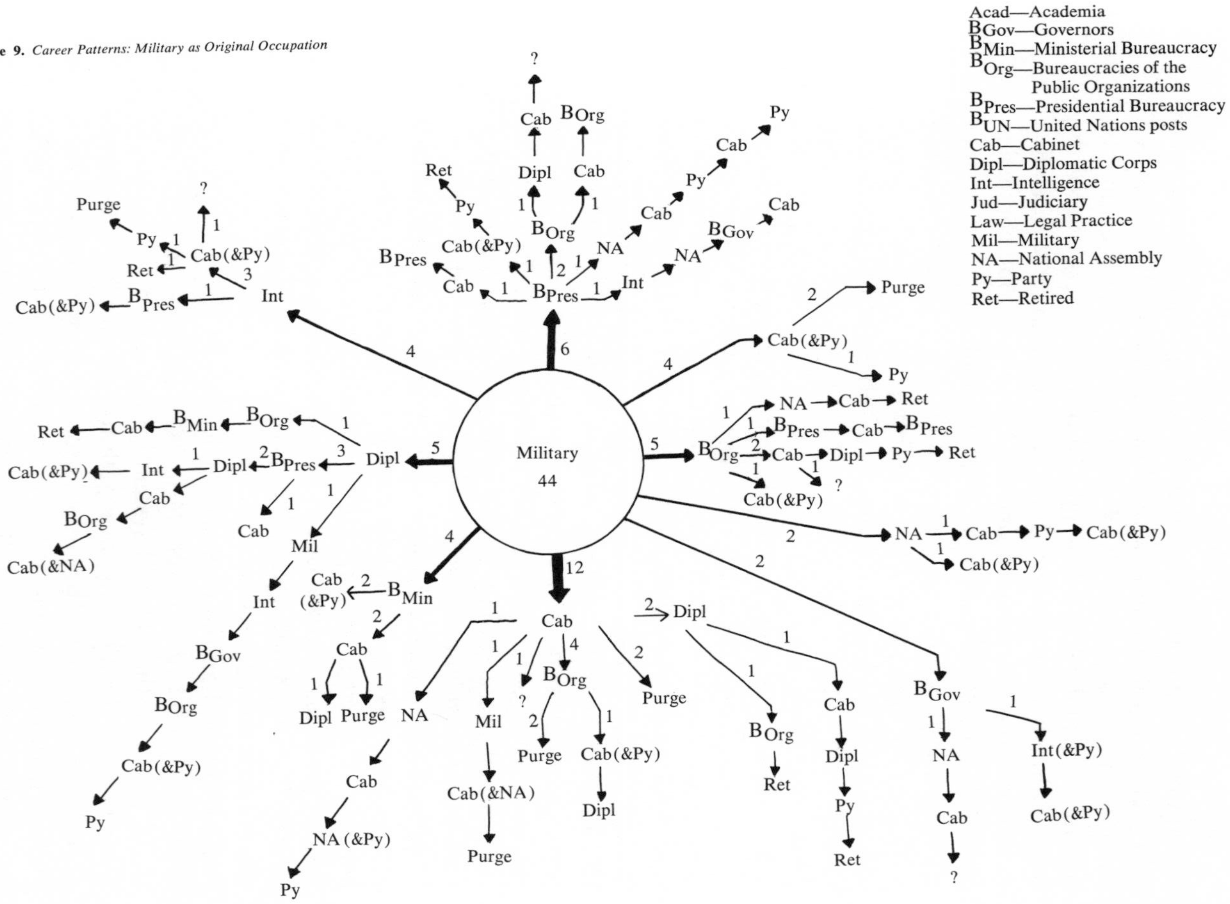
Acad—Academia
BGov—Governors
BMin—Ministerial Bureaucracy
BOrg—Bureaucracies of the Public Organizations
BPres—Presidential Bureaucracy
BUN—United Nations posts
Cab—Cabinet
Dipl—Diplomatic Corps
Int—Intelligence
Jud—Judiciary
Law—Legal Practice
Mil—Military
NA—National Assembly
Py—Party
Ret—Retired
Military
44

Figure 10. *Career Patterns: Academia as Original Occupation*

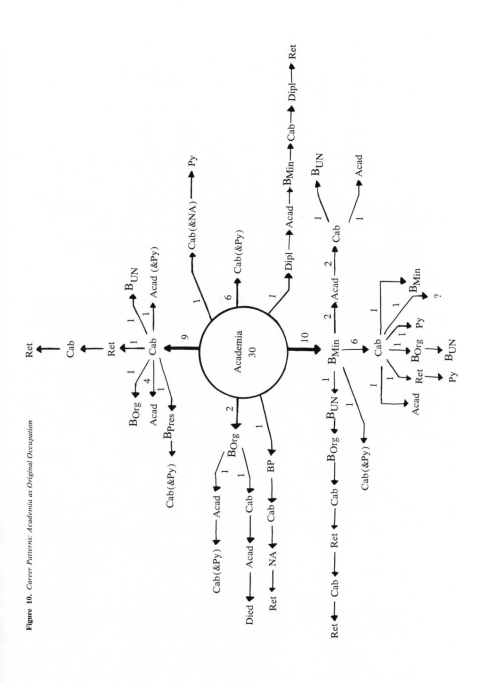

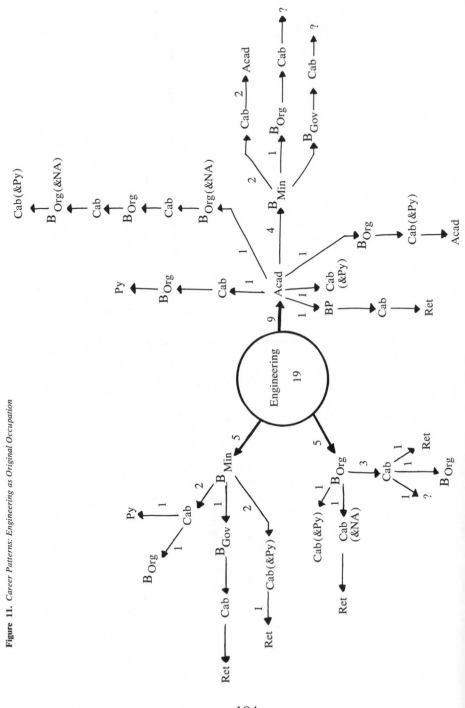

Figure 11. *Career Patterns: Engineering as Original Occupation*

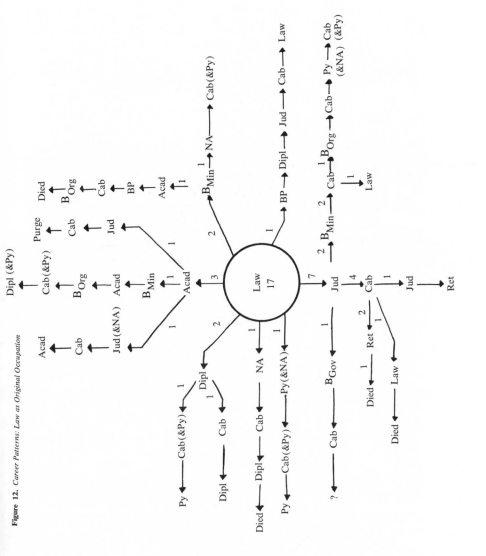

Figure 12. *Career Patterns: Law as Original Occupation*

195

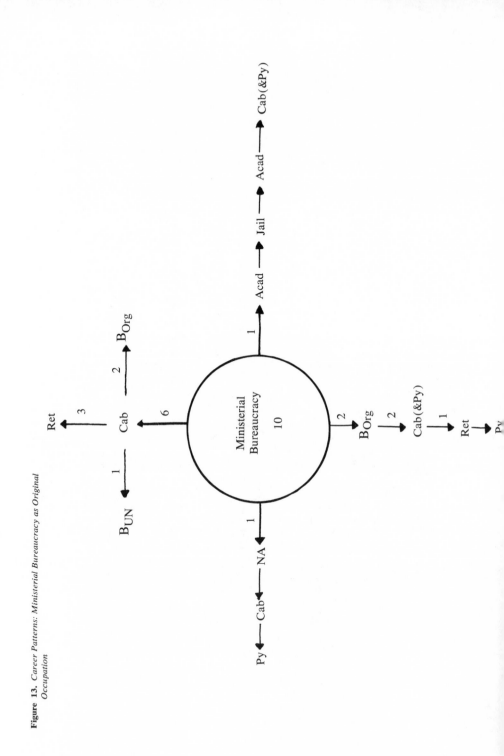

Figure 13. *Career Patterns: Ministerial Bureaucracy as Original Occupation*

196

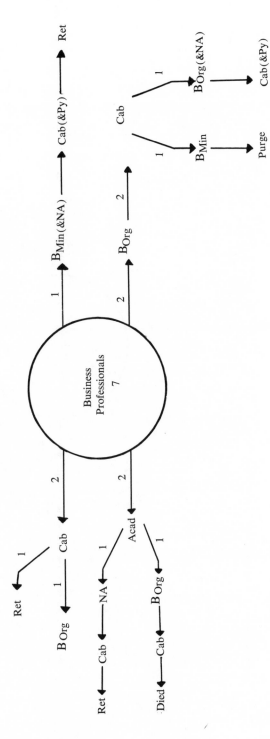

Figure 14. *Career Patterns: Business-Professional as Original Occupation*

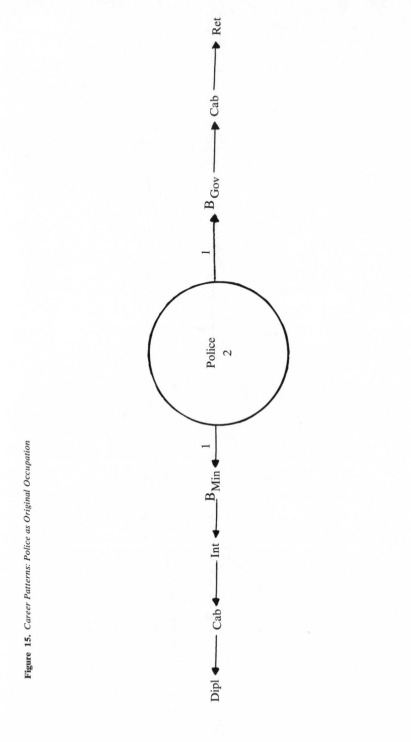

Figure 15. *Career Patterns: Police as Original Occupation*

Dipl ◀——— Cab ◀——— Int ◀——— B Min

Police 2

1 B Gov ——— Cab ——▶ Ret

Figure 16. *Career Patterns: Diplomatic Corps as Original Occupation*

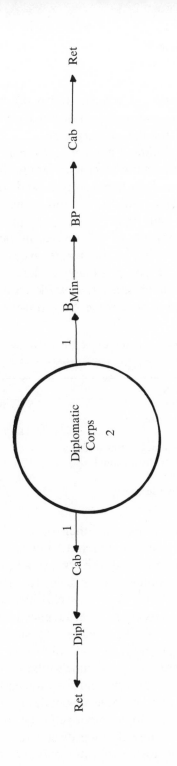

ficers in the cabinet—5 officers and 6 officer-technocrats—the presidential bureaucracy has constituted a main channel of upward movement for the military elite.

In addition to fulfilling control and supervisory functions, the officers in the various bureaucracies familiarized themselves with the administrative skills they sorely lacked. In this sense the bureaucracies provided the RCC and other officers with what J. C. Hurewitz calls their "political apprenticeship" [14] before cabinet office; a total of 23 served in bureaucracies before entering the cabinet, 11 of whom were officer-technocrats. Finally, at least 21 out of 44 officers had been associated with party organization or legislative work (ASU, National Union, and National Assembly), some on a full-time basis.

Table 14

Original Occupational Sources of Recruitment: Aggregate Count

OCCUPATION	N	%
Military	44	33.6
Academia	30	22.9
Engineering	19	14.5
Law	17	13.0
Bureaucracy (Ministerial)	10	7.6
Business-Professional	7	5.3
Police	2	1.5
Diplomatic Corps	2	1.5
	Total 131	

The second largest occupational source of elite recruitment is academia. The classification includes university professors, deans and rectors of colleges and universities, and heads of other top-level academic institutes. Lower-level teachers and military instructors were excluded from this classification.

There were no less than 30 academics constituting 22.9 percent of the total cabinet membership since September 1952. Their numerical position, second only to the military (see Table 14), is one indication of the regime's reliance on competent civilian experts. While relatively scarce in the early years of military rule, the number of recruitable academics greatly increased in the early sixties as a growing number returned from Western institutions of higher learning. Having discovered the potentialities of the academic road to the top, not only was there a rush to acquire Ph.D.s, but also, as Haykal pointed out, "every Ph.D. wanted to enter the cabinet." However, many of the new Ph.D.'s lacked visibility; they could not be recruited unless noticed by the men at the top. As a result, most of the academic recruits came from the upper-reaches of the university hierarchy—rectors, deans, department chairmen, institute heads, and full professors.

Figure 10 shows the different pathways taken by academics to reach the cabinet. Over half (16) went directly into the cabinet from positions in academia. The thirteen remaining took the bureaucratic route; 10 went to the ministerial bureaucracy (B_{Min}), two joined the public sector organisms (B_{Org}), and one became a diplomat.

The third largest source of leaders was the engineering profession (19) representing 14.5 percent of total cabinet members. None of the engineers went directly to the cabinet in contrast to a large portion of the academics. For 10 of them, the first step was either in the ministerial or the public-sector bureaucracies. The remaining 9 entered academia from which only 2 went directly to cabinet; 6 others had to enter the various bureaucracies before acquiring cabinet positions. Thus for 16 of the 19 professional engineers the bureaucracies were stepping stones to the top.

Law constituted the fourth largest category with seventeen members, or 13 percent of the total. As one would expect, a large number (10) served in the judiciary at some point prior to cabinet office (see Figure 11). Others used diplomatic service, party organization, academia, and ministerial bureaucracy, or a combination of these, as stepping stones to the top (see Figure 12). The relative scarcity of lawyers in the total elite reflected the incongruence of the legal profession with a revolutionary culture.

With 10 members (7.6 percent) the ministerial bureaucracy is the fifth largest source of elites. These represent the professional bureaucrats who made their way up the ladder to the undersecretary positions and thence into the cabinet. As the long-time servants of the bureaucratic apparatus, these ministers knew, more than anyone else, the intricacies of bureaucratic life—a type of experience that proved very useful for the ruling officers. Since sixteen of the engineer category entered the bureaucracy prior to the cabinet, and remained there for long periods of time, one may count them as bureaucrats. This would swell the bureaucratic component to 26, or 19 percent of the total (see Figures 11 and 13).

The three remaining occupational recruitment categories are businessman/professionals, the police, and diplomatic personnel, all of which accounted for 8.3 percent of the total leadership. The business/professional group of 7 members consisted of businessmen and physicians mostly active in the early months of the Revolution; although a few remained in power until the late 1950s (see Figure 13). With the advent of socialism, the business community ceased to be a source of leaders.

Overall, the number of leaders going from original occupation directly to cabinet was very high—41 or approximately 30 percent. Of the remaining leaders no less than 67 passed through one or more of the bureaucracies prior to cabinet office. Thus for over 50 percent of the elite, bureaucracy was one of the main occupational gateways to the top.

Table 15 presents a breakdown by cabinet of sources of elite recruitment. The fluctuating proportions of the military found in column 1 are exactly the same as those found in column 4 on Table 4 which shows background characteristics. The descriptive analysis, being the same, will not be repeated here. The ministerial bureaucracy registered a decrease as a source of elites from October 1953 to September 1962 when an upturn took place. As to the business/professional group, after a drop in December 1952, it fluctuated between 1 or 2 members until 1968. The legal profession as a source of elites registered a high of 29.4 percent in December 1952 after which it began a fluctuating decline to an all time low of 2.8 percent in September 1962; there were additional fluctuations after the upturn of March 1964, but the percentage of lawyers remained below 7 percent in recent years. This reinforces earlier conclusions on the general decline of the legal profession in the political system. After a brief appearance from 1962 to 1966 the police category disappears as a source of elites, as does the diplomatic service.

The two categories that showed gains since 1952 were academia and engineering. From 18.8 percent in September 1952, the academic component increased to a high of 23.5 percent by the

Table 15

Original Occupational Sources of Recruitment: Count by Individual Cabinet

CABINET	MILITARY		BUREAUCRACY-MINISTERIAL		BUSINESS-PROFESSIONAL		LAW		ACADEMIA		DIPLOMACY		ENGINEERING		POLICE		TOTAL
	N	%	N	%	N	%	N	%	N	%	N	%	N	%	N	%	
7 September 1952	1	6.3	3	18.8	3	18.8	4	25	3	18.8	2	12.5	—	—	—	—	16
8 December 1952	1	5.9	3	17.7	1	5.9	5	29.4	4	23.5	2	11.8	1	5.9	—	—	17
18 June 1953	5	26.3	2	10.5	1	5.3	5	26.3	3	15.8	1	5.3	2	10.5	—	—	19
4 October 1953	9	40.9	1	4.6	2	9.1	4	18.2	3	13.6	1	4.6	2	9.1	—	—	22
17 April 1954	11	45.8	1	4.2	2	8.3	4	16.7	3	12.5	1	4.2	2	8.3	—	—	24
1 September 1954	12	52.2	1	4.4	1	4.4	4	17.4	2	8.7	1	4.4	2	8.7	—	—	23
30 June 1956	8	36.4	1	4.6	2	9.1	4	18.2	3	13.6	1	4.6	3	13.6	—	—	22
5 March 1958	8	38.1	—	—	2	9.5	3	14.3	4	19.1	1	4.8	3	14.3	—	—	21
7 October 1958	16	48.5	1	3	2	6.1	2	6.1	7	21.2	1	3	4	12.1	—	—	33
17 August 1961	16	51.6	1	3.2	2	6.5	1	3.2	5	16.1	1	3.2	5	16.1	—	—	31
19 October 1961	15	51.6	1	3.5	1	3.5	1	3.5	6	20.7	1	3.5	4	13.8	—	—	29
29 September 1962	17	47.2	3	8.3	2	5.6	1	2.8	7	19.4	1	2.8	4	11.1	1	2.8	36
24 March 1964	16	36.4	2	4.6	2	4.6	3	6.8	10	22.7	1	2.3	9	20.5	1	2.3	44
2 October 1965	19	46.3	2	4.9	1	2.4	2	4.9	7	17.1	1	2.4	8	19.5	1	2.4	41
10 September 1966	21	55.3	2	5.3	1	2.6	2	5.3	3	7.9	1	2.6	7	18.4	1	2.6	38
19 June 1967	19	65.5	—	—	2	6.9	1	3.5	4	13.8	1	3.5	2	6.9	—	—	29
20 March 1968	13	39.4	2	6.1	2	6.1	2	6.1	9	27.3	1	3	4	12.1	—	—	33
28 October 1968	13	41.9	2	6.5	1	3.2	2	6.5	9	29	—	—	4	12.9	—	—	31

end of the year. There were successive declines beginning in October 1953 that reached a low of 8.7 percent in September 1954 as a result of growing military presence in the cabinet. In 1956 the proportion of academics began an upward trend reaching 21.2 percent in October 1958. After several fluctuations, there was a sharp drop in 1965 and an all-time low in the Muhyi al-Din cabinet of September 1966. Since the June War the proportion of academics has successively increased reaching 29 percent, an all-time high, in October 1968.

Engineering as an original source of recruitment showed an increase through 1953 and 1954. This upward trend persisted until March 1958 and after fluctuations an all-time high of 20.5 percent was reached in March 1964. The postwar cabinet of June 1967 brought a sharp drop in the engineering component, although there was a reversal in the 1968 cabinet.

Disposition of Elites

A study of circulation of elites is not complete without an inquiry into their occupational status after political office. An aggregate breakdown of disposition of Egyptian elites after cabinet office is presented in Table 16. Taking December 1968 as cut-off date, 31 of 131 leaders or 23.7 percent of the total were still in cabinet office. Of the rest, the largest group (22), had retired from both cabinet and political office. The second largest group (13) went to the bureaucracies of the various public organizations, usually as chairmen or as other top officials.

Another major depository of the Egyptian ministerial elite was academia. This group numbering 12 ministers had been originally recruited from the universities. The party provided still another repository. However, prior to ASU's 1968 reorganization, the acquisition of a party post after cabinet office constituted a demotion in most cases. In contrast, the party leadership posts in the new ASU, particularly at the Supreme Executive level, are considered more prestigious than cabinet membership. Therefore, while the 5 ministers who retired to party posts before 1968 were

Table 16

*Disposition of Elites after Cabinet Office:
Aggregate Count*

	N	%
Still in Office	31	23.7
Diplomatic Corps	11	8.4
Bureaucracy-United Nations	3	2.3
Bureaucracy-Organizational	13	9.9
Bureaucracy-Ministerial	2	1.6
Bureaucracy-Presidential	2	1.6
Law	3	2.3
Judiciary	1	0.8
Academia	12	9.2
Party	10	7.6
National Assembly	3	2.3
Retired	22	16.8
Purge	7	5.3
Died	1	0.8
Unknown	10	7.6
Total	131	

actually demoted, election to the Supreme Executive for the remaining 5 constituted a major promotion.

The postcabinet status of 10 ministers could not be ascertained. There were 7 clear-cut cases of purge where the cabinet member was known to have fallen out with the leadership and been dismissed from the cabinet. However, the actual number of those purged may have been larger since the real reasons for an individual's retirement were often not made public. Thus, a few placed in the retired category may have actually been purged.

A particularly attractive and desirable postcabinet position was the diplomatic corps where 11 ministers settled. The presidential and the ministerial bureaucracies each claimed 2 ministers and private legal practice claimed another 3. Three others received high posts in the United Nations, 3 became deputies, 1 entered the judiciary, and 1 died soon after leaving the cabinet.

Further analysis of each original occupational category reveals a number of interesting findings. For example, although the military enjoyed many privileges, it suffered the highest number purged—possibly exceeding the 7 indicated on Table 16. In terms of ultimate disposition (Table 17) as of January 1969, at least 9 of the 11 purged were ex-officers. Other postcabinet positions taken by officers included diplomatic corps (4) and party posts (6). Indeed the party possessed a certain attraction for the military generally; at various times during their political career, 21 of the ex-officer ministers had been involved in ASU activity. In addition 9 of the officers at some point were elected as assembly deputies. While 9 of the 30 academics returned to the universities after cabinet office, as far as known, only one officer returned to active military service.

Table 17
Ultimate Disposition of Elites (as of January 1969)

	N	%
Still in Office	31	23.7
Diplomatic Corps	5	3.8
Bureaucracy-United Nations	4	3.1
Bureaucracy-Organizational	9	6.9
Bureaucracy-Ministerial	1	0.8
Bureaucracy-Presidential	2	1.6
Law	2	1.6
Academia	11	8.9
Party	12	9.2
Retired	27	20.6
Purge	11	8.4
Died	6	4.6
Unknown	10	7.6
Total	131	

In terms of ultimate disposition, 27 ministers retired, 12 became party officials, 11 went to academia, 6 died, 5 went into diplomatic service, 2 reverted to law, and a total of 16 were serving in the various bureaucracies (Table 17). The total picture is not one of a political system characterized by a great deal of elite instability as has been the case in other revolutionary situations. In a great many cases outright purge was apparently replaced by demotion to a lesser, though still important post. It seems that unless a cabinet officer directly challanged the leadership, he was guaranteed high level position until retirement. Obviously the net effect of such a policy would be an ongoing circulation of the same leaders in the top echelons of government, party, public enterprises, and academia, thereby restricting the

Table 18
Positions Held Between Cabinet Offices

	FIRST INTER-CABINET POST	SECOND INTER-CABINET POST
National Assembly	1	
National Assembly and Party		1
Party	2	
Diplomatic Corps	1	
Military	1	
Bureaucracy-Organizational	4	
Bureaucracy-Organizational National Assembly	1	
Bureaucracy-Presidential	1	
Retired	2	1

infusion of new blood. While the available data do not indicate a closed system, Haykal's lament on the need for new leadership has considerable relevance.

For the 13 ministers who held cabinet positions more than once, the bureaucracies and the party provided between-cabinet jobs as seen in Table 18. Two others retired between their first and second cabinet jobs, one returned to the military, and another took a diplomatic post. In terms of the number of different cabinet positions held, a large majority (64.4 percent) occupied only a single post. Another 19.1 percent of the total occupied 2 different cabinet posts. As Table 19 shows there were 7 ministers who held as many as 4 different cabinet positions, and 2 individuals

Table 19
Number of Different Ministerial Positions Held

N OF POSTS	N OF OFFICIALS	%
1	87	66.4
2	25	19.1
3	10	7.6
4	7	5.3
5	2	1.5
	Total 131	

that occupied 5 different posts. The last two groups included some of the top RCC members as well as certain of their long-time civilian collaborators.

A total of 13 ministers held ministerial positions more than once as noted above. In terms of original occupation seven of the 13 were ex-officers—another measure of the military's influence in the system. Of the rest, 3 were academics, one an engineer, one a businessman, and the last a lawyer. Finally there was no circulation between the military and the academic group since the officers could teach only in military colleges and not in any of the major universities. On the other hand there was considerable circulation between academia and the bureaucracies; as many as 17 academics had held bureaucratic posts either before or after cabinet office. With respect to the party, 32 percent of the 131 ministers held high posts concurrently with ministerial positions. This indicates the extensive linkage between the top echelons of the old ASU and the government. It also reflects the degree to which the ASU relied on the government before 1968, corroborating some of the criticism in the press.

Regional Affiliation and Religion

The study of regional affiliation—a leader's identification with an area by virtue of residence, occupation, or birth—does not yield any great surprises. As Table 20 indicates about one-third of the 89 leaders on whom data was available came from the Cairo region. Given the traditional centrality of the capital and its dominance in all aspects of Egyptian life, one would expect Cairenes to constitute a large portion of the Egyptian elite. The second largest urban center, Alexandria, accounted for about 10 percent, with Gharbiyyah and Manufiyyah contributing 6.7 percent each. It should be noted that in a highly centralized political system such as Egypt's, regional identification does not play an important role. The utility of the partial data in Table 20 is to illustrate the predominance of Cairo thereby pointing to one of the leadership's concerns—how to limit the number of overeager Cairenes in government and party leadership posts and simulta-

Table 20

Regional Affiliation *

PROVINCE	NUMBER	PERCENTAGE
Alexandria	9	10.1
Assyut	5	5.6
Aswan	1	1.1
Bani Suayf	2	2.3
Buhayrah	2	2.3
Cairo	31	34.8
Daqahliyyah	3	3.4
Dumyat	2	2.3
Fayyum	2	2.3
Gharbiyyah	6	6.7
Giza	2	2.3
Isma'iliyyah	1	1.1
Kafr al-Shaykh	2	2.3
Manufiyyah	6	6.7
Minyah	2	2.3
Port Sa'id	1	1.1
Qalyubiyyah	3	3.4
Red Sea	1	1.1
Sharqiyyah	5	5.6
Sudan	3	3.4
Unknowns	42	
	Total 131	

* Regional affiliation—a general category that denotes an individual's identification with an area by virtue of residence, occupation, and / or birth.

neously prepare provincial leaders to assume a larger share of political responsibility and activity.

As an important political variable, religion applies mainly to the Coptic Christian minority in this predominantly Muslim society. The difficulty of ascertaining the approximate size of the Coptic community in Egypt has been dealt with in Chapter 7. It is safe to assume that the Coptic community is somewhat below 5 million, about one-sixth of the total population. After enjoying a disproportionately large presence in Egyptian political life under the *ancien régime,* the Coptic influence had been significantly reduced by the time of the revolution. Since September 1952 the revolutionary regime has maintained the practice of appointing at least one Coptic minister per cabinet. With the institution of multi-level cabinets after March 1964, two additional Coptic members were brought in as deputy ministers (see Table 4). This practice continued until the June 1967 cabinet. In the postwar period the government has attempted to strengthen the Copts' sense of identification with the regime as a part of its program to broaden the national consensus during a time of external peril. It is also possible that the government's more amicable attitude was partly prompted by the desire to acquire world Christian support against Israel. Two manifestations of the renewed official attention given to the Copts were the prominent role assumed by the regime in the building and consecration ceremonies of the new Saint Mark's Cathedral in mid-1968 and the favorable press-coverage of the apparition of Virgin Mary in the same year. At the leadership level, the Coptic ex-minister, Dr. Kamal Ramzi Stinu, was elected as one of the 8 members of the ASU Supreme Executive Committee, Egypt's most august political body.

Ideology and Socio-Economic Background

The study of ideological identification among cabinet and higher-level Egyptian leaders presents a number of major difficulties. These are due to the ideological changes instituted by the regime as well as the paucity of information on the ideological orientations of a considerable number of leaders. At the most general level the primary commitment among the officers and their civilian supporters was Egyptian nationalism. More specifically it was possible to identify leftist and rightist tendencies among the elite some of whom had had close association with the Brethren, the Wafd, the left, Misr al-Fatat, or the Ruwwad. Due to the post-1952 power struggles and the emergence of Nasir, official identification with any of the above groups and ideologies was rejected in favor of commitment to Egyptian nationalism and after 1955 to Pan-Arabism. As a result, those sympathizing with the outlawed political groups and their ideologies were either purged or reoriented themselves in keeping with the new political line. With the leftward evolution of the system in the late fifties and the official adoption of socialism in 1961, the elite ostensibly identified itself with the new ideological framework. There was no way of knowing the extent of each leader's commitment to the new faith. The techniques here utilized to discern ideological orientation of individual elites were content analyses of their pronouncements, the study of bits of circumstantial evidence derived from their policies, and press commentaries.[15] One of the main shortcomings of this approach was that a large number of leaders had made few ideologically oriented pronouncements. Hence, this contingent was labelled "tacit leftist." While operating within the general limits of the official ideology, these men simply did not manifest strong leftist or rightist doctrinal views.

After the suppression of the Brethren and the rest of the Egyptian political right, only the center and left-of-center range of the ideological spectrum remained operational. Therefore, beginning with the sixties, the right-of-center was not a useful category, since by definition there could be no right. The common identification of ex-Premier Muhyi al-Din as a rightist in the Western press is incorrect. In the present context he is labeled a "conservative-leftist" as are others who are noted for advocating a conservative to moderate and flexible approach to socialism internally, coupled with a generally more accommodating attitude toward the West. Nonetheless, it should be stressed that none of the leaders belonging to this category are likely to abandon socialism or to reduce significantly Egyptian militancy toward Israel.

The third ideological grouping one may label "vocal leftists." These are reputed to be more doctrinaire socialists; at the rhetorical level they use a heavy dose of socialist terminology. To be sure they are less evident in the cabinet than in the ASU and the press. It should be noted that being vocal in socialist jargon does not automatically mean a deep commitment to socialist ideology. Also, it is quite possible that some committed leftists exist in the large tacit left grouping, but it is difficult to identify them positively because they have refrained from making ideological pronouncements.

Since by definition the foregoing ideological classification applies only to cabinet leaders since the breakup of the UAR, a total of 94 leaders are subject to categorization. Of these, 70 were found to belong to the tacit left; another 16 were conservative leftists and 8 vocal leftists. Therefore, the tacit left is by far the largest category; it includes many of the officer-technocrats, engineers, and professionals. The 2 to 1 numerical strength of the conservative left over the vocal left may be considered a valid index of relative leftist weakness in the cabinet. Indeed, the real centers of leftist power have always been the ASU, the press, and to a certain extent the universities.

In terms of both definition and collection of data, the study of socioeconomic backgrounds of leaders presents major difficulties, especially in the Egyptian context. The notion of middle-class predominance in the elite may be somewhat exaggerated. To be sure, certain of the leaders came from families who could be classified as upper or upper-middle class by virtue of their wealth and social prestige. A well-known example is the family of the late Field Marshal Amir, which in terms of wealth (landowners) and prestige could not possibly be labeled as middle class. At the other extreme were a small number of leaders who came from poor rural and urban families. Needless to say, the whole question of socio-economic background as it relates to Egypt needs thorough reexamination and reformulation. Once this task has been accomplished, extensive field research must be undertaken to gather detailed socio-economic data. Neither of these has been attempted in the present study. What is presented here are some tentative conclusions based on incomplete data.

Approximately 42 of the 131 leaders came from upper/ upper-middle class families; 60 had middle-class backgrounds, and eight came from lower-class origins. The socio-economic backgrounds of 21 leaders could not be determined.

A great deal has been written about the rural middle-class background of the Egyptian military; of particular note are the studies of Eliezer Beeri [16] and Leonard Binder.[17] However, the real socio-political significance of the military's rural middle-class connection remains somewhat obscure. The relevant question in the present context is whether class loyalties persist among the top leadership, especially the ex-officers. Often one is given the impression by Egyptians that the rural connection (*umdah* class) has greatly withered and is not very significant politically. The type of attitudinal research necessary to shed light on these problems cannot be conducted in the foreseeable future because of the existing conditions in Egypt.

Political Opportunity

On the basis of the foregoing analysis, one may identify a number of prerequisite conditions or operating standards for admission into the political elite. First, political opportunity depends on the frequency with which cabinet positions become vacant. In contrast to the United States, where cabinet positions are usually (but not exclusively) filled every four or eight years, the Egyptian system shows no such regularity. Instead, cabinet changes or reshuffles have coincided with internal or external developments, e.g., the Nagib-Nasir contest, the formation and dissolution of the UAR, economic problems, the June War, internal instability (student riot of February 1968). But the lack of regularity of turnover has not appreciably reduced the frequency of vacancies in the past. However, since changeover has mostly depended on the occurrence of instability and crisis, the frequency of availability of future cabinet positions may also depend on these factors. In other words during future periods of general stability opportunities to enter the cabinet may actually decline and vice versa.

The other factor that affects opportunity is size of the cabinet. In the Egyptian case, cabinet size grew from 16 members to 24, between September 1952 and April 1954. In the next four years it declined to 21, but the second UAR cabinet reached a high of 33. The March 1964 multi-level cabinet of 44 members marked the peak in cabinet size; since then, the size has decreased due to successive reorganization schemes. In the last two years, cabinet size has not varied greatly; it has remained around 30 (see Table 4). It is not likely to become much smaller.

The Egyptian cabinet can be considered relatively large, especially when compared with British postwar cabinets of 16 to 18 members, the American cabinet of 12 members, or Lebanese cabinets which at times comprised as few as 4 members. Clearly, one effect of large size is to increase opportunity to serve at the top. Size, combined with the frequency of cabinet changes, has been responsible for the relatively large number of men who served in cabinet and higher level positions in Egypt since September, 1952. Momentarily disregarding the different positions that cabinets hold in different countries, the political opportunity-probability to serve in a cabinet position will tend to be higher in Egypt than in the United States or Lebanon, for example. Since 1952, 131 individuals have held cabinet posts; in the same period, the total number of individuals in American cabinets was less than a third of that number, while in Lebanon it was slightly over 100.

A cluster of other factors affect the political opportunity of aspiring individuals. These involve certain social, economic, and political prerequisites that determine the eligiblity of an individual for high office. In Egypt, as in all political systems, political reliability constitutes the most important prerequisite for cabinet appointment. Above all, political reliability meant loyalty to the person of Nasir and firm adherence to the goals of the revolution as delimited by the leader. For civilian aspirants, the lack of political-ideological coloration has usually been a requisite. In the fifties, most civilians recruited were specialists, not politicians. The few who were politicians before the revolution—Tarraf, F. Rudwan—soon became manifestly unpolitical as servants of the new order. The practice of recruiting apolitical civilian experts was maintained in the 1960s. More recently, in addition to political reliability and expertise, certain other political considerations may be emerging. One of these is the cabinet member's political role as the representative of various interest groups—economic, functional, religious, social. This has applied to the Coptic members of the elite since pre-revolutionary days. The similar role of the ex-officer ministers with respect to the military establishment has been elucidated in other chapters. No less important is the emerging role of popular professors in the cabinet, with respect to the increasingly restive student constituency. It appears that a primary determinant in Nasir's selection of several prominent professors in his March 1968 cabinet was the wide respect and support that these men commanded among the students. Other constituency-determined appointments may include the ministers of agriculture (S. Mar'i) and labor (A. Salamah; K. Rif'at). While he may have been given a cabinet post by virtue of being an ex-Free Officer, Rif'at's appointment as minister of labor may also have been prompted by his close association with workers.

Also to be considered are the socio-economic standards for eligibility. Though most individuals of the landowning and capitalist-entrepreneurial classes have been excluded since the early sixties, wealth did not constitute an impediment to high office in certain cases (Amir, Zaki). Nevertheless, considering the current drift of the political system, one would expect most future recruits to come from the middle class and perhaps from the activist elements of urban and rural lower-middle classes—i.e., peasants and workers. Similarly, in view of the changes since June 1967, previous membership in the military, even as an ex-Free Officer, may not be a determining factor of eligibility, as was the case previously. If the recent civilianization continues, and barring an army coup, military background may even become a hindrance for recruitment to cabinet-level positions.

A number of new standards controlling admission to the top leadership may be emerging. Given the existing cleavages in the ASU, ideological balance will probably play a greater role in cabinet recruitment. If the political system continues to evolve leftward, the operating standards controlling admission will have to include a firmer socialistic commitment among the new aspirants. Also, with the aging of the present leaders and the ferment among the students, youth may become a future requisite for eligibility. Furthermore, if the ASU successfully entrenches itself, an individual's service in the party bureaucracy may emerge as yet another determinant for admission to the cabinet.

Political Cost

Political cost refers to the rewards and deprivations that accompany entry to and exit from cabinet positions. Political cost is intimately tied to the value system of the society under study. It follows that cross-national analysis would have to consider the value differences of the societies being compared. In order to evaluate political cost comparatively, one needs information on such social, economic, and political variables as income, social prestige, political power, and personal risk as they relate to the particular political system. For example, in the American milieu, the acquisition or loss of a cabinet position gives one a set of rewards and deprivations that are quite different from those experienced in Egypt. Thus, in the United States, a cabinet position often means a considerable loss of income (McNamara, Connally, Hickel, Dillon). In contrast, cabinet office in Egypt usually means a higher income since most cabinet officials usually come from lower salaried positions. While a cabinet-level salary would not make an Egyptian affluent in the American sense (unless he accepts graft), it is more than sufficient to give him a comfortable livelihood. Conversely, a demotion from the cabinet would certainly mean a loss of income in Egypt; a loss of such office in the United States often results in a large net income gain from lucrative nongovernmental positions. In both countries, a cabinet position is tantamount to great social prestige, probably more so in Egypt than in the United States. Unless expressly fired, an American secretary's loss of office is not nearly so serious a blow to prestige as it can be in Egypt, except for those Egyptians retiring because of age. It appears that the only way for a minister to leave the cabinet without losing prestige would be election to ASU's Supreme Executive; indeed, this would produce a net gain.

The comparative analysis of ministerial power in Nasirite Egypt can focus on two related dimensions: decision-making and influence. Considering Nasir's personal power and propensity to intervene in the decision-making process, the typical Egyptian cabinet officer was given a smaller decisional role than his American counterpart, especially under such a passive president as Eisenhower. On the other hand, given the nature of political power in a semi-traditional society like Egypt, the influence of ministers on their subordinates in the bureaucracy has been infinitely greater than that of the Americans'. In simpler terms, an Egyptian minister may deal more arbitrarily with subordinates than an American secretary is able to do.

Finally, political cost involves an element of personal and/or political risk, especially in the event of loss of power. In contrast to the United States where cabinet officials can easily move into a variety of nongovernmental positions outside the state's influence, this cannot be done in Egypt where the elite's power is far more pervasive. The contrast is even greater for those purged for policy opposition to their respective leaders. In the United States, such opposition may bring dismissal or resignation; in certain cases, a politically vulnerable president may even tolerate a recalcitrant cabinet member (e.g., Harry Truman vs. Louis Johnson). In Egypt, any explicit opposition usually results in purging of the official concerned—a process that entails high political as well as personal risks. Not only is political opportunity reduced to zero, but the person may also find himself under detention. The only known case of continuous partial opposition to the leader is that of Marshal Amir until his dismissal after the June War and his subsequent house arrest and death.

The Atrophy of the Core

Since 1953, there has been a gradual weakening of the military group which was the backbone of the revolution. In view of their cental importance in the system, the core of revolutionary officers that organized the 1952 coup—the Free Officers Executive that transformed itself into the RCC—should be a primary focus of analysis. As indicated in Chapter 3, from July 1952 to April 1954 the Free Officers group experienced only moderate turnover in its membership. On the eve of the coup, the core of eleven or twelve officers under Abd al-Nasir had enlarged itself to include a number of key anti-status-quo officers like General Nagib. After the coup, this larger body of about eighteen officers reconstituted itself as the Revolutionary Command Council. It is significant that during the ensuing struggles for power, the RCC members ejected (except Khalid Muhyi al-Din) were late-comers to the inner core. The top officers remaining in power after the fall of Nagib were substantially the same persons that belonged to Abd al-Nasir's inner circle before the July 1952 coup d'etat. After the mid-fifties, two additional members of the original core —the Salim brothers—were ejected. In subsequent years the remaining eight leaders continued to occupy positions of great prominence in the governmental structure, along with a group of revolutionary officers who had newly risen to the top. It was not until March 1964 that two more inner core members were cashiered from the government. This expulsion of two of the foremost personalities of the revolution—Abd al-Latif al-Baghdadi and Kamal al-Din Husayn—has been shrouded in mystery. Some attribute their purge to policy differences over the Yemeni War and personality clashes with Abd al-Nasir. In Baghdadi's case serious illness also may have been a factor, however, it is known that Husayn had reacted angrily to what he considered a narrowing of his scope of action within the government. In addition to possible ideological or policy conflicts, the estrangement of some of his fellow revolutionaries from Nasir can be explained in terms of charisma. In the precharismatic stage often the leader is regarded as *primus inter pares*—first among equals—a situation that existed in the RCC before the coup and up to 1955. However, once the revolution is accomplished and the leader begins to acquire personal charisma through heroic performance and ideological propagation, his position vis-à-vis his former colleagues will invariably undergo a profound change. Indeed, as the charismatic symbol of the revolution, he is propelled into a position far above his former companions. In more practical terms, the leader does not need his former associates anymore in view of his new sources of mass support. As a result, a totally new relationship develops between the leader and his former associates. If the latter are unable to adjust to the leader's newly acquired charismatic position, they become estranged.

By March 1964 only seven of the original core of Free Officers were still active at the highest levels of leadership. These were Gamal Abd al-Nasir, Abd al-Hakim Amir, Zakariyya Muhyi al-Din, Kamal al-Din Rif'at, Husayn al-Shafi'i, Anwar al-Sadat, and Hasan Ibrahim.

During the mid-1960s, three additional members departed. Ibrahim became an ambassador to Czechoslovakia; Marshal Amir was dismissed after the June War and subsequently died; and Zakariyya Muhyi al-Din, the heir-apparent after 9 June 1967, was retired in March 1968 due to reported policy disagreements with the president. Of the remaining four, Rif'at became minister of labor while Shafi'i and Sadat were elected to the ASU Supreme Executive along with Nasir himself.

It should be remembered that the takeover of July 1952 was not solely the work of the core group; a large number of second-string officers were involved, many of whom were purged during the power struggles of 1953 and 1954. Those among them who had joined the Nasirite faction continued to play important roles in the intelligence services, the bureaucracy, and related fields. It was not until the late 1950s that some of these second-level Free Officers surfaced to positions of visibility in the cabinet. Led by Ali Sabri in 1957, six other ex-officers appeared in cabinet positions in 1958: Tawfiq Abd al-Fattah, Abbas Rudwan, Fathi Rizq, Husayn Zu al-Fiqar Sabri, Sarwat Ukasha, and Muhammad Nassar. Five others became cabinet ministers in the early 1960s: Abd al-Qadir Hatim, Ahmad Tu'aymah, Abd al-Muhsin Abu al-Nur, Tal'at Khayri, Sidqi Sulayman. In the mid-1960s, and up to the 1967 war, another large contingent of former revolutionary officers rose to the top, including Mahmud Riyad, Amin Huwaydi, Sha'rawi Guma'a, Nur al-Din Qurra, Ahmad Hamdi Ubayd, Mahmud Yunis, Muhammad Fa'iq, and Amin Shakir. In addition, there were a number of ex-officer cabinet members who may have been involved with the 1952 takeover, including Samir Hilmi, Salah Hidayat, Kamal Abadir, Ahmad Tawfiq al-Bakri, Abd al-Wahhab al-Bishri, and Hamdi Ashur. More than a score of others have remained in various governmental positions without achieving cabinet level office.

Composition of the Bureaucracy

While it is difficult to attempt a thorough study of the Egyptian bureaucracy without the benefit of field work, it is possible to assess the extent of military permeation in the bureaucracy during the early sixties.

The highest rank below the cabinet level [18] is that of undersecretary. There were approximately 137 persons who held this rank in the bureaucracy in the mid-sixties. In an officer-versus-civilian breakdown, the available evidence indicates that with few exceptions the positions of undersecretary were staffed overwhelmingly by civilians. In 1964, out of 137 undersecretaries no more than thirteen were officers, five of which held the active military rank of general officer.[19] This glaring paucity of active or ex-officers at the undersecretary level is not surprising considering the high degree of bureaucratic or technical expertise required in these key positions.

While no current figures are available about the composition of

Table 21

Distribution of Bureaucrats with Military Education *

MINISTRY OR AGENCY	TOTAL	MILITARY	
		N	%
Presidency of the Republic	65	13	20.00
National Assembly	63	–	–
Ministry of Treasury	3,163	1	.03
Ministry of Economy	838	2	.24
Ministry of Industry	688	1	.15
Ministry of Education	18,328	10	.05
Ministry of Interior	4,114	3,446	83.76
Ministry of Health	3,034	1	.03
Ministry of Housing and Utilities	1,051	–	–
Ministry of Justice	3,408	3	.07
Ministry of Public Works	1,818	–	–
Ministry of Agriculture	2,597	1	.04
Ministry of Agrarian Reform	88	–	–
Ministry of Transport	236	–	–
Ministry of Social Affairs and Employment	1,379	1	.07
Ministry of Supply	741	3	.40
Ministry of Culture and National Guidance	262	4	1.52
Ministry of Waqfs	625	–	–
Ministry of Local Affairs and Administration	1,944	37	1.90
Ministry of Foreign Affairs	698	65	9.31
Ministry of War	1,010	2	.20
Ministry of Higher Education	1,398	6	.42
Ministry of Planning	110	1	.90
Ministry of the High Dam	210	3	1.43
Other Agencies	9,898	114	1.15
	57,766	3,714	

* The left column represents the total number of persons with Baccalaureate degrees: the military degrees are considered Baccalaureates.

ranks below undersecretary, a 1962 government publication gives some illuminating statistics on the bureaucracy as of 1 November 1961.[20] Table 21 is a compilation of figures extracted from the above publication showing the distribution of individuals with officers' degrees within the various ministries and agencies at the level of undersecretary and below.

The most revealing statistic appearing above is what appears to be a massive military presence in the Interior Ministry. Out of a total 4,114 positions, 3,446 were held by officials who possessed a military baccalaureate. While this high proportion may indicate the regime's traditional interest in the Ministry of the Interior, not all of these holding military degrees were officers in the armed forces. It is quite possible that a large proportion possessed degrees from the Police Academy which was subsumed under the general category of military specialization.

The data further indicate that aside from the Interior Ministry the extent of the military's total presence in the bureaucracy may be less than commonly thought. This becomes apparent when the Interior Ministry figure (3,446) is subtracted from the total number of personnel with military degrees (3,714). The remaining 268 officers held positions in other ministries; and even these officers were not evenly distributed among the various ministries and agencies. Persons with military educational backgrounds were totally absent from the National Assembly staff and the Ministries of Housing and Utilities, Public Works, Agrarian Reform, Transport, and Waqfs. On the other hand it is significant to note that a disproportionately large group of ex-officers could be found in the Ministry of Local Affairs and Administration (1.9 percent) and the Ministry of Foreign Affairs (9.3 percent). In the Ministry of Local Affairs, the high officer count may be explained by the regime's desire to keep a close check on local developments, particularly in the provinces. The high percentage of military men in the Ministry of Foreign Affairs may reflect the regime's desire to reward loyal ex-officers with diplomatic posts and the well-known preference of certain ex-officers for "flashy" positions in the diplomatic services.

The officer-versus-civilian analysis may be meaningfully applied to several other key elite groups—the presidency, governorates, banks, universities, and the General Organizations.

Table 22

Miscellaneous Agencies—December 1964

	OFFICERS		CIVILIANS	
	N	%	N	%
The Presidency	11	45.83	13	54.16
Governors of the 26 Governorates	22	84.61	4	15.38
The General Organizations (11 in number)	6	16.21	31	83.78
Banks	1	10.00	9	90.00
Rectors and Vice-Rectors of Universities	–	—	19	100.00

The presence of a large number of ex-officers in the presidency—the entourage of an ex-officer president—is not surprising. One should note that the figure (11) for 1964 given in Table 22 does not vary greatly from the 1961 figure (13) of ex-officers working in the presidency found in Table 21. A more revealing statistic from the point of view of internal control is the overwhelming number of officers holding the position of governor. Out of twenty-six governors, twenty-two (84.6 percent) were active or retired security officers, nine with the rank of general.

The eleven General Organizations which functionally correspond to the government ministries are headed by about three dozen executives, who represent the top rank of Egypt's managerial class. The civilian predominance in this area (83.7 percent) as well as in the bank directorships (90 percent) can be attributed to the highly specialized training that managerial positions required—a qualification that was generally lacking to military officers.

Elite Unity and Disunity

The induction of a large number of civilians into the leadership points to the possible emergence of a new salaried "middle class" of modernizing elites in Egypt—as is the case in other developing states.[21] But the notion that these new elites are joined together by education and skills is not always true in Egypt. Furthermore, the assumption of some scholars that the new men are ideologically uncommitted, appears to be mistaken, at least for the time being. Indeed, beyond their self-image as "modern men," their commitment to rapid modernization, and their loyalty to Nasir, there existed few common bonds to unify the emerging new class.

Beginning in the early 1960s, there appeared unmistakable tendencies among the Egyptian elite to split along several lines. The events since June 1967 have confirmed the existence of these cleavages. First, there was the disunity among the remaining members of the Free Officers core of which the hidden Nasir-Amir controversy represented one aspect. This controversy was also symptomatic of division within the military establishment itself.

During the same period, there were growing signs of ideological cleavage among the elite, also confirmed by the controversies in the war's aftermath. In mid-1965, the ideological split was exemplified by the rivalry between Ali Sabri and Zakariyya Muhyi al-Din, as well as by Nasir's repeated mention of the role of "communists" in Egypt.[22] As indicated in Chapter 13, ideological differences have sharpened since the 1967 War.

Another potentially serious cleavage may be developing between ex-officers and civilian leaders. The growing number of civilians in the leadership constitutes a potential source of conflict. As the country develops industrially and politically, the regime inescapably and increasingly will have to depend on highly trained engineers, scientists, educators, and the like, whose administrative-technical expertise is greatly superior to the junior-college-level education of the officer class.[23] It is conceivable that in time this rapidly growing sector of the so-called middle class may challenge the predominant position of the officer class by virtue of its superior training and importance. Its members may resent the supervision of the less competent military and not only demand additional key posts in the power structure but also a larger voice in policy formulation.

Finally there is already a perceivable bifurcation within the civilian sector of this middle class. This may happen between in-groups and out-groups, as in the case of college professors and engineers who want to acquire high governmental positions, and/or between differing ideological factions. More crucial may be the alienation of the lower, less affluent levels of the middle class whose material and prestige expectations are often unfulfilled.

12
The Political System Under Stress (1965–1967)

THE origins of some of the complex problems confronting the Egyptian political system in the seventies can be found in the last decade of Nasirite rule. Among the difficulties is a rapidly expanding population in a country of very scarce resources, a large portion of which are channelled into unproductive enterprises such as maintaining a large military establishment. In addition there are the psychological, political, and economic burdens resulting from defeat in the June War. In another respect the regime has generated some of its own problems. As a modernizing elite that rules in the name of progress, the regime consciously pursues widespread socialization thereby widening the modern or "expectant" sector of the population. To maintain stability the expectations of this growing sector must be met. Essentially, this would be an economic rather than a political problem if there existed an abundance of resources. Under conditions of scarcity, however, as is the case in developing countries, it is plain that these expectations cannot be fulfilled in the near future and hence the need for politics. Thus, the problem confronting the political system is how to meet a minimum of popular demands and at the same time preserve stability by absorbing inevitable conflicts resulting from the socializational changes brought about by modernization. In this sense, the true measure of a political system is its absorptive capacity—its ability to resolve, neutralize, delay, and re-channel conflicts which are generated by the modernization process. The key mechanisms of conflict resolution include the establishment of reasonably efficient institutional frameworks capable of regulating conflicts and providing services, and the development of ideology to uphold the laws and regulations of these institutions.[1]

The absorptive capacity of the Egyptian political system since 1952 has been impressive in certain respects and less impressive in others. It is beyond doubt that during the past eighteen years the Egyptian regime has achieved a degree of internal legitimacy and stability uncommon in the world of developing nations. The supreme test of this came in June 1967. While the political system was unable to win a military victory, it was strong enough in terms of legitimacy and control to sustain itself, despite the enormity of defeat.

The dynamic factors responsible for the high degree of stability include the internal cohesion of the Free Officers group and the military, the systematic neutralization of competing elites, the legitimizing role of charismatic authority, the solidifying effect of foreign confrontations, the adoption and implementation of ideology, and the partial routinization of charisma. To be sure, these stabilizing features were not always introduced effectively and systematically. What is distinctive about the Egyptian political system is that they occurred at all in such a short time.

In the early years of the revolution the main mechanism of conflict resolution was systematic suppression, especially when the military was faced with a clear challenge to its position. It is to the credit of the military elite that this liquidation process was far less bloody than in other revolutionary systems. Yet after the final deposing of General Nagib and the suppression of the political groups, the military officers failed to proceed with the task of rapid internal transformation. The military continued to use the largely outmoded value system of Egyptian nationalism without making the slightest attempt to develop supplementary ideologies for internal change. Similarly, almost no institutional-organizational frameworks were set up for conflict resolution. Instead, the military's predisposition, no less than external events, produced a shift in the revolutionary dynamic from internal affairs to foreign politics—a development that had two significant consequences for the system. Because of his phenomenal success in foreign politics Abd al-Nasir acquired great popularity in Egypt and the Arab world which in turn prompted him to subscribe to the nationalist ideology of Pan-Arabism. The momentous adoption and successful propagation of this new value system by a popular leader introduced the charismatic element into what had been a military dictatorship.

One of the most crucial points stressed in this study is that after the mid-1950s the elite's position of power was sustained not by force (army) alone, but also by charismatic legitimacy; and to that extent the purely military nature of the system had been diluted. The combination of charismatic-military rule was so stable that the leadership felt little need for additional institutional props. The regime's externally focussed charismatic character tended to obscure the need for the ideological and institutional changes necessary for rapid modernization. The half-hearted attempt to create the National Union, an instrument of conflict resolution without a firm ideological base, demonstrated the elite's initial insensitivity to the inherent needs of the modernization process.

Therefore, it is no mere accident that serious attempts at comprehensive societal transformation and the routinization of charisma in various institutions and practices came after the Syrian secession. The inevitable erosion of charisma from external reverses (Syria, Yemen) increased the need for creating supplementary internal props. It is to be noted that each successive reverse since October 1961 intensified Abd al-Nasir's efforts to inject charismatic legitimacy into various political organizations. In retrospect, it is possible to state that the routinization of charisma —the implementation of a crystallized ideology and the development of organizational structures—was delayed by half a decade. Had the leader seriously pursued the work of routinization at the very zenith of the charismatic process—from 1957 to 1961—the chances for the success of his ideological and institutional schemes perhaps would have been greater.

A Time of Troubles

A number of interrelated and complex problems successively converged upon Egypt beginning in mid-1965 culminating in her defeat in June 1967. These included internal problems centering on the Brotherhood, Egypt's military involvement in the Yemen, and the general deterioration of the economy.

During August and September in 1965 reports of internal disturbances filtering out of Egypt were subsequently acknowledged by President Abd al-Nasir during his visit to the Soviet Union. The Egyptian press had put the blame squarely on the Brotherhood which was accused of plotting to assassinate many top political leaders and other personalities.[2] While it is reasonable to assume the complicity of this organization in creating disturbances in Dumyat and Cairo, almost certainly there existed other deep-seated causes that produced instability. Among the political causes was Nasir's inability to replenish his charismatic image by new military and diplomatic victories. The first venture of Egyptian arms since 1956 had proved to be an inglorious undertaking against the guerrilla forces of the Yemeni royalists. After almost three years of fighting, a clear-cut military victory had been denied to an army still suffering from an inferiority engendered by the lack of a military tradition and two successive defeats by Israel. Thus, Abd al-Nasir's reluctant trip to Saudi Arabia to end the hostilities could be regarded as an indication of growing popular discontent in Egypt resulting from the great human and economic sacrifices in the Yemen.

More critical perhaps were the serious food shortages that plagued the country during 1964-1965, which were compounded when the U.S. discontinued wheat shipments during 1966. As to the economy in general, the application of socialist laws, bureaucratic bungling, and the lack of development capital produced breakdowns in a number of enterprises. The serious lag in the economy was corroborated by the government's admission that the first five-year plan ending in June 1965 had been 33 percent short of its production goals.[3] Leadership and policy changes instituted early in October 1965 were in response to the deteriorating economic-political situation.

The three general tasks given to Prime Minister Zakariyya Muhyi al-Din's new government were precisely those in which the outgoing cabinet of Ali Sabri had failed—the rejuvenation of the lagging economy and amelioration of shortages, the strengthening of internal security, and the streamlining of the administrative machinery.[4] The new prime minister's words and deeds during October were sufficiently indicative of future ideological, political, and economic trends. After promising quick action on all three fronts, the prime minister asked for "further sacrifices" from the Egyptian people. While indicating his government's willingness to provide more consumer goods, he also pointed to the tremendous difficulty of coping with the needs of a growing population. More significantly, the relative absence of references to socialist dogma and his promise "to let the laws of supply and demand operate" pointed to a general relaxation of detailed planning and tight centralized control.[5] These, coupled with Muhyi al-Din's explicit invitation to Western firms to provide development capital for various enterprises, seemed to herald the beginning of a new period in which Egypt would avoid external confrontations in exchange for maximum European and American economic aid.

However, in no sense were the new policies to be understood as the end of socialist ideology and concomitant etatist practices in Egyptian society. In view of the regime's ideological commitment to socialism and etatistic controls, any major regressive step would automatically weaken its near monopoly of economic power and therefore hasten its demise. Similarly, the elite's strategically and ideologically motivated opposition to Israel excluded the possibility of long-term economic ties with the United States. The new policies constituted a reluctant but temporary step backward that would give the regime sufficient time and resources to strengthen itself economically and politically.

The Bureaucracy

One of the primary tasks of the pragmatic Muhyi al-Din government was to reorganize the inefficient and massive bureaucratic apparatus—a problem that had plagued Egypt long before the military's coming to power.[6]

While in normal circumstances a highly developed bureaucracy is considered a great asset to a developing system, by the early sixties, Egypt's bureaucratic establishment had become too cumbersome, costly, and inefficient. The greatly increased cost of financing the bureaucracy, largely caused by its growth in size, is reflected in Table 23.

The table indicates that the government payrole climbed from 50 percent to slightly over 52.9 percent of total governmental spending, in the first nine years of the revolution. The sharp increase came between 1962 and 1965, when the payroll rose from about 52.9 percent to about 73 percent of total government spending. The government's payroll had more than doubled between 1962 and 1965, from £E 101 million to a massive £E 234 million—an increase that at the very least meant the doubling of the bureaucracy during the interval. Obviously this phenomenal growth was due to the large-scale nationalization program effected by the promulgation of the Socialist Laws of 1961.

Table 23 *
Government Expenditures

	1952–53	1961–62	1965–66
Total government payroll (£E)	54.8 mil	101 mil	234 mil
Total government spending (£E)	108 mil	191 mil	318 mil

* Zakariyya Muhyi al-Din, *Ahdaf al-Marhalah al-Qadimah* [Aims of the Next Stage] (Cairo, 1965), pp. 37–38.

As a growing number of enterprises were brought under government control and management especially during 1961, the size of an already large bureaucracy increased greatly. The elite's passion for total coordination and integration of most aspects of social life—economic, political, and even religious—could not be realized except through a superbureaucracy which was formalized in the two-layer cabinet instituted in March 1964. By the end of the year the system's shortcomings were sufficiently acute to necessitate a "new look" at bureaucracy ordered by the president himself.[7] By early January 1965, the task of government reorganization was assigned to a control committee headed by Vice President Zakariyya Muhyi al-Din and composed of Deputy Prime Ministers Kamal al-Din Rif'at, Mustafa Khalil, and Abbas Rudwan. The committee was charged with "abolition of government red-tape and all the administrative complications which stand in the way of full working efficiency." [8] The ensuing discussions pointed to such shortcomings as excessive size and cost of ministerial bureaucracies, the duplication of functions, and deficiencies in administrative training.[9]

A second campaign in April 1965, aimed at "unstarching the white collars," was more aggressive and ideological in tone. The bureaucracy was accused of "burying the Revolution in the name of order and organization" [10] and deviating from the "revolutionary line" laid out by socialist principles because of its permeation with "capitalist tendencies." [11]

As premier, Muhyi al-Din pursued bureaucratic reforms with renewed vigor and pragmatism, without excessive resort to ideological rhetoric. His goals included reduction of spending and increasing efficiency through an expanded use of time-studies and "follow-up" methods, clearer delimitations of scope of bureaucratic responsibility, and more specialized administrative training. More specifically, the prime minister emphasized the need to allow bureau chiefs more liberty of action to make quick, on-the-spot decisions, rather than "passing the buck." [12] While stressing the necessity of making bureaucratic reform a permanent process, Muhyi al-Din candidly admitted the centrality of the human element which could be reformed, not through statutes, but by the infusion of social consciousness over a long period.[13] Further reforms included the amalgamation of the Ministries of Light Industry and Communications and Foreign Cultural Relations into other related ministries for purposes of reducing expenditures.[14] In all, thirteen members of the former cabinet were replaced or retired.

Given the time factor, there was little the new premier could do during his brief eleven-month tenure in office. No amount of dynamism and resourcefulness could break the entrenched pattern among Egyptian bureaucrats to work in Cairo, rather than in the provinces, or reduce significantly the absenteeism, sometimes as high as 50 percent among workers.[15]

The extent of bureaucratic reorganization was clearly visible. While the unwieldly sector system of 1964 was retained, the sectors were reduced from eleven to eight, and in the subsequent years virtually eliminated. At least fourteen of the ministries under the sectors were affected by reshuffles. It was no mere coincidence that these corresponded to areas of governmental activity which had encountered difficulties. One such area was the Sector for Scientific Affairs headed by Deputy Prime Minister Kamal Rif'at, whose military and revolutionary background had not prepared him to supervise the highly technical areas of higher education and scientific research. In any case, in the last eighteen months Rif'at had been increasingly concerned with ASU organizational work in addition to his special role as an ideologue of the socialist regime. Two of the three ministries of his sector were incorporated into other agencies apparently to reduce expenditures and bureaucratic red tape.[16] Also, the minister of higher education, Dr. Abd al-Aziz al-Sayyid, whose scheme for reorganizing the universities had come under heavy criticism in the National Assembly, was replaced.[17] Another sector eliminated was that encompassing the Ministries of Justice, Labor, and Youth, which were retained as independent ministries. In view of the unwieldy character of this sector headed by Dr. Nur al-Din Tarraf, presumably its breakup reflected the regime's policy of streamlining the bureaucracy. The third unit scrapped was the large and disjointed Sector for Local Government and Services, under Abbas Rudwan. Three of its ministries—Education, Public Health, Housing and Utilities —were retained. The Ministry of Social Affairs was merged into the Sector for Waqfs and Al-Azhar Affairs under al-Sharabasi, an action that may have been related to the regime's desire to emphasize its Islamic social orientation in the wake of the Ikhwan's recent conspiratorial activity.

An examination of personnel changes within the various ministries reveals strong evidence that the hardest hit was the Interior Ministry. No mere reshuffle, this outright purge indicated the regime's anxiety over the Brotherhood's plot and the general question of internal security. At the top no less than twenty-five functionaries with the rank of major general were involved. At least two of the four undersecretaries in charge of police and administrative-financial affairs were removed. Moreover, the director of prisons and the directors of security in the following governorates were replaced: Cairo, Asyut, Beni Suayf, Fayyum, Marsa Matruh, Red Sea, Manufiyya, Isma'iliyyah, Dumyat, Alexandria, Buhayrah. In five others, deputy directors were purged:

Qina, Suhag, Sharqiyyah, Port Sa'id, Kafr al-Shaykh. The fact that the purge at the top affected sixteen of the twenty-six governorates is a clear indication of the wide geographic dimensions of conspiratorial activity and general instability.[18] However, the most significant change was the prime minister's personal assumption of the post of interior minister by replacing Abd al-Azim Fahmi. It should be noted that more than anyone else, Mr. Muhyi al-Din had been responsible for modernizing and strengthening the Egyptian security apparatus which had been under his personal control until 1964.[19] Indeed, in view of his former success in suppressing the Brotherhood and the communists, his return to the Interior Ministry had also a symbolic significance. Furthermore, the appointment of Maj. Gen. Yusif Hafiz as deputy minister of interior meant that the prime minister intended to keep a personal hold on the ministry through a former associate.[20]

The most fundamental problem, however, that revealed itself during this period through the Brotherhood's abortive conspiracy, was the system's weaknesses in political socialization. The issue was not, essentially, the revelation and suppression of the conspiracy itself; once again the regime's coercive instrument— the *Mukhabarat*—had effectively dealt with its enemies. The more relevant question was the manifest failure of the elite to acquire legitimacy among the sector of the population represented by the Ikhwan. Significantly, many of the key conspirators were relatively young members of the new middle class—engineers, chemists, scientists, pilots, and students.[21] In short, none were peasants or belonged to the traditional sectors. But while occupationally modern, they did not share the prevailing value system. Only by technical training were they products of the system, which otherwise had failed to draw them into its political culture during the thirteen years of its existence. Thus, to the extent that the political system had failed in its highly important function of political socialization, it was ineffective and weak since it is through this process that the system perpetuates itself.[22]

It was to the credit of a sensitive elite that the need for a more effective socialization process was discerned and responses formulated. Aside from strengthening the leadership at the Ministry of National Guidance, under Amin Huwaydi, a well-organized and intensive campaign was started to contrast the "benefits" of the present system with the "destructive" nature of the Brotherhood. In addition to utilizing the mass media, the ASU arranged a series of conferences at all levels to keep the public "well-informed." Literally the whole of the Ministry of Waqfs and Al-Azhar University were put to work organizing conferences in mosques with the purpose of "explaining" the true meaning of Islam and giving the public "sound religious guidance" in order to guard against the Brotherhood's false interpretations.[23] Shaykh Hasan Ma'mun, the Great Imam of Al-Azhar, and ex-Brotherhood leader Shaykh Muhammad al-Ghazzali [24] took the lead in decrying the Brotherhood's fanatical beliefs and actions and reiterating the correctness of the regime's aims.[25] Thus, at a time of internal unrest and declining legitimacy the regime's strategy of control included the application of force to suppress counterelites (i.e., the Brethren); the intensification of socialization measures to compensate declining charismatic legitimacy by falling back on Islamic orthodoxy; and the resort to the device of "direct democracy" where Nasir would confront the regime's critics in face-to-face discussions to hear complaints and to explain his policies.[26] While the political formula worked well as a method of control maintenance, the real test of its utility and power came in the crucial months after the June War.

The Political System until June 1967

In retrospect, it is possible to identify certain changes in Egyptian internal and external politics during 1966 which had a direct bearing on the outbreak of the June War. While a great deal of hard evidence is still lacking, it is clear that these changes arose from an unusually close interaction of domestic and international politics and that monocausal economic theories (e.g., the West's stringent conditions attached to aid) did not constitute a fully satisfactory explanation for Egypt's new course.

The advent of the Muhyi al-Din government signalled Nasir's desire to reduce the level of conflict with the United States, primarily to facilitate the flow of financial aid and food shipments to Egypt. The anti-American manifestations of 1964, which continued until the summer of 1965,[27] had subsided by early August and the president had suddenly placed himself in the role of a neutral peacemaker in the Vietnamese conflict.[28] During October the press took a generally critical line toward communists in non-aligned states by questioning their loyalty to their home countries as exemplified in the unfolding PKI-Army struggle in Indonesia.[29] In November, the moderate Muhyi al-Din government had already reached agreement on the resumption of surplus food shipments in exchange for Egyptian currency and Nasir went in front of the National Assembly to hail the improvement of Egyptian-American relations. Further bilateral negotiations resulted in a new $55 million aid agreement signed on 3 January 1966 amid an atmosphere of growing cooperation and mutual confidence. The high point of the era of "good feeling" came on 21 February, with the visit to Washington of Speaker Anwar al-Sadat, who was to pave the way for an eventual official visit to the United States by Nasir himself.[30]

Ironically at the very peak of the American-Egyptian rapprochement during January and February, a number of potentially explosive problems came to the fore which eventually destroyed what had been accomplished. The first was the so-called Islamic Alliance conceived by King Faysal of Sa'udi Arabia to challenge the primacy of Nasir in the Arab orbit by uniting conservative-traditionalist Arab and non-Arab Islamic states. Considering the existing armed confrontation between Sa'udi Arabia and Egypt in the Yemen, the rising stature of the pro-American king seemed a threat to the UAR's position in the Middle East. A second unsettling issue centered on growing Egyptian fears of Israel's atomic capability.

Efforts to obtain Soviet atomic weapons in the future to counter this threat brought only a "nuclear guarantee" from the USSR—a promise that did not sufficiently alleviate Egyptian fears of insecurity. To complicate matters, there was the reported American sale of planes and tanks to Israel [31] and the sharpening of factional rivalries between the pragmatic moderates under Muhyi al-Din and the doctrinaire socialists led by ASU Secretary General Ali Sabri. It was believed that the latter group opposed the regime's new ties with the United States.

To be sure, it is difficult to establish the relative importance of the foregoing internal and external factors in shaping the course of Nasir's subsequent policies toward the United States. However, it is clear that in combination they pushed the Egyptian president to assail Britain and the United States on the very day his own peace emissary, Speaker al-Sadat, had reached Washington. Nasir accused the two powers of supporting a new type of Baghdad Pact through King Faysal and the Shah of Iran and warned of a possible Arab preventive attack should Israel manufacture atomic bombs. In the subsequent months relations further deteriorated when Egypt rejected the rigorous conditions placed upon a $70 million loan by the International Monetary Fund (IMF) which included devaluation of the Egyptian pound, tax increases, and reduction of government expenditures. Considering the widespread popular unrest over rising prices and the government's commitment to heavy expenditures for defense and industrialization, it was difficult for the regime to accept the West's offer.

The making of foreign policy and the behavior of states in the international arena are affected by a variety of complex factors including type of political system, character of leadership, flow of intelligence, ideology, tradition, and experience. Among these, experience and ideology are crucial in shaping a state's image of the external environment. Thus, foreign policies constitute the reactions of elites to their own images of a changing external environment. It is precisely the mutual perceptions (or misperceptions) of national leaders that determine the course of international politics and the issues of war and peace.[32] Any objective understanding of Egyptian foreign policy must be pursued within the foregoing context. The usual critical approach that has pervaded much of the Western journalistic and even scholarly literature since 1956 is of little value if objective analysis and explanation is the aim.

The Egyptian leadership and indeed Egyptians generally perceive the external world in terms of their recent national experience and through the prism of their particular ideology. The imperial past may have been a dead horse for the West, but it is recent history for Arabs, Chinese, Indians, and Africans. These "victims" of imperialism, as they regard themselves, possess very long and bitter memories, which the prevailing nationalist ideology constantly refreshes and reinforces.

Some of the recent events that have left their mark on the "national memory" of Egyptians are the 1948 defeat in Palestine, the Baghdad Pact, the Anglo-French-Israeli invasion of 1956, and the Eisenhower Doctrine—all of which produced deep suspicion of and animosity toward the West. Considering the Soviet opposition to Arab-unity schemes between Egypt, Syria, and Iraq in the late 1950s, even the Russians could not be trusted despite their massive economic and military contribution. Viewed through this historical perspective, the developments in the six years prior to the June War looked increasingly disconcerting and indeed ominous to the Egyptian leadership. One can easily conceive this period as one of general decline characterized by a succession of reverses—the Syrian secession of 1961, the frustration of repeated unity attempts with Syria and Iraq, containment of Egyptian influence in Africa, the quagmire of the Yemeni War, the rise of economic problems and the revival of Brethren opposition at home, the persistence of the Israeli threat, and the new challenge of the Islamic Alliance.

What further clouded the darkening Egyptian world view was the occurrence of these reverses in what seemed to be from 1963 onward an increasingly hostile international milieu. With the partial disintegration of the Bandung bloc of nonaligned states, Egypt, a founding member, lost an important source of diplomatic support. The Sino-Soviet rift, signalling the end of monolithic communism, introduced a disturbing disequilibrium into Egypt's perception of balance between East and West. More significant perhaps were the changes in the Egyptian view of the United States after President Kennedy's assassination. Kennedy's pro-Algerian stance, youthful vigor, and fresh approach to American-Egyptian relations through Ambassador John Badeau [33] had had a most favorable impact on Egypt. The Kennedy image was associated, in the Egyptian mind, with that of their own action-oriented president. This coupled with the resumption of American aid (i.e., food shipments) and the trust that Dr. Badeau inspired by virtue of his long years of educational work in the UAR, created the basis of a genuine rapprochement. Not only did

President Johnson lack his predecessor's attributes, but the Egyptians perceived him as being closer, politically and emotionally, to Israeli interests. In addition, Johnson was associated with a more aggressive phase of American foreign policy as exemplified by intervention in the Dominican and Vietnamese civil wars. Finally, there were the successive overthrows of Presidents Sukarno of Indonesia (1965–66) and Nkrumah of Ghana (February 1966)—both representatives of the nonaligned bloc of Afro-Asian nations. Against this backdrop came U.S. press reports during 1966 of wide-ranging CIA activities directed against certain foreign governments [34] that were hardly reassuring to a deeply suspicious Egyptian leadership.[35] It was against this background that *Al-Ahram* reflected what was perhaps Nasir's own view of international reality—". . . an imperialist reactionary advance is moving toward the Arab World, with the UAR as its focus." [36]

Despite these anxieties, in April 1966 the government formally requested an expansion of the Food for Peace program and invited Secretary Dean Rusk to visit the UAR. The proposed visit did not take place because of the Johnson Administration's preoccupation with Vietnam and the domestic concerns of a highly political president in an election year. On 14 July 1966, the House of Representatives voted against further aid to Egypt unless such assistance was judged clearly in the American interest by the president himself.[37] Yet apparently for reasons of economic need, the Egyptian side seemed eager to continue the rapprochement by consenting to the visit of two US destroyers, which arrived in Port Sa'id on 2 September for the first time in twelve years.

Cabinet Crisis

Not all of the reasons behind the unexpected cabinet shake-up of 10 September 1966, are discernible. Clearly there existed strong opposition within the ruling elite to Muhyi al-Din's policies of economic accommodation with the United States, encouragement of private foreign investment, and increasing prices and taxes. If Nasir's primary goal in bringing Muhyi al-Din to the premiership was the reinstitution of large-scale American economic aid, this

had not been achieved. While Muhyi al-Din's new economic policies had won some favor in the West, the response of the latter
was slow, incremental, and conditional upon financial reforms
and ultimate Egyptian withdrawal from the Yemen.[38] Apparently, Nasir felt he could meet neither of these two conditions
without creating additional problems for his regime. The financial reforms demanded by the West would have required a new
round of tax and price increases, further exacerbating domestic
discontent—precisely the condition that Nasir wanted to amelio-
rate by getting Western aid. A precipitous withdrawal from the
Yemen would have hurt his position in the Arab world and made
him vulnerable to the army's criticism for denying it victory on
the battlefield.

An examination of the cabinet reshuffle partially supports
some of these conclusions. Muhyi al-Din went back to his former
position of vice-president and three deputy premiers in charge of
all economic sectors—Dr. Abd al-Mun'im al-Qaysuni, Dr. Mustafa Khalil and Dr. Ramzi Stinu—were retired. Simultaneously,
the sector system was further reduced from eight to four, creating
a larger number of independent ministries. The total number of
cabinet ministers increased from thirty-two to thirty-three; the officer-civilian line-up changed in favor of the military, from thirteen officers and nineteen civilians in 1965, to sixteen officers and
seventeen civilians in 1966. Ex-officers not only controlled almost
half of the cabinet posts, but also the most important ones which
now included industry, communications, and supply and internal
trade. The rise in the military component could have been a
manifestation of Nasir's desire to take a more active and comprehensive role in policy formulation and / or the need to placate the
army. One should also note the appointment of Gen. Shams al-
Din Badran as war minister, in place of the officer-technocrat
Abd al-Wahhab al-Bishri—a changeover the significance of which
was not fully understood at the time. The replacement of the
apolitical Bishri by Badran represented a victory for First Vice-
President Marshall Amir, whose strange on-off relationship with
the president after 1961 remained a secret until the June War. As
a close associate of Amir, Badran was instrumental in further isolating the army from direct presidential control and ASU influence.
Finally, the appointment of Sidqi Sulayman as premier brought to

the fore a highly efficient officer-technocrat who had excelled himself as High Dam minister. Despite his former position as president of the Soviet-Egyptian Friendship Association, Sulayman's appointment did not signify a shift to the left. In view of his reputed piety and traditional background, he could at best be classified as a pragmatic socialist of the tacit left.

Under the Sulayman government, the belt-tightening policies of the previous cabinet continued, leading to growing unrest and a brief dockworkers' strike in early October at Port Sa'id. This coincided with a purge [39] directed both at the left (i.e., ASU, press, Socialist Institute) and the right (i.e., landowners) manifesting the regime's continued commitment to the ideological mainstream. In November, the Syrian-UAR defense treaty was concluded amid increasing anti-American manifestations which culminated in Egypt's cancellation of U.S. and British civilian and military overflights in mid-February 1967. Charges of a CIA-Sa'udi-Brethren plot against Nasir further exacerbated the situation. Nevertheless, Nasir finally backed down and agreed to IMF's stringent austerity measures,[40] despite the domestic political risks. The reported agreement in principle between the government and the IMF during April and May might have had a cooling effect barring contrary developments. Soon, however, a series of rapid developments pushed Egypt into the June 1967 War.

Prelude to War

A definitive analysis of the immediate causes of the 1967 Arab-Israeli War and of the war itself must await the publication of hitherto secret documents. There are too many moot questions concerning the precise intentions and roles of the two superpowers as well as of the combatants themselves. What is presented here is a brief analysis of the most visible factors in the conflict which had a direct bearing on the Egyptian political system. Of these, the role of the Palestine Liberation Organization (PLO) and the continuing struggle among the Arab states were perhaps the most important.

One of the primary catalysts that triggered the fateful process of events leading to the June War was the PLO and its *fida'iyin* units operating against Israel. It should be remembered that the guerrilla activities of the displaced Palestinian Arabs had played a similar role with respect to the Suez War of 1956.

In keeping with its traditional practice of massive retaliation, on 13 November 1966, Israel attacked the Jordanian village of Samu', reportedly a guerrilla base. One immediate effect of the raid was an intensification of the Arab cold war; indeed, it laid bare several basic realities. Despite Syria's persistent and open support of the Palestinian commandoes, Israel's punishment was directed at Jordan whose king was actively engaged in reducing commando activities. Israel's decision not to attack Syria may have been dictated by its reluctance to involve directly the UAR, which was in the process of concluding a joint defense treaty with Syria. The relatively higher cost of attacking Syria's well-entrenched positions in the Golan Heights may have also been a factor.

Beyond demonstrating Jordan's vulnerability, the Israeli raid triggered massive strikes and protests against King Husayn's opposition to full-scale PLO activity in border areas. The suppression of these demonstrations and the king's decision to accept a Sa'udi offer of 20,000 troops prompted Cairo to take an increasingly critical attitude toward Jordan. The king's government responded by blaming the UAR for not providing air protection during the Samu' raid. Amid the deepening turmoil, Israeli Foreign Minister Abba Eban came out with the improbable assertion that the Israeli raid had actually stabilized the situation. Nevertheless, the border conflict continued unabated during the first four months of 1967 mainly along Israel's frontiers with Syria and Jordan. The Egyptian border, guarded by UNEF units, remained conspicuously quiet, as it had been since 1956.

In early April, the UAR's de facto hands-off policy came under growing challenge by Jordan and Sa'udi Arabia as being "soft toward Israel." Indeed, because of its domestic economic problems and military involvement in the Yemen, the leading Arab state had done little to provoke Israel, except rhetorically. However, by mid-May Egyptian policy abruptly shifted for a number of reasons not all of which are readily identifiable. One possible explanation was the need to respond to Jordanian-Sa'udi charges of softness by taking some concrete though incremental action against Israel. If this was the only motivating factor, then Nasir's subsequent steps represented too rapid an escalation, in view of the grave risks involved. Having declared a state of alert on 15 May, the UAR requested from Secretary General U Thant an immediate withdrawal of UNEF from the Gaza Strip and Sinai. If a face-saving reassertion of Arab leadership was Egypt's aim, these steps would have been sufficient. However, the subsequent positioning of PLO troops in the north, the remilitarization of Sharm al-Shaykh on 21 May, and the declaration to close Aqaba to Israeli shipping on the next day may have been intended to provoke a larger confrontation.

One much-repeated explanation for Egypt's overreaction was a report of Soviet-supplied intelligence about Israeli armed concentrations on the Syrian border, which the subsequent Egyptian moves were designed to thwart. Another common explanation has been the contention that ultimately the Egyptian moves were to culminate in an attack on Israel. While this position serves as justification for the subsequent Israeli pre-emptive attack on 5 June, it hardly represents an objective assessment of Nasir's intentions. If one soberly considers the Egyptian situation before the war's outbreak, which presumably Nasir did, an immediate war with Israel was not feasible, even if Egypt could deliver the first blow. Considering the president's repeated misgivings concerning the ideological and technical efficiency of his troops, and the deployment of his best units in the Yemen,[41] it is difficult to believe that Nasir felt ready for the ultimate battle with Israel. To render the hypothesis plausible one must assume that Nasir was rational, that he did not overestimate the strength of the Syrian and Jordanian armed forces, and that he alone controlled the decision-making process, rather than the Egyptian military and/or PLO.

If the foregoing assumptions are correct then it is conceivable that Nasir's intention was not to "destroy Israel," as Radio Cairo's propaganda persistently threatened, but to engineer another political victory, as in years past, by going to the brink. The decision to dispatch his reputedly pro-Western vice-president, Muhyi al-Din, to Washington just prior to the Israeli attack may have been an attempt to withdraw from the brink. The resort to high-level diplomacy, coupled with the general disposition and unpre-paredness of Egypt's air force on 5 June, tends to strengthen the proposed thesis that Nasir did not intend to start an armed con-flict for the moment.[42] Even a limited political victory, such as the reestablishment of Egyptian sovereignty over Sharm al-Shaykh coupled with tacit guarantees for Israeli access, would have significantly strengthened the regime at home and in the Arab sphere.

The paucity of information on Egypt's intentions is matched by the obscurity of the Israeli decision-making process that cul-minated in the suprise attack of 5 June. For a long time to come diplomatic historians are bound to inquire about the reasons that compelled Israel to choose the ultimate of four basic options—a preemptive attack. Another option, diplomacy, was discarded after a brief two-week trial. A third possibility, the testing of the Egyptian blockade by dispatching an Israeli ship through the Tiran Straits, would have shifted the onus of armed aggression on the UAR, had the latter chosen to enforce the blockade. Fi-nally, Israel could have attempted a limited armed action to open the straits by force.

The limited scope of this study and the lack of data on Israeli decision-making preclude a detailed analysis of the factors deter-mining the choice of preemptive attack. One of the most basic considerations, however, that apparently escaped the attention of Egypt's policy-makers, was the pathological Israeli fear of encirclement and extermination. This central aspect of the Israeli national character springing from the ghetto experience of Jewish history manifested itself once again, only on a larger scale, with the massing of Arab armies on Israel's borders. Admittedly, the political ambitions of certain hawkish and expansionist Israeli leaders played a part in the final decision. But the resort to total war may have been ultimately dictated by the deep fear amongst the population. The crushing Arab defeat temporarily solved Israel's security problem; it also set into motion a constellation of powerful forces, the full impact of which will not be felt for several decades.[43]

13

Min Huna Nabda'*

THE most significant contemporary development for the student
of Middle Eastern politics is not Egypt's defeat in the June War;
few experts expected an Egyptian victory over Israel at that time.
Rather it is the great persistence of the Egyptian political system
to endure despite the enormity of defeat. While the "setback" of
June exposed many basic weaknesses of the Nasirite regime, its
ability to survive the war highlighted the system's inherent
strengths. In addition to providing insights into Egyptian politics,
a careful consideration of these strengths and weaknesses provides students of political development with a wealth of data for
cross-national analysis and could prove instructive to the policy-
makers of Egypt's friends and foes alike.

Charisma and Absorptive Capacity

Two general points need clarification before detailed analysis.
First, the regime's ability to maintain itself in the face of external
defeat and internal unrest does not preclude the possibility of difficulties or even collapse in the future. Second, while the political
order itself survived, a number of its features underwent marked
alteration. Yet the ability of the system to adjust itself to the conditions of severe stress after June 1967 testifies to its great absorptive capacity.

A primary element of strength identified in the first part of this

* "From here we start," taken from title of book by Khalid Muhammad Khalid, *Min Huna Nabda'* [From Here We Start], trans. by Isma'il
R. el-Faruqi, 3rd ed. (New York, 1953).

study was charismatic leadership. The central role of the charismatic phenomenon and its constituent ingredients was dramatically validated with the reinstitution of Abd al-Nasir on 9 June. When one considers how widespread and deep were the feelings shown by the demonstrators urging the president to withdraw his resignation, the full dimensions of the charismatic component come into clear view. Although the ASU seems to have played a guiding role in the demonstrations, the immensity of popular support surpassed that of a staged affair.[1]

As emphasized earlier, defeats do not bode well for charismatics as a basic rule. However, Nasir's reinstatement to power defied the established pattern for charismatic leaders for a number of reasons that are basic to an understanding of Egyptian politics. The most fundamental of these was the high degree of residual legitimacy that Nasir possessed by virtue of his leadership performance during the fifties—a legitimacy too great to be erased overnight by a defeat. After all, his activities as leader were the concrete manifestations of the nationalist ideological message which most Egyptians had shared and supported.

The great legitimacy that nationalist charismatics enjoy among their people even under an authoritarian system has always presented a painful reality for the West to accept or understand. Cuba is perhaps the best example. The fact remains that, regardless of political system, when popular beliefs and aspirations coincide with the policies of the leadership,[2] there is little that external pressure can do to erase the resulting legitimacy. Another primary factor in Nasir's reinstatement was the public reaction to the openly expressed Israeli and Western desire to witness his downfall. As in 1956, many Egyptians supported Nasir if only to deny the enemy the satisfaction of success. In a deeper sense, however, by reinstating the president, the Egyptians underlined their reluctance to accept defeat. Significantly, this emotionally determined popular choice may have been a supremely practical action as well, for no one except Nasir would have been able to avert chaos in a defeated and demoralized country. In the final analysis, charisma and the charismatic's compulsion to search for new victories that led Nasir to the disastrous brink in early June was also the force that helped him retain office after the defeat.

Beyond the purely charismatic dimension, there were other strengths that the system possessed which enabled it to endure after the war. One that should be emphasized was the general legitimacy the revolution derived from its "Egyptianness"—a characteristic that preceded Nasir's rise to power and development of charismatic legitimacy. The very act of expelling the non-Egyptian royal dynasty, no less than the Egyptianization of foreign-owned enterprises, had endowed the system with an initial legitimacy that still prevails. Despite the many deprivations and hardships suffered by the citizenry under the new order, there was always the psychological consolation that the rulers, however imperfect, were Egyptians themselves.

Legitimation and Routinization

The transference of legitimacy from the charismatic to other individuals and new institutions is an immensely difficult and complex task. The simple fact in Egypt was that the legitimacy Nasir possessed did not always encompass others in the leadership or the government itself. Certain privileged officials in the cabinet, the military, and the security establishment were barely tolerated by the general public, and the cumbersome bureaucracy was always a source of complaint. As a result, all the shortcomings of the regime before and even after the June War were blamed on incompetent and corrupt subordinates, but rarely on the *ra'is* himself. The halo of charismatic legitimacy and the president's reputation as an incorruptible, just, and puritanical patriot tended to place him beyond the range of popular criticism. The only area where legitimation had some success was the Arab Socialist Union. While it is by no means certain that this organism has taken root, it was strong enough to provide Nasir with a degree of support against his enemies in the military during the crucial days after the defeat.[3]

If the system's ability to absorb defeat was a measure of its strengths, the collapse of its armed forces in June 1967 was a manifestation of its inherent weaknesses. To knowledgeable observers, the surprising fact was not Israel's victory, but the rapidity of

Egypt's defeat. To be sure, a detailed description of the war itself falls outside the scope of this study. Nevertheless, any inquiry into the causes of defeat must consider several aspects of the war itself, before attempting to uncover the more basic weaknesses of the societal substructure.

A deeply held Egyptian view is that the conflict was not a fair fight because of Israel's preemptive air strike. There is no doubt that Egypt would have done better with the benefit of an air force. But even with a first air strike of their own, a clear-cut victory would have probably eluded the Egyptians considering the great technical and motivational strength of the Israelis. However, any evaluation of the Egyptian fighting-man should not overlook the military and psychological impact of Israel's surprise attack and control of the skies over the open desert. Since these conditions also existed during the Suez War of 1956, the precise fighting capabilities of the Egyptian soldier under offensive conditions advantageous to Egypt are simply not known.

Once shorn of air cover, the collapse of the Army of the Sinai was virtually assured. Yet its rapid disintegration can not be explained solely in terms of Israeli effectiveness on land and supremacy in the air. One would have expected a well equipped army of over 180,000 men to offer far greater resistance over a longer period than six days. Clearly insufficient technical training and lack of mobility in armored combat were important factors. Yet, ultimately the answer must be sought, not on the battlefield, but within the depths of Egyptian history and society.

History and National Character

When one considers the realities of the Egyptian historical experience as presented in earlier chapters, the three successive defeats by Israel come as no great surprise. Several points of central relevance need to be emphasized. More than any other collectivity, the inhabitants of the Nile Valley had experienced what is perhaps one of the longest periods of continuous servitude under numerous foreign rulers. With the nationalist awakening beginning in the late 1800s came a long crisis of national and personal identity which remains to be fully resolved. The sum total of these experiences was bound to leave its imprint on the psychology and behavior of modern Egyptians and, in a collective sense, shape their cultural patterns and national character.

The concept of national character, its definition and determination, have been the subject of lengthy scrutiny and debate.[4] According to Inkeles, national character has been variously studied. Some have focussed on institutional patterns, while others have viewed national character in cultural, behavioral, or racial terms.[5] Inkeles himself defines it as ". . . relatively enduring personality characteristics and patterns that are modal among the adult members of a society."[6] In the world of nation-states national character often constitutes one of the most basic elements in the determination of the national power.[7]

A great deal has been written about Arab national character by Arabs and non-Arabs, both before and after the June War. Although more field research needs to be done to reach valid conclusions, it is still possible to identify tentatively a few basic character traits of Arabs generally and Egyptians specifically. One is the tendency to exaggerate and indulge in rhetoric rather than concrete activity. More fundamental is the lack of mutual trust and the frequent manifestation of mutual suspicion and hostility.[8] The detrimental influence of these character traits on battle performance is not difficult to ascertain. The individual's view of reality becomes distorted through constant exaggeration and his feelings of hostility toward others doom all attempts to create group solidarity, cohesion, and organizational efficiency. The resulting sense of isolation is reported to be especially true of the peasants [9] who, until the recent induction of students, constituted a large portion of the Egyptian army's lower ranks. Further exacerbating the situation are class differences between the officers and the common soldier. The psycho-cultural gap that exists between a predominantly middle class officer corps and the lower class fighting-men is a problem of utmost seriousness for the national leadership, even more important than modern armaments. The evidence of the 1956 and 1967 wars suggests that not only did the officers fail to inspire their men in battle (although individual acts of bravery did occur), but they also mistreated them as a matter of practice in peacetime.

The absence of more systematic data renders the identification of the foregoing traits tentative. However, the existence of another pervasive national characteristic can be corroborated more reliably by survey data as well as descriptive studies. This is the deep sense of inferiority engendered during the centuries of foreign rule in Egypt—a social-psychological trait that could not be erased during the relatively short period since the revolution.

One should emphasize that these character traits are not peculiar to the Egyptian or the Arab psyche; many of them are discernible among virtually all ex-colonial peoples of the non-Western world in varying degrees. While any definitive conclusion must await the result of systematic cross-national studies, it would seem logical to hypothesize that due to the length and intensity of Egypt's colonial experience, certain character traits left a deeper imprint.

Egyptian feelings of inferiority toward the West, as well as a deep crisis of identity, was indicated by survey research conducted in 1951.[10] In many ways these findings are revealing despite the passage of time, especially those relating to the ambivalent character of nationalism among professionals. As nationalists, they identified Britain as their primary opponent and the British occupation as the country's main problem. Yet their responses reflected a general lack of a plan to end the British presence; and while some reportedly expressed a readiness to fight, no one seemed eager to do so. They had doubts about their ability to measure up to the West's standards.[11] Admittedly, this lack of enthusiasm for combat found stronger emphasis among professionals because of their middle and upper-middle-class status. Undoubtedly, there was a greater willingness to fight among the army officers and certain Muslim Brethren as evidenced by their repeated guerrilla raids against British installations. But there seems no reason to suppose that the ambivalent attitudes found among professionals were not shared by the military as well. Moreover, with the advent of military rule in July 1952, the officers corps acquired middle-class privileges—a situation that would tend to diminish their enthusiasm for sacrifice in the Sinai.

Daniel Lerner has observed that the sense of shame and humiliation generated by defeats and domination under Britain "scarred the Egyptian elite and confused its perception." [12] Significantly, these feelings were not erased by the British departure, since, in contrast to Kemalist Turkey, foreign occupation was ended by skillful diplomacy rather than military victory. The Egyptian sense of humiliation and inferiority was further reinforced by three successive defeats at the hands of Israel—a state founded and led by European Jews and their descendants. The defeat of 1948 came as a great shock precisely because of the unreal Egyptian and generally Arab perception of the Israeli state. Arab confidence at the war's outset was partly based on their image of the traditionally subservient Jewry of the Middle East, a far cry from the Zionist nationalists of Israel.

The problem of social-psychological inferiority has been frankly recognized and diagnosed by the political and intellectual leadership of Egypt, especially in the post-revolutionary period. Nasir repeatedly emphasized the theme of *karamah*—dignity—in an attempt to infuse the Egyptian/Arab with a sense of self-respect and pride. By making these values a part of his message he was utilizing his charismatic powers to bring about a psychological transformation and he may have succeeded to a degree. As a result, Nasir's charismatic appeal was strong enough to generate mass support for every one of his confrontations with the West and Israel, even in defeat. However, popular support through charisma was not transformed into effective fighting performance on the battlefield. While the individual soldier may have been willing to sacrifice himself for Nasir and Egypt as a result of a vertical charismatic bond, the crucial absence of a horizontal bond of trust with his fellow fightingmen rendered him psychologically impotent. In other words, despite the strength of his spiritual ties to the leader himself, the common soldier did not trust the leader's officers corps during the heat of the battle. This type of situation may have also obtained at each level of the military organization including the commissioned ranks, where despite a strong vertical relationship between individual officers and Nasir, the horizontal trust among officers remained weak. Finally, one might say that charisma can only inspire men, it cannot organize them.

It would seem that charismatically induced value transformations need certain concrete, practical manifestations to acquire permanence. In other words, while many Egyptians may have come to accept their leader's norms and values (e.g., dignity, self-respect, Arabism), these are likely to remain infirm until a victory is achieved. Nasir's victories were always political. Saddled with the burden of a history conspicuously lacking military prowess, Nasir failed to reverse the pattern of successive military defeats. The cry for a real military victory over Israel, however incremental, that Haykal raised in April 1969, was motivated by the need to reverse the ever-deepening sense of national frustration and inferiority.[13]

The campaign to combat the inferiority problem among Egyptians has been pursued beyond the purely military and political realms into the more private area of marriage. The tendency of many Afro-Asian students to marry Westerners while studying in the West is well known. In the Middle Eastern context, the increase of such marriages has caused deep social-political concern to the governments involved.[14] Interestingly, Egyptian sociologists have ascribed this tendency to the inferiority problem:

> When Egyptians used to marry foreigners this was because we felt inferior to them and by marrying them we felt uplifted. But now we do not feel inferior anymore. . . . Therefore we should marry our own kind . . . marrying foreigners is inconsistent with the principles of Arab nationalism. Marrying an Arab is a duty.[15]

This is a recognition of the existence of inferiority feelings in the recent past and as such reinforces Kendall's findings.[16] The very fact that the Egyptian writer goes on to emphasize that "now we do not feel inferior anymore . . ." points to the persistence of inferiority feelings.

Postwar Elite Strategy

It would be an understatement to say that the June 1967 defeat shook the very roots of the Egyptian political system. While the system was strong enough to withstand the shock, the need for basic social and political changes became obvious in the postwar period. However, the full consequences of the defeat will not be known for a long time.

The first order of business after Nasir's return to power was the reestablishment of full control in terms of its twin components, force and legitimacy. In times of instability, the reliability of the force component becomes extremely important to neutralize possible coups by counter-elites. The two available instruments of force, the army and the security apparatus, were rendered reliable by purges and retirements. Following the defeat, Nasir took over direct command of the armed forces in addition to holding the posts of president, prime minister, and party chief. Greater control was exercised through a new law requiring presidential approval on promotions to the rank of colonel or above. In view of the army's preoccupation with the enemy across the Suez, the security organization and the police emerged as the key tools of internal control. It was essential to keep the army involved with the enemy both to preserve its remaining military effectiveness and to neutralize its possible use against the ruling elite.

There were three instances of explicit challenge to the leadership since June 1967. These were ex-Marshal Amir's quasi-coup of September 1967 and the student-worker demonstrations of February and November 1968. The regime's success in dealing with these disruptions attested to the reliability of the force component; the security-police apparatus uncovered Amir's plot and suppressed the demonstrations, while the army remained at the front, seemingly uninvolved in domestic problems.[17]

The other aspect of control—legitimacy—was perhaps more important than force as a system-maintaining component in the long run. In the postwar period the elite augmented its legitimacy formula—i.e., charisma and Egyptianness—with a revival of traditional Islamic themes and symbols and a limited but significant reversion to Egyptian nationalism. These moves were designed to shoreup the regime's declining legitimacy among Muslim traditionalists and Egyptocentrists,[18] respectively. Without sacrificing the commitment to socialism or Arabism, the leadership broadened its legitimacy formula to neutralize the appeal of counter-elites (e.g., the Brethren) and to maximize popular support during a period of protracted crisis. The appeal to traditional Islamic legitimacy was manifested in the press and in Nasir's frequent references to Allah in his speeches. The presence of the top leadership headed by Nasir at mosque services commemorating the *mulid*—the birth of the Prophet—two days after the end of the June War symbolized the regime's identification with the Islamic ethos.[19]

Introspection and Self-Criticism

Despite the general legitimacy that the regime and its leader continued to enjoy, the commanding position of the military had been seriously compromised by the defeat. The public was exposed to many instances of laxity, corruption, and incompetence during the trials of both Marshal Amir's accomplices in the coup attempt and the generals held responsible for the June defeat. During the first part of 1968, grassroots anti-military sentiment reached a high point with the outbreak of student-worker rioting in February protesting the light sentences given to the accused generals.

These demonstrations, the first in over a decade, constituted enough of a danger signal for Nasir to initiate a series of both immediate and long-range reforms. The obvious sense of urgency explicit in his activities after March 1968 reflected a realization of the necessity of establishing new bases of legitimacy before it was too late. It was equally apparent that in order to survive and roll back the psychologically withering Israeli military presence across the canal, the home front had to be strengthened through basic reforms. The outcome was the "March 30 Program" promulgated by Nasir, amid continuing public debate concerning virtually all aspects of Egyptian life. Indeed, the period following the June War was one of genuine self-criticism and introspection among Egyptians, during which the most sacrosanct institutions and practices were questioned and dissent openly expressed. That a generally authoritarian regime would permit significant liberalization and dissent during a time of national emergency was a demonstration of systemic strength. One would find this type of behavior hard to conceive of even in the Western democracies under conditions of war and occupation similar to Egypt's.

Abd al-Nasir's basic strategy during 1968 seemed to be the maintenance of a balance between various power factions in an atmosphere of guided but genuine debate and inquiry. It was recognized that excessive criticism could easily alienate certain key groups thereby creating dissension and weakening the home front. Yet Nasir hoped to utilize the public debates to preserve national unity by forging as broad a consensus as possible until he could bring an end to the occupation. However, the more fundamental utility of open debate centered on the need to identify the basic problems afflicting the Egyptian body politic to avoid defeat in the future.

The most dangerous dilemma confronting the leadership was the irrepressible public criticism of the military's performance in the war. As a people who had bestowed special privileges and perquisites upon its officer corps since 1952, the Egyptians demanded not only punishment but also explanation. Yet realism dictated the immediate shoring up of the army's morale in the continuing military confrontation with Israel—a morale that had been shattered by the recent defeat, the widespread purge of its leadership,[20] and the biting criticism at home. Also, a protracted press campaign against the military could conceivably turn it against the regime itself. Despite the delicacy of the matter, press criticism of the military was extensive and vigorous, especially in late 1967. During 1968 the debate continued, but along more constructive and less emotional lines.

The fiercest and earliest attack came from the ASU, an organization generally more militant and leftist than the army or the government. The criticism centered on the military leadership's reluctance to permit the ASU's political vanguard horizontal access to the armed forces.[21] This provided official confirmation of what certain observers had suspected since the birth of the ASU. The precise relationship of the ASU to the military organization had never been clarified; it had been simply "left to the Supreme Executive Committee" during the mid-sixties. Apparently Marshall Amir had successfully kept the armed forces isolated from the ASU organizationally and from the rest of Egyptian society ideologically. Whatever the merits of the Soviet *zampolit* system in terms of ideological indoctrination and party control, it never existed in the Egyptian army. In the immediate postwar period the left demanded the immediate politicization of the military ranks by ASU cadres as the only way to assure victory in a future war.[22] Through revolutionary work the ASU's Political Vanguard would aim at "cementing" the armed forces to the rest of society.

A most intriguing revelation for both students of Egyptian politics and Egyptians generally was the strained relations between Nasir and Amir, and the latter's role in diluting presidential authority over the military which he had run as his personal fief. This type of power accumulation incensed not only the left but the entire political spectrum. Regardless of ideological coloration, the Egyptian press agreed on the need to prevent at all costs the rise of "centers of power" in the future.

What is a center of power? The press, represented by such distinguished editors as Haykal, Baha' al-Din, and Hamrush provided the answer without hesitation.[23] A center of power constituted the accumulation of illegal, illegitimate power in the absence of popular control (al-Riqabah al-Sha'biyyah). Significantly, the two main examples cited were the military and the police.[24]

Why were these centers permitted to exist before June 1967? While some maintained that only the 1967 defeat "revealed" the their existence, Haykal flatly asserted: "We could not talk about errors before 1967 because of political pressure." [25] There was also general agreement that these centers were the result of the political-organizational vacuum left unfilled by the ASU. The two questions that remained were how to prevent a recurrence of centers (i.e., the military and police) in the future, and in view of their continuing centrality in Egyptian security, how to reform them.

Assessments of the military establishment varied greatly and prescriptions for change ranged from total reform to specific remedies. The pressure for comprehensive change came most frequently, but not exclusively, from the left. In essence, they wanted the liquidation of the "exclusiveness" of the officer corps, the infusion of revolutionary ideology into the armed forces, and the "cementing" of the military to the "popular forces." [26] However, as time passed the leftist prescription to forge a strong army appeared to be shelved, at least temporarily. Not even the ASU-supported scheme for a popular defense army to guard the rear met with presidential approval.[27] Only after the Israeli commando raid of 31 October 1968 on electrical installations (Nagi Hamadi) did Nasir approve the establishment of such a force. The regime's reluctance to heed proposals for radicalization of the military may have been prompted by the fear of further alienating the officer corps and hurting its morale. While many agreed on the desperate need to politicize the army along revolutionary lines, a consensus emerged that the required ideological transformation could not be accomplished overnight and that any precipitous tampering with the existing military establishment might have disastrous consequences. Hence the regime adopted an incremental approach to military reform. While not explicitly expressed, it appears that under this alternative the military agreed to reform itself politically, with a minimum of outside (ASU) interference and a reduced level of press criticism. Meanwhile the efforts to cement the popular forces, as represented by the ASU and the armed forces, continued but only at the highest level. In January 1969 this task was assigned to Foreign Minister Mahmud Riyad, Interior Minister Sha'rawi Guma'a and National Guidance Minister Muhammad Fa'iq who reportedly "met with high ranking officers to discuss ways of ideologically cementing the people and the Armed Forces. . . ."[28] Significantly all three ministers were ex-officers and therefore more acceptable to their former military colleagues. Yet there was no firm evidence of lower level horizontal contacts between ASU cadres and the fighting-men. As in 1964,[29] "the mode of representation of the Armed Forces in the ASU," was once again left to the ASU Supreme Executive Committee.[30]

The bare outlines of the military's program for self-reform became discernible during the second half of 1968. Decisions emanating from the "political leadership" of the armed forces stressed certain basic themes, i.e., spirit of independent initiative at the front, the need for cohesion in each fighting unit between officers and men, and the imperativeness of ideological unity.[31] Changes in policy included the basing of promotions on merit rather than age and wider recruitment from among diploma and degree holders. This policy constituted a belated recognition of the importance of a better-educated army; also, it was the regime's response to student demands voiced during the February demonstrations for inclusion in the army. A new regulation placed those with diplomas and degrees in special units from which peasants and other less-educated soldiers were excluded.[32] There were optimistic reports that finally "natural integration" —*tafa'ul al-tabi'i*—was "beginning to occur in the army, integrating the soldiers, the leadership, and modern armaments." [33] Yet the optimism was tempered by the realization that a change of mentality—*taghyir aqliyyah*—was the crucial problem.[34] It remained for Haykal to remind everyone that the changes had "occurred in material fields and not in the moral area . . ." and that "according to knowledgeable sources, the changes in the armed forces are only imaginary." [35] At least one area of military endeavor showed unmistakable change. During 1969 evidence of tightening military discipline came to light when a number of commanders were summarily relieved of their duties and punished for unsatisfactory performance in the continuing battle at the canal front.[36]

The other center of power most frequently mentioned was the police apparatus, particularly the intelligence services. The public's dislike of police and security men had been a well-known fact even before the revolution. The persistence of this feeling after a decade of Nasirite rule periodically prompted the regime to institute "trust the police" campaigns which pictured the police as "servants of the people and the revolution." [37] The limited success of these campaigns could be explained by the arbitrary and high-handed behavior of the police, the efficiency of which had significantly increased since 1952. Therefore, in the postwar atmosphere of popular ferment it was natural for the police apparatus to become a main target of press criticism, especially after the arrest of Salah Nasr, Chief of Intelligence. Nasr was charged with involvement in the unsuccessful August 1967 coup and defamation of the Intelligence Service by arbitrary arrests and torture. However, the institution of reforms presented certain difficulties in view of the regime's reliance on the police organizations to combat counter-revolutionary attempts. Nasir's dilemma was how to infuse the police apparatus with a new sense of responsibility and restraint toward the public without reducing its efficiency. In contrast to the military, the crucial test for the attitudinal change among the police did not have to wait until the next war with Israel. The test came with the promulgation of Nasir's March 30 Program, and in the context of the new "open society," the police were found wanting.

The March 30 Program may well have been Nasir's most important contribution to Egypt after the revolution itself. His main problem was not the legitimation of the new order—this had been virtually accomplished with the help of charisma and because his program met the aspirational demands of most Egyptians. Rather than legitimation, the president was concerned with implementing his program without interference from the military, the police apparatus, or the bureaucracy. As to the program itself, it sought to retain and consolidate the lessons and gains achieved in the liberalizing period after the June defeat; it also provided a comprehensive and long-range plan for political and social reform.

In a more immediate sense Nasir's program aimed at absorbing and rechannelling the growing unrest and frustration as manifested in the widespread worker-student demonstrations in February 1968. The government's initial response combined the use of force with persuasion to quell the strikers. Almost immediately after the restoration of order the president intervened personally with a series of steps designed to meet certain of the demonstrators' demands. A retrial was ordered to mete out heavier sentences to the generals responsible for the June defeat and negotiations were started between student leaders and deputies at the National Assembly. On 3 March, the president addressed a workers' rally of thousands at Hilwan where the first demonstrations had originated. He skillfully placed himself on the side of the demonstrators by castigating the police for initially resorting to force and blamed a handful of "reactionary agitators" for the disturbances. Finally he promised the liberation of "every inch" of territory from Israel, as the strikers had demanded. On 20 March came the second installment of short-range reforms with the formation of a new thirty-three member cabinet with Nasir as prime minister. More than any of its predecessors since 1953, the March cabinet represented the infusion of new blood—fourteen new ministers, all civilians. While ex-officers still held many of the key ministries—i.e., Interior, Foreign Affairs, Communications,

Labor, War Production, Nation Guidance, Local Administration
—proportionately, the civilian component had been greatly increased.

As reflected in Table 24 there was a sharp decrease in the military's presence from 65.4 percent to 39.4 percent. The higher civilian presence corresponded to the antimilitary feeling among
Egyptians following the war. Significantly, at least half of the
fourteen new ministers were drawn from university faculties; and
almost all of these were highly respected and popular professors
with strong pro-student and reformist orientations. In this sense
the regime's policy to win over the students was clear and explicit.

Table 24
Postwar Changes in Cabinet Composition

CABINET	TOTAL N	MILITARY		CIVILIAN	
		N	%	N	%
June 1967	29	19	65.4	10	34.4
March 1968	33	13	39.4	20	60.6

On Muslim New Year's day came the March 30 Program—
the third installment of reform. Specifically, it provided for the
rebuilding of the ASU through a system of successive, multilevel
elections—a fundamental departure from the previous appoin-
tive procedures. Nasir stressed the necessity of bringing "new
blood" into the ASU, as well as "at all levels" of the government,
the diplomatic corps, and the economic bureaucracy. In addition, the president proposed ten guidelines for the drafting of a
permanent constitution which stipulated that:

1. The Constitution should stipulate and affirm that Egypt
is an organic part of the Arab nation, by history, struggle
and destiny . . .
2. The Constitution should stipulate that all socialist gains
must be protected and strengthened. Such gains include the
proportional representation given to peasants and workers
in all elected popular councils by the Charter; and participation of workers in management and their sharing of profits; the right to free education, health and social insurance;
the emancipation of women; and protection of the rights of
children, mothers, and families.

3. The Constitution should stress the strong link between social and political freedom, and should provide every guarantee of individual freedom, and security for all citizens in all circumstances, and every guarantee of freedom of thought, expression, publication, opinion, scientific research and the press.

4. The Constitution should provide for the establishment of a modern State and its administration. Having a modern State is no longer a question of one individual, nor does it depend on political organization alone. Science, and technology now play a vital part. Accordingly, it must be clear that the President performs the duties of government through ministers and expert councils which combine the cream of efficiency and national experience . . .

5. The Constitution should clearly define the government establishments and their jurisdictions, including the Head of State, the legislative body and the executive body. It is desirable that the authority of the National Assembly is stressed. As the legislative body, the Assembly also controls the Government and participates in drafting and carrying out the general plan for political organization and economic and social development . . .

6. The Constitution should stress the importance of work as the only criterion of the value of man.

7. The Constitution should guarentee the protection of public property, cooperative property, and private property as well as the limits and social role of each.

8. The Constitution should stress the immunity of the judiciary. The right to seek justice must be guaranteed. No measure by the authorities must be above being contested in the courts, because the judiciary is the scale of justice which gives everyone his rights and prevents any violation of rights or freedoms.

9. The Constitution should provide for the establishment of a supreme constitutional court having the right to decide on the constitutionality of laws and to see that they conform to the Charter.

10. The Constitution should specify the term of office for

senior executive political posts to ensure constant renewal
and regeneration.[38]

In short, Nasir's constitutional guidelines comprised a liberal
and progressive document by any standard. The key provisions
stressed Egypt's continuing Arabism and socialism. Welfare-statist
measures and the new role of workers and peasants in various organizations were to be preserved and strengthened. More significant were the explicit guarantees relating to the basic freedoms
and the supremacy of the law, maintained by an independent judiciary. To assure circulation at the top, the projected constitution would specify terms of office for senior political leaders.
Furthermore, the National Assembly's authority would be
stressed within the context of a modern state which ". . . is no
longer a question of one individual . . ."—a clear reference to
the need to depersonalize power and to reduce the dependence of
the political system on Nasir himself. All of these proposals
would be eventually incorporated into a permanent constitution.
The question remained as to *when* and *to what extent* would the
new reform provisions become operational; more specifically,
would they be applicable under the prevailing emergency situation?

In the period following 30 March, these questions were only
partly answered. The press, led by *Al-Ahram,* continued to maintain a consistently critical yet constructive approach toward public affairs, and on several key issues came down on the side of
moderation and liberalization. After the student-worker disorders
of February, Haykal took pains to explain that "while the coun-
ter-revolution does exist, crushing it by force is not the way to
save the revolution." [39] It was generally recognized by the
press and affirmed by Nasir that the youth and the masses had
reason to protest in view of the defeat and the exposés of its aftermath.[40] Haykal's prescription for Egyptian society was "political work" by the ASU, in an atmosphere of free discussion.

The acid test of the "open society" came on 13 October, with
Haykal's attack on the military security and state security organizations (*Jihaz Mukhabarat*). The subsequent dramatic confrontation between Haykal and the security organs finally convinced

many students of the Egyptian scene that genuine change was taking place. The incident centered on the arbitrary arrest and two-week detention of a statistician by the security organizations without charges. Acting under legal procedures, the scientist had released statistical information on nutrition for use by a Japanese firm against the wishes of Lt. Gen. Gamal Askar, the chairman of the Statistics and General Mobilization Organization, who had him arrested. The subsequent release of the scientist did not satisfy Haykal, who reaffirmed the nation's commitment to freedom of thought and scientific research and the supremacy of the law —two of the principles of the March 30 Program. The lengthy defense that the Minister of State for Security Amin Huwaydi included in a letter to *Al-Ahram* did not deter Haykal who declared that "a man is innocent until proven guilty." [41] Similar incidents concerning the Justice Ministry's unlawful detention of citizens were revealed in August 1969 leading to the resignation of Justice Minister Abu Nusayr.[42] A major judicial reorganization followed, involving 800 new appointments and promotions. While Haykal stressed once again the need to keep centers of power liquidated, it was clear that these still persisted in Egyptian society; nevertheless, Haykal had demonstrated that now they could be challenged.

In two subsequent articles during October 1968, Haykal continued to expound the concept of an open society, the preservation of which depended on eliminating the centers of power. More fundamental to Haykal, however, was how to prevent the emergence of these centers—a problem that led him to promulgate a system of "controlled equilibrium."

A Controlled Pluralistic Democracy?

Despite his denials, Haykal's role as Nasir's unofficial spokesman was known for many years.[43] The president used Haykal's weekly column in *Al-Ahram* for trial balloons to gauge public reaction to new ideas and programs. In a given editorial, however, it was impossible to distinguish Nasir's ideas from Haykal's. Whatever the case, the notion of a pluralistic political system represented a clear departure from earlier monolithic concepts that bore some of the markings of totalitarian rule. Specifically, Haykal's formulation envisaged the creation of various "institutions" which would at once blunt attempts of personal control and at the same time articulate their conflicting interests before decision-making bodies.[44] The only way to influence the decision-making process would be to work through these institutions, none of which would have absolute control over the others within the ASU and the government in general. A scheme of horizontal separation of powers à la Polybius, Montesquieu, or the American Founding Fathers, was not what Haykal had in mind. Instead he favored a situation of "controlled and stable equilibrium" among the popular forces represented by various "institutions," which would perpetually check and balance one another. Simultaneously, these institutions would be in a condition of check and balance with respect to various governmental agencies, which in turn would check and balance one another.[45] Haykal specifies concrete examples as follows:

to check

Universities and scientific research institutions———————→All governmental planning organizations and operations
Judicial branch—————→All security organizations
Local popular councils——→Local government agencies
Legislative branch (National Assembly)——→Ministerial power
The free press——→All aspects of governmental policy making and execution

What emerges is a pluralist scheme within a single-party organization—the ASU.[46] In his frequent use of Britain as a model, Haykal is confronted with the key role of political parties in pluralist democracies. However, in analyzing the dilemma he simply notes the absence of parties in Egypt and proceeds to assert that "traditional government is shaken" and the emerging institutions are still too weak to take its place.[47]

Opposition to Haykal and his views revealed itself dramatically during November 1968. There were unofficial reports of an assassination attempt against him and press criticism of his "open society" views appeared in *Akhbar al-Yawm*. His critics opposed the expansion of democratic liberties to elements not represented in the ASU, as Haykal may have implied. If the basic freedoms were given to "bourgeois classes" and "counter-revolutionary elements," then the "open society" would become "a place of social chaos." [48] This clearly indicated basic disagreements regarding future political development in Egypt; it also reflected a serious split among the top leadership.

Despite these debates, the liberalization program continued, especially in the legal area. On 3 November, republican decrees were issued limiting the authority of the military police to arrest civilians and liberalizing prison laws and other emergency restrictions imposed since the war.[49] However, the extent to which these measures were implemented could not be readily ascertained.

The second wave of student demonstrations in late November 1968 did not strengthen the hand of the liberalizers. Peaceful marches by precollege students protesting the cancellation of automatic admission to universities soon turned into violent clashes with the police claiming more than twenty lives. *Al-Ahram* reported "a hidden hand" behind the demonstrations and Nasir blamed them on "Israeli and foreign financing and planning." [50] Foreign Minister Mahmud Riyad described the students' restlessness as "a world disease" and Haykal came to their defense by asserting that Egyptian youth were not the drug-addicted deviationists found in other countries. He urged a continuing "dialogue" between the generations.[51] He and others defended the students' right to differ with their elders at a time when defeat in war had laid bare the gap between promise and performance.[52] The reaction from the hard-liners was equally adamant. Husayn Fahmi of *Al-Akhbar* called for "severe punishments" for student agitators, since at a time of external peril, the regime should "uproot the counter-revolutionary forces from within." [53] He pointed at what he considered to be a conflict in Egypt's educational system, between socialist and nonsocialist elements; Fahmi's solution—"to inject the youth with socialism." [54] Ahmad Baha' al-Din was equally uncompromising; the well-known editor of *Al-Musawwar* spoke of the students' lack of clear perception of the difficulties involved in successfully overcoming Israel's strength. He told them to express their opinions through "orderly channels" not through demonstrations.[55] Cognizant of the need for long-range solutions, the government reorganized the ASU's youth sector and placed renewed emphasis on the political education of youth.[56] In addition, the regime seemed to encourage student involvement in the political process [57] and introduced a new system of student participation in university administration.[58]

What is an Egyptian?

Few areas of national endeavor escaped critical evaluation in the two years following the 1967 War. However, one aspect of the political process which remained relatively unchallenged was the sacrosanct realm of ideology. If a primary function of ideology is the legitimation of the elites, then it is clear why they are reluctant to make it a subject of debate. It would have been suicidal for the Egyptian leadership to modify significantly its basic ideological creeds of Arabism and socialism. One might even argue that despite the disappointment that Egyptian leaders and citizens alike felt with these ideological orientations there existed no pressing need to change creeds. While no field survey is feasible at this stage of Egypt's history, it is safe to assume that Arabism and socialism still enjoy a wider degree of legitimacy than any other ideological construct. Thus in the postwar period, ideological change occurred at the micro level, centering on important shifts of emphasis.

Realizing the need to maximize national unity, the leadership effected a subtle shift of emphasis from Pan-Arabism to Egyptian nationalism. While maintaining Egypt's basic commitment to Arabism,[59] there was a growing awareness that at a time of external danger Egyptians had to rely primarily upon themselves for their salvation.[60] This reidentification with Egypt soon reopened the debate on the "Egyptian personality," which had laid dormant since the mid-1950s. The writings of Taha Husayn and Tawfiq al-Hakim—the patron saints of Egyptian nationalism— once again assumed some of their former credibility, as ASU's *Al-Jumhuriyyah* reminded Egyptians "not to forget the pharaonic past, since this is a part of Egypt's personality, as are the Arabic language and the Islamic religion." [61] A more devastating attack on the historical censorship of the late 1950s came from Haykal who asserted that "during the Syrian unification it was an unforgivable mistake to mention the pharaonic origin of Egypt." [62] He also charged the leadership for taking too long to identify the Egyptian personality, thereby exacerbating the bewildering identity crisis which had left Egyptians hanging between the Islamic, Arab, and European societies. In order to resolve the national personality crisis Haykal advanced the following definition of "Egyptian personality." [63]

I. Name (*Ism*)—The Egyptian people
II. Family (*Usrah*)—The Arab nation
III. Race (*Jins*)—A mixture of several cultures, the most important being that of early Egypt in the Nile valley.
IV. Address (*Inwan*)—Between Asia and Africa, where the White and Red Seas meet.

A more balanced view of the Egyptian past had finally emerged. The massive onrush of the late fifties toward Arabism had been checked. One could even detect a pervasive feeling of self-assurance with respect to the Arabism of the Arab East. Indeed, having made certain sacrifices on behalf of Arabism during the last decade, the Egyptians felt they needed no further proof of their Arabness.

Education and Literature

The criticism of education centered mainly on the curricula of preparatory and secondary schools. At the general level, the existing curriculum was criticized for having failed to give the student a correct view of the internal and external world. Specifically, the textbooks for certain required courses—history, politics, geography, sociology—needed updating and rewriting to insure a more well-rounded and sophisticated analysis of national and world problems. A more serious charge against the Ministry of Education was that textbooks of all levels lacked a comprehensive treatment of the origins and development of the Arab-Israeli conflict. These shortcomings were seen as causing serious misconceptions about Israel and the international scene in general.[64] Finally, the disjointed nature of course work in Egyptian history was seen as a factor in retarding the development of a "national personality." [65]

A related problem was the distorted picture of reality given the public by the press. The campaign for a truthful and freer press was led by Haykal who advocated a policy of "sticking to the truth." In January 1970, at the height of the highly successful Israeli incursions, Haykal termed "unacceptable" the government's attempt to hide the nature and magnitude of Egypt's losses.[66] Others analyzed the general shortcomings of Egyptian journalism prior to and during the June War—e.g., preoccupation with sex and sports, misleading public opinion on the economic problems before the June War and on the war itself, and lack of sufficient concern with workers and peasants.[67]

The demands for a freer press and a more objective school curriculum were bound to lead to the more fundamental question of literary censorship. It is well known that such censorship did exist both before and after the June War, although to a much milder degree than in most communist states, including Yugoslavia. In October 1968, no less a person than the noted writer, Abd al-Rahman al-Sharqawi, called for the lifting of governmental censorship on literature; but the issue remains unresolved.[68]

General Criticism of the Past (1952–1967)

Out of the torrent of criticism and debate a synthesis began to appear in late 1968, which provided a diagnostic consensus among journalists and the intelligentsia concerning the period since the 1952 Revolution. In several important aspects, the emerging view of Egypt's recent past resembles the analysis presented in earlier chapters.

One major area of criticism centered on the shortcomings of military rule. The psychological inability of the officers' corps to undertake the functions of rulership was analyzed by Haykal and others in considerable detail. Operating in a political and ideological vacuum and lacking political experience, "some of these leaders were not qualified to handle rationally the tremendous power of the state." [69] This resulted in "an extension of authority . . . magnified by the advent of socialism." [70]

Haykal also criticized the tendency among the military toward overcommitment, secrecy, and ambition. He recognized the corrupting influence of power on the military elite. It is asserted that in their quest for total control, they overcommitted themselves by promising to move Egypt into the twentieth century. To further complicate their task of modernization, they threw a veil of secrecy over Egypt's political life—"the secrecy of revolutionaries." Hence there emerged the "centers of power." [71]

Another consequence of the military's influence in the pre-1967 regime was the alienation of intellectuals. It is maintained that the military's presence and its ideological orientation prevented a genuine rapprochement between the elite and the intelligentsia. The inherent anti-intellectualism of most military men also existed in Egypt. As Haykal related, the regime generally "belittled the intellectuals," yet some of its military members "tried to get doctorates by any means. . . ." [72] Undoubtedly, these men wanted to combine the power of their political roles with the prestige of intellectuals, thereby enjoying the best of two worlds. One should add that certain of the ruling officers did not even attempt to acquire doctorates, but simply assigned themselves the tasks of intellectuals. The outcome was the appearance of half-baked journalists, authors, ideologues, political scientists, economists—roles that had been the preserve of the intelligentsia.[73] Finally, as Haykal pointed out, the political system could not absorb the "rightist traditional intellectuals" because of their class position; neither could the system absorb the "leftist intellectuals" because of their political position.[74] The coming of socialism liquidated the traditional classes and discredited its rightist intellectuals. However, the resulting vacuum remained substantially empty not only because the "new classes [peasants, workers] were not ready" [75] to take an active role, but also because of the military's suspicion and reluctance to use the leftist intelligentsia.

How did the system sustain itself for fifteen years under the burdens of these shortcomings? Hamrush [76] of the left and

Haykal [77] of the mainstream maintained that the system worked because of the leader's personality.[78] Despite the conceptual difficulties imposed by a Marxist orientation, Hamrush was remarkably successful in evaluating the spiritual role of the leadership: "During the ten years prior to the formation of the ASU, . . . the regime relied on the tremendous magnetic force of its leadership . . . this magnetism literally spellbound the people." [79] Hamrush went on to relate that the failure to organize party structures until 1962 came from an overwhelming reliance on "magnetic leadership" whereby "too heavy a load was placed on it, more than it could carry. . . ." [80] This observation confirms the thesis advanced in previous chapters that the great legitimacy and support accorded Nasir blinded the regime to the need for party organization.

There exists a striking resemblance between Khalid Muhammad Khalid's indirect criticism of the regime during the early 1960s [81] and the critical attitudes expressed after the June War. Khalid's stress on the basic freedoms, popular elections, and limitation of state power were precisely the subjects that became central to the discussions and reforms of 1968.

The New ASU

Nasir's problem of party organization in 1968 was what Manfred Halpern had diagnosed in 1963. Halpern viewed the political party as a means to create a viable political culture by binding together charisma, ideology, organization, and accountability.[82] In the Egyptian case, charisma emerged foremost, followed by ideology and a modicum of organization. Least developed was accountability to a growing constituency—a function haphazardly filled by the president and more recently by the National Assembly. It was precisely this lack of accountability that became one of the main issues of the postwar period. Therefore, the electoral process chosen to maximize the popular legitimacy of the new ASU also contained the ingredients for making the organization an instrument of accountability.

In order to give the March 30 Program popular legitimacy

Nasir initiated a wide-ranging personal campaign directed at the various groups comprising the ASU. His stated aim was to obtain a rational, popular affirmation of the mandate placed upon him on 9–10 June 1967. Thus he saw the forthcoming referendum on the March 30 Program as a test of rational, popular commitment in contrast to the emotional, popular commitment of 9–10 June 1967.[83] During the month of April he delivered campaign speeches to students and intellectuals, soldiers at the front, workers, and peasants explaining his program of reform and reconstruction. On 2 May 1968 more than 7 million citizens (98.2 percent turnout) went to the polls; the announced results of the voting indicated a 99.98 percent affirmative vote, 798 negative votes, and 887 empty ballots.

Once the stamp of popular legitimacy was obtained, the rebuilding of the ASU began. On 5 May all ASU senior executives resigned and on 16 May Nasir appointed a fifty-member ASU Supervisory Electoral Committee. Its membership (see Table 25) was derived from the constituent groups of the ASU including five heads of professional syndicates, four academies, two National Assembly deputies, two ambassadors, one student, fifteen workers, nine peasants, and a general category of twelve miscellaneous personalities. Further scrutiny along occupational lines yields a different breakdown (See column 2 of Table 25). Under the new categorization the number of academics rises to seven; five ex-ministers emerge, as well as one journalist and one bureaucrat. However, the two most suspect groups of the official classification are the workers and peasants. A careful reading of the job descriptions of the sixteen workers clearly shows that all of these men occupied leading positions in the syndicates. While it is safe to assume that they are workers, it is possible that their leadership posts occupied a large part of their time. As to the nine peasants, virtually all occupied local leadership positions, thereby making it difficult to state with certainty that they worked their land full time. In summary, the syndicalists were overrepresented, in contrast to the National Assembly, the governmental bureaucracy, and particularly the students, despite their rioting in February 1968. The combination of ex-ministers and academics was high enough to provide effective political leadership. There were no less than twelve Ph.D.s, or 24 percent of the total committee.

Significantly, the sole member with a military background was an army physician. The appointment of politically neutral and widely respected personalities and the election of Dr. Mahmud Fawzi as chairman, endowed the Committee of 50 with an aura of impartiality.

In late May and early June the Committee of 50 set out to organize the hierarchical sequence of ASU elections, the first of which was held on 25 June when 180,239 candidates campaigned for 75,840 local committee posts in 7,584 basic units. Over 5 million citizens voted. The next task of basic-unit members was to elect the 1,648 members of the National Congress which took place on 14 July 1968, according to the regulations set by the Basic Law of the ASU.[84] It is difficult to reconstruct a clear picture of the composition of the National Congress because of conflicting sources of official and unofficial information. It appears that the new stricter definition of peasants and workers had been generally applied during the electoral process. According to this definition a peasant is one whose personal and family holdings should not exceed ten *faddans;* agriculture should be his main occupation and source of income; and he should live in the countryside.[85] A laborer (worker) is one who is not eligible for membership in the professional unions; and not a graduate of a university, higher institute, or military college.[86] These definitions contrast sharply with those employed after 1962 which stipulated landholdings up to twenty-five *faddans* for peasants and a loose definition for workers that included technicians and intellectuals as well.[87] According to Egyptian sources over 50 percent of the National Congress was comprised of peasants and workers as defined above.[88] The same sources, however, admit that this percentage included heads of general syndicates, their deputies and general secretaries, directors of cultural centers, heads of agricultural reform societies and cooperatives, and local clerical officials—in short the local peasant and worker leadership. While a large number of these may not be functioning as full-time peasants and workers, there is little evidence to suggest that they have moved into other occupational categories. The other half of the National Congress included intellectuals, physicians, lawyers, professors, students, merchants, property owners, and the managerial class. In addition, all cabinet ministers but one were elected, as were all governors, all but three ex-ASU secretariat members and all but two ASU governorate secretaries. Surprisingly, certain prominent personalities were defeated—a possible indication that the elections were conducted impartially. Among these were ex-minister Abd al-Qadir Hatim; the prominent writer Yusif Siba'i; Minister of Culture Sarwat Ukasha; editor of *Ruz al-Yusif,* Ahmad Hamrush; the director of ASU's Institute for Socialist Studies, Dr. Ibrahim Sa'd al-Din; and President Nasir's two brothers.

In many respects the Congress reflected the sense of balance that the regime had striven to obtain since the war. Ideologically, the left was strong but not preponderant as indicated by the defeats of two of its leaders, Hamrush and Sa'd al-Din. The right was represented by Azharite religious men and various profes-

Table 25

ASU Committees: Occupational Breakdown

	COMMITTEE OF 50		COMMITTEE OF 100
	Official Breakdown	*Actual Occupational Classification*	*Official Breakdown*
Professionals (Engineers, M.D.s, Lawyers)	—	—	14
Heads of Professional Syndicates	5	5	—
Managers	—	—	4
Journalists	—	1	6
Bureaucrats	—	1	4
Academics	4	7	9
Instructors	—	—	3
Students	1	1	4
National Assembly Deputies	2	2	5
Ex-Ministers	—	5	2
Ambassadors	2	2	—
Workers	15	—	33
Workers' Syndicalists	—	16	—
Peasants	9	6	16
Executives of Peasants' Syndicates, Cooperative and Agrarian Reform Societies	—	4	—
Miscellaneous	12	—	—

sionals and bureaucrats. The rest of the members, however, were centrists, representing the "wide, middle, silent majority." [89] Among the centrists one might count the key category of "national capital" which won 15 percent of the National Congress seats.[90] According to the press, these included men of finance and property,[91] company directors, board chairmen, cultivators, and merchants. The inclusion of these men constituted another indication that the regime intended to broaden the base of the new national consensus during a time of external danger.

The statistics of the National Congress also reflect the relative strength of the workers when compared with the peasants. Of the 859 in the worker-peasant category, 578 were identified as workers and 281 as peasants. The relative weakness of the peasants was due to the lack of effective leadership as well as a lower level of political consciousness—factors that are plausible explanations if the stricter definition of peasant was enforced. In contrast the workers exhibited a higher level of ideological and group consciousness as manifested in greater campaigning activity and better organization and leadership. It was reported that in certain areas workers' candidates, by allying themselves with members of the Socialist Youth Organization, successfully challenged the workers' slates supported by factory management.[92]

Nasir was elected president of the ASU National Congress at its first session, and a Committee of 100 was chosen to prepare the agenda and direct the proceedings. This committee was constituted by the election of two to four representatives from each governorate. No ministers or governors could be elected, thus giving greater opportunity to National Congress members. At the same time Mahmud Fawzi was elected chairman and Abd al-Salam Zayyat as secretary general to preside over the affairs of the committee through five subcommittees.

A comparison of the membership of the Committee of 100 and the earlier Electoral Committee of 50 points to certain marked trends in the building of the ASU. The semi-official breakdowns of the two committees are provided in Table 25. While the committee size doubled, the peasant contingent did not increase proportionately, but the worker component went up from 15 to 33, partly cutting into peasant representation. The new strength of the workers was another indication of the gains

Chart 2. *ASU Organizational Structure (1968)*

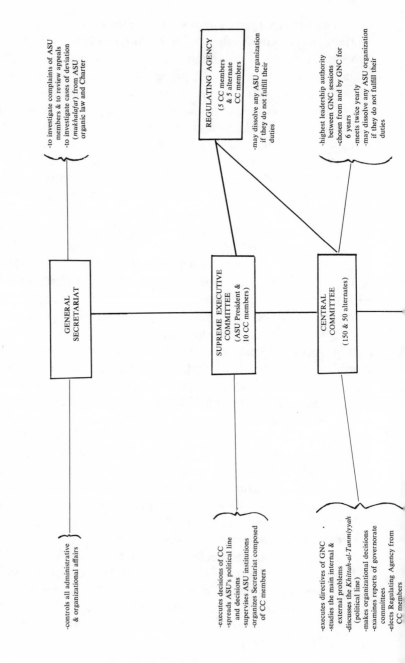

GENERAL SECRETARIAT

-to investigate complaints of ASU members & to review appeals
-to investigate cases of deviation (*mukhalafat*) from ASU organic law and Charter

-controls all administrative & organizational affairs

SUPREME EXECUTIVE COMMITTEE (ASU President & 10 CC members)

-executes decisions of CC
-spreads ASU's political line and decisions
-supervises ASU institutions
-organizes Secretariat composed of CC members

REGULATING AGENCY (5 CC members & 5 alternate CC members)

-may dissolve any ASU organization if they do not fulfill their duties

CENTRAL COMMITTEE (150 & 50 alternates)

-highest leadership authority between GNC sessions
-chosen from and by GNC for 6 years
-meets twice yearly
-may dissolve any ASU organization if they do not fulfill their duties

-executes directives of GNC
-studies the main internal & external problems
-discusses the *Khittah-al-Tanmiyyah* (political line)
-makes organizational decisions
-examines reports of governorate committees
-elects Regulating Agency from CC members

274

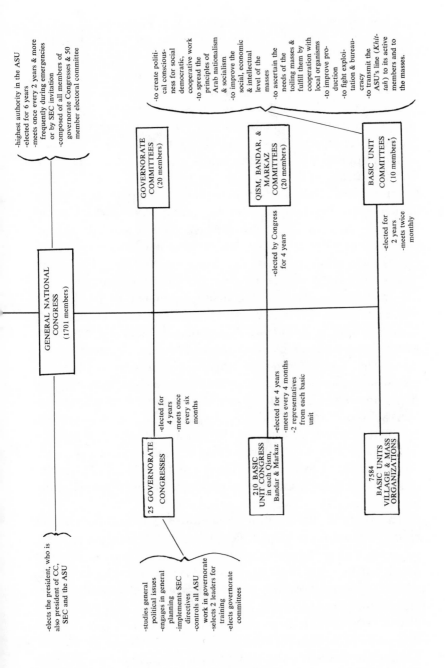

they had registered in the National Congress elections. Other categories with increased representation were the academics, National Assembly deputies, and students.[93] These, combined with 6 well-known journalists were expected to provide intellectual leadership in the preparation of the agenda.

The Committee of 100 submitted its agenda to the first working session of the National Congress on 14 September 1968. It provided for comprehensive mobilization of military and economic resources to oppose the Israeli presence across the canal. The first order of business was the election of ASU's Central Committee (al-Lajnah al-Markaziyyah)—a subject that generated considerable discussion among National Congress delegates. Especially controversial were the composition and modality of choosing the Central Committee. Among intellectuals and jour-. nalists there was substantial opposition to extending the 50 percent worker and peasant quota into the Central Committee; Haykal and Abaza recommended a larger number of intellectuals instead of peasants and workers.[94] Also, there was some apprehension about a presidentially appointed Central Committee, which was put to rest by Nasir during National Congress discussions. The electoral procedure finally instituted was a complex one which combined the leadership's preference with congressional approval. The first step was the election of 250 candidates by ASU Governorate Councils of which 125 full members and 50 alternates were selected by the "political leadership"—in effect President Nasir. The remaining 25 full members were directly appointed from above. Thus, a slate of 150 full members and 50 alternate members was presented to the National Congress, which gave its unanimous approval.[95]

The study of the Central Committee's composition presents certain difficulties in view of conflicting data published in newspapers as well as the ambiguity of classifying individuals who can be placed in more than one category. For example, there was wide disagreement over the number of workers elected; the workers' newspaper Al-Ummal, claimed 68 workers and syndicalists elected, while Akhir Sa'ah put the number at 51.[96] Nevertheless, it is possible to identify most of the components of the Central Committee through a rigorous analysis of the members' occupational background. Such a breakdown is presented in Table 26 which provides as close an approximation to reality as possible.

Of the 150 full members, 24 were incumbent ministers, including presidential advisor, Mahmud Fawzi. This group functioned as an essential connecting link between the top echelons of the party and the government. An important consideration regarding these 24 were their backgrounds: 9 ex-officers and 15 civilians. The 9 ex-officer ministers constituted the sole military representation in the Central Committee, aside from Nasir himself. Indeed, one puzzling aspect of the new ASU was precisely the glaring absence of direct military representation in the various levels of the organizations.

Another important group consisted of 21 full time party workers (*apparatchiki*). These men were expected to provide the organizational backbone of the new ASU. While neither the ministerial component nor the *apparatchiki* had been represented in the Committees of 50 and 100, the academics were found in all three organizations. The 7 academics and the 2 journalists were expected to provide intellectual leadership in the Central Committee.[97] Smaller groups included 2 ex-ministers, 3 bureaucrats, 3 lawyers, 2 teachers, 7 deputies,[98] 3 company board members, 2 national-level professional syndicalists, and 1 agriculturalist. In attempting to determine the extent of actual worker-peasant representation, Table 26 differentiates between the common workers and peasants and their leading elements. A scrutiny of background data shows that of those officially designated under the worker category, 7 were actually national-level workers' syndicalists and 3 local-level workers' syndicalists. Another 35 appear to be common workers [99] although the 3 National Assembly Deputies among them may not be functioning as full-time workers. In contrast, newspaper electoral claims ranged from 51 to 68 workers, both well above the estimate in Table 26. Although Egyptian sources conceded the inclusion of syndicalists in their figures, they did not numerically differentiate between syndicalists and common laborers. In the case of peasants it is possible to identify 1 national-level syndicalist, 4 local syndicalists, and 5 directors of agrarian reform. While 18 appear to be common peasants, it is quite possible that some of the local level agricultural syndicalists and agrarian reform directors are engaged as full-time peasants.[100] Regardless of the figures used, the workers maintained in the Central Committee the two-to-one margin [101] over the peasants that they had held in the Committees of 50 and 100.[102]

It should be emphasized that a significant number of the peasant-worker leadership (syndicalists and other executive personnel)

Table 26
Central Committee Composition

	FULL MEMBERS		ALTERNATE MEMBERS	
OCCUPATIONAL BACKGROUND	N	%	N	%
ASU Regulars (Provincial secretaries)	21	14	–	–
Deputies	7	4.7	1	2
Ministers	24	16	3	6
Ex-Ministers	2	1.3	2	4
Bureaucrats	3	2	1	2
Lawyers	3	2	2	4
Academics	7	4.7	5	10
Teachers	2	1.3	–	–
Journalists	2	1.3	–	–
Chairmen of Boards and Board Members	3	2	7	14
National-level Professional Syndicalists	2	1.3	–	–
Peasants				
Agriculturalists	1	0.7	1	2
Common Peasants	18	12	6	12
National-level Agricultural Syndicalists	1	0.7	1	2
Local-level Agricultural Syndicalists	4	2.7	1	2
Directors of Agrarian Reform	5	3.3	–	–
Workers				
Common Workers	35	23.3	12	24
National-level Worker Syndicalists	7	4.7	4	8
Local-level Worker Syndicalists	3	2	2	4
Unknown	–	–	1	2
Total	150		50	

probably were workers and peasants previously. In the final analysis the important fact about the new ASU was that it actually included real workers and peasants in significant proportions. In percentage terms, using the minimum figures on Table 26, the real peasant-worker total in the Central Committee was 53, or 35.3 percent, of the whole membership, the remaining 14.7 percent of the official quota being filled by syndicalists and agrarian reform leaders. It is not at all clear what this might portend for

the political system. If the new ASU is granted a greater importance, then the sizeable worker-peasant contingent may assume a
key role in Egyptian politics. It would certainly mean broadening
popular participation. And if the political system evolves in a
radical-leftist direction, the worker-peasant component in the
ASU might very well provide the revolutionary cadres of the future.

Table 27

Supreme Executive Committee Candidates

NAME	VOTES	BACKGROUNDS
Ali Sabri	134	officer
Husayn Shafi'i	130	officer
Mahmud Fawzi	129	civilian
Anwar Sadat	119	officer
Ramzi Stinu	112	civilian
Diya' al-Din Dawud	104	civilian
Abd al-Muhsin Abu al-Nur	104	officer
Labib Shuqayr	80	civilian
Kamal Hinnawi	64	officer
Ali Sayyid Ali	62	civilian
Kamal Rif'at	50	officer
Hasan Abbas Zaki	37	civilian
Jabir Jad Abd al-Rahman	34	civilian
Sayyid Mar'i	33	civilian
Aziz Sidqi	33	civilian
Ahmad Fahim Abd al-Mu'ti	30	civilian
Khalid Muhyi al-Din	20	officer
Sayyid Darwish	14	civilian
Mustafa Abu Zayd Fahmi	12	civilian
Fahmi Mansur	10	civilian

The culmination of the ASU electoral process came with the
election of the Supreme Executive Committee on 19 October
1968. As in the election of the Central Committee, the electoral
formula combined a measure of membership participatión with
presidential authority. Contrary to expectations, Nasir declined
to appoint the Supreme Executive Committee. Thus 20 Central
Committee members submitted their candidacy applications to
Interior Minister Sha'rawi Guma'a who was placed in charge of
ASU organizational work. Through his interior minister, Nasir
was in a position to prevent the candidacy of undesirables,

although there is no evidence that he exercised this perogative. Next, the Central Committee elected a ten-man Supreme Executive Committee from the officially approved list of 20 candidates. Only 8 candidates received the required majority of votes and election of the remaining two was postponed by presidential suggestion. Those elected were Sabri, Shafi'i, Fawzi, Sadat, Stinu, Dawud, Abu al-Nur, and Shuqayr. In keeping with the president's wishes, the four ministers (as well as Dr. Fawzi) who were elected to the Supreme Executive Committee, resigned their cabinet posts.

Several noteworthy observations can be made about the men who ran for the Supreme Executive Committee. Out of 20 candidates, 7 were ex-officers and 13 were civilians. Twelve were either ministers or ex-ministers. There were 3 academics, 1 worker syndicalist, 1 agriculturalist, and 3 former ASU leaders. Seven of the 20 held Ph.D.s. Ideologically, the candidates represented the whole political spectrum (with the exception of the Brotherhood). For example, the presence of Khalid Muhyi al-Din and Ali Sabri on the left was counterbalanced by Shafi'i and Sadat.

Assuming that the voting represented the relative strength of each candidate in a fair election, in certain cases the outcome acquired special significance. The defeat of Labor Minister Rif'at was unexpected in view of his former identification with the RCC as well as his more recent involvement in labor affairs and ideological questions. Similarly, Khalid Muhyi al-Din's failure to gain more than 20 votes reflected the Central Committee's unwillingness to strengthen the far left wing of the ASU. The voting also showed the inability of long-time associates of the regime—Zaki, Mar'i, Sidqi—to draw support from a Central Committee partly composed of newcomers to politics. The worker-peasant vote was insufficient to assure the victory of either the worker syndicalist or agriculturalist candidate.

Among the winners there were also several surprises, especially the election of Diya' al-Din Dawud and Labib Shuqayr. At 42, Dawud was a latecomer to the leadership with a background of law and provincial party work. Only in March 1968 had he become a minister. Dr. Labib Shuqayr's rise to power was equally meteoric although he only polled 80 votes to Dawud's 104. Also 42, Shuqayr was better known than Dawud, with several years of

Min Huna Nabda' 281

cabinet service as minister of planning and higher education. As a lawyer with a doctorate in political economy from the Sorbonne, Shuqayr is the only intellectual of the SEC.

The election of the remaining 6 members was no surprise. Ali Sabri's election with the highest number of votes (134) was probably due to his former position as ASU General Secretary as well as his identification with ASU's left wing. In contrast Husayn Shafi'i (130 votes) probably drew his strength from the center and right of center. A founding member of the Free Officers group, Shafi'i's public reputation for uprightness and his close identification with Nasir helped assure his election. Dr. Mahmud Fawzi's (129 votes) role as chairman of the Committees of 50 and 100, coupled with his service as foreign minister since the revolution, were undoubtedly responsible for his election. The voting also showed strong support for National Assembly Speaker Anwar al-Sadat (119 votes), another founding member of the Free Officers group, and Dr. Ramzi Stinu (112 votes), a respected ex-minister and the only Copt in the leadership. Finally, the selection of ex-officer Abd al-Muhsin Abu al-Nur (104 votes) brought in a noncontroversial and efficient minister who had been in charge of agrarian reform and local government since the early sixties.

In terms of age Dr. Fawzi was senior member at 68 with Dawud and Shuqayr the junior members at 42; the average age was 50. Not counting the ninth member of the SEC, Nasir himself, the military-vs.-civilian breakdown stood at 4 apiece. Two of the 4 ex-military—Sadat and Shafi'i—had been original members of the Free Officers inner core, in addition to Nasir. Sabri and Abu al-Nur were relative latecomers as second-string Free Officers. There were a total of three Ph.D.s, and in specialization and experience, the SEC included foreign affairs, economics and finance, law, party organization, legislative work, and religious, military and social affairs—again an overall balance.

Soon after its election, the SEC organized itself into five permanent committees: political affairs (Sadat); administration (Sabri); internal affairs (Abu al-Nur); economic development (Shuqayr); culture and information (Dawud). The five permanent committee heads and Interior Minister Sha'rawi Guma'a constituted a joint committee in charge of the ASU's General Secretariat. In this key committee the military presence was especially marked with four ex-officers and only two civilians. Particularly notable was the increasingly powerful position of Interior Minister Guma'a who was neither elected through ASU's electoral procedures nor was he required to resign his cabinet post. Thus, Guma'a became the only man, except the president, who combined governmental and party posts.

Needless to say there are striking similarities, organizationally, between the Arab Socialist Union and prototype communist parties like that of the Soviet Union. These similarities exist at almost every level of the party structure including the Secretariat. However, there are also significant differences between the two, one of the most important being what seems a greater reliance in the ASU on democratic electoral forms. A more basic difference, however, is the immutable fact that the ASU was the handiwork of the regime while the CPSU was the creator of the Soviet state. Indeed, this is the fundamental weakness of the ASU which has given the organization a sense of artificiality and impermanence. As Haykal's writings [103] indicate, since the June War there has been an increasing awareness among the Egyptian elite that the ASU's birth was not crowned with a victorious revolutionary struggle as had been the case with other revolutionary parties. Thus the prevailing circumstances of protracted conflict with Israel are viewed as the only chance for the ASU to prove itself by contributing to the liberation of occupied territory.[104] It was maintained that only through such a struggle would the ASU acquire permanence and grass-roots legitimacy.

Since the completion of the new ASU in the fall of 1968 several problems have remained unresolved. One of these was the modality of military representation in the ASU. The leadership seems to have postponed consideration of this critical issue until after the removal of the Israeli occupation. In the meantime, the ex-officer ministers in the Central Committee, the 4 ex-officer members of the Supreme Executive Committee, and the president constituted the main links between the military establishment and the ASU.

A second unresolved question was that of vanguardism.[105] Instead of initially committing itself to the formation of a purely vanguard organism, the leadership seems to have decided first to create as wide an alliance (*tahaluf*) of popular forces as possible. This was to be followed by the organization of a vanguard party (*Hizb al-Tali'i*) selected from the most active elements of the alliance. Such a cautious policy may have been prompted by the danger of alienating popular opinion through the creation of a privileged, elitist vanguard.

The third and probably the most dangerous problem facing the political system and the ASU was the continuing bifurcation between left and center, with the leadership taking a generally neutral position. More vocal and better organized, the left favored change along radical-revolutionary lines. These included a highly selective and more ideologically motivated vanguard party, a people's militia, and a tighter restructuring of society and the ASU excluding the remaining upper middle class of entrepreneurs, merchants, and landowners often described as national capitalists.[106] It seemed that the only person who could create a *modus vivendi* between the various ideological groups was Nasir. At the National Congress and Central Committee sessions the president had been able to minimize overt manifestations of ideological conflict through the sheer weight of his personality, reinforced by popular support.

Finally there existed the twin problems of defining the ASU's relationship to the press and the National Assembly. Both issues were important enough to generate heated public discussion and press controversy. In late December 1968 Haykal editorially rejected a proposal to establish an ASU Supreme Press Council to control and supervise the press.[107] A week later Haykal's vehement defense of a free press came under frontal attack from Mahmud Alim, the editor of *Akhbar al-Yawm*. Alim accused the Egyptian press of being anti-regime and anti-revolutionary and advocated the application of state power to assure press support for "the principles of the revolution."[108] He further declared that a party without a press would be one lacking authority and opinion and demanded close coordination between the ASU and the press.[109]

Equally explosive was the developing rivalry between the ASU and the National Assembly. Because the Assembly had been relatively more effective than the old ASU, its deputies viewed the strengthening of the party organization with misgivings and alarm. Already there had been a discernible decline in Assembly power in the postwar period and deputies feared that Assembly functions would be taken over by various ASU bodies. In early November 1968, Nasir personally acknowledged the existence of the rivalry and took a number of steps to minimize it.[110] The first task was the delimitation of the ASU's and the National Assembly's respective functions and areas of competence.

The ASU was to be "the supreme popular authority, which assumed the leadership role in the people's name." [111] In this capacity the ASU exercised "popular political control on the governmental organism." [112] Under the guidance of the Central Committee, the ASU would draw "the political line" which would be binding upon all governmental organizations and by implication on other aspects of national life. The basic problem as seen by the regime was how to bind the Central Committee and the National Assembly.

The National Assembly, on the other hand, represented the supreme state authority. Its functions included general supervision over the execution of ASU directives and the legislation of statutes in accordance with the political line of the Central Committee. Thus as the parliamentary arm of the ASU, the Assembly would exercise constitutional control over the state apparatus.[113] It was expected that in practice the ASU and the National Assembly would control and balance each other. While the ASU would not give the Assembly "direct orders," it would be in a position to pressure it by mobilizing the masses or working through the president.[114]

Despite these clarifications of the Assembly's role vis-à-vis the party, the rivalry persisted. On 7 November 1968, by exercising his constitutional rights, the president dissolved the Assembly, several months in advance of its legal expiration date. It was feared that by calling the legislature back into session the rivalry would intensify and some deputies would have to resign their posts in view of the more restrictive laws redefining the categories of workers and peasants. To reassure the deputies, Nasir reiterated his belief in the indispensability of the National Assembly.

On 8 January 1969, seven million Egyptians voted for a new National Assembly of 350 deputies. The electoral results showed that the turnover of deputies between the 1964 Assembly and the new one was very large, about 73 percent; only 92 had been in the 1964 legislature. In all probability this was due to the automatic elimination from candidacy of those ex-deputies whose occupational-financial status did not conform with the tighter laws regarding the workers and the peasants. This hypothesis is strengthened by the fact that only 117 of the 350 former deputies became candidates in 1969.[115]

The dearth and the unreliability of biographical data on the new deputies does not permit a comprehensive analysis of sources of recruitment. However, according to occupational figures provided by the Egyptian press, the following trends were discernible. As in the various ASU organizations, the worker representation in the Assembly increased and that of the peasants declined—both by significant margins. In 1964 there were 75 deputies identified as workers and 108 described as peasants; in 1969 the number of workers increased by 44 to a total of 119, and peasants decreased by the same number to a mere 64 members.[116] In other words, the peasant dominance of 1964 had been replaced by an equal worker dominance in 1969. A number of tentative explanations may be advanced for the workers' electoral success. As in the ASU elections held earlier, the workers' leadership had assumed a very active role in the campaign.[117] It appeared that the workers had better leadership and organization and a higher level of ideological consciousness than the peasants. Also it is possible that the new definition of peasant disqualified a number of effective ex-peasant candidates from the race.

A second development of perhaps greater long-range significance was the election of 23 deputies who had run on their own without ASU support. The ASU had formally sponsored 350 candidates against 643 others who ran privately. The ASU's candidates won in every electoral district except those won by the 23 independents. Herein may lie the seeds of a two-party system in Egypt.

In effect the regime had permitted a list of opposition candidates to run against its chosen candidates. After their election, the Central Committee declared its willingness to utilize "these positive elements." The fact that the twenty-three had successfully surmounted stiff competition by marshalling mass support was sufficient proof to the Central Committee that they possessed leadership qualities.[118] As a result, the party went out of its way to welcome the independents and pledged to give them the same treatment as party-backed deputies.[119] All this was in keeping with the flexibility of the regime since the June War.

The Assembly elections brought the reorganization of Egypt's political system to its culmination. While many dark areas remain undefined regarding the legislature's relationship with the ASU and the government, the elections of certain leading personalities as deputies, may have provided a temporary solution. Among the elected were eight ministers—Fa'iq, Sidqi, Nusayr, Badawi, Huwaydi, Hijazi, Jaballah, and Zaki—who would be in a position to link the National Assembly with the government. In addition, Labib Shuqayr of the Supreme Executive Committee was elected a deputy and subsequently Speaker of the National Assembly, thus tying together the party and the legislature at the very top.

14

The Politics of
Protracted Conflict

SINCE the Arab-Israeli War of 1967, it has become increasingly clear that the protracted struggle with Israel is having a profound influence on social-political change in Egypt. The emergency conditions arising from the prolonged Israeli occupation, no less than the defeat itself, have forced the Egyptian people to confront painful and sobering realities as never before in their recent history.

A major reality Egyptians have come to recognize since the war is their limited capability, both diplomatic and military, to remove the Israeli presence across the Canal. Diplomatically, their hopes for an externally imposed solution were tempered by their perception of the world situation. Unlike the aftermath of the Anglo-French-Israeli invasion of 1956, the June War elicited neither a Soviet-American alignment nor an aroused world public opinion against Israel. Moreover, a better understanding of the American political process has prompted the Egyptians to tone down earlier expectations of a major American role in ending the Israeli occupation.[1] They have been aware of the changes since 1956 in the American elites' external priorities. What especially bewildered pro-Western Egyptians was not the U.S. involvement in Vietnam, but the Johnson administration's seeming disinterest in maintaining America's power position in the Arab orbit. After a temporary heightening of expectations during ex-Governor Scranton's Middle East mission late in 1968, the Egyptian (and Arab) attitude reverted to the earlier view of the United States policy. While the Egyptians perceived a greater Republican awareness of American interests in the Middle East, they also realize that President Nixon's domestic vulnerability makes it unlikely that he could repeat the forceful Eisenhower performance of 1956–57 in ending the occupation.[2] However, with the Rogers peace initiative in 1970, Egyptian hopes for a positive American role were rekindled.

The Egyptian expectations of Soviet support were also limited. Despite persistent feelings of suspicion, Egyptians are grateful to the USSR for its massive military and economic assistance. But they are also aware of the lack of Soviet militancy toward the United States and Israel. To be sure, the Egyptians do not expect the Soviets to join them in attacking Israel, nor have they advocated a Cuban-type Soviet-American confrontation in the Middle East.[3] What they desire to see is a greater Soviet military commitment to Egypt's defense as exemplified by the dispatch of pilots and missiles during 1970. The USSR's cautious policy is attributed to her growing concern with China and reluctance to endanger the emerging detente with the United States.[4]

The War of Attrition

The regime's limited diplomatic capabilities were matched by the inability to mount a full-scale military campaign against Israel. The political and economic stabilization of the home front had been barely completed when in September 1968 Nasir announced a policy shift from "passive resistance" to "preventive defense," i.e., a long war of attrition against Israel. Through a combination of commando attacks and massive artillery barrages, the Egyptians were pursuing several internal and external political-military objectives. These included: 1) the need to calm the growing public clamor, especially in the army, to undertake large-scale military action against the enemy; 2) the destruction of Israeli positions across the Canal to prevent the transformation of cease-fire lines into permanent borders; 3) the maximization of Israeli war costs, especially in human terms; and 4) the need to increase pressure on the great powers to impose a settlement based on the lifting of the occupation.[5]

Israel responded with massive air raids, artillery attacks, and commando activity aimed at denying the Egyptians what Haykal described as "the need for a single victorious battle . . . to destroy the legend which Israelis are trying to engrave in our minds, that the Israeli Army is undefeatable." [6] Subsequent military encounters illustrated that the Egyptian quest "to erase . . . the psychological fear" [7] of Israel would not materialize in circumstances of overwhelming Israeli air superiority. Egyptian success in battle was limited to commando raids and artillery attacks across the Canal, both of which took an increasingly heavy toll among the Israelis. However, these were more than counterbalanced by highly effective Israeli raids on Egyptian positions along the Canal and in the Gulf of Suez area. In a July 1969 speech, President Nasir implied rejection of the cease-fire agreements amid a flurry of diplomatic activity aimed at maintaining a precarious balance between the superpowers. In the course of a single month he paid a double debt to the Soviets by extending recognition to East Germany and the Vietnamese National Liberation Front; simultaneously, he congratulated the U.S. on its successful moon landing and announced the opening of UAR ports to American merchant ships. These acts were meant to signal a new rapprochement with the U.S. but met with failure. In the Egyptian view, the continued American reluctance to force a withdrawal upon Israel, coupled with President Nixon's declared intention to maintain Israeli air superiority, prevented any rapprochement. The Israeli persistence in using American-supplied Phantoms evoked massive anti-American outcries in Egypt, especially as civilian casualties began to mount.

Judging from Israel's intensified air offensive and large-scale raids in the Gulf of Suez beginning in September 1969, the Egyptian "war of attrition" seemed a serious miscalculation. Soon, however, the Egyptian miscalculations were matched by Israeli errors in judgment—the consequences of which may have left a deep and lasting impact on Middle Eastern politics.

In September 1969 the Israelis began the systematic destruction of the Egyptian radar network and SAM-2 missile systems through intensified air attacks and combined amphibious operations in the Gulf of Suez. Early in January, Israel's air force started attacking targets deep inside Egypt, including the outskirts of Cairo, taking an inevitable toll of civilian casualties. Egyptian resistance was minimal due to the shortage of competent pilots, the lack of radar and missile defenses against low-level attacks, and the technical inferiority of the MIG 21 jets compared to Israel's Phantoms. Faced with such a situation, Nasir appealed to the Soviet Union and received air protection for Egypt after mid-February 1970, the installation of SAM-3 missile sites was begun around large cities as Soviet pilots arrived to fly protective missions over Egypt's interior. Meanwhile, the central purpose of Israel's extended bombing raids became clear when Prime Minister Golda Meir and Foreign Minister Abba Eban explicitly spoke of their desire to see the collapse of the Nasir regime.[8]

It was painfully apparent by mid-1970 that history had once again repeated itself with all of its fateful consequences, as it had done since the days of Israel's raid on Gaza in February 1955. The evidence strongly suggests the tragic obsession of Israel's leadership since 1955 with the person of Abd al-Nasir.[9] The relationship between his demise and Israel's well-being had been a part of the Israeli perception—a notion which has obscured the more organic forces that transcended Nasir's person—e.g., Arab nationalism, Egyptian nationalism, Palestinian nationalism. Within this perspective, the air campaign of early 1970 emerged as the latest in a series of abortive Israeli attempts to overthrow the Nasir regime that were preceded by the Gaza raid of February 1955, the Suez War of 1956 and the Six-Day War of 1967. Each time policy was made on distorted perceptions of Egyptian social-psychological reality. The Israeli strategists failed to understand the charismatic role of Nasir, the force of nationalism, and the historically-conditioned resilience of Egyptians that contributed to their ability to absorb defeat.[10]

Diplomatic and military difficulties, no less than the manifest inability of the other Arab states to coordinate their actions, led the Egyptians to view themselves as being alone facing a powerful enemy. In the absence of an externally imposed settlement and psychologically unwilling to accept a victor's peace dictated by Israel, the Egyptians realized that they themselves had to continue the struggle against Israel despite enormous sacrifice. They had finally begun to perceive the magnitude of hardships required. The passivity of earlier years seemed to have declined, as it became apparent that the leadership was no longer capable of solving the country's problems through "magic," without mass participation. For in the past, all that Nasir required of Egyptians was support, obedience, and certain economic sacrifices; his chain of victories were personal triumphs requiring no sustained mass participation. As the Israeli occupation came to be viewed as unalterable, the necessity and opportunities for true mass participation, both military and political, greatly increased. Pressures generated by the emergency, as well as the elite's specific actions, encouraged participation. In other words, because of the nature of charismatic rule, psychological mass participation had been maximized, but actual political participation had remained at a low level during the prewar period.[11] Since the war, however, force of circumstance and elite encouragement seem to have increased actual mass involvement.

If the greater participation and self-reliance generated by the defeat prove to be genuine and enduring, the Israelis may eventually find themselves confronted with two unintended and unwelcome consequences of their victory. Since the adoption in 1955 of a policy of massive retaliation against Arab commando attacks and verbal threats, a pattern of Israeli psychological strategy has gradually emerged. This is founded on the compulsion "to teach a lesson" to the enemy so that he will eventually "learn" to accept the existence of the Israeli state. In psychological terms, these raids, coupled with the successive defeats of 1948, 1956, and 1967, may have been designed to perpetuate indefinitely the Egyptian and Arab sense of social inferiority and personal inadequacy. Fearful of Arab encirclement and convinced of Arab intransigence to grant the Jewish state regional legitimacy, the Israeli leadership seems to have made pre-emptive attack an integral part of its overall, long-range strategy. Yet the learning process, explicit in Israeli doctrine, can become a two-way phenomenon; instead of learning to leave Israel alone, the Arabs may learn to express their hostilities more effectively. Repeated humiliation and defeat may prolong and perpetuate Arab feelings of inferiority and helplessness, or it may produce a fundamental shift in Arab national character with incalculable consequences for Israel.

Although changes in national character usually occur slowly over a period of centuries, it would be a mistake to consider it a constant as does Professor Morgenthau. One may hypothesize that in today's technologically conditioned milieu of accelerated change, abrupt shifts of character traits are possible. This can be discerned in China since 1949; yet the best example of such a shift is Israel itself. Centuries of Jewish subjugation as a minority in the diaspora had created a generally pliable collectivity possessed by a mentality of subservience. It was not until the half-century preceding 1948 that a value transformation began among European Jewry within the context of modern nationalism, centering on an implacable resolve to resist domination.

It is quite possible that a similar development is taking place currently in the Arab national character. Needless to say, not all the aspects of the proposed Arab-Jewish parallel are comparable or similar. Yet, at least three main factors that caused the Jewish transformation are also discernible in the Arab situation. These include a long history of subservience, subjugation, and defeat; the existing nationalist milieu; and the increasing recognition that in view of Israeli territorial demands the sole alternative is to fight regardless of cost.

Class Cleavages

While the long-range effects of this emerging Egyptian-Arab perception of the enemy and the world are difficult to forecast, a number of avenues of development can be enumerated. One of the most fundamental of possible changes may be the shifting of the revolutionary base from the middle class to the peasants and to their lower and lower-middle-class offshoots, the workers.

In a sense, it is ironic that despite the progressive alienation of Egyptians from the West during the first half of the twentieth century, an intimate identification with certain Western middle-class values persisted among professionals and intellectuals.[12] Despite increasing alienation and the concomitant adoption of a socialist-etatist model, the deep-seated Egyptian aspiration to enter the middle class seems to have remained unchanged. Under the guidance of a basically middle-class military-civilian elite, Egypt's is still essentially a middle-class revolution that aims

. . . to enlarge the middle class [*al-tabaqah al-mutawas-sitah*]; Arab Socialism hopes to force everyone into the middle class by reducing the capitalists, the bourgeoisie and the landlords, and pushing up the workers and the peasants.[13]

Nothing would seem peculiar about this noble and revolutionary goal were it not for the frequent parallels drawn by certain Egyptian writers between the Vietnamese "liberation war" and themselves after June 1967. Among the factors that falsify the parallel is the absence of suitable terrain (like the Vietnamese jungle) and a spread-out friendly population in the Sinai. A more serious difference between the Egyptian and Vietnamese cases is dissimilarity of the revolutionary base. The Vietnamese revolutionary struggle (as the Chinese) is peasant-based, a feature that even persists in North Vietnamese urban centers. In sharp contrast to the Egyptian case, the Vietnamese revolutionary culture encourages no large-scale upward rush into the comforts of the middle class. Given the continuing aspirational attachment of many Egyptians to the middle class, they may be disinclined to undertake the high order of self-sacrifice that is the hallmark of guerrilla warfare. Nevertheless, the continued Israeli presence at the Canal may push many aspirants to and members of the middle class to forsake, at least temporarily, their preoccupation with upward mobility and devote themselves to armed resistance.

Beyond this possibility, there have been concrete signs of a gradual downward thrust in the revolution toward the workers and peasants. As noted previously, this movement was significantly accelerated by the formation of the new ASU during 1968. This is not to suggest that the epicenter of the revolution and political system has shifted to the emergent worker-peasant classes; indeed, it still remains firmly in the middle class itself. Yet, the revolutionary potential of the Egyptian lower classes —the peasants and the newly urbanized worker-laborers— should not be underestimated. The politicization of the peasantry undertaken by the regime soon after its takeover in 1952 had progressed sufficiently by 1956 for Hirabayashi and El-Khatib to report the emergence of "a nationally conscious group." [14] Their survey data taken from a study of five villages in the Delta province of Manufiyyah showed an increasing and spreading political awareness and international consciousness, chiefly as a result of the mass media.[15] Since 1956, a great deal has happened to aid this politicization process among peasants; not only have they finally been brought into the middle-level political leadership, but more importantly, many of them have been given land, becoming owners for the first time in their lives. Thus, it is just possible that something unprecedented in Egyptian history is taking place—the peasant is beginning to identify himself with the political system and the nation as a whole.

To be sure, despite their numerical strength and growing political consciousness, the peasants are still too weak to take a leading role in the revolution, even in coalition with the more politicized urban laborers. Yet they have now become a major interest group with clearly identifiable demands and expectations from the leadership. The further reduction of maximum individual ownership from 100 to 50 *faddans* in July 1969 releasing additional land for redistribution is a case in point.[16] Any attempt by a more conservative leadership to halt or reverse the land reform program will surely create peasant opposition against Egypt's middle-class rulers. Ultimately, if the present leadership continues to discredit itself by its impotence against Israel, one may well expect in the long-range a peasant-worker attempt to assume leadership of the Egyptian revolution.

Given the predominantly middle-class and upper-middle-class background of the leadership and its middle-class revolutionary aims, the potential for class conflict in Egyptian society remains real. As the newly politicized children of the revolution, the peasant-worker class may eventually challenge the leading position of its middle-class benefactors—a challenge that is likely to acquire ideological coloration in the hands of the Egyptian left. Since 1967 evidence has been accumulating to reinforce this hypotheses concerning class conflict.

The most explicit critics of the middle class have been the leftists within the ASU and in the press. Paradoxically, these members of the intelligentsia are themselves of middle and upper-middle-class origin; yet frequently they defend peasant-worker interests.

At the most general level the left's criticism of the middle class (bourgeoisie) [17] has centered on its predominant role in the ASU and the government establishment.[18] It is pointed out that due to advantages in education and experience, the middle class possesses a disproportionately large share of power within the National Alliance (*al-Hilf al-Watani*) as represented by the ASU.[19] To the leftists, the most disquieting result of this phenomenon is the "exploitation of the peasants" by middle-class landlords and bureaucrats who control the farmers' cooperative societies.[20] They claim that the predominant social-economic position of the landowning middle class, reinforced by middle-class bureaucrats, produces "capitalist" exploitation in the rural areas.[21] Clearly, the focal point of attack in the *umdah* class (village chiefs)—a group intimately related in social background to the revolution's power elite.[22] It is proposed that the candidacy of all *umdahs, shaykhs,* and landowners be prohibited in rural elections,[23] so that poorer peasants will have a chance to participate in the political process. Less explicitly, the left has pressed for the liquidation of rural middle-class land holdings and their redistribution among the poorer peasants.

Two other foci of leftist attack on the middle class are the military and the intellectuals, especially writers. For obvious political reasons the "centers of class power in the military command" are passed over lightly,[24] while the social background of writers is given closer scrutiny. Among the contradictions the left sees between a middle-class and a lower-class revolution is the largely "petit bourgeois" background of Egypt's men of literature.[25] It is maintained that these writers "must overcome" their class identification by becoming revolutionaries.[26] It is clear that the prerequisites for class conflict exist in Egyptian society. The charismatic presence at the top tended to neutralize these class cleavages. However, one may anticipate future conflict if the left is permitted to politicize the lower class (peasant-workers) along its ideological lines now that Nasir is no more.

In the immediate future, a more rapid radicalization of the peasant and worker class would probably occur only in the event of Israeli occupation of the thickly populated Delta, across the

Canal. The net result of such an action might be the forceful and unintended conversion of the traditionally docile Egyptian fallah into an effective fighter. In contrast to earlier times, the fallah will have something to fight for—his newly acquired piece of land. If the peasant emerges as a guerrilla fighter, his effectiveness will be enhanced by the teeming millions of the Delta.

Parameters of Change

The Egyptian-Israeli conflict is not the only factor in determining the direction of systemic evolution in Egypt. While a move to the left had been advocated by leftists and many centrists soon after the June War, subsequent events have not reflected the massive leftward evolution that many Egyptian and non-Egyptian observers had anticipated. There were five major restraining influences working against the adoption of a more leftist course: 1) the continuing strength of the Islamic religion and institutions centered upon Al-Azhar; 2) the generally centrist orientation of the armed forces; 3) the relative weakness of the Egyptian left in comparison to the army and the religious establishment; 4) the desire to retain ties with the U.S. to counterbalance the growing Soviet influence and as a possible intermediary with Israel; and 5) the leadership centered around Abd al-Nasir's person.

Considering the importance of the first three factors, it is plausible that Nasir could not have successfully embarked on an extreme leftward course, even if he had been willing to do so. According to the available evidence, he seems to have played the key role in preventing a more leftist evolution; evidently he believed in the capacity of his moderately leftist Arab nationalist formula of consensus to overcome Egypt's difficulties with Israel.

Nonetheless, one should not exclude a future adoption of an extreme leftist or communist ideological program of internal-external action. While a great deal depends on the U.S. and Israel, the fragmented state of the world revolutionary movement may also hinder the development of communism in Egypt. Had it not been for the simmering Sino-Soviet conflict and the general disarray in the communist ranks, there might have been a greater Egyptian willingness to choose the Marxist path as a way out of their Isra-

eli problem. In contrast to the late 1950s, the Marxist alternative has lost its internal cohesion and dynamism and therefore its relevance and attractiveness as a mobilizational formula
for non-Western developing states. However, Israeli reluctance to
vacate the Sinai, coupled with further Egyptian defeats and humiliation, might still orient the regime toward an extremely leftist
position. In desperation, the leadership might abandon its middle-class base and moderate socialist stance and try to build a
new left-revolutionary movement similar to Fidel Castro's based
on the peasant-worker classes. After all, Castroite Marxism
accommodates both nationalism and religion; such an accommodation may be reached in Egypt as well.

Nasir may well have contemplated these possibilities after the
June defeat or during the extensive Israeli bombings of early
1970. However, there is no evidence to that effect. On the contrary, the government granted special privileges to the private
sector and its middle and upper-middle-class supporters. The
peasants and public-sector workers were also given higher rates
of compensation. The clear aim was to neutralize popular discontent arising from the lack of material satisfactions. Despite impa-
tience with Nasir's reluctance to order an all-out attack against
Israel, the military seemed under control, in contrast to 1967.
However, signs of inter-elite conflict persisted. In September 1969
the leftist ex-Premier Ali Sabri lost his post as an ASU Secretary
and was replaced by the fast rising Interior Minister Sha'rawi
Guma'a. Although certain of Sabri's partisans in the ASU and
the press were demoted, he did remain a member of ASU's Supreme Executive Committee. The press, led by Haykal's *Al-Ahram,* persisted in maintaining the relative openness established
after the June War. After years of reluctance to accept political office, Haykal emerged as minister of information in the cabinet reshuffle of 16 April 1970, despite continued criticism from left-
of-center editors.[27] Simultaneously, President Nasir appointed
Ali Sabri as ASU secretary for foreign affairs in what appeared
to be a restoration of the ideological balance within the elite.

The UAR's position in the Arab orbit remained paramount
during 1969, although shifts of emphasis were discernible. Regarding the eastern front states of Syria, Iraq, and Jordan, the
Egyptian traditional policy of full military-political coordination
against Israel registered only partial success. The former enmity

between Egypt and Sa'udi Arabia remained muted as Sa'udi financial aid continued and Nasir mediated the Sa'udi-South Yemeni border dispute in December 1969. Similar mediation efforts helped contain conflict between Lebanon and the Palestinian guerrillas. However, the bloody encounters of June 1970 between Palestinians and Jordanian troops demonstrated Egypt's inability to moderate extremists on both sides. Equally frustrated were Nasir's efforts to create a united front of Islamic and Arab states after the burning of Al-Aqsa Mosque in Jerusalem. Both the Islamic Summit Conference (September 1969) and the Arab Summit Conference (December 1969) held at Rabat, Morocco, were ineffective. However, these reverses were more than offset by pro-Nasirite military revolutions in the Sudan (25 May 1969) and in Libya (1 September 1969) which contributed to the strategic, economic, and political position of the UAR vis-à-vis the West, the Arabs, and Israel. Both of these revolutionary regimes modelled themselves after the Egyptian revolution and the beginnings of tripartite regional integration efforts were already discernible.

In the foreseeable future, however, the direction and rate of social-political change in Egypt will depend on the course of the Arab-Israeli conflict. Despite the many changes prompted by the Six-Day War, its long-range impact on Egyptian society still cannot be properly measured. The great unknown is whether the 1967 defeat will produce an Egyptian social reformation thorough enough to develop an internally and externally stronger society. As related in previous chapters, a number of significant changes did occur on the internal scene since June 1967. The political system did not disintegrate as some had expected; the armed forces were rebuilt, and under austerity conditions the economy registered gains more impressive than the prewar years. Under these emergency conditions, the new trends toward liberalization and consensus promoted greater cohesion in society—a cohesion further strengthened by the deep Israeli air attacks after January 1970. Nevertheless, it is still too early to detect whether these changes are actually reshaping the deep-rooted relationships among Egyptians. A large degree of fatalism and passivity still remain. All that can be stated with surety is that many more Egyptians now perceive the need for basic change; and some have even acquired a clearer perception of what needs to be changed.

Another unknown is whether the postwar reformation will produce an improvement in Egyptian military performance. Even if social change continues to occur slowly and incrementally, it is inconceivable that the Egyptians (and Arabs) can do any worse than in previous encounters with Israel. And unless one assumes that they are incapable of learning from past experience, it is quite plausible to expect some improvement in battle performance. On the other hand, as shown in the last two wars against Egypt, the Israelis have operated virtually at peak efficiency. Thus, any improvement in Egyptian (and Arab) military performance, however marginal, may cause disproportionately greater human and material harm to the Israelis, especially when one considers the Arab-Egyptian numerical superiority. This is precisely the type of sacrifice Israel can least afford, given her numerical inferiority as well as the psychological inability of a highly developed Western culture to sustain human losses.[28] The prospect of having over 80 million antagonistic Egyptians across the Sinai in the next three decades should be enough to give any Israeli leader concerned with the future some sobering thoughts.[29]

In the next decade, the Soviet role in the Middle East may be a crucial if not decisive factor in Egypt's political development and in the Arab-Israeli conflict. Due to the West's generally pro-Israeli orientation and its unwillingness to provide large-scale military and economic aid to key Arab countries, American-Western influence has been replaced by a growing Soviet presence in the UAR, Syria, Iraq, Algeria, Sudan, and the Yemen. In contrast to the U.S. role in Southeast Asia, the Soviet involvement in Egypt and the Arab world has been through express invitation. Because of its military and economic aid to the Arabs against Israel, the USSR enjoys indigenous mass support. A growing naval presence in the Mediterranean and the Persian Gulf, with friendly ports of call at Mirs al-Kabir, Alexandria, Port Sa'id, and Latakia, has underlined the new Soviet position in the region.

Despite these gains, however, the USSR is likely to remain an anti-status-quo power in the Middle East. Not only there remain a lingering American presence in the region, but also the large Soviet investment has not been translated into concrete political or territorial gains. After nearly two centuries of Russian effort, the Straits remain a blocking factor both militarily and psychologically. Moreover, the huge Soviet military-economic assistance program to the Arab states has failed to produce a single convert to Soviet-style communism. Although Marxist and Soviet systemic (ideological and organizational) influences can be discerned in several Arab states, their Arab nationalist and Islamic orientations have blocked more rapid evolution toward the Soviet system.[30]

These considerations raise fundamental questions with respect to the goals of the USSR in Egypt. If the ultimate aims include communization, there is no overt sign indicating a Soviet drive in that direction. Yet given the fluid nature of international and domestic politics a number of possibilities may be entertained. For example, an Israeli occupation of Cairo could produce an Egyptian request to join the Warsaw Pact for military protection. Assuming the presence of an accommodating leadership in the Kremlin, the Arabs might be asked to form communist-led popular-front governments as the price for Warsaw Pact or Soviet protection. On the other hand, if the Soviets chose to assume a less pro-Arab policy, a Sino-Arab alignment in the context of a Chinese-led world revolutionary movement emerges as a distinct possibility. Already there exist elements in the Arab orbit who envisage such a development in the next few decades.

Given the nature of nationalist man and the realities of international politics, the prospects of lasting peace between Arabs and Israelis do not seem promising. During the next decade the Egyptian political system is likely to confront far greater problems than in the past as a result of social change at home, even if Israel did not exist. But the existence and threat of Israel is very real to Egyptians, even more real than the problems at home, thus necessitating a continued division of the nation's resources and capabilities between the foreign and the home fronts. Undoubtedly, this type of a two-front involvement is more taxing to the Egyptian than the Israeli political system. The burdens and costs of modernization of the home front are far greater for Egypt's relatively less developed society.

Saddled with a greater burden of modernization than Israel,

Egypt is also confronted by a unique and powerful enemy. In many ways the Israeli experience in nation-building can be considered *sui generis;* certain of the features of the Israeli political system as well as the nature of its international demands are unprecedented in politics among nations. The founding of a nation-state in a few short decades upon successive crests of victories, and the advancement of a morally justified demand for total and perpetual security are not commonplace occurrences in a hostile world of nations. Given the great built-in strengths of the Jewish state, the Egyptians' manifold difficulties and defeats become easily explainable. Few developing nations have had to confront a challenge of Israel's magnitude.

Nevertheless, although unique in the history of nations, Israel has behaved in the international arena according to the rules of the game, both in times of war and peace. However harsh and amoral, these old rules of international politics may eventually produce a semblance of peace in the Middle East. As old-fashioned as it may be, the crucial determinant of peace may be a balance of power between a strong Israel and a strengthened Egypt in the larger context of a Soviet-American detente in the Middle East. Accordingly, Egypt's capacity to strengthen itself might ultimately emerge as the keystone of a more durable peace in the Middle East.

15

The End of an Era

THE sudden death of President Nasir on 28 September 1970
brought to an end an era of intensive political activity in the
Egyptian and larger Arab sphere. To appraise a leader of Nasir's
proportions is no easy task. The complexity and pervasiveness of
his role, no less than the myths and controversies that surrounded
him, greatly hinder a balanced analysis. Undoubtedly, the basic
question centers on one's choice of perspectives as well as criteria
of judgment. For the student of Egyptian politics, however, the
most relevant perspective in evaluating Ňasir is that of the Egyptian people.

One of the main theses of this work has been the existence of a
peculiar spiritual bond between Nasir and the Egyptian and Arab
masses. Regardless of one's own view of Nasir, the reality and
strength of this charismatic relationship has to be acknowledged
and properly analyzed within the context of Egypt and the Arab
milieu.

From the psychological perspective of Western man, the charismatic relationship is rarely understood; in the case of Nasir it
was often misinterpreted—eighteen years after the 1952 Revolution, he was still labelled a military dictator by Western media.
Ironically, despite the conceptual difficulties imposed by Marxist
ideology, the Soviets quickly recognized Nasir's special charismatic role after his brief skirmish with Khrushchev during 1959.
The supreme confirmation of this strong charismatic bond came
on 9 June 1967, when unprecedented mass support returned
Nasir to the presidency; however, the ultimate proof of charisma
was the unabashed outpouring of popular sorrow at Nasir's
funeral—a phenomenon equalled only by the passing of Nehru
and Gandhi.

None of the above should be taken to suggest that Nasir
lacked detractors and enemies in Egypt and the Arab world. To
the Muslim Brethren and their theocratic supporters outside

Egypt, Nasir remained the perpetual antagonist. Other opponents included the various economically and politically dispossessed groups of Egypt—large landowners, capitalist enterpreneurs, Wafdists, extreme leftists, some students, and the remaining non-Muslim and non-Egyptian minorities—all of whom constituted a relatively small percentage of the country's population. In the wider Arab context, virtually every Arab leader regarded Nasir as an immediate or potential enemy by definition: indeed, in its ultimate logic, Nasir's call for Arab unity meant the eventual displacement of the various ruling Arab elites who often enjoyed less support than the Egyptian leader in their own respective countries. Without question the 1967 defeat eroded some of his Pan-Arab following, especially among the Palestinians; the Nasir of 1970 was not the exuberant president of a united Syria and Egypt whose 1960 visit to the U.N. had been widely acclaimed by the Arabs. Yet despite the progressive erosion of the Nasirite myth in the intervening ten years, the centrality of Egypt and Nasir in the Arab orbit persisted to a significant degree. Arab leaders of differing persuasions and backgrounds continued to flock to Cairo to settle disputes and/or receive the touch of legitimacy, the *baraka,* of Abd al-Nasir as an indispensible reinforcement to their own rulership.

As a charismatic leader Nasir had to deal with two distinct publics—his own Egyptians and the Arabs outside Egypt. While in the past the support of these two constituencies reinforced each other in maximizing the leader's position, there were also underlying contradictions in their demands. What the Syrians, Palestinians, or Algerians asked from Nasir was not always in the Egyptian interest and vice versa. Indeed, activity on the Pan-Arab level often required Egyptian sacrifices of time, money, resources, and blood, which resulted in some muted Egyptian resentment of their president's overinvolvement in Arab affairs; this was true especially after the June War. Conversely, the members of Nasir's Pan-Arab constituency—Palestinian guerrillas, Syrians, Iraqis, Lebanese, Yemenis—often felt that Nasir and the Egyptians were not sacrificing enough for the cause of Pan-Arabism. Until the end, Nasir was torn between these two diverging sets of expectations. The task of determining which set he favored must be left to the careful scrutiny of future scholars. Significantly, however, Nasir's last major official act belonged to the Pan-Arab realm—he died soon after presiding over an exhausting conference of Arab leaders in Cairo which had framed a peace agreement between the Jordanian army and the Palestinian guerrillas.

It is clear that Nasir's death has created a charismatic void in the Egyptian political system and the larger Arab sphere. While the full implications of his departure will not become apparent for some time to come, a number of factors are already discernible. Obviously, the main symbol of the Arab-unity movement is no more; it is difficult to envisage the emergence of another dynamic figure to lead this movement in the foreseeable future. In view of his followers' great psychological dependence upon him, Nasir's removal may eventually produce demoralization and identity crises among many Arabs. Equally apparent is the leadership vacuum in the decisional sense. His Arabist followers depended on him for support and guidance against local rulers; the guerrillas and King Husayn wanted him to frame an agreement favorable to both; the Syrians expected him to help defend them against Israel; the new Libyan and Sudanese military leaders wanted Nasir's support to sustain their power; Israel wanted him to sign a peace treaty and render it acceptable to the Arabs; the Soviets and at times even the Americans depended on him as one of the few constant realities in the unstable world of Arab politics. These, coupled with the expectations of his own Egyptians, had placed upon Nasir a decision-making load of major proportions, one that he could not physically bear. While his death may have been secretly greeted with relief by Arab and non-Arab adversaries, it is also true that now all face a new element of long-range uncertainty and instability. Arabs, Egyptians, foes, friends, and neutrals have to recast their politics and policy styles to fit the new noncharismatic situation. After operating for a decade and a half in a milieu of charismatic politics, the transition will not be an easy task to accomplish.

The consequences of the charismatic void may be still more serious in Egypt—the leader's home constituency. Egypt depended on Nasir with a completeness only found in other charismatic political systems. In view of his proven ability to extricate the country from difficulties, the common man was content to leave everything to the president. A similar trend characterized the governmental bureaucracy. Unwilling to make decisions, bureaucrats tended to pass the buck upward to the presidency. The prevailing bureaucratic culture and the political costs of failure militated against a flowering of decisional initiative in the ranks. These factors, operating within a highly centralized structure, further increased Nasir's already staggering burden of decision-making. His several attempts to diffuse some of his responsibilities before 1967 were unsuccessful. During the mid-1960s, he spoke of a desire to withdraw from the government in favor of becoming party chief—Secretary General of the Arab Socialist Union. However, Egypt's economic troubles and military defeat in 1967 caused the abandonment of such plans. In the wake of a defeat that demonstrated the incompetence of some of his trusted aides, the president assumed even greater burdens when he took over as prime minister and ASU secretary.

In retrospect, one of the great tragedies of Egypt and the Arab world of the 1960s was the great disparity between Nasir's leadership style and the Arab political culture. Nasir responded to each challenge with great bursts of energy, dedication, and hard work rarely matched in the Arab-Egyptian milieu. Few among the Egyptian elite, or the larger Arab leadership, could match his dynamism; nor was he successful in imparting his life style to the bulk of his followers. In this respect neither Egypt nor the Arab world were ready for him.

Basic value transformations occur slowly, especially in societies where popular attachments to the traditional culture remain strong. Indeed, it was unrealistic to expect Nasir to achieve thoroughgoing ideological and social modernization within the brief sixteen years since his rise to power. Whenever he demanded support, he received it in generous amounts from the masses as well as from most of his government colleagues. However, his attempts to evoke the degree of disciplined response necessary to achieve rapid change were not always crowned with success. Rather than being the culminator of the value transformation process, Nasir was its initiator and catalyst. In this respect, he played a central role as propagator of Pan-Arabism. He did not invent Pan-Arabism, he was not even an early convert; yet his espousal of its goals in the context of his emergence as charismatic leader, made Pan-Arabism a part of the psychic makeup of every Arab. In this sense, the Egyptian president made himself the major agent of *isti'rab*—the Arabization process—even in such culturally mixed areas as the Maghrib. More than any other leader in modern times, Nasir tried to infuse the Arabs with a sense of dignity.

The second major ideological change that Nasir initiated was the introduction of Arab socialism. While its initial formulation predated Nasir's rise, his espousal of the doctrine made it respectable and legitimate in an Islamic society deeply suspicious of the atheistic elements found in leftist ideologies.

Besides his achievements, Nasir experienced several major failures. In retrospect, these seem the result of his misperceptions of Israel and the United States as well as his distorted view of the Arab world. Despite his deep realization of Egypt's great internal weaknesses, he attempted to play too ambitious a role in Middle Eastern and international politics. Through dramatic exploits and skillful diplomatic maneuvering he tried to compensate for Egypt's internal weaknesses. Without transforming Egypt—the base of the Arab revolution—he reluctantly allowed the Ba'athists to persuade him into a premature union with Syria. Nasir had responded to the widespread unionist sentiments in Syria without considering the deep religious, ethnic, and sectional cleavages in Syrian society which would make it highly ungovernable.

Similar misconceptions clouded Nasir's Yemen policy which turned that country into Egypt's Vietnam. There is little evidence that Egyptians were aware of the prevailing conditions in the Yemen, i.e., royalist strength, tribal factionalism, mountainous terrain, Sa'udi assistance, to mention a few. However, until the mid-1960s commitment to Pan-Arabist ideology tended to blind Nasir and the Nasirites to the objective realities in each Arab country. In their eagerness to promote Arab unity, the Pan-Arabists tended to view the Arab social realm as a relatively homogenous one; nothing could be further from the truth. Although some of these differences were acknowledged in the UAR Charter (1962), Nasir still committed some of his best troops to the Yemen in response to the appeals of the Republican government. Ironically, at the time of the Egyptian involvement, Arab nationalism had barely made its appearance in the Yemen, a country newly emerging from centuries of total isolation.

Another shortcoming of Nasir was his conspiratorial approach to politics. This can be traced to his early experiences with the king's police as well as the internal struggles after the 1952 military takeover. Most revolutionaries have difficulty abandoning their conspiratorial mentality after seizing power, and Nasir was no exception. In one sense this approach served him well, helping him suppress each of the internal and external plots against the regime, especially those of the Muslim Brotherhood. However, the conspiratorial approach often poisoned inter-Arab relations even though Nasir merely followed the prevailing operational code among the Arab states and in the international arena.

The one challenge that immobilized the Nasirite dynamic was Israel. More than most of his compatriots he recognized the great strengths of the Jewish state as well as the weaknesses of the Arabs. What he probably failed to perceive clearly was the mentality of a beleaguered people who had long suffered massacres and oppression. Had Nasir comprehended this psychological reality and its logical extension—massive preemptive attack—he would have refrained from the fiery rhetoric and brinksmanship of May 1967 or at least prepared better to confront Israel's sudden attack. Similarly, he was consistently careless in his choice of terminology to attack the United States—a practice that frequently caused unnecessary strains in American-Egyptian relations.

One must now return to Egypt and examine the leader's patrimony in ideology, institutions, and processes. Ultimately Nasir would have judged himself by how well and how long the Nasirite revolution and political system would survive in Egypt. Clearly this constitutes a most important question considering the centrality of Egypt in Middle Eastern politics.

Among the charismatic leaders of the neutralist bloc who emerged after World War II, Nasir was perhaps the most successful in reordering the social-political life of his country. He held power longer than everyone except Tito. Unlike Sukarno and Nkrumah, the Egyptian president was able to create a viable political order which could not be overthrown despite repeated internal and external efforts. Finally, Nasir's feat in surviving the 1967 defeat more than equalled Nehru's in surviving the Chinese incursion. Indeed, Nehru and Nasir disproved the assumption that reverses destroy the charismatic bond between leader and followers. It remains to be seen whether the post-Nasirite evolution of the Egyptian political system will disprove another commonly held theoretical assumption—that systematic instability and turmoil follow the leader's departure.

Judging from the swift and orderly transfer of power during October 1970, the regime seemed secure. The legitimacy that Anwar al-Sadat derived from his long association with Nasir as well as his position as vice-president were instrumental in his assumption of Nasir's mantle. This transfer of legitimation culminated with Sadat's election by 85 percent of the votes. While the vote count fell 15 percent short of Nasir's tally of 99.9 percent, it still constituted a strong popular endorsement. Under Sadat a collective leadership first emerged centering on the eight-member ASU Supreme Executive. The most senior member of this body, ex-Foreign Minister Mahmud Fawzi, was made prime minister. Significantly, Dr. Fawzi is Egypt's first civilian prime minister since Ali Mahir, who resigned in September 1952. Despite rumors, there were no signs of a major power struggle although cabinet changes did occur. Information Minister Haykal returned to the editorship of *Al-Ahram* while former Vice-President and Interior Minister Zakariyya Muhyi al-Din was not returned to power as some had expected.

Since his assumption of power President al-Sadat repeatedly stressed his government's intention to pursue Nasir's Arabist and socialist policies. The first clear indication of continuity of policy came on 8 November, with the formation of a new federation joining the United Arab Republic, Libya, and the Sudan. This marked the culmination of Nasir's efforts since September 1969 to achieve a united front with Egypt's two revolutionary neighbors against Israel. In contrast to the Syrian-Egyptian union of 1958, the new Arab entity was looser in form and more realistic in goals. It represented a more African type of Arabism, darker in shade, and possessing territorial and cultural continuity; however, Syria's subsequent adherence to it may alter the initial character of the federation.

Another indication of continuity of policy could be found in Sadat's repeated extension of the cease-fire agreement with Israel, originally concluded under Nasir. Despite criticism from Egyptian militants, President Sadat has skillfully pursued a flexible diplomacy to dislodge the Israelis from the Sinai. Striving to enlist American support and attract world public opinion, Sadat's

peace offensive succeeded in putting Israel on the defensive diplomatically. However, difficulties remain. Israel's demands
might be greater from an Egypt weakened by Nasir's death; and
Sadat's government can probably offer fewer concessions than
Nasir could have in view of his greater prestige.

On 18 April 1971, the Arab unity movement took a further
step as Egypt, Syria, and Libya announced their intention to establish the Federation of Arab Republics after a September
plebiscite. On 2 May, U.S. Secretary of State William Rogers
visited Egypt amid signs of improving American-Egyptian relations. These two developments, coupled with Sadat's need to
consolidate his position, seem to have triggered a power struggle
of significant proportions. Just before the Rogers visit, Sadat
fired Ali Sabri of the ASU's Supreme Executive Committee.
Less than two weeks later he proceeded to purge the party and
the government after announcing the discovery of a conspiracy.
At the party level, three members of the ASU Supreme Executive Committee—Abu al-Nur, Shuqayr, and Dawud—were
fired, as was Sha'rawi Guma'a who was also Minister of Interior.
Of the cabinet members, General Muhammad Fawzi (war),
Sami Sharaf (state), Muhammad Fa'iq (information), Sa'd Zayid
(housing), and Hilmi al-Sa'd (electricity) lost their positions. In
one stroke, Sadat had eliminated almost everyone in the collective leadership that could conceivably pose a threat to him. With
such major personalities of the previous regime as Sabri, Guma'a,
Fawzi, Sharaf, and Abu al-Nur, Sadat was *primus inter pares;*
now he is master of his house—if he can prevail upon the
United States to pressure the Israelis into a complete withdrawal.

While the first priority of the new leadership remains the ending
of Israeli occupation, there are growing signs of a desire to return
to normalcy. War fatigue is apparent at both the leadership and
mass levels. If the new leaders are given the opportunity to conclude an acceptable peace, the likelihood of a new war may recede for at least a decade.

To assure its long-range survival, the present leadership needs
to go beyond securing Israeli withdrawal; it must quickly occupy
itself with the pressing social and economic needs of a rapidly increasing population. Sadat's failures on either front would inevitably produce dissatisfaction and even radicalization, especially
among the military, workers, and intellectuals. In such circum-

stances, it is quite possible that a military and/or leftist counter-elite would emerge seeking to seize power by evoking the unfulfilled policies and promises of Abd al-Nasir. In the event of such a power struggle, the left could expect support from intellectuals (university professors and journalists), students, and the worker-peasant leadership. The opposition would probably center on a broad grouping of antileftist politicians, the military leadership, and the Islamic clerical establishment. As the scope of conflict widens, the formerly dispossessed traditionalist elements of Egyptian society—the Brethren and Wafdists—could be expected to align themselves with the anti-left coalition. In any confrontation, the left may lost initially due to the army's presence in the opposite camp. Yet the army itself may exhibit divided loyalties. The common lower-class base shared by the soldiers and the worker-peasant class may be a decisive factor in neutralizing the army's role as a coercive instrument. In any case one should not overestimate the strength and capabilities of the antileft coalition, nor should the army be regarded as a reliable instrument to arrest a leftward drift in the long-range.

Indeed, Nasir himself had been the best guarantee against a military or leftist takeover. He had repeatedly blocked pressures from either direction, first by purging the military and then by refusing the left's prescriptions of militant radicalization. In the turbulent period after June 1967, the temptation and pressures to adopt a radically leftist course of revolutionary action were indeed great for the Egyptian leader. He continued to press for increased worker-peasant participation in government thereby introducing two new potentially revolutionary elements into the political system; however, he did not envisage leading a new revolution based upon these two classes. In social background, experience, temperament, and ideology, Nasir was ill-suited to play the role of a Castro or Ho Chi Minh. In essence his was a middle-class revolution which, despite the prevailing Soviet and Marxist influences, possessed a muted desire to emulate the Western model of socio-economic development. His socialism was tempered with religious belief. Abd al-Nasir was born a Muslim Egyptian; he propounded a secular and fierce nationalist doctrine; he died a Muslim Arab and was laid to rest in his neighborhood mosque.

Notes

1. The Framework of Analysis

1. See Jack L. Walker, "A Critique of the Elitist Theory of Democracy," *American Political Science Review,* vol. 60, no. 2 (June 1966): 285–295, and Robert A. Dahl, "Further Reflections on 'The Elitist Theory of Democracy'," *American Political Science Review,* vol. 60, no. 2 (June 1966): 296–305. Also Peter Bachrach, *The Theory of Democratic Elitism: A Critique* (Boston, 1967).

2. Robert A. Dahl, *Modern Political Analysis* (Englewood Cliffs, 1963), p. 19.

3. H. H. Gerth and C. Wright Mills, *From Max Weber: Essays in Sociology* (New York, 1946), pp. 78–79. As Weber relates, in the real world these types of authority are usually found in combinations.

4. K. J. Ratnam, "Charisma and Political Leadership," *Political Studies,* vol. 12, no. 3 (Oct. 1964): 341–354. Peter M. Blau, "Critical Remarks on Weber's Theory of Authority," *American Political Science Review,* vol. 57, no. 2 (June 1963): 305–316. Carl J. Friedrich, "Political Leadership and the Problem of the Charismatic Power," *Journal of Politics* 23 (Feb. 1961): 3–24. Claude Ake, "Charismatic Legitimation and Political Integration," *Comparative Studies in Society and History,* vol. 9, no. 1 (October 1966): 1–13. For other works on Weber see Wolfgang Mommsen, "Max Weber's Political Sociology and His Philosophy of World History," *International Social Science Journal,* vol. 17, no. 1 (1965): 23–45. Hans Gerth, "The Nazi Party: Its Leadership and Composition," *American Journal of Sociology,* vol. 45, no. 4 (1940): 519. Ann Ruth Willner and Dorothy Willner, "The Rise and Role of Charismatic Leaders," *The Annals* 358 (March 1965): Reinhard Bendix, *Max Weber, An Intellectual Portrait* (New York, 1960). Dennis H. Wrong, "Max Weber: The Scholar as Hero," *Columbia University Forum,* vol. 5, no. 3 (Summer 1962): 31–37. Claude Ake, *A Theory of Political Integration* (Homewood, Ill., 1967), pp. 51–67.

5. William H. Friedland, "For a Sociological Concept of Charisma," *Social Forces,* vol. 43, no. 1 (October 1964): Actually in another version, Weber deemphasized the psychological aspects of charismatic leadership. See Gerth and Mills, *op. cit.,* p. 295.

6. Max Weber, *The Theory of Social and Economic Organization,* trans. A. M. Henderson and Talcott Parsons (New York, 1947), pp. 358–359. Gerth and Mills, *op. cit.,* pp. 295–297.

7. Henderson and Parsons, *op. cit.*, p. 359. Friedland, *op. cit.*, pp. 19–21.

8. James C. Davies, "Charisma in the 1952 Campaign," *American Political Science Review* 48 (December 1954: 1083. Amitai Etzioni, *A Comparative Analysis of Complex Organizations* (New York, 1961), p. 204. Friedland, *op. cit.*, p. 212. Dankwart A. Rustow, *A World of Nations: Problems of Political Modernization* (Washington, 1967), p. 160. Willner and Willner, *op. cit.*, pp. 82–83.

9. George Devereux, "Charismatic Leadership and Crisis," *Psychoanalysis and the Social Sciences* 4 (1955): 146–151.

10. Devereux goes further to state that a crisis infantilizes people who demand a leader who conforms to their childish expectations. *Ibid.*, pp. 149–151.

11. On psychological vulnerability in mass society see William Kornhauser, *The politics of Mass Society* (Glencoe, 1959), pp. 114–115. Hans H. Toch, "Crisis Situations & Ideological Revaluation," *Public Opinion Quarterly* 19 (Spring 1955): 53–67.

12. See, James C. Davies, *Human Nature in Politics* (New York, 1963), p. 305. As Professor S. N. Eisenstadt points out, Weber did not explicitly deal with the problem of the appeal of charismatic leaders. See S. N. Eisenstadt, ed., *Max Weber: On Charisma and Institution Building* (Chicago, 1968), p. xxii. On the interplay between the leader's ideology and the people's interests see Karl Mannheim, *Ideology and Utopia* (New York, 1946), p. 142.

13. On the possibility of achieving personal charisma while in office see Etzioni, *op. cit.*, p. 205.

14. As Professor Bendix points out, Weber did not foresee this possibility. Bendix goes on to observe that it would be a mistake to infer that charisma cannot develop in today's technologically conditioned milieu. See Reinhard Bendix, "Reflections on Charismatic Leadership," *Asian Survey*, vol. 7, no. 6 (June 1967): 348–349. One may add that the mass media accords the potential charismatic unprecedented opportunities for success.

15. As Shils points out, the leader's "order-creating" and "order-destroying" capabilities will become the building blocks of charismatic power. See Edward Shils, "Charisma, Order and Status," *American Sociological Review* 30 (April 1965): 204.

16. Etzioni, *op. cit.*, pp. 203–204.

17. *Ibid.*

18. Richard R. Fagen, "Charismatic Authority and the Leadership of Fidel Castro," *Western Political Quarterly*, vol. 18, no. 2, pt. 1 (June 1965): 275.

19. John T. Marcus, "Transcendence and Charisma," *Western Political Quarterly* 14 (March 1961): 237; also Willner and Willner, *op. cit.*, pp. 82–83.

20. On the process of dispersion of charisma from the political into the economic sphere see Edward Shils, "The Concentration and Dispersion of Charisma—Their Bearing on Economic Policy in Underdeveloped Countries," *World Politics* 11 (1958–59): 4.

21. However, as Wallerstein suggests, the erosion of charisma can be checked by the staging of ceremonies to glorify the leader. See Immanuel Wallerstein, *Africa, the Politics of Independence* (New York, 1961), pp.

100–101. The effects of these measures would be temporary and eventually erosion will set in, in the absence of victories and other payoffs.

22. Often some charismatics are skillful at organizational work from the very outset, especially those aiming at revolutionary capture of power. Examples are Lenin, Ataturk, and Nasir.

23. Friedrich, *op. cit.*, p. 16.

24. David Easton, *A Systems Analysis of Political Life* (New York, 1965), pp. 303–305.

25. See, especially, George Devereux, *op. cit.*, pp. 145–157. Erik H. Erikson, *Young Man Luther* (New York, 1958) and *Gandhi's Truth*, (New York, 1969). *Journal of Social Issues* 24 (July 1968): 3. E. V. Wolfenstein, *The Revolutionary Personality* (Princeton, 1967). *Daedalus*, vol. 97, no. 3 (Summer 1968). Dankwart A. Rustow, ed, *Philosophers and Kings* (NY 1970); Fred Greenstein, *Personality and Politics* (Chicago, 1969).

26. Karl Loewenstein questions the utility of the concept of charisma in the study of contemporary politics, especially with respect to democratic systems because of their increasingly secular context. He considers democratic leaders as becoming popular rather than charismatic. See Karl Loewenstein, *Max Weber, Staatspolitische Auffassungen in der Sicht Unserer Zeit* (Frankfurt, 1965), pp. 74–85. For charisma in democratic societies see Arthur Schlesinger, Jr., "On Heroic Leadership," *Encounter* (December 1960): 3–11. Also Mattei Dogan, "Le Pérsonnel Politique et la Personnalite Charismatique," *Révue Francaise de Sociologie*, vol. 6, no. 3 (July–September 1965): 305–324. Seymour Martin Lipset, *The First New Nation* (New York, 1963), pp. 18–23.

27. On the role of charismatic authority in Ghana see David Apter, *The Gold Coast in Transition* (Princeton, 1955), p. 303; also, David Apter, *Ghana in Transition*, rev. ed. (New York, 1963), p. 305. Lionel Tiger, "Bureaucracy and Charisma in Ghana," *Journal of Asian and African Studies* 1 (1966), pp. 13–26; and W. G. Runciman, "Charismatic Legitimacy and One-Party Rule in Ghana," *Archives Européennes de Sociologie*, vol. 4, no. 1 (1963): 148–165.

28. Accordingly, Ataturk, Lenin and the Gandhi-Nehru combination may be classified as leaders who have successfully completed the charismatic cycle.

29. Strictly speaking, C is also a variable. In other words, L and F are the determinants of Control. The level of C = level of Legitimacy + quality (effectiveness) of Force.

30. On the concept of political stability see Rustow, *A World of Nations*, pp. 156–157. To Rustow, political stability equals stability of institutions and rulers.

31. Strictly speaking reserve force should also be treated as a variable since its actual control by elites often fluctuates over time.

2. A Background of Protracted Turmoil

1. Tu'aymah Al-Jarf, *Thawrat 23 Yulyu wa Mabadi' al-Nizam al-Siyasi fi al-Jumhuriyyah al-Arabiyyah al-Muttahidah* [The July 23 Revolution and the Principles of the UAR Political System] (Cairo, 1964), p. 150.

2. For brief periods these groups assumed some importance in the

struggle for power. Thus, the Sa'dist movement between 1946 and 1949 severely persecuted the Brotherhood and the communists. Also after the Wafd's return to power in January 1950, these parties attempted to check the excesses of the uneasy alliance between Faruq and the Wafd. For an account of political parties in Egypt see Jacob M. Landau, *Parliaments and Parties in Egypt* (Tel Aviv, 1953).

3. For a comprehensive analysis of the pre-Revolutionary period see P. J. Vatikiotis, *The Egyptian Army in Politics; Pattern for the New Nations?*, (Bloomington, Ind., 1961).

4. The right to the individual interpretation of Islamic law which ceased to be exercised after the tenth century.

5. White-collar workers, industrial workers, unemployed graduates of high schools and universities.

6. On the history of the Muslim Brethren see Christina Phelps Harris, *Nationalism and Revolution in Egypt: The Role of the Muslim Brotherhood* (The Hague, 1964), and Richard P. Mitchell, *The Society of Muslim Brothers* (New York, 1969). Also, Vatikiotis, *op. cit.*, pp. 29–30.

7. Several leading anti-regime officers had been killed during the war; among them was Lt. Col. Ahmad Abd al-Aziz who had been influential among the younger officers many of whom were his former students. See Abu al-Hajjaj Hafat, *Al-Batal Ahmad Abd al-Aziz* [The Hero, Ahmad Abd al-Aziz] (Cairo, 1961).

8. Vatikiotis, *op. cit.*, p. 65.

9. Rashid al-Barawi, *The Military Coup in Egypt* (Cairo, 1952). Anwar El-Sadat, *Revolt on the Nile* (London, 1957). Tom Little, *Egypt* (New York, 1958). Jean and Simonne Lacouture, *Egypt in Transition* (New York, 1958). Amin Sa'id, *Al-Thawrah* [The Revolution] (Cairo, 1959). Ahmad Atiyyat Allah, *Qamus al-Thawrah al-Misriyyah* [Dictionary of the Egyptian Revolution] (Cairo, 1955). For a detailed analysis of bibliographical sources on Abd al-Nasir see Khalil I. H. Semaan, "A New Source for the Biography of Jamal Abd al-Nasir," *Muslim World,* vol. 58, no. 3 (July 1968): 242–252.

10. Eliezer Beeri, "On the History of the Free Officers in Egypt," *Hamizrah he-Hadash,* vol. 13, no. 3 (A.E. 5751/1963), p. xiv.

11. Ishak Musa Husaini, *The Moslem Brethren* (Beirut, 1956), pp. 127–128.

12. Vatikiotis, *op. cit.*, p. 46.

13. Beeri, *op. cit.*, p. xv.

14. On the concept of leadership as a process of communication see Karl W. Deutsch, *The Nerves of Government* (New York, 1963), pp. 157–160.

15. Especially after their success in electing their slate in the Officers' Club Affair.

3. The Advent of Military Dictatorship

1. For a more detailed treatment see chap. 9.

2. One recent author puts the number of the original group of Free Officers at ten. See Eliezer Beeri, "On the History of the Free Officers in Egypt," *Hamizrah he-Hadash,* vol. 13, no. 3 (A.E. 5751/1963), p. xv.

3. Anwar El-Sadat, *Revolt on the Nile* (London, 1957), p. 109.

4. Beeri, *op. cit.*, p. xv.

5. On the crucial relationship between success in battle and choice for leadership, see Majid Khadduri, "The Role of the Military in Middle Eastern Politics," *American Political Science Review,* vol. 47, no. 2 (June 1953): 511–524.

6. A good index of Abd al-Nasir's position at that time can be found in radio broadcasts where he is described as ". . . General Nagib's assistant . . ." Radio Cairo, 27 February 1953.

7. Mahmud Mutwalli, *Al-Ittihad al-Ishtiraki al-Arabi* [The Arab Socialist Union] (Cairo, 1964), p. 33.

8. On RCC-Brotherhood relations see, Muhammad Taha Badawi and Muhammad Hilmi Mustafa, *Tharwat Yuliu* [July Revolution] (Alexandria, 1966), pp. 336–340.

9. Anouar Abdel-Malek, *Egypte, Société Militaire* (Paris, 1962), pp. 72–73.

10. Tom Little, *Egypt* (New York, 1958), p. 203.

11. Mohamad Neguib, *Egypt's Destiny* (London, 1955), p. 150.

12. Abdel-Malek, *op. cit.,* p. 97.

13. This split became apparent as early as 1953. See P. J. Vatikiotis, *The Egyptian Army in Politics, Pattern for New Nations?* (Bloomington, Ind., 1961), p. 87.

14. In this case, the Ikhwan pictured the RCC as being "soft" toward Britain and therefore guilty of betraying Egyptian national interests. For the Anglo-Egyptian Agreement on the Sudan see J. C. Hurewitz, *Diplomacy in the Near and Middle East: A Documentary Record (1914–1956),* 2 vols. (Princeton, 1956), vol. 2, p. 335.

15. *New York Times,* 1 March 1954.

16. Jean and Simonne Lacouture, *Egypt in Transition* (New York, 1958), pp. 183–185. Abdel-Malek, *op. cit.,* pp. 98–99. Vatikiotis, *op. cit.,* p. 90.

17. On Egyptian historiography concerning the period 1952–1954, see pp. 140–144.

18. Colonel Sadiq broke with the junta early in 1953 and left for Paris, only to be arrested upon returning to Egypt in 1954. See Lacouture, *op. cit.,* pp. 264–265.

19. Beeri, *op. cit.,* p. xv.

20. Note the striking similarity with the Stalin-Trotsky struggle: socialism in one country vs. world revolution. Without a doubt, of the two Trotsky was by far the more natural leader with great popularity and charismatic potential. Yet he did not win. On the relationship of power, policy, and ideology see Zbigniew K. Brzezinski, *Ideology and Power in Soviet Politics* (rev. ed., New York, 1967), pp. 4–5, 104–105.

21. Richard C. Neustadt, *Presidential Power: The Politics of Leadership* (New York, 1960), pp. 181–184.

22. In addition to Khalid Muhyi al-Din's expulsion to Europe, the aristocratic Ahmad Shawqi and sixteen leftist officers were imprisoned during April 1954. See Abd al-Rahman al-Rafi'i, *Thawrat 23 Yulyu 1952* [The Revolution of 23 July 1952] (Cairo, 1959), p. 103; and *Al-Akhbar,* 1 July 1954; Lacouture, *op. cit.,* p. 265. Abdel-Malek, *op. cit.,* pp. 100–101. Ahmad Anwar headed the military police and later became ambassador.

23. Ahmed Abul-Fath, *L'affaire Nasser* (Paris, 1962), pp. 163–173.

24. Neguib, *op. cit.,* p. 233.

25. *Al-Ahram,* 26 September 1954.

26. *Al-Ahram,* 31 May 1954. In addition Mustafa Kamal Sidqi and twenty officers, including some leftists were jailed; see Rafi'i, *op. cit.,* pp. 129–130.

27. Hurewitz, *op. cit.,* pp. 383–384.

28. Ishak Musa Husaini, *The Moslem Brethren* (Beirut, 1956), pp. 135–136; Little, *op. cit.,* p. 251.

29. Husaini, *op. cit.,* p. 136; Keith Wheelock, *Nasser's New Egypt* (New York, 1960), p. 45.

30. *New York Times,* 5 December 1954; Little, *op. cit.,* p. 252.

31. On the trials see Lacouture, *op. cit.,* pp. 253–254.

32. Rafi'i, *op. cit.,* p. 135.

33. Husaini, *op. cit.,* p. 137.

34. In view of the events of mid-1965, the brotherhood still constitutes an underground force to reckon with. See *Al-Nahar,* 29 and 31 August 1965. On the modern role of Islam and the actions of the Brotherhood see Hamilton A. R. Gibb, "The Heritage of Islam in the Modern World (II)," *International Journal of Middle East Studies,* Vol. 1, no. 3 (July 1970): 228–230.

35. These measures of domestic conflict are similar to those utilized by Rummel. See Rudolph J. Rummel, "Dimensions of Conflict Behavior Within and Between Nations," *General Systems Yearbook* 8 (1963): 5.

36. Another possible variable affecting the decrease in reported incidents of violence could be the RCC's control over the press and radio; although eyewitness reports from foreigners living in Egypt, corroborate the above findings.

4. The Emergence of Charismatic Authority

1. Gamal Abdel Nasser, *The Philosophy of the Revolution* (Buffalo, 1959), pp. 36–37.

2. Majid Khadduri, "The Role of the Military in Middle Eastern Politics," *American Political Science Review,* vol. 47, no. 2 (June 1953): 511–512. Article by Fathi Uthman al-Mahlawi in *Al-Dimuqratiyyah fi al-Alam al-Arabi* [Democracy in the Arab World] (Beirut, 1959), p. 113. On the reasons for the decline of Western democracy see Hisham Sharabi, "The Transformation of Ideology in the Arab World," *Middle East Journal,* vol. 19, no. 4 (Autumn 1965): 471–486.

3. For an official account of communism and its role in Egypt, see, Gamal Abd al-Nasir, *Nahnu wa al-Iraq wa al-Shuyu'iyyah* [We, Iraq and Communism] (Beirut, 1960?), pp. 77–91.

4. *Al-Ahram,* 17 January 1954; 18 April 1954.

5. *Ibid.*

6. *Al-Ahram,* 9 August 1954; 12 August 1954.

7. On the concept of excessive "load" on the political systems, see, Karl W. Deutsch, *The Nerves of Government* (New York, 1963), p. 189.

8. On the transformation of Egyptian nationalism to Arab unity or Pan-Arab nationalism, see chap. 7 and 8.

9. Also many Arabs outside Egypt began to look at Abd al-Nasir and his ideology as a means for Arab success and grandeur.

10. Often it has been argued that one major factor responsible for the heightened Egyptian interest in the Arab East especially after the rise of Abd al-Nasir was oil.

11. For a fuller analysis see chap. 7.

12. In early December 1954 there were mass protests in Syria, Iraq, and Jordan against the Egyptian suppression of the Ikhwan. See *New York Times,* 6 and 9 December 1954; and Robert St. John, *The Boss* (New York, 1960), p. 186.

13. Erskine B. Childers, *The Road to Suez* (London, 1962), pp. 127–129.

14. J. C. Hurewitz, *Diplomacy in the Near and Middle East: A Documentary Record (1914–1956),* 2 vols. (Princeton, 1956), pp. 309, 401–402; and Abd al-Mun'im Shumays, *Al-Thawrah al-Arabiyyah al-Kubrah* (The Great Arab Revolution) (Cairo, 1960), p. 540.

15. Tom Little, *Egypt* (New York, 1958), p. 263.

16. On the decline of the West in the Arab world see Charles Issawi, "Negotiations from Strength?" *International Affairs,* vol. 35, no. 1 (1959): 1–9.

17. On Nasir's perception of the relationship between popular desires and his choice of issues see, Charles D. Cremeans, "Nasser's Approach to International Politics," in Benjamin Rivlin and Joseph S. Szyliowicz, ed., *The Contemporary Middle East,* (New York, 1965), pp. 514–515.

18. Shumays, *op. cit.,* p. 410. On the Bandung Conference see Georgiana Stevens, "Arab Neutralism and Bandung," *Middle East Journal,* vol. 11, no. 2 (Spring 1957): 139–152.

19. K. J. Ratnam, "Charisma and Political Leadership," *Political Studies,* vol. 12, no. 3 (Oct. 1964): 341–354.

20. Sulayman Mazhar, *Adwa' ala Waqi'ina* [Focus on Our Situation] (Cairo, n.d.), p. 19.

21. The Gaza raid signalled the end of the period of relative calm between Egypt and Israel that was marked by secret negotiations between Nasir and Prime Minister Moshe Sharett. The return of ex-Prime Minister Ben Gurion from retirement coincided with a more militant phase of Israeli policy that started with the Gaza raid of 28 February 1955. An appraisal of the consequences of the Gaza raid is found in Kennett Love, *Suez, The Twice Fought War* (New York, 1969).

22. John S. Badeau, "Non-Alignment and the UAR," [Union College] *Symposium,* Summer 1965; and J. C. Hurewitz, "Our Mistakes in the Middle East," *Atlantic Monthly* 198 (December 1956): 51.

23. On the Western position, see Herbert Feis, "Suez Scenario: A Lamentable Tale," *Foreign Affairs* 38 (July 1960): 1–15; and Sir Anthony Eden, *Memoirs: Full Circle* (London, 1960); and Herman Finer, *Dulles Over Suez* (Chicago, 1964). George E. Kirk, *Contemporary Arab Politics* (New York, 1961), pp. 43–89. Kennett Love points out that the U.S. offer to finance the High Dam was designed to counteract the effect of the Soviet arms deal. See, Love, *op. cit.,* p. 317.

24. It is clear that the Egyptians would have nationalized the Canal eventually regardless of the nature of the U.S. decision on the dam. Therefore Dulles' sudden withdrawal of U.S. financial support simply hastened the Egyptian takeover.

25. In this connection Professor Malcolm Kerr observes that "Nasir-

ism's first property is motion." See Malcolm Kerr, "Coming to Terms with Nasser," *International Affairs* 43 (1967): 67.

26. On the war in the Sinai, see S. L. A. Marshall, *Sinai Victory* (New York, 1958); Robert Henriques, *100 Hours to Suez* (New York, 1957); Edgar O'Balance, *The Sinai Campaign 1956* (London, 1959); Serge and Merry Bromberger, *Secrèts of Suez* (London, 1957); Childers, *op. cit.,* pp. 225–304. Most accounts of the Sinai War, except Childers', have a distinct pro-Israeli tinge. It is only fair to state that an Israeli campaign in the Sinai without French air support and in the absence of the Anglo-French ultimatum and attack would have been a costlier operation. On British foreign policy, see, Elizabeth Monroe, *Britain's Moment in the Middle East,* (Baltimore, 1963), pp. 178–206.

27. A further gain was the destruction of a large part of the Egyptian forces in the Sinai and the capture of large amounts of Soviet-made military hardware.

28. Izzat Sami, *Muzakkarat Al-Liwa' Mahmud Tal'at* [Memoirs of General Mahmud Tal'at] (Cairo, 196?), p. 50; Imil al-Ghuri, *Sira' al-Qawmiyyah al-Arabiyyah* [Struggle of Arab Nationalism] (Damascus, UAR, 1958), p. 74.

29. *Ibid.*

30. UAR, *The Charter* (Information Department, Cairo, n.d.), p. 14.

5. The Ideological Imperative

1. Daniel Bell, *The End of Ideology* (New York, 1962), pp. 402–403. For another view see Henry David Aiken, "The Revolt Against Ideology," *Commentary,* vol. 37, no. 4 (April, 1964): 29–39.

2. Robert E. Scott, "Nation-Building in Latin America," in *Nation-Building,* ed. Karl W. Deutsch and William J. Foltz (New York, 1963), pp. 76–77. On the role of ideology see also Manfred Halpern, "The Rate and Costs of Political Development," *The Annals* 358 (March 1965): 25.

3. Lewis Coser, *The Functions of Social Conflict* (New York, 1956), p. 118.

4. For an explanation of ideology see David E. Apter, ed., *Ideology and Discontent* (London, 1964), pp. 16–17. See also, George I. Blanksten, "Ideology and Nation-Building in the Contemporary World," *International Studies Quarterly* Vol. 11, No. 1 (March 1967): 3–4.

5. Zbigniew K. Brzezinski, *The Soviet Bloc* (Cambridge, Mass. 1960), p. 385. On the need for ideology in nation-building see Blanksten, *op. cit.,* pp. 10–11.

6. It has been suggested that nationalist appeals need constant replenishment including a concern with domestic problems. See Douglas E. Ashford, "Contradictions of Nationalism and Nation-Building in the Muslim World," *Middle East Journal,* vol. 18, no. 4 (Autumn 1964): 423–424, 430.

7. Patricia L. Kendall, "The Ambivalent Character of Nationalism Among Egyptian Professionals," *Public Opinion Quarterly* 20 (1956): 277–289.

8. For the meaning of the term "nationalist-statehood" as distinct from "nation-statehood" see J. C. Hurewitz in William Theodore de Bary and Ainslie T. Embree, ed., *Approaches to Asian Civilizations* (New York, 1961), p. 136.

9. Hanna Abu Rashid, *Tarikh Nahdat Misr al-Hadithah* [History of the Modern Awakening of Egypt] (Beirut, 1960), p. 29; and Mahmud Mutwalli, *Al-Ittihad al-Ishtiraki al-Arabi* [The Arab Socialist Union], (Cairo, 1964), pp. 36–37.

10. John C. Campbell, *Defense of the Middle East* (New York, 1958), p. 109. On the roles of Castro and Nasir see Zbigniew K. Brzezinski, *Ideology and Power in Soviet Politics,* (rev. ed., New York, 1967), p. 7.

11. Mutwalli, *op. cit.,* pp. 112–114.

12. *Ibid.* For a brief analysis of the weaknesses of the Liberation Rally, see, Manfred Halpern, *The Politics of Social Change in the Middle East and North Africa* (Princeton, 1963), pp. 308–310.

13. Mutwalli, *op. cit.,* pp. 119–120.

14. Articles by Butros Ghali and Ahmad Mahaba in *Al-Dimuqratiyyah fi al-Alam al-Arabi* [Democracy in the Arab World] (Beirut, 1959), pp. 98–103, 138–152.

15. Mutwalli, *op. cit.,* pp. 121–133.

16. *Ibid.;* and President Abd al-Nasir's Speech of 16 October 1961. Text in *Press Release,* Press Bureau of UAR Mission to the United Nations, p. 426. For an informative analysis of the National Union and the political system in the mid-1950s see Don Peretz, "Democracy and the Revolution in Egypt," *Middle East Journal,* vol. 13, no. 1 (Winter 1959): 34–40.

17. Georges Sorel, *Reflections on Violence,* trans. T. E. Hulme (New York, 1914), p. 32. Concepts similar to Sorel's myth include: Plato's "noble lie," Mosca's "political formula," Pareto's "derivations," and Lasswell's "political myth."

18. George Sabine, *A History of Political Theory,* 3rd ed. (New York, 1961), p. 894.

19. Sati' al-Husari, *Abhath Mukhtara fi al-Qawmiyyah* (Selected Studies in Arab Nationalism), (Cairo, 1964), p. 28 and Abdallah al-Rimawi, *Al-Qawmiyyah wa al-Wahdah,* (Nationalism and Unity), (Cairo, 1961), pp. 41–44.

20. Gamal Abdel Nasser, *The Philosophy of the Revolution* (Buffalo, 1959), pp. 59–62; also, John S. Badeau, "The Role in Search of a Hero: A Brief Study of the Egyptian Revolution," *Middle East Journal* 9 (Fall 1955): 373–384; Abd al-Hafiz Abd Rabbuh, *Thawrah wa Thuwwar* [Revolution and Revolutionaries] (Cairo, 1962). For an incisive account of the relationship between Arab national traits and the emergence of charismatic leadership see Majid Khadduri, *Political Trends in the Arab World* (Baltimore, 1970), pp. 24–26.

21. President Abd al-Nasir's speech of 16 October 1961. Text in *Press Release,* Press Bureau of UAR Mission to the United Nations, pp. 9–10.

22. Mahmud Fathi Umar and Hafiz al-Hammud, *Nadharat Hawl Falsafat al-Thawrah* [Views on the Philosophy of the Revolution] (Cairo, 1961), pp. 176–177.

23. Muhammad Hasanayn Haykal, "Lonely at the Top," *Arab Observer* (1 February 1965): 50. Similar attributes proliferated in publications honoring the president's reelection. The following is a sample from more than thirty favorite attributes to Abd al-Nasir: The Revolutionary Giant; Father Gamal; Exploder of the Revolution; Destroyer of Imperialism; Builder of the High Dam; Hero of Heroes; Lover of Millions; See, *Ruz al-Yusif,* Golden Issue, 31 March 1965; and Ahmad Muhammad al-

Hufi, *Butulah wa Batal* [Heroism and a Hero] (Cairo, 1963), pp. 131–138.

24. Halpern, *Politics,* p. 311.

25. Other factors contributing to the formation of the UAR were Syrian President Shukri al-Quwwatli's and the Ba'athists' fears of a Communist takeover in Syria.

26. The coercive force had been weakened by the controversy between Field Marshall Amir, Egyptian proconsul in Syria and Minister of Interior, Col. Abd al-Hamid Sarraj. As a result, Sarraj's very effective Maktab al-Thani (Deuxieme Bureau) became weakened. Amitai Etzioni, *Political Unification: A Comparative Analysis of Leaders and Forces* (New York, 1965), pp. 109, 119–120. Patrick Seale, "The Break-up of the UAR," *World Today* 17 (1961). On the break-up also see Monte Palmer, "The United Arab Republics: An Assessment of its Failure," *Middle East Journal,* vol. 20, no. 1 (Winter 1966), pp. 50–67. For a perceptive analysis of the Egyptian-Syrian negotiations concerning renewed attempts at unification see, Malcolm Kerr, *The Arab Cold War, 1958–1967,* 2nd ed., (London, 1969) and *Muhadir Muhadathat al-Wahdah,* (Cairo, 1963).

27. President Abd al-Nasir's speech of 5 October 1961. Text in *Press Release,* Press Bureau of UAR Mission to the United Nations, pp. 1–6.

28. *Ibid.,* pp. 5–6.

29. *Ibid.*

30. On the detention of at least forty persons and other police measures taken by Vice President Zakariyya Muhyi al-Din for "internal vigilance" see *Arab Observer,* 29 October 1961, pp. 10–11; also *Scribe* (September–October 1961): 13; *Scribe* (October–November 1961): 5–7.

31. Moreover, there were serious economic reasons as those caused by Nile floods and a bad cotton crop, both of which pushed the regime toward precipitate action; see Charles Issawi, *Egypt in Revolution* (London, 1963), p. 61.

32. President Abd al-Nasir's speech of 16 October 1961. Text in *Press Release,* Press Bureau of UAR Mission to the United Nations, pp. 4–5.

33. Marcel Colombe, "Ou va l'egypte?" *Orient* vol. 5, no. 20 (1961): 61.

34. Ahmed Abul-Fath, *L'affaire Nasser* (Paris, 1962), and Anouar Abdel-Malek, *Egypte Société Militaire* (Paris, 1962).

35. Khalid Muhammad Khalid, *Azmat al-Hurriyyah fi Alamina* [The Crisis of Freedom in Our World] (Cairo, 1964), p. 5.

36. *Ibid.,* pp. 249–250.

37. *Ibid.,* pp. 258–281.

38. *Al-Ahram,* 27, 30 November 1961; also *Al-Tariq ila Al-Dimuqratiyya* [The Path to Democracy] (Cairo, 1962), pp. 191–215, 262–280.

6. The Revolutionary Present and the Recasting of the Past

1. President Gamal Abdel Nasser, *Speeches and Press Interviews, 1958* (Cairo, UAR, Information Dept., n.d.), pp. 291–292; also, Muhammad Farid Abu Hadid, *Ummatuna al-Arabiyyah* [Our Arab Nation], (Cairo, 1961), p. 309.

2. Edward Hallett Carr, *The New Society* (Boston, 1951), p. 2.

3. Clearly any such effort on the part of the officers would have given substance to the Brotherhood's antiregime propaganda.

4. On the post-1960 Communist Chinese reinterpretation of Chinese and world history, which clearly reflects "Sinocentric" tendencies, see R. V. Viatkin and S. L. Tikhvinskii, "Some Problems of Historical Scholarship in the Chinese People's Republic," *Soviet Review* 5 (Summer 1964): 48–64.

5. Carr, *op. cit.*, p. 13.

6. Various peoples living in the Hapsburg Empire were also engaged in rewriting and inventing history.

7. Ahmad Khaki, *Falsafat al-Qawmiyyah* [Philosophy of Nationalism] (Cairo, 1962), pp. 174–175; Mahmud Fathi Umar and Hafiz al-Hammud, *Nadharat hawl Falsafat al-Thawrah* [Views on the Philosophy of the Revolution] (Cairo, 1961), pp. 80–83.

8. Molotov subsequently apologized for the statement. See *Kommunist* (October 1955), and Robert Conquest, *Power and Policy in the USSR* (London, 1962), pp. 268, 281. In August 1963 the task of rewriting an official history of Egypt was assigned to the Ministry of National Guidance and Culture, see, *Arab Observer*, 5 August 1963, p. 18.

9. Khaki, *op. cit.*, p. 174; and UAR, *The Charter* (Information Dept., Cairo, n.d.), pp. 18–20.

10. Umar and al-Hammud, *op. cit.*, p. 131.

11. UAR, *Charter*, pp. 20–21.

12. Umar and al-Hammud, *op. cit.*, pp. 80–95.

13. Khaki, *op. cit.*, pp. 175–177.

14. UAR, *Charter*, p. 21; and Ibrahim Ahmad al-Adawi, *Qadat al-Tahrir al-Arabi* [Leaders of the Arab Liberation] (Cairo, 1964), pp. 104–121.

15. Abd al-Mun'im Shumays, *Al-Thawrah al-Arabiyyah al-Kubrah* [The Great Arab Revolution] (Cairo, 1960), p. 205; and UAR, *Charter*, pp. 21–27.

16. UAR, *Charter*, pp. 21–27.

17. Shumays, *op. cit.*, p. 205.

18. Abu al-Futuh Rudwan, Muhammad al-Hadi Afifi and Muhammad Ahmad al-Ghannam, *Usul al-Alam al-Hadith* [The Origins of the Modern World] (Cairo, 1963), pp. 334–335; also UAR, *Charter*, p. 26.

19. UAR, *Charter*, p. 22.

20. The Syrian Ba'athists Salah al-Bitar and Michel Aflaq have gone further by calling the "Arabness" of Egypt a "sentimental" phenomenon. See Mahmud Abd al-Rahim, *Al-Sha'b al-Arabi Yudin al-Aflaqiyin* [The Arab People Condemn the Aflaquites] (Cairo, 1963), pp. 372–378.

21. UAR, *Charter*, p. 23.

22. *Ibid.*, pp. 27–28. On the self-isolation of Egypt from the Arab world in the immediate post-World War I period see Muhammad Ali al-Ghatit, *Thawrat al-Arab fi 1919, Thawrat Misr* [Arab Revolutions in 1919: The Egyptian Revolution], vol. 2 (Cairo, 196?), pp. 353–354.

23. UAR, *Charter*, pp. 25–26.

24. Fathi Uthman al-Mahlawi, in *Al-Dimuqratiyyah fi al-Alam al-Arabi* [Democracy in the Arab World] (Beirut, 1959), p. 113.

25. Umar and al-Hammud, *op. cit.*, p. 168.

26. UAR, *Charter*, pp. 25–26.

27. *Ibid.*, p. 28.

28. Anwar El-Sadat, *Revolt on the Nile* (New York, 1957), pp. 38–42.

29. Instead the roles are reversed and Israel is called "an aggressive racial movement" see UAR, *Charter*, p. 27.

30. *Ibid.*, p. 28.

31. Muhammad Ali's conquest of other Arab lands is not an exception since it is considered as being "foreign" sponsored.

32. UAR, *Charter*, pp. 28–29.

33. *Ibid.*, pp. 29–30.

34. Sulayman Mazhar, *Adwa'ala Waqi'ina* [Focus on Our Situation] (Cairo, 1963), p. 6.

35. UAR, *Charter*, pp. 28–30.

36. Umar and al-Hammud, *op. cit.*, pp. 80–85.

37. Abdallah al-Rimawi, *Al-Mantiq al-Thawri* [The Revolutionary Logic] (Cairo, 1961), pp. 31–32.

38. Shumays, *op. cit.*, pp. 85–86.

39. *Ibid.*

40. Muhammad Shadid, "Ma'rakat Ayn Jalut," *Al-Talabah al-Arab* (Cairo, 13 February 1965), p. 12; Sayyid Abd al-Hamid Mursi, *Min al-Thahawwul ila al-Intilaq* [From Transition to the Take-off Point] (Cairo, 1964), pp. 54–55. On the role of Arab historians see Anwar G. Chejne, "The Use of History by Modern Arab Writers," *Middle East Journal*, vol. 14, no. 4 (Autumn 1960): 382–396.

41. On the theory of "the base" and the "indivisibility" of the Arab Revolution see Abd al-Rahim, *op. cit.*, pp. 371–378.

42. Husayn Fawzi al-Najjar, *Wahdat al-Tarikh al-Arabi* [The Unity of Arab History] (Cairo, 1963), pp. 15–52.

43. See Abd al-Aziz Sayyid al-Ahad, *Ayyam Salah al-Din* [The Days of Salah al-Din] (Beirut, 1960).

44. Such as the Ba'ath, Hashimis, and Sa'udis.

45. Philip K. Hitti, *History of the Arabs*, 4th ed. rev. (London, 1949), pp. 452–455.

46. The Tulunids conquered Syria, and the Ikhshidids added Palestine and Arabia.

47. Hitti, *op. cit.*, pp. 617–618.

48. The unity of Syria and Egypt is also stressed by recalling earlier instances of joint Egyptian-Syrian action. One such example is UAR Navy Day, celebrated on 29 August, commemorating the Egyptian-Syrian naval victory over Byzantium in the Battle of Masts (A.D. 655); see *Arab Observer*, 6 September 1965, p. 12.

49. Note the use of Salah al-Din's eagle as national emblem in the UAR and several other Arab countries. On the symbolic significance of the Battle of Hittin against the Crusaders (A.D. 1187); see Atayyah al-Qusi, *Ma'rakat Hittin wa al-Wahdah al-Arabiyyah* [The Battle Hittin and Arab Unity] (Cairo, 1963). It should be noted that Salah al-Din was born a Kurd in Iraq.

50. Muhammad Sa'id al-Aryan and Gamal al-Din al-Shayyal, *Qissat al-Kifah Bayna al-Arab wa al-Isti'mar* [The Story of Struggle Between the Arabs and Imperialism] (Cairo, 1960), pp. 13–24; and Umar and al-Hammud, *op. cit.*, p. 157.

51. Umar and al-Hammud, *op. cit.*, pp. 157–158.

52. UAR, *Charter*, p. 17.

53. Gamal Abdel Nasser, *Speeches and Press Interview, 1960* (October–December), p. 116; (April–June), pp. 100–104.

54. UAR, *Charter*, p. 18.

55. Khaki, *op. cit.*, pp. 168–169; also Ahmad Izzat Abd al-Karim, Abd al-Hamid al-Batriq, Abu al-Futuh Rudwan, *Tarikh al-Alam al-Arabi fi al-Asr al-Hadith* [The History of the Arab World in Modern Times] (Cairo, 1957), pp. 50–51.

56. Khaki, *op. cit.*, pp. 168–169.

57. Rudwan, Afifi, al-Ghannam, *op. cit.*, p. 13; and UAR, *Charter*, pp. 17–18.

58. Rudwan, Afifi and al-Ghannam, *op. cit.*, pp. 24–25, 115. The crucial Syrian-Christian translators of Greek texts into Arabic are treated as Arabs.

59. *Ibid.*, pp. 60–61.

60. *Ibid.*, pp. 68–80.

61. Bertram D. Wolfe, "Totalitarianism and History," *Totalitarianism*, ed. Carl J. Friedrich (New York, 1964), p. 264.

62. On the "wrong analysis" of "some historians" see UAR, *Charter*, pp. 18 and 22.

7. Pan-Arabism and the Arabization of Modern Egypt

1. Copts and other Christians. There seem to be varying opinions about the periodization of the *isti'rab*. One view states that the *isti'rab* and the resulting unity of Arab history began with the spread of Islam. See Husayn Fawzi Najjar, *Wahdat al-Tarikh al-Arabi* [The Unity of Arab History] (Cairo, 1963), p. 15; another view traces the *ist'i rab* back to early times and Arabizes the following: Egyptians, Phoenicians, Babylonians, Canaanites, Hebrews, Chaldeans, Akkadians, etc. (exceptions: Sumerians, Hittites); see Mahmud Kamil, *Al-Dawlah al-Arabiyyah al-Kubra* [The Great Arab State] (Cairo, 1964?), pp. 15–95. Muhammad Izzat Darwazah, *Urubat Misr* [The Arabism of Egypt], (Saida, 1963), pp. 95–99.

2. The Turkic groups arrived mostly as conquerors (Kipçak Mamluks, Ottomans, etc.). See Philip K. Hitti, *History of the Arabs*, 4th ed. rev. (London, 1949), p. 622; Cilician Armenians are evident in Egypt in the tenth and eleventh centuries; see *Abu-Salih al-Armani* (Oxford, 1895). Syrian Christians came during the nineteenth century. After World War I, a new influx of Armenians began from former Ottoman territories.

3. See chap. 9.

4. This "anti-Christian" sentiment is often manifested in the form of attacks on the Crusaders who are pictured as having returned under the guise of European imperialism. See Mahmud Fathi Umar and Hafiz al-Hammud, *Nadharat hawl Falsafat al-Thawrah* [Views about the Philosophy of the Revolution] (Cairo, 1961), pp. 157–159.

5. This notion was clearly manifested in the interviews conducted with members of some Egyptian minority groups who have immigrated to the United States.

6. This was done very gracefully by the promulgation of the Socialist Laws of July 1961, and similar measures since that date; see *New York Times*, 13 August 1963.

7. Such royal "favorites" as Karim Thabit, Antoine Pulli and Elias

Andraos may be regarded as occupying positions of access, thereby providing the various ethnic minorities with symbols of identification with the state. As to the Armenians who lacked special access to the king, the symbols of identification with Egypt included Prime Minister Boghos Nubar Pasha. More recently, Nubar Pasha has been replaced by the eleventh century Egyptian-Armenian General Badr al-Jamali. See, Muhammad Jamal al-Din Surur, "Badr al-Jamali: The Armenian Mamluk," *Al-Ahram*, 21 December 1964; also *Cahaqir* and *Lusaper* newspapers, 1961–1964.

8. *New York Times*, 9 November 1963.

9. John A. Wilson, *The Culture of Ancient Egypt* (Chicago, 1954), pp. 135, 261.

10. Yitzhak Oron, "The Nationalist Myth in Contemporary Egypt," *Hamizrah he-Hadash*, vol. 10, no. 3 (A.E. 1539/1960).

11. While there are no statistics available, some Copts are said to be assimilating readily because of their linguistic identity and other cultural similarities. Of particular interest is the size of the Coptic community. While most Western sources estimate it to be 4,000,000, U.N. sources place the total number of Christians in Egypt at approximately 1.9 million. It is assumed that the latter figure is supplied by the Egyptian government; see U.N., *Demographic Year Book, 1963*, p. 332.

12. Other minorities are rapidly shrinking in number. Almost all of the 50,000 Italians have disappeared. The Greek community has shrunk to less than 40,000; see *New York Times*, 21 May 1962. After the Six-Day War the Jewish community shrank to less than 1,000.

13. Alan H. Gardiner, *Egyptian Grammar*, 3rd ed. (Oxford, 1957), p. 5; and also Georg Steindorff, *Lehrbuch der Koptisohen Grammatik* (Chicago, 1951), p. 1; G. E. Von Grunebaum, *Modern Islam* (New York, 1964), p. 162.

14. Abu al-Futuh Rudwan, Muhammad al-Hadi Afifi and Muhammad Ahmad al-Ghannam, *Usul al-Alam al-Hadith* [The Origins of the Modern World] (Cairo, 1963), p. 13. UAR, *The Charter* (Information Dept., Cairo, n.d.), pp. 17–18. The negative Egyptian view of Ottoman rule predates the revolution; a similar view was advanced by Taha Husayn see Albert Hourani, *Arabic Thought in the Liberal Age, 1798–1939* (London, 1962), p. 331.

15. Ahmet Riza, *La faillité morale de la politique occidentale en orient* (Paris, 1922), p. 5.

16. See Ziya Gökalp, *Yeni Türkiyenin Hedefleri* [The Aims of the New Turkey] (Ankara, 1956); M. Necmeddin Deliorman, *Balkan Türklerinin Tarihi* [The History of Balkan Turks] (Ankara, 1941), pp. 81–83.

17. Ali Abd al-Raziq, *Al-Islam wa Usul al-Hukm* [Islam and the Principles of Authority] (Cairo, 1925), pp. 78–103. On secularization in Islam see Majid Khadduri, *Political Trends in the Arab World* (Baltimore, 1970), pp. 212–252. Hourani, *op. cit.*, pp. 324–340.

18. A comprehensive account of these developments is found in Nadav Safran, *Egypt in Search of Political Community* (Cambridge, Mass., 1961).

19. *Ibid.*, p. 143.

20. A critical account of the "Egypt First" group is found in Sati' al-Husari, *Al-Urubah Awwalan* [Arabism First] (Beirut, 1965), pp. 136–165.

21. However, it should be noted that the Fascist-Nazi alternative began to gain adherents especially during World War II.

22. Muhammad Husayn Haykal, *Fi Manzil al-Wahy* [In the Descending place of the Revelation] (Cairo, 1936), p. 19. A similar metamorphosis occurred in Ahmad Amin, who during the last years of his life manifested anti-Western and anti-Zionist tendencies. See A. M. H. Mazyad, *Ahmad Amin* (Leiden, 1963), pp. 33, 68. At the mass level a similar Islamic revivalism was propagated by the Brotherhood. On the intellectual influence of Muhammad Abduh and Rashid Rida see Malcolm Kerr, *Islamic Reform* (Los Angeles, 1966).

23. Haykal, *op. cit.*, p. 19. For a detailed account see Safran, *op. cit.*, pp. 173–175.

24. This political role of Islam is reflected in Abd al-Nasir's notion that one function of the *hajj* is a political one; see Oron, *op. cit.*, p. 1.

25. The social protest was led by such intellectuals as Tawfiq al-Hakim, Taha Husayn, and Khalid Muhammad Khalid.

26. Mazyad, *op. cit.*, p. 51.

27. Muhammad al-Ghazzali, *Our Beginning in Wisdom* (Washington, D.C., 1953), pp. 130–137.

28. Similarity of the intellectual metamorphosis between these Egyptian thinkers and the German philosopher Fichte on internationalism vs. nationalism is striking.

29. For an analysis of these trends, see Anwar G. Chejne, "Egyptian Attitudes toward Pan-Arabism," *Middle East Journal*, vol. 2, no. 3 (Summer 1957): 253–268. One of the strongest proponents of Pan-Arabism in this period was Sati'al-Husari. On the rise of Pan-Arabism also see, Elie Kedourie, "Pan-Arabism and British Policy," in Walter Z. Laqeueur, ed., *The Middle East in Transition* (New York, 1958), pp. 100–101.

30. Harold Lasswell, Nathan Leites, and Associates, *Language of Politics: Studies in Quantitative Semantics* (New York, 1949), pp. 40–126, 173–368, Bernard Berelson, *Content Analysis in Communication Research* (Glencoe, 1952), pp. 9–146. Robert C. North, Ole R. Holsti, George M. Zaninovich, and Dina A. Zinnes, *Content Analysis: A Handbook with Applications for the Study of International Crisis* (Evanston, 1963). Alexander L. George, *Propaganda Analysis* (Evanston, 1959).

8. The Nasirite Theory and Practice of Arab-Unity Nationalism

1. This ideology is often described as "Nasirism."

2. It would seem that Nasir would fit all four of Lasswell's leadership skill categories. See Harold D. Lasswell, *Psychopathology and Politics* (New York, 1960), pp. 38–64, and *Power and Personality* (New York, 1962), pp. 22–26.

3. On the process of political socialization see Richard E. Dawson and Kenneth Prewitt, *Political Socialization* (Boston, 1969).

4. It has been suggested that strained relations with the father, resulting in low self-esteem, prompts certain men to turn to revolutionary politics to compensate for their unfavorable self-view. See Alexander L. George and Juliette L. George, *Woodrow Wilson and Colonel House: A Personality Study* (New York, 1964).

5. In psychological analysis Nasir's strained relations with his father

may be interpreted as stemming from the father's role in the mother's pregnancy, which resulted in her death in childbirth. For biographical details see, Robert St. John, *The Boss*, (New York, 1960), pp. 13–36.

6. Although Nasir's father was born a peasant in Bani Murr (Upper Egypt), he had managed to acquire enough education to enter the civil service as a postal clerk. Nasir himself was born in Alexandria.

7. Gamal Abdel Nasser, *Speeches and Press Interviews, 1958* (Cairo, n.d.), pp. 44–45. Sati' al-Husari, *Ara' wa Ahadith fi Al-Qawmiyyah al-Arabiyyah* [Opinions and Discourses on Arab Nationalism] (Beirut, 1951), p. 85–86. On Husari's views see L. M. Kenny, "Sati al-Husri's Views on Arab Nationalism," *Middle East Journal*, vol. 17, no. 3 (Summer 1963): 231–256.

8. The term "intuition" is used here in its Bergsonian meaning. See G. T. W. Patrick, *Introduction to Philosophy*, rev. ed. (Cambridge, Mass., 1952), p. 231.

9. Abdallah al-Rimawi, *Al-Qawmiyyah wa al-Wahdah* [Nationalism and Unity] (Cairo, 1961), pp. 46–52.

10. *Ibid.*, p. 44.

11. *Ibid.*

12. *Ibid.*

13. UAR, *Charter*, p. 6.

14. *Ibid.*, p. 31.

15. *Ibid.*, p. 13.

16. *Ibid.*, p. 36.

17. Gamal Abdel Nasser, *The Philosophy of the Revolution* (Buffalo, 1959), pp. 59–62.

18. *Ibid.*, p. 70.

19. UAR, *Charter*, p. 91; also see Sati' al-Husari, *Abhath Mukhtarat fi al-Qawmiyyah al-Arabiyyah* [Selected Studies in Arab Nationalism] (Cairo, 1964), p. 54.

20. Muhammad al-Tammawi, *Al-Tatawwur al-Siyasi li al-Mujtama al-Arabi* [The Political Evolution of Arab Society] (Cairo, 1961), pp. 223–224; on the importance of Arabic as a unifying force see Abd al-Rahman Bazzaz, *Min Wahyi al-Urubah* [From the Inspiration of Arabism] (Cairo, 1963), pp. 291–313.

21. United Arab Republic, *Arab Political Encyclopedia* (Cairo, January–February 1962), p. 155; also *Scribe* (September–October 1961), p. 2.

22. Abdallah al-Rimawi, *Al-Bayan al-Qawmi al-Thawri* [The National Revolutionary Manifesto] (Cairo, 1966), p. 16. *Press Release of the UAR Mission to the U.N.*, October 1961, p. 6.

23. UAR, *Political Encyclopedia*, p. 155.

24. UAR, *Charter*, p. 93.

25. *Ibid.*, p. 94.

26. *Ibid.*

27. *Ibid.*, p. 93.

28. Several types of frameworks to achieve unity have been proposed. See Muhammad Taha Badawi and Abu al-Fattah Sayfi, *Al-Wahdah al-Arabiyyah* [Arab Unity] (Cairo, 1966), p. 146.

29. UAR, *Political Encyclopedia*, p. 155; also Munif Abd al-Razzaz, *Ma'alim al-Hayat al-Arabiyyah al-Jadidah* [Features of the Modern Arab Life] (Beirut, 1959), pp. 123, 263–264.

30. Abdel Nasser, *Philosophy*, pp. 61–62.

31. UAR, *Political Encyclopedia*, p. 155.

32. UAR, *Charter*, p. 16. Also Abdallah al-Rimawi, *Al-Bayan*, (Cairo, 1966), pp. 120, 137; and Sati' al-Husari, *Ara' wa Ahadith* (Beirut, 1951), p. 97.

33. UAR, *Charter*, p. 93.

34. *Arab Observer*, 2 December 1963, p. 20. In addition to Ba'athist doctrines of unity, the Fertile Crescent and Greater Syria schemes are vehemently rejected. See Muhammad Rif'at, *Al-Tawjih al-Siyasi li al-Fikrah al-Arabiyyah al-Hadithah* [The Political Orientation of Modern Arab Thought] (Cairo, 1964), pp. 348–351.

35. Gamal Abdel Nasser, *Speeches and Press Interviews, 1960, October–December* (Cairo, n.d.), p. 57. Also see Gamal Abdel Nasser, *Speeches and Press Interviews, 1958* (Cairo, n.d.), p. 34.

36. UAR, *Charter*, p. 94.

37. *Ibid.*, p. 95.

38. Note the striking resemblances between this Nasirite position and the Khrushchevian policy of peaceful coexistence, which encourage wars of liberation.

39. al-Tammawi, *op. cit.*, p. 341.

40. *UAR Declaration of the Union Accord* (Cairo, 17 April 1963).

41. On the various interpretations of positive neutralism by Arab writers see Leonard Binder, *The Ideological Revolution in the Middle East* (New York, 1964), pp. 230–257. Also Fayez A. Sayegh, ed., *The Dynamics of Neutralism in the Arab World* (San Francisco, 1964). Majid Khadduri, *Political Trends in the Arab World* (Baltimore, 1970), pp. 273–281.

42. This was especially true in Syria.

43. Ahmet Riza, *La faillité morale de la politique occidentale en orient* (Paris, 1922), pp. 132, 171.

44. Anwar El-Sadat, *Revolt on the Nile* (London, 1957), pp. 25–43.

45. *Ibid.*, p. 21.

46. J. C. Hurewitz, *Diplomacy in the Near and Middle East: A Documentary Record, (1914–1956)*, 2 vols. (Princeton, 1956), vol. 2, p. 329.

47. For a detailed analysis see, Binder, *op. cit.*, p. 233–234.

48. Sulayman Mazhar, *Adwa' ala Waqi'ina* [Focus on Our Situation] (Cairo, 1963), pp. 219–221.

49. *Radio Cairo*, 23 July 1954.

50. Hurewitz, *op. cit.*, pp. 401–402; also Abd al-Mun'im Shumays, *Al-Thawrah al-Arabiyyah al-Kubra* [The Great Arab Revolution] (Cairo, 1963), p. 540.

51. Shumays, *op. cit.*, pp. 408–410.

52. Mazhar, *op. cit.*, p. 46.

53. Gamal Abdel Nasser, *Speeches and Press Interviews, 1960 October–December*, p. 31.

54. UAR, *Charter*, p. 101.

55. Shumays, *op. cit.*, pp. 411–419.

56. Mazhar, *op. cit.*, pp. 220–221; also UAR, *Charter*, p. 101.

57. UAR, *Charter*, p. 101.

58. *Ibid.*, p. 102.

59. *Ibid.*, p. 103.

60. *Ibid.*

61. *Ibid.*

62. *Ibid.*, p. 100.

63. A good example was the Egyptian refusal to condemn the Soviet occupation of Czechoslovakia in August 1968.

9. The Nasirite Theory and Practice of Arab Socialism

1. Jean and Simonne Lacouture, *Egypt in Transition* (New York, 1958), p. 19; on power in "hydraulic" systems see Karl Wittfogel, *Oriental Despotism* (New Haven, 1957), pp. 166–167. On the relationship of centralized authority and control of the Nile see Gabriel Baer, *Studies in the Social History of Modern Egypt* (Chicago, 1969), p. 63. Charles Issawi, *Egypt in Revolution* (London, 1963), p. 50.

2. Charles Issawi, *Egypt at Mid-Century: An Economic Survey* (London, 1954), p. 169.

3. *Ibid.*, p. 216.

4. Issawi, *Egypt in Revolution*, p. 247.

5. UAR, *Charter*, (Information Department, Cairo, n.d.), p. 5.

6. National Bank of Egypt, *Economic Bulletin*, vol. 5, no. 3 (1952): 216–217.

7. *Ibid.*, vol. 4, no. 3 (1961): 278. For a leftist interpretation of the structure of landownership in Egypt see Hasan Riad, *L'Egypte Nasserienne* (Paris, 1964), pp. 10–31.

8. Issawi, *Egypt in Revolution*, p. 52.

9. *Ibid.*, p. 53.

10. Leonard Binder, *The Ideological Revolution in the Middle East* (New York, 1964), pp. 223–224.

11. *Ibid.*

12. UAR, *Charter*, p. 5. On the steps in socialistic development, see Hamdi Hafiz, *Al-Ishtirakiyyah wa al-Tatbiq al-Ishtiraki fi al-Jumhuriyyah al-Arabiyyah al-Muttahidah* [Socialism and the Application of Socialism in the UAR] (Cairo, 1966), p. 207.

13. *Révue égyptienne de droit internationale*, vol. 12, no. 1 (Cairo, 1956): 151–152.

14. National Bank of Egypt, *Economic Bulletin*, vol. 10, no. 1 (1957): 38–39. For an incisive analysis of the socialist laws see, Raymond Reynolds Thompson, *The Emergence of Abd al-Nasir's Socialism*, (unpublished Masters Essay, Columbia University, 1962).

15. *Ibid.*, p. 37.

16. *Ibid.*, vol. 12, no. 1 (1960), p. 38.

17. *Ibid.*, vol. 11, no. 3 (1958), p. 255.

18. *Ibid.*, vol. 11, no. 2 (1958), p. 57.

19. *Ibid.*, vol. 11, no. 3 (1958), p. 255.

20. Gamal Abdel Nasser, *Speeches and Press Interviews 1958*, (Cairo, n.d.), p. 249.

21. *Ibid.*, pp. 291–292.

22. National Bank of Egypt, *Economic Bulletin* vol. 14, no. 1 (1961): 8.

23. *Ibid.*, p. 36.

24. *Scribe*, 1 June 1960, p. 3.

25. Hanna Abu Rashid, *Tarikh Nahdat Misr al-Hadithat* [History of the Modern Awakening of Egypt] (Beirut, 1960), pp. 353–354.

26. For a concise account see Malcolm H. Kerr, "The Emergence of a Socialist Ideology in Egypt," *Middle East Journal,* vol. 16, no. 2 (Spring 1962): 127–144. Also, see Thompson, *loc. cit.*

27. Law No. 108 decreed that all cotton exports were to be made through government-owned companies.

28. National Bank of Egypt, *Economic Bulletin* vol. 14, no. 3 (1961): 325.

29. *Ibid.,* vol. 14, no. 4 (1961): 441.

30. *Ibid.,* pp. 326–328.

31. *Ibid.,* pp. 324–333.

32. *Ibid.,* pp. 324–326.

33. *New York Times,* 12 August 1963.

34. *New York Times,* 16 August 1963.

35. Patrick O'Brien, *The Revolution in Egypt's Economic System* (London, 1966), p. 294. Central Bank of Egypt, *Economic Review,* vol. 4, no. 3–4 (1964): 332.

36. Central Bank of Egypt, *Report of the Board of Directors 1964–5,* (Cairo, 1965), p. 25. As of 1971, the number of landless peasants had reached three million. See *Al-Tali'ah,* January 1971, pp. 20–34.

37. Central Bank of Egypt, *Economic Review,* vol. 8, no. 1–2 (1968): 60.

38. See article by Salah al-Mukhaymir, *Al-Talabah al-Arab,* 27 June, 1964; also Abd al-Mun'im Shumays, *Al-Thawrah al-Arabiyyah al-Kubra* [The Great Arab Revolution] (Cairo, 1960), pp. 192–193; and *Al-Talabah al-Arab,* 6 June 1964; and Abd al-Hamid Mursi, *Min al-Tahawwul ila al-Intilaq* [From Transition to the Take-off Point] (Cairo, 1964), p. 235. On socialist elements in Al-Afghani's thought see Sami A. Hanna, "Al-Afghani: A Pioneer of Islamic Socialism," *Muslim World* vol. 57, no. 1 (January 1967): 24–32.

39. Shumays, *op. cit.,* pp. 198–200; also Mahmud Shalabi, *Ishtirakiyyah Abi Bakr* [Abu Bakr's Socialism] (Cairo, 1963); Mustafa al-Siba'i, *Ishtirakiyyat al-Islam* [The Socialism of Islam] (Cairo, 1960), p. 135. For a translation of excerpts from al-Siba'i's work see George H. Gardner and Sami A. Hanna, "Islamic Socialism," *Muslim World* vol. 56, no. 2 (April 1966): 73–86.

40. Note the clash between Chairman Khrushchev and Presidents Abd al-Nasir and Arif on the question of nationalist ideology: "unity of workers of all nations" vs. "Arab unity," see *New York Times,* 16 May 1964 and 20 May 1964. For the Soviet view see I. Beliaev and V. Cheprokov, "The UAR at a New Stage," *Kommunist* 9 (June 1964): 87–96.

41. These sources are identified as the Sa'udis, and to a lesser extent, the Hashimites; see, Sulayman Mazhar, *Adwa' ala Waqi'ina* [Focus on Our Situation] (Cairo, 1963), p. 15.

42. Muhammad Abd Allah al-Arabi, "Basic Characteristics of the Ties of Arab Nationalism," *Al-Talabah al-Arab,* 2 May 1964.

43. Abd al-Majid Abd al-Rahim, *Falsafat al-Mujtama' al-Arabi* [Philosophy of Arab Society] (Cairo, 1964), pp. 15–29.

44. *Ibid.*

45. Mahmud Fathi Umar and Hafiz al-Hammud, *Nadharat hawl Fal-*

safat al-Thawrah, [Views on the Philosophy of the Revolution] (Cairo, 1961), pp. 160–170.

46. Salah al-Mukhaymir, "What is the philosophy of our Arab Socialism?" *Al-Jumhuriyyah,* 16 February 1963.

47. See Chap. 8.

48. UAR, *Charter,* p. 36.

49. See Chap. 8.

50. UAR, *Charter,* p. 36.

51. *Ibid.;* also Mazhar, *op. cit.,* p. 156.

52. al-Mukhaymir, *Al-Jumhuriyyah,* 16 February 1963.

53. *Ibid.*

54. UAR, *Charter,* p. 49.

55. al-Mukhaymir, *Al-Jumhuriyyah,* 16 February 1963.

56. *Ibid.*

57. *Ibid.* On the "flexibility" of Arab socialism, in contrast to "dogmatic" Marxism, see Yahya al-Jamal, *Al-Ishtirakiyyah al-Arabiyyah* [Arab Socialism] (Cairo, 1966), pp. 186–192.

58. UAR, *Charter,* p. 37; and Karam Habib Barsum, *Dirasat al-Mujtama'* [Study of Society] (Cairo, 1964), pp. 43–50. Kamal ed-Din Rifaat, "Development of Socialist Relationships in the U.A.R.," *Middle East Forum,* vol. 42, no. 1, (Winter 1966): 37, 40.

59. UAR, *Charter,* p. 37.

60. Abdallah al-Rimawi, *Al-Harakah al-Arabiyyah al-Wahidah* [The United Arab Movement] (Beirut, 1963), pp. 275–276.

61. Muhammad Hasanayn Haykal, *Al-Talabah al-Arab,* 11 July 1964; also UAR, *Charter,* p. 42.

62. *Arab Observer,* 30 July 1961, pp. 8–9.

63. *Al-Talabah al-Arab,* 4 April 1964.

64. Under Lenin, soldiers were included in the proletariat as well as the farmers on a more ambivalent basis. On the other hand, Maoist communism at the outset based itself squarely on the peasants.

65. *Arab Observer,* 30 July 1961, pp. 8–9.

66. Muhsin Ibrahim, "Arab Socialism in the Making," *Arab Journal* vol. 1, no. 2–3 (Spring–Summer 1964), pp. 19–22.

67. UAR, *Charter,* p. 43.

68. Zbigniew K. Brzezinski, *The Permanent Purge* (Cambridge, Mass., 1956).

69. UAR, *Charter,* p. 50.

70. *Ibid.,* pp. 37–38; also Husayn Kamil Baha' al-Din, "The Revolution," *Al-Talabah al-Arab,* 13 February 1965.

71. *Ibid.,* 21 March and 13 June 1964.

72. The list condensed from UAR, *Charter,* pp. 73–74.

73. Barsum, *op. cit.,* pp. 65–66.

74. Yusif al-Himadi, Ibrahim al-Tarazi, Muhammad Mustafa Hadarat, Abu al-Hasan Ibrahim Hasan, *Al-Qira'ah al-Thanawiyyah* [Secondary Readings] (Cairo, 1962), pp. 295–297. A more democratic socialism was envisioned by Salamah Musa, see Kamel S. Abu Jaber, "Salamah Musa: Percursor of Arab Socialism," *Middle East Journal,* vol. 20, no. 2, (Spring 1966): 196–206.

75. UAR, *Charter,* p. 82.

76. Barsum, *op. cit.,* pp. 110–111, and UAR, *Charter,* p. 82.

77. Muhammad Jamal Saqr, *Al-Ishtirakiyyah wa al-Tarbiyah* [Socialism and Education] (Cairo, 1964?), pp. 50–56.

78. *Ibid.*, pp. 20–32, 104.

79. Luwis Awad, *Al-Ishtirakiyyah wa al-Adab* [Socialism and Literature] (Beirut, 1962), p. 12.

80. Hasan Muhammad Hasan, *Al-Fann fi Rakb al-Ishtirakiyyah* [Art in the Realm of Socialism] (Cairo, 1966), pp. 7, 128, 170.

81. UAR, *Charter*, p. 81; and al-Hammud et al., *op. cit.*, pp. 75–79.

82. UAR, *Charter*, p. 82.

83. Saqr, *op. cit.*, p. 23. It is further held that a person's status is determined by "how much work and what quality of it" he is prepared to do. Thus, there is no notion of a classless society. The president himself once defended the high salaries given to managers (£E 4,000) see *Arab Observer*, 8 March 1965, pp. 12–13 and 24 May 1965, pp. 6–7.

84. UAR, *Charter*, p. 84.

85. *Al-Talabah al-Arab*, 4 April 1964; and UAR, *Charter*, pp. 57–58.

86. UAR, *Charter*, p. 63.

87. *Ibid.*, p. 64.

88. *Ibid.*, pp. 88–89; and Gamal Abdel Nasser, "The Science of Revolution," *Arab Observer*, 21 December 1964, pp. 9–10.

89. Gamal Abdel Nasser, *Arab Observer*, 21 December 1964, pp. 9–10.

90. UAR, *Charter*, p. 50.

91. Gamal Abdel Nasser, *Arab Observer*, 21 December 1964, p. 9.

92. Mahmud Abd al-Rahim, *Al-Sha'b al-Arabi Yudin al-Aflaqiyin* [The Arab People Condemn the Aflaqites] (Cairo, 1963), p. 304.

93. Gamal Abdel Nasser, *Arab Observer*, 21 December 1964, p. 10.

94. *Ibid.*, p. 11.

95. UAR, *Charter*, pp. 61, 104; on the textbook level see al-Himadi, et al., *op. cit.*, pp. 123–129.

10. Routinization of Charisma: The First Phase

1. *Arab Observer*, 31 May 1965, p. 9.

2. Often the term "Central Committee of the ASU" is used. See *Arab Observer*, 7 December 1964, p. 8.

3. On the organization of the ASU, see *The Arab Socialist Union* (Information Dept., Cairo, 1963).

4. *Statute of the Arab Socialist Union* (Information Dept., Cairo, n.d.), p. 41.

5. Concerning the role of the "vanguard" see *Al-Tali'ah*, July 1968, pp. 19–20.

6. *Arab Socialist Union*, p. 4.

7. *Arab Observer*, 31 May 1965, p. 9.

8. Gamal al-Atifi, "Hawl al-Mu'tamar al-Qawmi," *Al-Ahram*, 20 May 1968.

9. *Al-Ahram*, 25 June 1968; *Al-Tali'ah*, July 1968, p. 95.

10. *Arab Observer*, 31 May 1965, p. 9.

11. *Arab Socialist Union*, p. 8.

12. *Ibid.*

13. *Ibid.*, p. 9.

14. *Arab Observer,* 17 May 1965, pp. 10–11.

15. *Ibid.*

16. *Arab Observer,* 5 April 1965, p. 11. On the curriculum of the Institute see Claude Estier, *L'Egypte en Revolution* (Paris, 1965), pp. 135–139.

17. *Statute of the ASU,* pp. 8–9; on the ASU's function as "the mother of the People" see Mahmud Mutwalli, *Al-Ittihad al-Ishtiraki al-Arabi* [The Arab Socialist Union] (Cairo, 1964), p. 218. Also Lutfi al-Khuli, *Dirasat fi al-Waqi' al-Misri al-Mu'asir* [Studies in Contemporary Egyptian Reality] (Beirut, 1964), pp. 118–122.

18. *Statute of the ASU,* pp. 6–7.

19. *Arab Observer,* 5 April 1965, pp. 12–13.

20. *Ibid.*

21. *New York Times,* 17 October 1965. On the ways to "absorb" communists into the ASU, see Muhammad Ali Abu Rayyan, *Al-Nuzum al-Ishtirakiyyah* [Socialist Systems] (Cairo, 1965), p. 398.

22. *Arab Observer,* 7 December 1964, p. 9.

23. Ahmad Baha 'al-Din, "Al-Tariq ila al-Mu'tamar al-Qawmi," *Al-Musawwar,* 19 July 1968.

24. Atifi, *loc. cit.*

25. Baha' al-Din, *op. cit.*, and Haykal, *Husaper,* 29 October 1968.

26. *Ibid.*

27. *Ibid.*

28. *Ibid.*

29. *Al-Ahram,* 13 May 1968.

30. *Ibid.;* Atifi, *op. cit.*

31. *Al-Ahram,* 8 August 1966.

32. *New York Times,* 5 July 1967.

33. Part of this section is taken from the author's "The U.A.R. National Assembly: A Pioneering Experiment," *Middle Eastern Studies,* vol. 4, no. 4 (July 1968): 361–375.

34. *Al-Talabah al-Arab,* 14 March 1964.

35. *Arab Observer,* 7 June 1965, p. 13.

36. P. J. Vatikiotis, *The Egyptian Army in Politics, Pattern for New Nations?* (Bloomington, Ind., 1961), p. 106.

37. U.S., Embassy, Cairo, *UAR Directory of Personages,* (December 1964).

38. Leonard Binder, "Political Recruitment and Participation in Egypt," in *Political Parties and Political Development,* Joseph Lapolombara and Myron Weiner, eds. (Princeton, 1965), pp. 236–239.

39. *Al-Talabah al-Arab,* 23 March 1964.

40. For a full text of the Provisional Constitution, see *Arab Observer,* 30 March 1964, pp. 21–26. The drafting of a permanent constitution was assigned to a committee of seven deputies. See *Al-Ahram,* 10 May 1966. A redrafting was ordered during 1968.

41. *Arab Observer,* 14 June 1965, p. 13; *Egyptian Gazette,* 24 November 1964.

42. *Arab Observer,* 18 January 1965, pp. 8–9.

43. *Egyptian Gazette,* 3 December 1964; *Arab Observer,* 7 December 1964, p. 13.

44. *Egyptian Gazette,* 1 December 1964, 3 December 1964; *Arab Observer,* 7 December 1964, pp. 12–13.

45. *Arab Observer,* 4 January 1965, p. 9.

46. *Arab Observer,* 4 January 1965, p. 13.

47. *Al-Talabah al-Arab,* 27 February 1965, 6 March 1965; *Arab Observer,* 8 March 1965, p. 14.

48. *Arab Observer,* 28 June 1965, pp. 6–7; 5 July 1965, p. 7–8.

49. *Arab Observer,* 5 July 1965, p. 8.

50. Muhammad al-Sayyid al-Jazzar, *Dirasat fi al-Muhasabah al-Ammah* [Studies in General Accounting] (Cairo, 1965), pp. 367–68.

51. *Al-Talabah al-Arab,* 20 November 1965; *Arab Observer,* 15 November 1965, p. 8.

52. On the functional specialization of legislative committees, see, Abd al-Hamid Bakhit, *Al-Mujtama' al-Arabi wa al-Islami* [The Arab and Islamic Society] (Cairo, 1965), p. 486.

53. See *Al-Ahram,* 3 May 1966. Also see the recommendation on the "Committee of Six" endorsing public hearings, *Ruz al-Yusif,* 6 June 1966, p. 4.

54. *Al-Ahram,* 6 December 1965.

55. *Al-Ahram,* 15 December 1965.

56. *New York Times,* 15 December 1965; *Arab Observer,* 20 December 1965, p. 5.

57. *Arab Observer,* 20 December 1965, pp. 4–5.

58. *New York Times,* 15 December 1965.

59. *Al-Ahram,* 16 December 1965; *Arab Observer,* 20 December 1965, p. 5.

60. *Al-Ahram,* 9 December 1965.

61. *Al-Ahram,* 15 December 1965.

62. *Al-Ahram,* 20 December 1965.

63. *Ibid.*

64. *Arab Observer,* 28 March 1966, p. 14.

65. *Ruz al-Yusif,* 11 July 1966, p. 25.

66. *Arab Observer,* 30 May 1966, pp. 6–7.

67. *Arab Observer,* 30, May 1966, p. 13.

68. *Al-Jumhuriyyah,* 22 June 1966, *Ruz al-Yusif,* 27 June 1966, pp. 8–9 and *Arab Observer,* 27 June 1966, pp. 6–7.

69. In the case of the Supreme Soviet, there have been indications that its role is to be strengthened with respect to the governmental bureaucracy, see *New York Times,* 14 December 1966.

70. On this subject see Professor John Badeau's remarks to the Arab League in *Arab Observer,* 7 March 1966, p. 51.

71. *Arab Observer,* 8 March 1965, p. 12.

72. *Arab Observer,* 24 May 1965, p. 5; and *Al-Talabah al-Arab,* 22 May 1965.

73. *Arab Observer,* 28 December 1964, p. 15.

74. *Ruz al-Yusif,* 6 June 1966, p. 4.

75. *Arab Observer,* 24 May 1965, p. 7.

76. *Al-Ahram,* 7 August 1966.

77. *Arab Observer,* 7 June 1965, p. 3. On the trend toward a greater Assembly role in the political system see Alan Horton, "A Note on Syria, the Sudan, and the United Arab Republic," *American Universities Field Staff,* vol. 13, no. 1 (June 1965): 17.

11. The Power Elite (1952–1969)

1. For a comprehensive criticism of Lasswell's concept of political elites, see, Peter Bachrach, *The Theory of Democratic Elitism: A Critique* (Boston, 1967), pp. 69–82.

2. *Ibid.,* p. 77.

3. For a review of theoretic and case studies of elites, see, Donald R. Matthews, *The Social Background of Political Decision-Makers* (New York, 1954). Other relevant studies include Carl Beck and James M. Malloy, "Political Elites: A Mode of Analysis," (Geneva, 1964); Lewis J. Edinger and Donald D. Searing, "Social Background in Elite Analysis," *American Political Science Review* 61 (June 1967): 429–445; Morris Janowitz, "The Systematic Analysis of Political Biography," *World Politics,* 6 (April 1954): 405–412; Dwaine Marvick, ed., *Political Decision-Makers* (New York, 1961); Lester G. Seligman, "Elite Recruitment and Political Development," *Journal of Politics* 26 (August 1964): 612–624; W. L. Guttsman, *The British Political Elite,* (New York, 1963); Fredrick W. Frey, *The Turkish Political Elite,* (Cambridge, Mass., 1965); M. P. Gehlen and M. McBride, "The Soviet Central Committee: An Elite Analysis," *American Political Science Review* 62 (December 1968): 1232–1241; Manfred Halpern, *The Politics of Social Change in the Middle East and North Africa* (Princeton, 1963); Harold D. Lasswell and Daniel Lerner, *World Revolutionary Elites* (Cambridge, Mass., 1965); R. V. Presthus and L. V. Blankenship, *Men at the Top* (New York, 1964); William B. Quandt, *Revolution and Political Leadership: Algeria, 1954–68* (Cambridge, Mass., 1969); Austin Ranney, *Pathways to Parliament* (Madison, Wis., 1965); J. A. Schlesinger, *Ambition and Politics: Political Careers in the United States* (Chicago, 1966); and Geraint Parry, *Political Elites* (New York, 1969). Jose Imaz, *Los Que Mandan,* trans. by Carlos A. Astiz, (Albany, 1970).

4. The concept of "circulation of elites" has been used frequently since Vilfredo Pareto. See T. B. Bottomore, *Elites and Society* (New York, 1964), p. 53.

5. *Who's Who in the Arab World; Kessing's Contemporary Archives; Arab Report and Record; International Who's Who; Cahier d'Orient Contemporain; Europa Yearbook; Whitaker's Almanac; New York Times;* and *Facts on File.*

6. Specifically, *Al-Ahram; Al-Akhbar; Akhbar al-Yawm; Akhir Sa'ah; Al-Musawwar; Al-Jumhuriyyah; Al-Anwar; Al-Nahar; Scribe; Daily Star* (Beirut), and *Arab Observer.*

7. Many of the other officers, including Nasir, had attended civilian colleges and universities; they are excluded from the officer-technocrat category because they left school before completion of academic degrees.

8. The Syrian leadership is *not* included in the computation.

9. Research in progress in collaboration with Paul Smith on, "Cross-national Circulation of Elites: United States, Lebanon, Egypt": Center for Comparative Political Research, State University of New York at Binghamton.

10. Muhammad Hasanayn Haykal, "An al-Tajribah an al-Dimuqratiyyah fi Zamanina" [On Experience in Democracy in Our Times], *Al-Ahram,* 15 November 1968.

11. The activism of the French left and its relatively more cohesive ideology may have contributed to the spread of leftist, French intellectual influences in Egypt.

12. Actually this number represents a minimum since data are lacking on several leaders. Table 9 shows a total of 54 foreign degrees granted; but several held more than one foreign degree.

13. Needless to say the author admits a certain bias in favor of specialists, although some may consider Husayn's depolitization of students as an important achievement.

14. J. C. Hurewitz, *Middle East Politics: The Military Dimension* (New York, 1969), p. 127.

15. The final breakdown was checked by a panel of three judges, two Egyptian and one American.

16. Eliezer Beeri, "Social Class and Family Background of the Egyptian Army Officer Class," *Asian and African Studies* 2 (1966): 1–38.

17. Leonard Binder, "Egypt: The Integrative Revolution," in Lucian Pye and Sidney Verba, ed., *Political Culture and Political Development* (Princeton, 1965), pp. 396–449.

18. It is to be noted that there are only four ministries that retained the intermediate rank of deputy minister, which is a cabinet position. In these cases the undersecretary level is the next lowest position.

19. Four of these were undersecretaries in the Ministry of Interior, and one in the War Ministry. These findings are based mostly on the author's confidential communications with Egyptians. The accuracy of the information is ascertained by checking and collating the various sources against each other.

20. UAR, Bureau of Census and Statistics, *Nashrah Ihsa' Muwazzafi al-Hukumah wa al-Hay'at* [Report on Statistics of Employees of the Government and Agencies] (Cairo, 1962), pp. 52–53.

21. On the concept of the new middle class see Manfred Halpern, *The Politics of Social Change in the Middle East and North Africa* (Princeton, 1963), pp. 51–78; and William R. Polk, *The United States and the Arab World* (Cambridge, Mass., 1965), pp. 215–28. Also, Morroe Berger, "The Middle Class in the Arab World," in Walter Z. Laqueur, ed., *The Middle East in Transition,* (New York, 1958), pp. 61–71.

22. *Arab Observer,* 8 March 1965, p. 13; 15 March 1965, p. 11; 12 July 1965, p. 11; 2 August 1965, p. 12; 30 August 1965, p. 9.

23. "Officer-technocrats" are exceptions.

12. The Political System Under Stress (1965–1967)

1. S. N. Eisenstadt, "Modernization and Conditions of Sustained Growth," *World Politics,* vol. 16, no. 4 (July 1964): 576–594.

2. *Arab Observer,* 13 September 1965, pp. 8–12.

3. *New York Times,* 23 October 1965.

4. *Daily Star* (Beirut), 2 October 1965.

5. *Al-Nahar,* 6 October 1965; *New York Times,* 23 October 1965.

6. For comparative data on size of bureaucracy see Morroe Berger, *Bureaucracy and Society in Modern Egypt* (Princeton, 1957), pp. 82–84. On the shortcomings of Egypt's bureaucracy see Morroe Berger, "Patterns of Communication of Egyptian Civil Servants with the Public," *Public Opinion Quarterly* 20 (1956): 292–296.

7. *Arab Observer,* 4 January 1965, pp. 17–18.

8. *Ibid.,* p. 18.

9. *Ibid.,* and Muhammad Mukhtar Amin Makram, *Hawl al-Ishtirakiyyah al-Arabiyyah* [About Arab Socialism] (Cairo, 1966), pp. 183–195.

10. *Bina' al-Watan,* April 1965.

11. See speeches by Premier Ali Sabri in *Arab Observer,* 13 April 1964, p. 11, and 26 April 1964, pp. 18–19.

12. Zakariyya Muhyi al-Din, *Ahdaf al-Marhalah al-Qadimah* [Aims of the Next Stage] (Cairo, 1965), pp. 38–54.

13. *Ibid.,* p. 39.

14. *Daily Star* (Beirut), 2 October 1965.

15. Muhyi al-Din, *op. cit.,* pp. 43–54.

16. *Daily Star* (Beirut), 2 October 1965.

17. *Al-Nahar,* 6 October 1965.

18. *Al-Ahram,* 7 October 1965. Some officers reportedly were purged because of errors and others because of their "relationships" with the Ikhwan; see *New York Times,* 14 October 1965.

19. *Al-Siyasah al-Ammah li al-Thawrah fi al-Wizarah al-Dakhiliyyah* [General Policy for the Revolution in the Interior Ministry] (Cairo, 1962); Sadiq Halawi, *Al-Amn al-Am* [Public Security] (Cairo, 1962).

20. *Al-Nahar,* 2 October 1965.

21. *Arab Observer,* 13 September 1965, pp. 8–12.

22. Gabriel A. Almond and James S. Coleman, ed., *The Politics of Developing Areas* (Princeton, 1960), p. 27.

23. *Arab Observer,* 27 September 1965, p. 11.

24. The well-known Shaykh al-Ghazzali is the head of the Islamic Orientation Department in the Waqfs Ministry.

25. *Arab Observer,* 27 September 1965, p. 11.

26. For example, his "fireside chats" in early December 1965 and his marathon meetings with intellectuals in August 1966. See *New York Times,* 5 December 1965. Also see *Al-Ahram,* 8–11 August 1966.

27. During July 1965 the regime announced the arrest of publisher Mustafa Amin amid charges of a CIA-sponsored coup. *Al-Jumhuriyyah,* 29 July 1965.

28. *New York Times,* 4 August 1965.

29. *New York Times,* 17 October 1965.

30. *New York Times,* 22 February 1966. In January 1966, Averell Harriman visited Nasir in connection with Vietnam peace efforts.

31. It has been suggested that the U.S. decision to sell planes and tanks to Israel was prompted by the UAR criticism of the renewed American bombing in North Vietnam and the opening of NLF offices in Cairo.

32. Joseph H. de Rivera, *The Psychological Dimensions of Foreign Policy,* (Columbus, 1968), pp. 21–64; Ross Stagner, *Psychological Aspects of International Conflict* (Belmont, 1967), pp. 5–16.

33. For an account of President Kennedy's new policy in the Middle East written by one of its foremost practitioners see John S. Badeau, *The American Approach to the Arab World* (New York, 1968), pp. 133–49.

34. See the series of articles on the CIA in *New York Times,* 25–29 April 1966.

35. For an Egyptian view of the CIA, see, *Al-Ahram,* 20 February

1967. Ambassador Badeau retired six months after Johnson assumed office.

36. *Al-Ahram,* 8 April 1966; 27 January 1967.

37. For a revealing account of American policies toward Egypt and their detrimental affect on the Egyptian government's actions leading to the June War see interview with ex-U.S. chargé d'affaires in Cairo, David Ness, *Arab World* vol. 16, no. 3–4 (March–April 1970): 7–10. See also *New York Times,* 6–9 February 1968.

38. *Economist* (London), 5 November 1966, p. 589.

39. *Arab Report and Record,* 15 October 1966, 30 November 1966.

40. For a critical Egyptian view of the IMF see *Al-Musawwar,* 20 January 1967, pp. 20–21.

41. In 1966 one third of Egypt's military manpower was in the Yemen. See J. C. Hurewitz, *Middle East Politics: The Military Dimension,* (New York, 1969), p. 140. Also, the *New York Times* reported on 24 May 1967 that 50,000 Egyptian troops had initiated a new thrust against the Yemeni Royalists.

42. According to former American chargé d'affaires in Cairo, David Ness, he had been given explicit assurances by the Egyptian government that they would not attack Israel first. See Ness, *loc. cit.*

43. For a perceptive analysis of the prewar period see Alan W. Horton, "The Arab-Israeli Conflict of June 1967," *American Universities Field Staff,* vol. 14, no. 3 (September 1967): 1–15.

13. Min Huna Nabda'

1. For an Egyptian perspective on the events of 9–10 June 1967 see Sayyid Hamid al-Nassaj, *Thawrat al-Jamahir al-Sha'biyyah* [The Popular Mass Revolution] (Alexandria, 1969).

2. This view is similar to Lipset's who notes that "groups regard a political system as legitimate or illegitimate according to the way in which its values fit in with their primary values." Seymour Martin Lipset, "Some Social Requisites of Democracy," in Nelson Polsby, Robert A. Dentler, and Paul A. Smith, eds., *Politics and Social Life,* (Boston, 1963), p. 554.

3. *New York Times,* 5 July 1967.

4. Alex Inkeles, "National Character and Modern Political Systems" in Nelson W. Polsby, et. al., *op. cit.* pp. 172–174.

5. *Ibid.;* also see H. C. J. Duijker and N. H. Fridja, *National Character and National Stereotypes* (Amsterdam, 1960); Daniel Lerner and Harold Lasswell, ed., *The Policy Sciences—Recent Developments in Scope and Method* (Stanford, 1951).

6. Inkeles, *op. cit.,* p. 173.

7. Hans Morgenthau, *Politics Among Nations* (New York, 1967), pp. 127–129.

8. Morroe Berger, *The Arab World Today* (London, 1962), pp. 155–161; Sania Hamady, *Temperament and Character of the Arabs,* (New York, 1960), pp. 39, 100, 230; H. Ammar, *Growing Up in an Egyptian Village* (London, 1954), p. 10.

9. Henry Habib Ayrout, *The Egyptian Peasant* (Boston, 1963), p. 112–113.

10. Patricia L. Kendall, "The Ambivalent Character of Nationalism

Among Egyptian Professionals," *Public Opinion Quarterly* 20 (1956): 277–98.

11. *Ibid.,* pp. 278–282. As Lucian Pye points out, there is a close relationship between the pervasive crisis of identity in transitional societies and the prevalence of mutual distrust. See Lucian W. Pye, *Politics, Personality, and Nation Building: Burma's Search for Identity* (New Haven, 1962), pp. 52–56.

12. Daniel Lerner, "A Note on Ambivalent Nationalism and Political Identity," *Public Opinion Quarterly* 20 (1956): 289–292.

13. *Al-Ahram,* 11 April 1969.

14. Even such notable figures as Taha Husayn and Habib Buraqiba had been criticized for taking European wives.

15. *Al-Tawjih al-Qawmi* [National Orientation] (Cairo, 196?), pp. 495–496.

16. Kendall, *loc. cit.*

17. This only pertains to general army involvement. Nevertheless, military intelligence has been active on the domestic scene.

18. This group consisted of individuals like Khalid Muhammad Khalid who had resisted the rapid evolution of Egyptian nationalism into Arabism.

19. For the symbolic significance of the event, see, *Akhir Lahzah,* 12 June 1967. A large number of Muslim Brethren were released from jail as a gesture of Islamic goodwill. On the revival of Islam after June 1967 see, Sami A. Hanna, "Islam, Socialism, and National Trials," *Muslim World,* vol. 58, no. 4 (October 1968): 284–294.

20. Marshall Amir had enjoyed great popularity among the military, regardless of his incompetence. As to the purges in the military, 200 officers were retired in June 1968; the total number of those purged was probably much higher. See *Le Monde,* 5 July 1968.

21. For an interesting analysis see, Ahmad Hamrush, "Man Yahmi al-Thawrah," [Who Defends the Revolution], *Ruz al-Yusif,* 31 July 1967, pp. 6–7. *Al-Tali'ah,* October 1968, pp. 106–7.

22. Ahmad Hamrush, "Min Ajl Himayat al-Thawrah," [In Order to Defend the Revolution], *Ruz al-Yusif,* 7 August 1967, p. 7.

23. Ahmad Baha' al-Din, "Al-Tariq ila al-Mu'tamar al-Qawmi," [The Way to the National Congress], *Al-Musawwar,* 19 July 1968; Ahmad Hamrush, "La Tariq ila al-Hizb" [No Way But the Party], *Ruz al-Yusif,* 14 August 1967, pp. 9–16; Muhammad Hasanayn Haykal, "Hadith An al-Ittihad al-Ishtiraki al-An" [Discussion on the ASU, Now], *Al-Ahram,* 1 November 1968. Nasir had referred to centers of power in criticizing the ASU in March 1966.

24. *Ibid.* Sayyid Hamid Nassaj, *Misr wa Zahirat al-Thawrah* (Egypt and the Phenomenon of the Revolution) (Cairo, 1969), pp. 329–333.

25. Muhammad Hasanayn Haykal, "An al-Tajribah An al-Dimuqratiyyah fi Zamanina" [On Experience in Democracy in Our Times], *Al-Ahram,* 15 November 1968.

26. Hamrush, "La Tariq," pp. 8–9; Naji Allush, "Awamil Siyasiyyah li al-Hazimah al-Askariyyah" [Political Factors of Military Defeat], *Dirasat Arabiyyah* (November 1967), pp. 22–31.

27. At the ASU National Congress on 14 September 1968, Nasir had rejected the proposal of a popular army for lack of sufficient weapons. See *Al-Jumhuriyyah,* 15 September 1968.

28. *Al-Jumhuriyyah*, 20 January 1969.

29. Abd al-Hamid Bakhit, *Al-Mujtama' al-Arabi wa al-Islami* [The Arab and Islamic Society] (Cairo, 1965), p. 468.

30. See Article 20 of "The Basic Law of the ASU," in *Al-Jumhuriyyah*, 10 May 1968.

31. *Al-Ahram*, 16 September 1968. Also, Nassaj, *Misr wa Zahirat*, p. 329–330.

32. *Akhir Sa'ah*, 21 August 1968, p. 16. A worker's journal asserted that "the soldiers of socialism need to develop not only muscles, but also brains." See *Al-Ummal*, 3 October 1968.

33. *Akhir Sa'ah*, 21 August 1968, p. 16.

34. Haykal quoted in *Housaper*, 14 August 1968; *Akhir Sa'ah*, 21 August 1968, p. 16.

35. Muhammad Hasanayn Haykal, "Hal Tahaqqaq al-Taghyir?" [Did the Change Occur?] *Al-Ahram*, 11 October 1968.

36. *Al-Ahram*, September 21 1969, and *Le Monde*, 20 September 1969.

37. Baha' al-Din Ibrahim Mahmud, *Al-Shurtah wa al-Sha'b* [The Police and the People] (Cairo, 196?), pp. 63–64.

38. *Arab Report and Record*, 16–31 March 1968, p. 80.

39. As reprinted in *Housaper*, 23 and 24 April 1968.

40. *Ibid.;* On the youth see *Akhir Sa'ah*, 27 March 1968, pp. 8–9; also see Nasir's speech of 25 April 1968 in *Le Progrès Egyptien*, 26 April 1968.

41. For a full account of the episode see *Al-Ahram*, 13, 14, 15, 17 October 1968.

42. See *Arab Report and Record*, 16–31 August 1969, p. 348. This long-time cabinet member was reportedly disliked by senior judges for unduly influencing court decisions.

43. Muhammad Hasanayn Haykal, "Al-Ma'na al-Haqiqi li-Kulli ma Takashshaf Ba'd al-Naksah" [The True Meaning of All That Has Been Exposed After the Setback], *Al-Ahram*, 8 November 1968.

44. Muhammad Hasanayn Haykal, "Al-Mujtama' al-Maftuh" [The Open Society], *Al-Ahram*, 18, 25 October 1968; also Muhammad Hasanayn Haykal, "An al-Tajribah," *Al-Ahram*, 15 November 1968. Haykal notes the lack of an Arabic word for "institution."

45. Haykal, "An al-Tajribah," *Al-Ahram*, 15 November 1968.

46. Interestingly, Haykal's examples do not include the military.

47. Haykal, "An al-Tajribah," *Al-Ahram*, 15 November 1968.

48. *Akhbar al-Yawm*, 16 November 1968.

49. *Al-Ahram*, 3 November 1968.

50. *Al-Ahram*, 29 November 1968; 3 December 1968.

51. *Al-Ahram*, 29 November 1968.

52. *Ruz al-Yusif*, 23 December 1968, p. 6; *Al-Ahram*, 6 December 1968.

53. *Al-Akhbar*, 2 December 1968.

54. *Ibid.*

55. Ahmad Baha' al-Din, "Kalimah an al-Muzaharat," [A Word on the Demonstration] *Al-Musawwar*, 29 November 1968, p. 13.

56. *Al-Ahram*, 1 December 1968.

57. *Al-Ahram*, 3 and 6 December 1968, and *Al-Jumhuriyyah*, 2 December 1968.

58. *Al-Ahram,* 10 October 1969.

59. The first article of Nasir's Constitutional Guidelines reads: "Egypt is an organic part of the Arab nation."

60. For a striking parallel note Stalin's temporary reversion to indigenous Soviet nationalisms—Russian, Ukrainian, Georgian, Armenian, etc. —to insure maximum unity at home during the German onslaught.

61. Amin Iskandar, "Al-Bahth an al-Shakhsiyyah al-Misriyyah" [The Search for the Egyptian Personality], *Al-Jumhuriyyah,* 24 October 1968. One writer had gone as far as to argue that historically the notion of Arab unity and nationalism had been vague among the Egyptian leadership and people and that Arab nationalism did not have strong roots in Egypt. See, Abd al-Mun'im Muhammad Badr. *Al-Thawrah al-Arabiyyah al-Ishtirakiyyah* [The Arab Socialist Revolution] (Cairo, 1967), pp. 317–318.

62. Muhammad Hasanayn Haykal, "An al-Tajribah," *Al-Ahram,* 15 November 1968.

63. *Ibid.*

64. For a detailed criticism see Abdallah Imam, "Likay la Tafham Shay'an an Isra'il Iqra Kutub al-Madaris" [In Order Not to Learn Anything About Israel, Read School Textbooks], *Ruz al-Yusif,* 17 July 1967, pp. 24–25.

65. Ahmad Abd al-Mu'ti Hijazi, "Tarikhuna al-Qawmi Mali' bi al-Tanaqud" [Our National History is Full of Contradictions], *Ruz al-Yusif,* 17 July 1967, p. 26.

66. Haykal was specifically referring to the press secrecy surrounding the Israeli capture of radar equipment. See *Al-Ahram,* 23 January 1970.

67. Fathi al-Ibyari, *Al-Sahafah al-Iqlimiyyah wa al-Tanzim al-Siyasi* [The Provincial Press and Political Organization] (Cairo, 1969), p. 75.

68. See, *Al-Ta'awun,* 20 October 1968. See, *Al-Musawwar,* 21 February 1969, pp. 28–29.

69. Haykal, "An al-Tajribah," *Al-Ahram,* 15 November 1968.

70. *Ibid.*

71. *Ibid.*

72. *Ibid.*

73. For data and analysis, see chapter on elites.

74. Haykal, "An al-Tajribah," *Al-Ahram,* 15 November 1968.

75. *Ibid.*

76. Hamrush, "Min Yahmi," *Ruz al-Yusif,* 24 July 1967, pp. 6–7.

77. Haykal, "An al-Tajribah," *Al-Ahram,* 15 November 1968.

78. *Ibid.*

79. Hamrush, "Min Yahmi," *Ruz al-Yusif,* 24 July 1967, pp. 6–7.

80. *Ibid.* As early as 1962 two American consultants had observed the tremendous administrative load that pressed upon the President. See Luther Gulick and James K. Pollock, *Government Reorganization in the UAR, A Report Submitted to the Central Committee for the Reorganization of the Machinery of Government* (mimeographed, Cairo, June 1962), p. 16.

81. Khalid Muhammad Khalid, *Azmat al-Hurriyyah fi Alamina* [The Crisis of Freedom in Our World] (Cairo, 1964), p. 5. Shaykh Khalid had been a vocal spokesman of liberalization at the National Congress of Popular Forces in 1961. See *Al-Ahram,* 27, 31 November 1961.

82. Manfred Halpern, *The Politics of Social Change in the Middle East and North Africa* (Princeton, 1963), pp. 281–284, 312.

83. *Le Progrès Egyptien,* 26 April 1968.

84. For the text of ASU's Basic Law see *Al-Jumhuriyyah,* 16 May 1968.

85. *Al-Ahram,* 15 November 1968.

86. *Ibid.*

87. Ahd al-Wahid al-Wakil, *Adwa' ala al-Ittihad al-Ishtiraki al-Arabi* [Focus on the Arab Socialist Union] (Cairo, 1963), pp. 23–24.

88. *Al-Akhbar,* 17 July 1968 and *Al-Jumhuriyyah,* 17 July 1968.

89. *Al-Ahram,* 1 November 1968.

90. *Al-Akhbar,* 17 July 1968.

91. The examples given were Ministers Hasan Abbas Zaki and Abd al-Aziz Hijazi; and bankers Ahmad Fu'ad and Muhammad Khawaja. *Ibid.*

92. *Al-Ummal,* 27 June 1968.

93. *Al-Ummal,* 25 June 1968.

94. *Housaper,* 18 September 1968; also see Fikri Abaza, "Ala Hamish al-Mu'tamar" [Relating to the Congress], *Al-Musawwar,* 27 September 1968.

95. *Al-Jumhuriyyah,* 21 September 1968.

96. *Al-Ummal,* 26 September 1968; *Akhir Sa'ah,* 25 September 1968.

97. Twenty-one of the full-time members and 13 of the alternate members held doctorates.

98. In actuality there were 15 additional deputies who were counted as part of the other categories.

99. The types of workers included carpenters, railroad workers, steelworkers, dyers, mechanics, hospital workers, electricians, oil men, lumbermen, weavers, and a few white collar workers.

100. This might account for the difference between the press estimate of 24 peasants elected and the number, 18, as determined in Table 26.

101. The two-to-one proportion between workers and peasants was also maintained in the number of alternate members to the Central Committee; see Table 26.

102. Twenty of the 50-man Committee became full Central Committee members while 2 became alternate Central Committee members.

103. Haykal, "Hadith," *Al-Ahram,* 1 November 1968.

104. *Ibid.*

105. *Al-Ahram,* 22 November 1968.

106. For a rare view of the cleavage see the pro-Egyptian Beirut newspaper *Al-Anwar,* 21 September 1968. Also, Hamrush, "Min Ajl," *Ruz al-Yusif,* 7 August 1967.

107. *Al-Ahram,* 20 December 1968.

108. *Akhbar al-Yawm,* 27 December 1968.

109. *Ibid.*

110. *Al-Akhbar,* 7 November 1968.

111. *Al-Ahram,* 22 November 1968.

112. *Ibid.*

113. *Al-Ahram,* 9, 22 November 1968.

114. *Ibid.*

115. *Al-Jumhuriyyah,* 20 January 1969. Constitutionally, of a total of

360 deputies, 350 are elected and the remaining 10 appointed by the president.

116. *Ibid.*

117. *Ibid.*

118. *Ibid.*

119. It should be stressed that the 23 independently elected deputies were also ASU members.

14. The Politics of Protracted Conflict

1. A detailed analysis of the Egyptian view of the American role is presented by Haykal. See *Al-Ahram,* 13 June 1969; 15, 22, 29 August 1969.

2. *Ibid.,* and *Al-Ahram,* 13 March 1970. *Al-Akhbar,* 9 April 1970.

3. See, Haykal in *Al-Ahram,* 20, 27 March 1970; *Arab Report and Record,* 1–15 May 1970, pp. 279.

4. In this context, reference is made to ex-Premier Bulganin's threat to dispatch volunteers to fight in the Suez War of 1956, in contrast to the relative silence of the Soviet leaders during the June War.

5. For a similar analysis see Eric Rouleau, *Le Monde,* 7–9 April 1970.

6. He made clear that "the single limited battle" would have to involve the destruction of two or three Israeli divisions. See *Al-Ahram,* 11 April 1969.

7. *Ibid.*

8. See *Le Monde,* 18–19 January 1970, and *Arab Report and Record,* 16–31 January 1970, pp. 80.

9. Kennett Love, *Suez, the Twice Fought War* (New York, 1969), p. 104.

10. For an analysis of the adaptability of Egyptian society to the war of attrition see Isma'il Sabri Abdallah, "Harb al-Istinzaf," *Al-Tali'ah,* September 1969, pp. 8–12.

11. Professor Binder maintains that during the early sixties there had been deliberate attempts by the leadership to limit real political participation. See, Leonard Binder, "Political Recruitment and Participation in Egypt," in Joseph La Palombara and Myron Weiner, ed., *Political Parties and Political Development* (Princeton, 1966, pp. 217–240. On the shortcomings of "party charisma" in creating mass participation see I. L. Horowitz, *Three Worlds of Development* (New York, 1966), pp. 230–231.

12. Patricia Kendall, "The Ambivalent Character of Nationalism Among Egyptian Professionals," *Public Opinion Quarterly* 20 (1956): 277–289.

13. Muhammad Ali Abu Rayyan, *Al-Nuzum al-Ishtirakiyyah* [Socialist Systems] (Cairo, 1965), pp. 441–442.

14. Gordon Hirabayashi and M. Fathalla El-Khatib, "Communication and Political Awareness in the Villages of Egypt," *Public Opinion Quarterly,* vol. 22, no. 3 (Fall 1958): 357–363.

15. *Ibid.,* p. 363.

16. The ASU Third National Congress approved Nasir's suggestion to reduce maximum individual ownership of land from 100 to 50 *faddans;*

the previous maximum limit for each family was retained at 100 *faddans*. See *Al-Ahram*, 24 July 1969. Central Bank of Egypt, *Economic Bulletin*, vol. 22, no. 4 (1969): 349–350. See Fahmi al-Baz, in *Al-Musawwar*, 28 December 1969, p. 25.

17. Many Egyptian writers use the terms middle class and bourgeoisie interchangeably.

18. "Min Ajl Mumarasah Haqiqiyah Lil-Dimuqratiyyah" [For the Sake of a Real Practice of Democracy], *Al-Tali'ah*, July 1968, p. 18.

19. *Ibid.*

20. Hilmi Yasin, "Majalis al-Idarah" [Boards of Directors], *Al-Tali'ah*, September 1968, p. 109.

21. "Min Ajl," *Al-Tali'ah*, July 1968, p. 18; Hilmi Yasin, "Majalis," *Al-Tali'ah*, September 1968, p. 109.

22. Leonard Binder, "Egypt: The Integrative Revolution," in Lucian W. Pye and Sidney Verba, ed., *Political Culture and Political Development* (Princeton, 1965), pp. 397–398.

23. Mishil Kamil, "Mashakil al-Quwa al-Ijtima'iyah" [The Problems of Social Forces], *Al-Tali'ah*, May 1969, p. 14. This is to apply to landowners "up to grade 4."

24. *Ibid.*

25. Lutfi al-Khuli, "Jil al-Thawrah" [The Generation of the Revolution], *Al-Tali'ah*, September 1969, pp. 80–87.

26. *Ibid.*

27. Dr. Muhammad Anis, *Al-Jumhuriyyah*, 4 December 1969.

28. For a penetrating analysis of future social and military trends in Israel and Egypt, see Rebecca Grajower, "Zionism and Militarism," *New Left Forum* (September 1967): 32–44.

29. Egyptian military planners place great stress on what they consider to be a sixteen-to-one superiority in numbers over Israel. See *Al-Nahar, Arab Report*, 1, 2, 16 March 1970.

30. Khalid Muhyi al-Din finds no contradiction between socialism and Islam. See *Al-Tali'ah*, January 1970, p. 159.

Bibliography

Books

Abd al-Karim, Ahmad Izzat, Abd al-Hamid al-Batriq, and Abu al-Futuh Rudwan. *Tarikh al-Alam al-Arabi fi al-Asr al-Hadith* [The History of the Arab World in Modern Times]. Cairo, 1957.

Abd al-Nasir, Gamal. *Falsafat el-Thawrah* [Philosophy of the Revolution]. Cairo: n.d.

————. *Nahnu wa al-Iraq wa al-Shuyu'iyyah* [We, Iraq, and Communism] Beirut, 1960?

Abd al-Rahim, Abd al-Majid. *Falsafat al-Mujtama' al-Arabi* [Philosophy of Arab Society]. Cairo, 1964.

Abd al-Rahim, Mahmud. *Al-Sha'b al-Arabi Yudin al-Aflaqiyin* [The Arab People Condemn the Aflaqites]. Cairo, 1963.

Abd al-Raziq, Ali. *Al-Islam wa Usul al-Hukm* [Islam and the Principles of Authority]. Cairo, 1925.

Abdel-Malek, Anouar. *Égypte Société Militaire*. Paris: Editions du Seuil, 1962.

Abdel Nasser, Gamal. *The Philosophy of the Revolution*. Buffalo, N.Y.: Economica Books, 1959.

Abu Hadid, Muhammad Farid. *Ummatuna al-Arabiyyah* [Our Arab Nation]. Cairo, 1961.

Abu Rashid, Hanna. *Tarikh Nahdat Misr al-Hadithat* [History of the Modern Awakening of Egypt]. Beirut, 1960.

Abu Rayyan, Muhammad Ali. *Al-Nuzum al Ishtirakiyyah* [Socialist Systems]. Cairo, 1965.

Abul-Fath, Ahmed. *L'affaire Nasser*. Paris: Plon, 1962.

al-Adawi, Ibrahim Ahmad. *Qadat al-Tahrir al-Arabi* [Leaders of the Arab Liberation]. Cairo, 1964.

al-Ahad, Abd al-Aziz Sayyid. *Al-Ayyam Salah al-Din* [The Days of Salah al-Din]. Beirut, 1960.

Ake, Claude. *A Theory of Political Integration*. Homewood, Ill.: Dorsey Press, 1967.

Almond, Gabriel A. and James S. Coleman, eds. *The Politics of the Developing Areas*. Princeton: Princeton University Press, 1960.

Ammar, H. *Growing Up in an Egyptian Village*. London: Routledge & Paul, 1954.

Apter, David. *Ghana in Transition*, rev. ed. New York: Atheneum Publishers, 1963.

————. *The Gold Coast in Transition*. Princeton: Princeton University Press, 1955.

————, ed. *Ideology and Discontent*. London: Free Press, 1964.

al-Armani, Abu-Salih. *Abu-Salih al-Armani*. Oxford, 1895.

al-Aryan, Muhammad Sa'id and Gamal al-Din al-Shayyal. *Qissat al-Kifah Bayna al-Arab wa al-Isti'mar* [The Story of Struggle between the Arabs and Imperialism]. Cairo, 1960.

Al-Siyasah al-Ammah li al-Thawrah fi al-Wizarah al-Dakhiliyyah [The General Policy of the Revolution in the Interior Ministry]. Cairo, 1962.

Al-Tariq ila al-Dimuqratiyyah [The Path to Democracy]. Cairo, 1962.

Al-Tawjih al-Qawmi [National Orientation]. Cairo, 196?.

Atiyyat Allah, Ahmad. *Qamus al-Thawrah al-Misriyyah* [Dictionary of the Egyptian Revolution]. Cairo, 1955.

Awad, Luwis. *Al-Ishtirakiyyah wa al-Adab* [Socialism and Literature]. Beirut, 1962.

Ayrout, Henry Habib. *The Egyptian Peasant*. Boston: Beacon Press, 1963.

Bachrach, Peter. *The Theory of Democratic Elitism: A Critique*. Boston: Little, Brown & Co., 1967.

Badawi, Muhammad Taha, and Mahmud Hilmi Mustafa. *Thawrat Yulyu* [July Revolution]. Alexandria, 1966.

Badawi, Muhammad Taha, and Abu al-Fattah Sayfi. *Al-Wahdah al-Arabiyyah* [Arab Unity]. Cairo, 1966.

Badr, Abd al-Mun'im Muhammad. *Al-Thawrah al-Arabiyyah al-Ishtirakiyyah* [The Arab Socialist Revolution]. Cairo, 1967.

Badeau, John S. *The American Approach to the Arab World*. New York: Harper & Row, Publishers, 1968.

Bakhit, Abd al-Hamid. *Al-Mujtama' al-Arabi wa al-Islami* [The Arab and Islamic Society]. 2 vols. Cairo, 1965.

Baer, Gabriel. *Studies in the Social History of Modern Egypt*. Chicago: University of Chicago Press, 1969.

al-Barawi, Rashid. *The Military Coup in Egypt*. Cairo, 1952.

Barsum, Karam Habib. *Dirasat al-Mujtama'* [Studies of Society]. Cairo, 1964.

Bazzaz, Abd al-Rahman. *Min Wahy al-Urubah* [From the Inspiration of Arabism]. Cairo, 1963.

Bell, Daniel. *The End of Ideology*. New York: Free Press, 1962.

Bendix, Reinhard. *Max Weber, An Intellectual Portrait*. Garden City, N.Y.: Doubleday & Co., 1960.

Berelson, Bernard. *Content Analysis in Communication Research*. Glencoe, Ill.: Free Press, 1952.

Berger, Morroe. *Bureaucracy and Society in Modern Egypt*. Princeton: Princeton University Press, 1957.

————. *The Arab World Today*. Garden City, N.Y.: Doubleday & Co., 1962.

Binder, Leonard. *The Ideological Revolution in the Middle East*. New York: John Wiley & Sons, 1964.

————. "Egypt: The Integrative Revolution," in *Political Culture and Political Development*, ed. by Lucian W. Pye and Sidney Verba. Princeton: Princeton University Press, 1965.

————. "Political Recruitment and Participation in Egypt," in *Political Parties and Political Development*, ed. by Joseph LaPalombara and Myron Weiner. Princeton: Princeton University Press, 1965.

Bottomore, T. B. *Elites and Society*. New York: Basic Books, 1964.

Bromberger, Serge and Merry. *Secrets of Suez*. London: Pan Books, 1957.

Brzezinski, Zbigniew K. *Ideology and Power in Soviet Politics*. New York: Frederick A. Praeger, 1967.

————. *The Permanent Purge*. Cambridge, Mass.: Harvard University Press, 1956.

————. *The Soviet Bloc*. Cambridge, Mass.: Harvard University Press, 1960.

Campbell, John C. *Defense of the Middle East*. New York: Harper & Row, Publishers, 1958.

Carr, Edward Hallett. *The New Society*. Boston: Beacon Press, 1951.

Childers, Erskine E. *The Road to Suez*. London: MacGibbon & Kee, 1962.

Conquest, Robert. *Power and Policy in the USSR*. London: Macmillan & Co., 1962.

Coser, Lewis. *The Functions of Social Conflict*. New York: Free Press, 1956.

Dahl, Robert. *Modern Political Analysis*. Englewood Cliffs, N.J.: Prentice-Hall, 1963.

Darwazah, Muhammad Izzat. *Urubat Misr* [The Arabism of Egypt]. Saida, 1963.

Davies, James C. *Human Nature in Politics*. New York: John Wiley & Sons, 1963.

Dawson, Richard E. and Kenneth Prewitt. *Political Socialization*. Boston: Little, Brown & Co., 1969.

DeBary, William Theodore, and Ainslie T. Embree, ed. *Approaches to Asian Civilization*. New York: Columbia University Press, 1961.

Deliorman, M. Necmeddin. *Balkan Turklerinin Tarihi* [The History of Balkan Turks]. Ankara, 1941.

Deutsch, Karl W. and William J. Foltz, eds. *Nation-Building*. New York: Atherton Press, 1963.

Deutsch, Karl W. *The Nerves of Government*. London: Collier-Macmillan, 1963.

Duijker, H. C. J. and N. H. Fridja. *National Character and National Stereotypes*. Amsterdam: North-Holland Publication Co., 1960.

Easton, David. *A Systems Analysis of Political Life*. New York: John Wiley & Sons, 1965.

Eden, Sir Anthony. *Memoirs: Full Circle*. Boston: Houghton, Mifflin & Co., 1960.

Eisenstadt, S. N., ed. *Max Weber: On Charisma and Institution Building*. Chicago: University of Chicago Press, 1968.

Erikson, Erik H. *Gandhi's Truth*. New York: W. W. Norton & Co., 1969.

————. *Young Man Luther*. New York: W. W. Norton & Co., 1958.

Estier, Claude. *L'Egypte en Revolution*. Paris: R. Julliard, 1965.

Etzioni, Amitai. *A Comparative Analysis of Complex Organizations*. New York: Free Press, 1961.

————. *Political Unification: A Comparative Analysis of Leaders and Forces.* New York: Holt, Rinehart & Winston, 1965.

Finer, Herman. *Dulles over Suez.* Chicago: Quadrangle Books, 1964.

Friedrich, Carl J., ed. *Totalitarianism.* New York: Grosset & Dunlap, 1964.

Frey, Fredrick W. *The Turkish Political Elite.* Cambridge, Mass.: M.I.T. Press, 1965.

Gardiner, Alan H. *Egyptian Grammar.* 3rd ed. Oxford: Oxford University Press, 1957.

George, Alexander L. *Propaganda Analysis.* Evanston: Row & Peterson & Co., 1959.

George, Alexander and Julliette L. George. *Woodrow Wilson and Colonel House: A Personality Study.* New York: Dover Publications, 1964.

Gerth, H. H. and C. Wright Mills. *From Max Weber: Essays in Sociology.* New York: Oxford University Press, 1946.

Ghali, Butros and Ahmad Mahaba. Untitled chapter in *Al-Dimuqratiyah fi al-Alam al-Arabi* [Democracy in the Arab World]. Beirut, 1959.

al-Ghatit, Muhammad Ali. *Thawrat al-Arab fi 1919, Thawrat Misr* [Arab Revolutions in 1919: The Egyptian Revolution]. vol. 2. Cairo, 196?.

al-Ghazzali, Muhammad. *Our Beginning in Wisdom.* Washington: American Council of Learned Societies, 1953.

al-Ghuri, Imil. *Sira' al-Qawmiyyah al-Arabiyyah* [Struggle of Arab Nationalism]. Syria, UAR, 1958.

Gökalp, Ziya. *Yeni Turkiyenin Hedefleri* [The Aims of the New Turkey]. Ankara, 1956.

Greenstein, Fred L. *Personality and Politics.* Chicago: Markham, 1969.

Gulick, Luther and James K. Pollock. *Government Reorganization in the UAR, A Report Submitted to the Central Committee for the Reorganization of the Machinery of Government.* Mimeographed. Cairo, 1962.

Guttsman, W. L. *The British Political Elite.* London: MacGibbon & Kee, 1963.

Hafat, Abu al-Hajjaj. *Al-Batal Ahmad Abd al-Aziz* [The Hero, Ahmad Abd al-Aziz]. Cairo, 1961.

Hafiz, Hamdi. *Al-Ishtirakiyyah wa al-Tatbiq al-Ishtiraki fi al-Jumhuriyyah al-Arabiyyah al-Muttahidah* [Socialism and the Application of Socialism in the UAR]. Cairo, 1966.

Halawi, Sadiq. *Al-Amn al-Am* [Public Security]. Cairo, 1962.

Halpern, Manfred. *The Politics of Social Change in the Middle East and North Africa.* Princeton: Princeton University Press, 1963.

Hamady, Sania. *Temperament and Character of the Arabs.* New York: Twayne Publishers, 1960.

Hanna, Sami A. and George H. Gardner. *Arab Socialism.* Salt Lake City: University of Utah Press, 1969.

Harris, Christina Phelps. *Nationalism and Revolution in Egypt: The Role of the Muslim Brotherhood.* The Hague: Mouton, 1964.

Hasan, Hasan Muhammad. *Al-Fann fi Rakb al-Ishtirakiyyah* [Art in the Realm of Socialism]. Cairo, 1966.

Haykal, Muhammad Husayn. *Fi Manzil al-Wahy* [In the Descending Place of the Revelation]. Cairo, 1967.

Henriques, Robert. *A Hundred Hours to Suez*. New York: Viking Press, 1957.

al-Himadi, Yusif; Ibrahim al-Tarazi, Muhammad Mustafa Hadarat, and Abu al-Hasan Ibrahim. *Al-Qira'ah al-Thanawiyyah* [Secondary Readings]. Cairo, 1962.

Hitti, Phillip K. *History of the Arabs,* 4th ed. rev. London: Macmillan & Co., 1949.

Horowitz, I. L. *Three Worlds of Development*. New York: Oxford University Press, 1966.

Hourani, Albert. *Arabic Thought in the Liberal Age, 1798–1939*. New York: Oxford University Press, 1962.

Al-Hufi, Ahmad Muhammad. *Butulah wa Batal* [Heroism and a Hero]. Cairo, 1963.

Hurewitz, J. C. *Diplomacy in the Near and Middle East: A Documentary Record (1914–1956),* vol. 2. Princeton: D. Van Nostrand Co., 1956.

————. *Middle East Politics: The Military Dimension*. New York: Frederick A. Praeger, 1969.

Husaini, Ishak Musa, *The Moslem Brethren*. Beirut, 1956.

al-Husari, Sati'. *Abhath Mukhtarat fi al-Qawmiyyah al-Arabiyyah* [Selected Studies in Arab Nationalism]. Cairo, 1964.

————. *Al-Urubah Awwalan* [Arabism First]. Beirut, 1965.

————. *Ara' wa Ahadith fi al-Qawmiyyah al-Arabiyyah* [Opinions and Discourses on Arab Nationalism]. Beirut, 1951.

al-Ibyari, Fathi. *Al-Sahafah al-Iqlimiyyah wa al-Tanzim al-Siyasi* [The Provincial Press and Political Organization]. Cairo, 1969.

Imaz, José Luis de. *Los Que Mandan*. Translated by Carlos A. Astiz. Albany: State University of New York Press, 1970.

Issawi, Charles. *Egypt at Mid-Century: An Economic Survey*. London: Oxford University Press, 1954.

————. *Egypt in Revolution: An Economic Analysis*. London, Oxford University Press, 1963.

al-Jamal Yahya. *Al-Ishitirakiyyah al-Arabiyyah* [Arab Socialism]. Cairo, 1966.

al-Jarf, Tu'aymah. *Thawrat 23 Yulyu wa Mabadi al-Nidham al-Siyasi fi al-Jumhuriyyah al-Arabiyyah al-Muttahidah*. (The July 23 Revolution and the Principles of the UAR Political System). Cairo, 1964.

al-Jazzar, Muhammad al-Sayyid. *Dirasat fi al-Muhasabah al-Ammah* [Studies in General Accounting]. Cairo, 1965.

Kamil Mahmud, *Al-Dawlah al-Arabiyyah al-Kubra* [The Great Arab State]. Cairo, 1964.

Kerr, Malcolm. *The Arab Cold War, 1958–1967,* 2nd ed. London: Oxford University Press, 1969.

————. *Islamic Reform*. Berkeley: University of California Press, 1966.

Khadduri, Majid. *Political Trends in the Arab World*. Baltimore: Johns Hopkins Press, 1970.

Khaki, Ahmad. *Falsafat al-Qawmiyyah* [Philosophy of Nationalism]. Cairo, 1962.

Khalid, Khalid Muhammad. *Azmat al-Hurriyyah fi Alamina* [The Crisis of Freedom in Our World]. Cairo, 1964.

————. *Min Huna Nabda'* [From Here We Start], 3rd ed. Translated by Isma'il R. el-Faruqi. Washington: American Council of Learned Societies, 1953.

Kirk, George E. *Contemporary Arab Politics*. New York: Frederick A. Praeger, 1961.

al-Khuli, Lutfi. *Dirasat fi al-Waqi' al-Misri al-Mu'asir* [Studies in Contemporary Egyptian Reality]. Beirut, 1964.

Kornhauser, William. *The Politics of Mass Society*. Glencoe, Ill.: Free Press, 1959.

Lacouture, Jean and Simonne. *Egypt in Transition*. New York: Criterion Books, 1958.

Landau, Jacob M. *Parliaments and Parties in Egypt*. Tel Aviv: Israeli Publishing House, 1953.

Lapalombara, Joseph and Myron Weiner, eds. *Political Parties and Political Development*. Princeton: Princeton University Press, 1965.

Laqueur, Walter Z., ed. *The Middle East in Transition*. New York: Frederick A. Praeger, 1958.

Lasswell, Harold D. *Power and Personality,* New York: W. W. Norton & Co., 1962.

————. *Psychopathology and Politics*. New York: Viking Press, 1960.

Lasswell, Harold D.; Leites, Nathan; and Associates. *Language of Politics: Studies in Quantitative Semantics*. New York: G. W. Stewart, 1949.

Lasswell, Harold D. and Daniel Lerner, eds. *The Policy Sciences— Recent Developments in Scope and Method*. Stanford: Stanford University Press, 1951.

————. *World Revolutionary Elites*. Cambridge, Mass.: M.I.T. Press, 1965.

Lipset, Seymour Martin. *The First New Nation*. New York: Basic Books, 1963.

Little, Tom. *Egypt*. New York: Frederick A. Praeger, 1958.

Loewenstein, Karl. *Max Weber, Staatspolitische Auffasungen in der Sicht Unserer Zeit*. Frankfurt am Main: Athenäum Verlag, 1965.

Love, Kennett. *Suez, the Twice Fought War*. New York: McGraw-Hill Book Co., 1969.

al-Mahlawi, Fathi Uthman. Untitled chapter in *Al-Dimuqratiyyah fi al-Alam al-Arabi* [Democracy in the Arab World]. Beirut, 1959.

Mahmud, Baha' al-Din Ibrahim. *Al-Shurtah wa al-Sha'b* [The Police and the People]. Cairo, 196?.

Makram, Muhammad Muhktar Amin. *Hawl al-Ishtirakiyyah al-Arabiyyah* [About Arab Socialism]. Cairo, 1966.

Mannheim, Karl. *Ideology and Utopia*. New York: Harcourt, Brace & World, 1946.

Marshall, S. L. A. *Sinai Victory*. New York: William Morrow & Co., 1958.

Marvick, Dwaine, ed. *Political Decision-Makers*. New York: Free Press, 1961.

Matthews, Donald R. *The Social Background of Political Decision-Makers*. Garden City, N.Y.: Doubleday, 1954.

Mazhar, Sulayman. *Adwa' ala Waqi'ina* [Focus on Our Situation]. Cairo, n.d.

Mazyad, A. M. H. *Ahmad Amin*. Leiden: E. J. Brill, 1963.

Mitchell, Richard P. *The Society of Muslim Brothers*. New York: Oxford University Press, 1969.

Monroe, Elizabeth. *Britain's Moment in the Middle East, 1914–1956*. Baltimore: John Hopkins University Press, 1963.

Morgenthau, Hans J. *Politics Among Nations*. New York: Alfred A. Knopf, 1967.

Muhyi al-Din, Zakariyya. *Ahdaf al-Marhalah al-Qadimah* [Aims of the Next Stage]. Cairo, 1965.

Mursi, Abd al-Hamid. *Min al-Tahawwul ila al-Intilaq* [From Transition to the Take-off Point]. Cairo, 1964.

Mutwalli, Mahmud. *Al-Ittihad al-Ishtiraki al-Arabi* [The Arab Socialist Union]. Cairo, 1964.

al-Najjar, Husayn Fawzi. *Wahdat al-Tarikh al-Arabi* [The Unity of Arab History]. Cairo, 1963.

al-Nassaj, Sayyid Hamid. *Misr wa Zahirat al-Thawrah* (Egypt and the Phenomenon of the Revolution). Cairo, 1969.

———. *Thawrat al-Jamahir al-Sha'biyyah* [The Popular Mass Revolution]. Alexandria, 1969.

Neguib, Mohammed. *Egypt's Destiny*. London: Gollancz, 1955.

Neustadt, Richard E. *Presidential Power: The Politics of Leadership*. New York: John Wiley & Sons, 1960.

North, Robert C.; Ole R. Holsti, George M. Zaninovich, and Dina ·A. Zinnes, *Content Analysis: A Handbook with Applications for the Study of International Crisis*. Evanston: Northwestern University Press, 1963.

O'Balance, Edgar. *The Sinai Campaign 1956*. New York: Frederick A. Praeger, 1959.

O'Brien, Patrick. *The Revolution in Egypt's Economic System*. London: Oxford University Press, 1966.

Parry, Geraint. *Political Elites*. New York: Frederick A. Praeger, 1969.

Patrick, G. T. W. *Introduction to Philosophy,* rev. ed. Boston: Houghton Mifflin Co., 1952.

Polk, William R. *The United States and the Arab World*. Cambridge, Mass.: Harvard University Press, 1965.

Polsby, Nelson W.; Robert A. Dentler, and Paul A. Smith, eds. *Politics and Social Life*. Boston: Houghton Mifflin Co., 1963.

Presthus, R. V. and L. V. Blankenship. *Men at the Top*. New York: Oxford University Press, 1964.

Pye, Lucian W. *Politics, Personality, and Nation-Building: Burma's Search For Identity*. New Haven: Yale University Press, 1962.

Pye, Lucian W. and Sidney Verba, eds. *Political Culture and Political Development*. Princeton: Princeton University Press, 1965.

Quandt, William B. *Revolution and Political Leadership: Algeria 1954–68*. Cambridge, Mass.: M.I.T. Press, 1969.

al-Qusi, Atiyyah. *Ma'rakat Hittin wa al-Wahdah al-Arabiyyah* [The Battle of Hittin and Arab Unity]. Cairo, 1963.

al-Rabbuh, Abd al-Hafiz Abd. *Thawrah wa Thuwwar* [Revolution and Revolutionaries]. Cairo, 1962.

al-Rafi'i, Abd al-Rahman. *Thawrat 23 Yulyu 1952* [Revolution of 23 July 1952]. Cairo, 1959.

Ranney, Austin. *Pathways to Parliament*. Madison, Wisc.: University of Wisconsin Press, 1965.

al-Razzaz, Munif. *Ma'alim al-Hayat al-Arabiyyah al-Jadidah* [Features of the Modern Arab Life]. Beirut, 1959.

Riad, Hassan. *L'Egypte Nasserienne*. Paris: Editions de Minuit, 1964.

Rif'at, Muhammad. *Al-Tawjih al-Siyasi li al-Fikrah al-Arabiyyah al-Hadithah* [The Political Orientation of Modern Arab Thought]. Cairo, 1964.

al-Rimawi, Abdallah. *Al-Bayan al-Qawmi al-Thawri* [The National Revolutionary Manifesto]. Cairo, 1966.

————. *Al-Harakah al-Arabiyyah al-Wahidah* [The United Arab Movement] Beirut, 1963.

————. *Al-Mantiq al-Thawri* [The Revolutionary Logic]. Cairo, 1961.

————. *Al-Qawmiyyah wa al-Wahdah* [Nationalism and Unity]. Cairo, 1961.

Rivera, Joseph H. de. *The Psychological Dimensions of Foreign Policy*. Columbus, O.: Charles E. Merrill Books, 1968.

Rivlin, Benjamin and Joseph S. Szyliowicz, eds. *The Contemporary Middle East*. New York: Random House, 1965.

Riza, Ahmet. *La faillité morale de la politique occidentale en orient*. Paris, 1922.

Rudwan, Abu al-Futuh; Muhammad al-Hadi Afifi, and Muhammad Ahmad al-Ghannam. *Usul al-Alam al-Hadith* [The Origins of the Modern World]. Cairo, 1963.

Rustow, Dankwart A., ed. *Philosophers and Kings*. New York: George Braziller, 1970.

Rustow, Dankwart A. *A World of Nations: Problems of Political Modernization*. Washington: Brookings Institution, 1967.

Sabine, George. *A History of Political Thought,* 3rd ed. New York: Holt, Rinehart & Winston, 1961.

El-Sadat, Colonel Anwar. *Revolt on the Nile*. London: Allan Wingate Publishers, 1957.

Safran, Nadav. *Egypt in Search of Political Community*. Cambridge: Harvard University Press, 1961.

Sa'id, Amin. *Al-Thawrah* [The Revolution]. Cairo, 1959.

St. John, Robert. *The Boss*. New York: McGraw-Hill Book Co., 1960.

Sami, Izzat. *Muzakkarat Al-Liwa' Mahmud Tal'at* [Memoirs of General Mahmud Tal'at]. Damascus, UAR, 1958.

Saqr, Muhammad Jamal. *Al-Ishtirakiyyah wa al-Tarbiyah* [Socialism and Education]. Cairo, 1964?

Sayegh, Fayez A., ed. *The Dynamics of Neutralism in the Arab World*. San Francisco: Chandler Publishing Co., 1964.

Shalabi, Mahmud. *Ishtirakiyyat Abi Bakr* [Abu Bakr's Socialism]. Cairo, 1963.

Shumays, Abd al-Mun'im. *Al-Thawrah al-Arabiyyah al-Kubra* [The Great Arab Revolution]. Cairo, 1960.

al-Siba'i, Mustafa. *Ishtirakiyyat al-Islam* [The Socialism of Islam]. Cairo, 1960.

Sorel, Georges. *Reflections on Violence*. Translated by T. E. Hulme. New York: B. W. Huebsch, 1914.

Stagner, Ross. *Psychological Aspects of International Conflict*. Belmont, Calif.: Wadsworth Publishing Co., 1967.

Statistical Pocketbook, United Arab Republic, 1952–1962. Cairo, April 1963.

Steindorff, George. *Lehrbuch der Koptischen Grammatik*. Chicago: University of Chicago Press, 1951.

al-Tammawi, Muhammad. *Al-Tatawwur al-Siyasi li al-Mujtama' al-Arabi* [The Political Evolution of Arab Society]. Cairo, 1961.

Thompson, Raymond Reynolds. *The Emergence of Abd al-Nasir's Socialism*. (unpublished Masters Essay) New York: Columbia University, 1962.

Umar, Mahmud Fathi. *23 Yulyu* [23 July]. Cairo, 1963.

Umar, Mahmud Fathi, and Hafiz, al-Hammud. *Nadharat hawl Falsafat al-Thawrah* [Views on the Philosophy of the Revolution]. Cairo, 1961.

Vatikiotis, P. J. *The Egyptian Army in Politics: Pattern for New Nations?*. Bloomington: Indiana University Press, 1961.

Von Grunebaum, Gustave E. *Modern Islam: The Search for Cultural Identity*. New York: Vintage Books, 1964.

al-Wakil, Abd al-Wahid. *Adwa' Ala al-Ittihad al-Ishtiraki al-Arabi* (Focus on the Arab Socialist Union). Cairo, 1963.

Wallerstein, Immanuel V. *Africa, the Politics of Independence*. New York: Vintage Books, 1961.

Weber, Max, *The Theory of Social and Economic Organization*. Translated by A. M. Henderson and Talcott Parsons. New York: Oxford University Press, 1947.

Wheelock, Keith. *Nasser's New Egypt*. New York: Frederick A. Praeger, 1960.

Wilson, John A. *The Culture of Ancient Egypt*. Chicago: University of Chicago Press, 1954.

Wittfogel, Karl. *Oriental Despotism*. New Haven: Yale University Press, 1957.

Wolfe, Bertram D. "Totalitarianism and History," in *Totalitarianism*, ed. by Carl J. Friedrich. New York: Grosset & Dunlap 1964.

Wolfenstein, E. V. *The Revolutionary Personality*, Princeton: Princeton University Press, 1967.

Articles

Abaza, Fikri. "Ala Hamish al-Mu'tamar," *Al-Musawwar*, 27 September 1968.

Abdallah, Isma'il Sabri. "Harb al-Istinzaf" *Al-Tali'ah*, September 1969.

Abdel Nasser, Gamal. "The Science of Revolution," *Arab Observer*, 21 December 1964.

Abu Jaber, Kamel S. "Salamah Musa: Precursor of Arab Socialism," *Middle East Journal*, 20 (Spring 1966): 196–206.

Aiken, Henry David. "The Revolt Against Ideology," *Commentary* 37 (April 1964): 29–39.

Ake, Claude. "Charismatic Legitimation and Political Integration," *Comparative Studies in Society and History* 9 (October 1966): 1–13.

Allush, Naji. "Awamil Siyasiyyah li al-Hazimah al-Askariyyah," *Dirasat Arabiyyah,* November 1967.

Ashford, Douglas E. "Contradictions of Nationalism and Nation-Building in the Muslim World," *Middle East Journal* 18 (Autumn 1964): 421–430.

al-Arabi, Muhammad Abdallah. "Basic Characteristics of the Ties of Arab Nationalism," *Al-Talabah al-Arab,* 2 May 1964.

al-Atifi, Gamal. "Hawl al-Mu'tamar al-Qawmi," *Al-Ahram,* 20 May 1968.

Badeau, John S. "Non-Alignment and the UAR," *Symposium,* Summer 1965.

———. "The Role in Search of a Hero: A Brief Study of the Egyptian Revolution," *Middle East Journal* 9 (Fall, 1955): 373–384.

Baha' al-Din, Ahmad. "Al-Tariq ila al-Mu'tamar al-Qawmi," *Al-Musawwar,* 19 July 1968.

———. "Kalimah an al-Muzaharat," *Al-Musawwar,* 29 November 1968.

Baha' al-Din, Husayn Kamil. "The Revolution," *Al-Talabah al-Arab,* 13 February 1965.

Beck, Carl and James M. Malloy. "Political Elites: A Mode of Analysis." Unpublished paper, presented at Sixth World Congress, International Political Association, Geneva, 1964.

Beeri, Eliezer. "On the History of the Free Officers in Egypt," *Hamizrah he-Hadash* 13 (1963): xiv–xv.

———. "Social Class and Family Background of the Egyptian Army Officer Class," *Asian and African Studies* 2 (1966): 1–38.

Beliaev, I. and V. Cheprokov. "The UAR at a New Stage," *Kommunist* 9 (June 1964): 87–96.

Bendix, Reinhard, "Reflections on Charismatic Leadership," *Asian Survey* 7 (June 1967): 341–352.

Berger, Morroe. "Patterns of Communication of Egyptian Civil Servants with the People," *Public Opinion Quarterly* 20 (1965): 292–298.

Blanksten, George I. "Ideology and Nation-Building in the Contemporary World," *International Studies Quarterly* 11, (March 1967): 3–11.

Blau, Peter M. "Critical Remarks on Weber's Theory of Authority," *American Political Science Review* 57 (June 1963): 305–316.

Chejne, Anwar G. "Egyptian Attitudes toward Pan-Arabism," *Middle East Journal* 2 (Summer 1957): 253–268.

———. "The Use of History by Modern Arab Writers," *Middle East Journal,* vol. 14, no. 4 (Autumn 1960): 382–396.

Colombe, Marcel. "Où va l'Egypte?" *Orient* 5 (1961): 57–66.

Dahl, Robert A. "Further Reflections on 'The Elitist Theory of Democracy.' " *American Political Science Review,* 60 (June 1966): 296–305.

Davies, James C. "Charisma in the 1952 Campaign," *American Political Science Review* 48 (December 1954): 1083–1102.

Dekmejian, R. H. "The UAR National Assembly: A Pioneering Experiment," *Middle Eastern Studies* 4 (July 1968): 361–375.

Devereux, George. "Charismatic Leadership and Crisis," *Psychoanalysis and the Social Sciences* 4 (1955): 146–151.

Dogan, Mattei. "Le Personnel politique et le personnalité charismatique," *Revue francaise de sociologie* 6 (July-September 1965): 305–324.

Edinger, Lewis J. and Donald D. Searing. "Social Background in Elite Analysis," *American Political Science Review* 61 (June 1967): 428–445.

Eisenstadt, S. N. "Modernization and Conditions of Sustained Growth," *World Politics* 16 (July 1964): 576–594.

Fagen, Richard R. "Charismatic Authority and the Leadership of Fidel Castro," *Western Political Quarterly* 18 (June 1965): 275–284.

Feis, Herbert. "Suez Scenario: A Lamentable Tale," *Foreign Affairs* 38 (July 1960): 598–612.

Friedland, William H. "For a Sociological Concept of Charisma," *Social Forces* 43 (October 1964): 18–25.

Friedrich, Carl J., "Political Leadership and the Problem of the Charismatic Power," *Journal of Politics* 23 (1961): 3–24.

Gardner, George H. and Sami A. Hanna. "Islamic Socialism," *Muslim World* 56 (April 1966): 69–86.

Gehlen, M. P. and M. McBride. "The Soviet Central Committee: An Elite Analysis," *American Political Science Review* 62 (December 1968): 1232–1241.

Gerth, Hans. "The Nazi Party: Its Leadership and Composition," *American Journal of Sociology,* 45 (January 1940): 517–541.

Gibb, Hamilton A. R. "The Heritage of Islam in the Modern World (II)," *International Journal of Middle East Studies,* vol. 1, no. 3 (July 1970): 221–237.

Grajower, Rebecca. "Zionism and Militarism," *New Left Forum* (September 1967): 32–44.

Halpern, Manfred. "The Rate and Costs of Political Development," *The Annals of the American Academy of Political and Social Science* 358 (March 1965).

Hamrush, Ahmad. "La Tariq ila al-Hizb," *Ruz al-Yusif,* 14 August 1967.

———. "Min Ajl Himayat al-Thawrah," *Ruz al-Yusif,* 7 August 1967.

———. "Man Yahmi al-Thawrah," *Ruz al-Yusif,* 31 July 1967.

Hanna, Sami A. "Al-Afghani: A Pioneer of Islamic Socialism," *Muslim World* 57 (January 1967): 24–32.

———. "Islam, Socialism, and National Trials," *Muslim World* 58 (October 1968): 284–294.

Haykal, Muhammad Hasanayn. *Al-Talabah al-Arab,* 11 July 1964.

———. "Al-Ma'na al-Haqiqi li-Kulli ma Takashshaf Ba'd al-Naksah," *Al-Ahram,* 8 November 1968.

———. "Al-Mujtama' al-Maftuh," *Al-Ahram,* 18, 25 October 1968.

———. "An al-Tajribah an al-Dimuqratiyyah fi Zamanina," *Al-Ahram* 15 November 1968.

———. "Hadith An al-Ittihad al-Ishtiraki al-An" *Al-Ahram,* 1 November 1968.

———. "Hal Tahaqqaq al-Taghyir?" *Al-Ahram,* 11 October 1968.

———. "Lonely at the Top," *Arab Observer,* 1 February 1965.

Hijazi, Ahmad, Abd al-Mu'ti. "Tarikhuna al-Qawmi Mali' bi al-Tanaqud" *Ruz al-Yusif,* 17 July 1967.

Hirabayashi, Gordon, and M. Fathalla El Khatib. "Communication and Political Awareness in the Villages of Egypt," *Public Opinion Quarterly* 22 (Fall 1958): 357–363.

Horton, Alan W. "A Note on Syria, the Sudan, and the United Arab Republic," *American Universities Field Staff: Reports Service* 12 (1965): 1–24.

————. "The Arab-Israeli Conflict of June 1967," *American Universities Field Staff: Reports Service* 14 (1967): 1–15.

————. "The Officer who Chose Progress," *American Universities Field Staff: Reports Service* 14 (1967): 1–14.

Hurewitz, J. C. "Our Mistakes in the Middle East," *Atlantic Monthly* 198 (December 1956): 46–52.

Ibrahim, Muhsin. "Arab Socialism in the Making," *Arab Journal* 1 (Spring-Summer 1964): 15–25.

Imam, Abdallah. "Likay la Tafham Shay'an an Isra'il, Iqra' Kutub al-Madaris," *Ruz al-Yusif,* 17 July 1967.

Iskandar, Amin. "Al-Bahth an al-Shakhsiyyah al-Misriyyah," *Al-Jumhuriyyah,* 24 October 1968.

Issawi, Charles. "Negotiations from Strength?" *International Affairs* 35 (January 1959): 1–9.

Janowitz, Morris. "The Systematic Analysis of Political Biography," *World Politics* 6 (April 1954): 405–412.

Kahin, G. McT.; G. Pauker, and L. W. Pye. "Comparative Politics of Non-Western Countries," *American Political Science Review* 49 (1955): 1022–1041.

Kamil, Mishil. "Mashakil al-Quwa al-Ijtima'iyyah," *Al-Tali'ah,* May 1969.

Kendall, Patricia L. "The Ambivalent Character of Nationalism Among Egyptian Professionals," *Public Opinion Quarterly* 20 (1956): 277–288.

Kenny, L. M. "Sati al-Husri's Views on Arab Nationalism," *Middle East Journal,* vol. 17, no. 3 (Summer 1963): 231–256.

Kerr, Malcolm. "Coming to Terms With Nasser," *International Affairs* 43 (1967): 65–84.

————. "The Emergence of a Socialist Ideology in Egypt," *Middle East Journal* 16 (Spring 1962): 127–144.

Khadduri, Majid. "The Role of the Military in Middle Eastern Politics," *American Political Science Review,* 47 (June 1953): 511–524.

al-Khuli, Lutfi. "Jil al-Thawrah," *Al-Tali'ah,* September 1969.

Lerner, Daniel. "A Note on Ambivalent Nationalism and Political Identity," *Public Opinion Quarterly* 20 (1956): 289–292.

Marcus, John T. "Transcendence and Charisma," *Western Political Quarterly,* 14 (March 1961): 236–241.

Mommen, Wolfgang, "Max Weber's Political Sociology and His Philosophy of World History," *International Social Science Journal,* 17 (1965).

Al-Mukhaymir, Salah. "What is the Philosophy of Our Arab Socialism?" *Al-Jumhuriyyah* 16 February 1963.

Ness, David. "Interview," *The Arab World* 16 (March-April 1970).

Oron, Yitzak. "The Nationalist Myth in Contemporary Egypt," *Hamizrah he-Hadash* 10 (1960): 153–177.

Palmer, Monte. "The United Arab Republic: An Assessment of its

Failure," *Middle East Journal,* vol. 20, no. 1 (Winter 1966): 50–67.

Peretz, Don. "Democracy and the Revolution in Egypt," *Middle East Journal* 13 (Winter 1959): 26–40.

Ratnam, K. J. "Charisma and Political Leadership," *Political Studies* 12 (October 1964): 341–354.

Rummel, Rudolph. "Dimensions of Conflict Behavior Within and Between Nations," *General Systems Yearbook* 8 (1963).

Runciman, W. G. "Charismatic Legitimacy and One-Party Rule in Ghana," *Archives Europeenes de Sociologie* 4 (1963): 148–165.

Schlesinger, Arthur, Jr. "On Heroic Leadership," *Encounter* (December 1960): 3–11.

Seale, Patrick. "The Break-up of the UAR," *World Today* 17 (1961).

Seligman, Lester G. "Elite Recruitment and Political Development," *Journal of Politics* 26 (August 1964): 612–624.

Semaan, Khalil I. H. "A New Source for the Biography of Jamal Abd al-Nasir," *Muslim World* 58 (July 1968): 242–252.

Shadid, Muhammad. "Ma'rakat Ayn Jalut," *Al-Talabah al-Arab* 13 February 1965.

Sharabi, Hisham. "The Transformation of Ideology in the Western World," *Middle East Journal,* vol. 19, no. 4 (Autumn 1965): 471–486.

Shils, Edward. "Charisma, Order and Status," *American Sociological Review* 30 (April 1965).

———. "The Concentration and Dispersion of Charisma—Their Bearing on Economic Policy in the Underdeveloped Countries," *World Politics* 11 (1958–9): 1–19.

Stevens, Georgiana. "Arab Neutralism and Bandung," *Middle East Journal* 11, (Spring 1957): 139–152.

Surur, Muhammad Jamal al-Din. "Badr al-Gamali: The Armenian Mamluk," *Al-Ahram,* 21 December 1964.

Tiger, Lionel. "Bureaucracy and Charisma in Ghana," *Journal of Asian and African Studies* 1 (January 1966): 13–26.

Toch, Hans. "Crisis Situations and Ideological Revaluation," *Public Opinion Quarterly* 19 (Spring 1955): 53–67.

Ulman, A. H. and R. H. Dekmejian. "Changing Patterns in Turkish Foreign Policy, 1959–1967," *Orbis* 11 (Fall 1967): 772–785.

Viatkin, R. V. and S. L. Tikhvinskii. "Some Problems of Historical Scholarship in the Chinese People's Republic," *Soviet Review* 5 (Summer 1964): 48–63.

Walker, Jack L. "A Critique of the Elitist Theory of Democracy," *American Political Science Review* 60 (June 1966): 285–295.

Willner, Ann Ruth and Dorothy, "The Rise and Role of Charismatic Leaders," *The Annals of the American Academy of Political and Social Science* 358 (March 1965).

Wrong, Dennis H. "Max Weber: The Scholar as a Hero," *Columbia University Forum* 15 (Summer 1962): 31–37.

Yasin, Hilmi. "Majalis al-Idarah," *Al-Tali'ah,* September 1968.

Newspapers and Periodicals

Ahram, Al-, 1954, 1959, 1961, 1964, 1965, 1966, 1967, 1968, 1969, 1970
Akhbar, Al-, 1 July 1954, 1968, 1970.
Akhbar al-Yawm, 1965, 1968.
Akhir Lahzah, 1967
Akhir Sa'ah, 1968
Anwar, Al-, 1968
Arab Observer, 1961–1966
Atlantic Monthly, December 1956
Bina' al-Watan, April 1965
Cahagir, 1961–1964
Central Bank of Egypt, *Economic Review,* 4, 3–4, 1964; Vol. 8, No. 1–2
     1968.
Central Bank of Egypt, *Report of the Board of Directors, 1964–65*
Daedalus, 97, 3 (Summer 1968)
Daily Star, The, 1961, 1965
Economist, The, 1966
Egyptian Gazette, The, 1964
Housaper, 1968
Jerusalem Post, 1965
Journal of Social Issues, July 1968
Kommunist, October 1955; June 1964
Monde, Le, 1968, 1969, 1970
Les Progres Egyptian, 1968
Lusaper, 1960–1964
Musawwar, Al-, 1968, 1969
Nahar, Al-, 1965
Nahar, Al-, Arab Report, 1970
National Bank of Egypt, Economic Bulletin, vol. 5, no. 3 (1952); vol. 10,
     no. 1 (1957); vol. 11, no. 2 (1958); vol. 11, no. 3 (1958); vol. 12,
     no. 1 (1960); vol. 14, no. 1 (1961); vol. 14, no. 3 (1961); vol. 14,
     no. 4 (1961).
Revue Egyptienne de droit internationale, vol. 12, no. 1 (1956).
Ruz al-Yusif, 1959, 1965, 1966, 1967, 1968, 1969
Scribe, The, 1960–1964
Ta'awun, Al-, 1968
Talabah al-Arab, Al-, 1964, 1965, 1966
Tali'ah, Al-, 1968, 1969, 1970, 1971
New York Times, The, 1952, 1953, 1954, 1962, 1963, 1964, 1965, 1966,
     1967, 1968, 1969
Ummal, Al-, 1968

General Reference Books

Arab Record and Report
Cahier d'Orient Contemporaine
Europa Yearbook

Facts on File
International Who's Who
Keesing's Contemporary Archives
U.N. Demographic Yearbook
Whitaker's Almanac
Who's Who in the Arab World

Public Documents

Abd al-Nasir, President, *Press Release.* Press Bureau of UAR Mission to the United Nations, 1961.

Abdel Nasser, President Gamal, *Speeches and Press Interviews, 1958, 1959, 1960, 1961.* Cairo, Information Dept., n.d.

The Arab Socialist Union. Information Dept., Cairo, 1963.

The Charter. Information Dept., Cairo, n.d.

Muhadir Muhadathat al-Wahdah. Cairo, 1963.

Statute of the Arab Socialist Union. Information Dept., Cairo, n.d.

UAR Arab Political Encyclopedia. Information Dept., January-February 1962.

UAR Declaration of the Union Accord. Cairo, 17 April 1963.

UAR Yearbook, 1963. Cairo: Information Dept., 1963.

United Arab Republic, Bureau of Census Statistics, *Nashrah Ihsa' Muwazzafi al-Hukumah wa al-Hay'at* [Reports on Statistics of Employees of the Government and Agencies].

U.S., Department of State, Embassy in Cairo, *Directory of UAR Personages.* December 1964, December 1965, December 1966.

Index